Mark Twain
A Literary Life

Everett Emerson

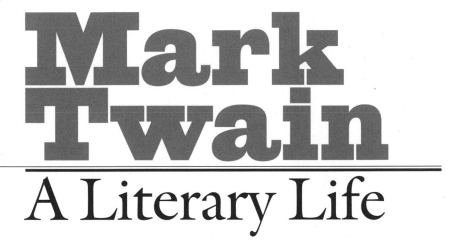

Mark Twain

A Literary Life

PENN

University of Pennsylvania Press

Philadelphia

10 9 8 7 6 5 4 3 2 1

Published by
University of Pennsylvania Press
Philadelphia, Pennsylvania 19104-4011

Library of Congress Cataloging-in-Publication Data
Emerson, Everett H., 1925–
    Mark Twain : a literary life / Everett Emerson.
        p.   cm.
    Includes bibliographical references and index.
    ISBN 0-8122-3516-9 (alk. paper)
    1. Twain, Mark, 1835–1910.   2. Humorists, American —
19th century Biography.   3. Authors, American — 19th
century Biography.   4. Journalists — United States
Biography.   I. Title.
PS1331.E48   1999
818'.409 — dc21
    [B]   99-34173
                                                           CIP

Frontispiece: Samuel Clemens / Mark Twain in 1906, etching by
Otto Schneider, National Portrait Gallery, Smithsonian
Institution, Washington, D.C. NPG 69–67.

FOR MY SCHOLARLY FRIENDS

Louis Budd and Alan Gribben

Contents

Preface

ark Twain endures. Readers sense his humanity, enjoy his humor, and appreciate his insights into human nature, even into such painful experiences as embarrassment and humiliation. No matter how remarkable the life of Samuel Clemens was, what matters most is the relationship of Mark Twain the writer and his writings. That is the subject of this book. While I have made use of the materials in my earlier book, *The Authentic Mark Twain*, which appeared in 1984, the differences between the two books are nevertheless substantial. My increased understanding and knowledge of Mark Twain's life have led me to realize that in order to see his writings in focus one must give proper attention to aspects of his life that I had either insufficiently recognized or quite neglected in the earlier volume.

The assumption behind this book is that one can understand virtually all of Mark Twain's works better if one can read them in their biographical context. It is therefore distinctly different from other biographies, including Andrew Hoffman's *Inventing Mark Twain: The Lives of Samuel L. Clemens* (1997), in which much that Mark Twain wrote is ignored.

Samuel Clemens himself, I like to think, would approve of my undertaking. In the next to last year of his life he wrote an essay entitled "The Turning Point of My Life." In it he asserted, "To me, the most important feature of my life is its literary feature." My purpose here has been to comprehend that literary feature, which requires a recognition of the constantly changing circumstances of his literary career.

Mark Twain is one of America's greatest writers. Unlike some of his peers — Walt Whitman, Herman Melville, and William Faulkner, for example — he is widely read. Moreover, he and his writings are still frequently in the news: the discovery of the first half of the *Huckleberry Finn* manuscript in California, new information about Mark Twain's support of a black student at Yale Law School and a black artist who wanted to study in Paris, the likely extinction of the kind of Calaveras County frog Mark Twain wrote about, the question of whether high school students should be assigned *Huckleberry Finn*.

Mark Twain's literary career is truly fascinating in its strangeness. How could this genius have had so little sense of what he should do with himself? A contemporary observer of the writer's life could not have imagined where his career would subsequently take him and what he would write next, if anything, though the unoriginal idea of writing sequels was always a strong temptation.

The connections between the writings of Mark Twain and the life of Samuel L. Clemens begin early. Clemens was blessed by a childhood that as Mark Twain he could often use in his most memorable novels, in his autobiography, and even at times in his travel books. In *Tom Sawyer* he asserted that "most of the adventures in this book really occurred; one or two were experiences of my own, the rest those of boys who were schoolmates of mine." Thereafter, in young Sam's first vocation, that of journeyman printer, he was able to travel far from home to the sights of New York, Philadelphia, and Washington. He made extensive literary use of this printing experience in the posthumous book-length fragment "No. 44, The Mysterious Stranger," in which the narrator is a printer's apprentice. Sam's work in printshops also had much to do with his much later investing many thousands of dollars in a machine that would have replaced the typesetter had it worked properly. Its failure had major consequences for the writer.

His next vocation gave him an identity. He became a Mississippi steamboat pilot, where he heard the leadsman's call "MARK TWAIN," announcing that the water was just deep enough for the boat to proceed. Choosing "Mark Twain" as his pen name identified him permanently with the great river, as did such books as *Life on the Mississippi* and *Huckleberry Finn*.

All along in his early years he was sporadically writing for publication, but only when he went west to Nevada and, after an unsuccessful try at silver mining, had to find a new means of survival did he become a newspaperman — specifically, a humorist. For a time he followed a second career as well, that of lecturer; his success in this endeavor would provide him with a reliable source of funds when he was financially pressed. After he went bankrupt, he devoted most of a year to making a lecture tour around the world and then writing a book about his experience.

Mark Twain's first success was an account of his 1867 trip to Europe and the Holy Land, and thereafter his writing career often took him back to Europe. To a large extent he defined himself and his America vis-à-vis Europe, especially in *A Connecticut Yankee in King Arthur's Court,* but also in *Huckleberry Finn,* which in its way amounts to an international novel. In time he resided in London, Berlin, Florence, and most notably Vienna, where he and his family lived for nearly two years. His Austrian experiences enriched and conditioned his thinking at the end of the century and brought new life to his writing.

An especially powerful force in Samuel Clemens's career was his marriage and the associations to which it led. His choice of a wife from genteel Eastern society and his consequent adoption of Hartford, Connecticut, as his home often created contradictions with his earlier life. Was he the irreverent, satirical humorist of the West, or was he the husband of Olivia Langdon Clemens and conventional father of three daughters? Susy, his oldest daughter, was quite aware of her father's divided identity. She, like her mother, favored the author of *The Prince and the Pauper,* not the one who wrote *Huckleberry Finn.* Moreover, the hectic social life that Clemens adopted in Hartford limited his writing time to the summer, when he would hide out on a hillside farm nestled above Elmira, New York, his wife's hometown.

These tendencies are examined here, in addition to many others: Mark Twain's continuing interest in the theater and playwriting; his substantial business interests and other distractions from writing; his preference for publishing by subscription rather than by the usual retail method; his preoccupation with religion and his changing views of the Deity; his many unfinished manuscripts, most of which have been published in recent years; the place of illustrations in his books; his on-again, off-again interest in writing his autobiography, and his involvement, again on and off, with politics.

Because during his lifetime Mark Twain was, in his own words, the "most conspicuous person on the planet,"[1] how he presented himself is crucial — and interesting. Therefore I have provided many images of the man, photographs taken over the years, some of them little known. In reporting the author's life I have endeavored to permit Mark Twain to tell his own story through his letters and autobiographical writings. The reading and research undertaken for this book have been a great satisfaction to me, since I have an abiding affection for both Samuel Clemens and his extraordinary legacy.

ACKNOWLEDGMENTS

My work was made possible by the extensive resources of the Mark Twain Project at the University of California, Berkeley. In its riches critics and scholars have access to sources such as are available for no other American author: thousands of Mark Twain's letters and thousands of letters he received, his notebooks (including still unpublished ones), the manuscripts of many of his writings, published and unpublished, copies of the collections of other repositories, *and* dedicated scholars who staff the collection and prepare the marvelous editions that the University of California publishes, such as the first five magisterial volumes of Mark Twain's letters that have now appeared. For a Mark Twain specialist, being there is to be in heaven, surrounded by angels. To say that I am grateful to Harriet E. Smith, Victor Fischer, Michael Frank, Lin Salamo, Kenneth Sanderson, Louis Suarez-Potts, Anh Bui, and particularly Dr. Robert Hirst, David Briggs, and Brenda Coker would be an understatement, and their support has been personally very gratifying. I am deeply grateful for permission to publish Mark Twain's previously unpublished words, which I located in the Mark Twain Papers, to reproduce photographs found there, and to make use of the papers of Isabel Lyon, housed there. Quite as important, truly indispensable, has been the support my wife Katherine has given me through dark days.

I am grateful for the assistance of colleagues, associates, and friends, especially Alan Gribben, who read the entire manuscript in its penultimate stage and made hundreds of suggestions; R. Kent Rasmussen, author of the invaluable *Mark Twain A to Z,* who identified a shocking number of mistakes; Louis J. Budd, Great Authority on Mark Twain, my friend and neighbor, and always helpful; Carl Dolmetsch, whose work on Mark Twain's years in Vienna is arguably the most important contribution to Mark Twain biography in the last twenty years; another friend and neighbor, Mary Boewe; Michael Kiskis, an authority on Mark Twain's autobiography; Herbert S. Bailey; Howard Baetzhold; Salli Benedict; Alberta A. Booth; Kevin J. Bochynski; Isabelle Budd; Gregg Camfield; Sherwood Cummings; Hamlin Hill; Horst Kruse; Joe McCullough; Bruce Michelson; Paula Miller; Elaine Durham Otto, a superb copyeditor; Tracy Sayles; Barbara Schmidt; Gretchen Sharlow; Kenneth Silverman; Laura Skandera-Trombley; David E. E. Sloane; Thomas A. Tenney; and Jim Zwick. I am also grateful to the Pierpont Morgan Library in New York City for permission to quote from Mark Twain's autobiographical sketch, MA 1405, which it owns. I thank the heirs of Isabel Lyon for permission to quote from her diary, and both the Mark Twain House, Hartford, and the Vassar College

Library for permission to reproduce photographs owned by those institutions. I have made use, with gratitude, of the scholarship and insights that other commentators have made during the past two decades. The resources of the libraries of the University of North Carolina at Chapel Hill has been a constant boon.

CHAPTER ONE

Mark Twain Assembled

etween the birth of Samuel Langhorne Clemens and his trimphant success as a writer, the path was long and crooked. A seven-months child, Sam was born in the tiny hamlet of Florida, Missouri — population one hundred — on November 30, 1835. His family had arrived there from Tennessee only six months before. Two years later the Clemenses moved thirty-five miles northeast to Hannibal, the Mississippi River town now celebrated for its famous son. The connections between the town and the writer are especially close because the author was to draw on his childhood experiences again and again in his most enduring works, in both fiction, especially *Tom Sawyer,* and in some of the best passages of his mostly factual autobiography. He especially celebrated summers at his Uncle Quarles's farm.

He was just sixteen when he first described Hannibal in the *Philadelphia American Courier.* "This town is situated on the Mississippi river, about one hundred and thirty miles above St. Louis, and contains a population of about three thousand. . . . Among the curiosities of this place we may mention the *Cave,* which is about three miles below the city. It is of unknown length; it has innumerable passages, which are not unlike the streets of a large city."[1] This cave, Hannibal's steep hill, the steamboats (over a thousand arrived each year), the islands in the river, his uncle's farm not far from Florida — Mark Twain would utilize all of these in memorable scenes within the American literary landscape.

Of his boyhood summers he was to recall in "Early Days" (1897–98):

I spent some part of every year at the farm until I was twelve or thirteen years old. The life which I led there with my cousins was full of charm, and so is the memory of it yet. I can call back the solemn twilight and mystery of the deep woods, the earthy smells, the faint odors of the wild flowers, the sheen of rain-washed foliage, the rattling clatter of drops when the wind shook the trees, the far-off hammering of woodpeckers and the muffled drumming of wood pheasants in the remoteness of the forest, the snapshot glimpses of disturbed wild creatures scurrying through the grass — I can call it all back and make it as real as it ever was, and as blessed.[2]

For several pages he conjured up the sights, tastes, touches, sounds, and smells of his past. Sentence after sentence begins hypnotically "I know how" and "I know" and "I can remember."

Sam's father, John M. Clemens, justice of the peace, carried the title of Judge Clemens. He was described in the *St. Louis Republican* as

a stern, unbending man of splendid common sense . . . the autocrat of the little dingy room on Bird Street where he held his court. . . . Its furniture consisted of a dry-good box which served the double purpose of a desk for the Judge and table for the lawyers, three or four rude stools and a puncheon for the jury. And here on court days when the Judge climbed upon his three-legged stool, rapped on the box with his knuckles and demanded, "Silence in the court" it was fully expected that silence would reign supreme.[3]

Like Judge Driscoll in Mark Twain's *Pudd'nhead Wilson,* he was "very proud of his Virginian ancestry, and in his hospitalities and his rather formal and stately manners he kept up its traditions"; he was "a free-thinker" (chap. 1). Judge Clemens was a man of dignity with a good standing in the community, but at his death in 1847 he left his family very little. He had supposed that riches might be found in the thousands of acres in Tennessee he had purchased in the 1820s and 1830s, and for years members of his family imagined that this land speculation was to make them rich. They were, however, mistaken.[4]

Sam's mother was no doubt a stronger influence on the writer-to-be. (Much later he assumed considerable responsibility for his mother's financial well-being until her death in 1890.) Jane Lampton Clemens saw to it that young Sam went to Sunday school, first at the Methodist church and later at the Presbyterian church that she had joined. Subsequently, the writer was to recall his Sunday school experiences when he wrote *Tom Sawyer.*

The author's affectionate description of his mother is much lengthier and more emotional than that of his father. Among the characteristics he described, two may be mentioned.

> She had a slender small body, but a large heart; a heart so large that everybody's griefs and everybody's joys found welcome in its hospitable accommodation. The greatest difference which I find between her and the rest of the people I have known, is this, and it is a remarkable one: those others felt a strong interest in a few things, whereas to the very day of her death [at age eighty-seven] she felt a strong interest in the whole world and everything and everybody in it. . . . When her pity or her indignation was stirred by hurt or shame inflicted upon some defenceless person or creature, she was the most eloquent person I have heard speak. It was seldom eloquence of a fiery or violent sort, but gentle, pitying, persuasive, appealing; and so genuine and so nobly and simply worded and so touchingly uttered, that many times I have seen it win the reluctant and splendid applause of tears.[5]

Clearly, Sam's lifelong humanitarianism owed a debt to his mother.

Sam was a troublesome child, plagued by illnesses. In 1882 he wrote, "During the first seven years of my life I had no health — I may almost say that I lived on allopathic medicines."[6] His behavior was often eccentric, and he had a tendency to wander away from home. His formal education (soon to be interrupted) was such as a small town could offer. He himself referred to it dismissively in the early 1870s: "Attended the ordinary western common school in Hannibal, Mo., from the age of 5 till near the age of 13. That's all the schooling — if playing hookey & getting licked for it may be called by that name."[7] Of necessity his later education was picked up elsewhere than in schools. As a boy he read adventure stories of pirates and knights in the heroic fiction and poetry of such authors as Sir Walter Scott, Lord Byron, and James Fenimore Cooper. Had he not chosen initially to think of these writers as exemplary, he would not have become the highly original writer that in time he became. He was always a reader, though he usually chose to present himself as far from being bookish.

Sam was only eleven years old when his father died in 1847. Already poor, the Clemens family now became almost destitute. Before 1849, when his schooling came to a close, Sam undertook part-time work that would lead to a career. After serving as delivery and office boy, he became a printer's apprentice for the hometown newspaper, the *Hannibal Courier*. He was following in the footsteps of his brother Orion, nearly six years his elder, who had become an apprentice in 1839. Twenty years later Sam Clemens wrote, "Education continued in the offices of the Hannibal 'Courier' & the 'Journal,' as an apprenticed printer."[8] Sam served in all capacities, including staff work. The *Courier*'s makeshift library introduced him to humorous publications such as *The Spirit of the Times,* regularly drawn on for "fillers." In early 1851, having completed his apprenticeship, Sam went to work for Orion as a journeyman printer on the *Hannibal Western Union.*

Even before this time, Sam had published "A Gallant Fireman" in the *Western Union* for January 16. Soon he was showing incipient signs of genuine literary ambition. On May 1, 1852, a Boston comic weekly, *The Carpet-Bag,* published his short sketch entitled "The Dandy Frightening the Squatter." Although the piece is not in itself striking (it resembles a sketch that its author may well have read in the *Hannibal Courier* of 1850, "Doin' a Dandy"), it is notable that this short sketch appeared in remote Boston. It was signed "S.L.C." Sixty years later, the writer would say of this sketch and of his description of Hannibal published the same year, "Seeing them in print was a joy which rather exceeded anything in that line I have ever experienced since."[9]

His Boston publisher was B. P. Shillaber, creator of Mrs. Partington, a character who was later to influence the creation of Tom Sawyer's Aunt Polly. Shillaber's publication was only one of many comic periodicals flourishing in America at this time, and these had a strong influence on young Clemens. The first comic weekly was created as early as 1831 by William T. Porter, a Vermonter: *The Spirit of the Times* described itself as a "Chronicle of the Turf, Agriculture, Field Sports, Literature, and the Stage." Addressing a masculine audience, it is remembered chiefly for its publication of tales based on the oral humor of the frontier, especially the Southern frontier. Many other magazines soon followed its example. Although not far removed from the real life of the people they portrayed, the stories they published were frequently tall tales. To increase his credibility and enhance the sense of contrast, the narrator was likely to maintain a poker face while he provided a "report." The theme of many of these tales is the distinction between the false and the real and between the pretentious and the unsophisticated. Sometimes the teller is himself the unconscious victim in his story; often it is an Easterner who is outsmarted, even humiliated, for he is likely to be innocent, ignorant, naive. (Sometimes it is the reader who is taken in as well.)

Clemens found this concern with victimization and humiliation particularly congenial to his talents and attitudes. *Huckleberry Finn* and "The Man That Corrupted Hadleyburg" deal with these themes, to mention two examples. For a short time, Clemens adopted from the southern frontier stories the use of slang and elaborate misspellings. Also, like many of the writers of this school, he adopted a pen name. Among the writers familiar to Clemens in one way or another were George Horatio Derby, who became John Phoenix and told of his adventures in the California of the 1850s; H. W. Shaw, who, as Josh Billings, wrote about farming, exploration, and riverboating; and David Ross Locke, who adopted the name "Petroleum Vesuvius Nasby, late pastor uv the Church uv the New Dispensation, Chaplain to his excellency the President, and p. m. at Confederate roads, Kentucky." Most successful of all was Charles Farrar Browne, later to become Artemus Ward, a comic lecturer and crusader against insincerity and sentimentality. Clemens met Ward in 1863 and later made his humor the subject of a much-repeated lecture.

Young Clemens's "Dandy" anecdote only faintly reflects the coarse and violent humor of these writers. Set in Hannibal when "the now flourishing young city . . . was but a 'woodyard,'" it tells of a would-be gentleman, obviously from the East, who seeks to demonstrate his manliness to some young women by frightening a woodsman. But the Easterner, who ends up in the river, is "astonished" and humiliated. Clemens gives no characterization to his narrator, and the story is not told in dialect.

A sometimes overlooked fact about Clemens's youth is that he smoked "immoderately," one hundred cigars a month, according to his own account, when he was eight years old![10] Many years later, at the party given to celebrate his seventieth birthday, he noted, "I do not know just when I began to smoke, I only know that it was in my father's lifetime, and that I was discreet. He passed from this life early in 1847, when I was a shade past eleven: ever since then I have smoked publicly. . . . Today it is all of sixty years since I began to smoke the limit."[11] The limit? Not specified, but apparently Clemens meant as often as he possibly could.

After demonstrating that his work could be published in the East, Clemens turned his attention to local publication. While Orion was absent from home in September 1852, Sam was able to publish several items, some as a consequence of his getting into an argument with the editor of the *Hannibal Tri-Weekly Messenger,* whom he tried to embarrass. Nearly forty pieces in all have been located in Hannibal newspapers: verses, burlesques, local items. They show much energy but little control. Several are signed "W. Epaminondas Adrastus Perkins," later simply "Blab" or the initials, W.E.A.B. Other brief pieces used famous pen names of the period such as the Rambler and the Grumbler. Somewhat more personal is "Oh, She Has a Red Head!" by a redhead who signs himself "A Son of Adam" and who argues that "red is the natural color of beauty." In this piece the future public personality acknowledges his love of open display, which was to be lifelong. A satire of the Democratic governor and legislature, "Blabbing Government Secrets," anticipates another of his future interests, public affairs.

In May 1853, Orion Clemens awarded young Sam "Our Assistant's Column." Not only did the column criticize newspapers that borrowed without credit: it attacked one "Mr. Jacques," whose drunken mistreatment of his children he believed should be punished with tarring and feathering and being ridden out of town on a rail. (Huck considered this form of punishment cruel when applied to the Duke and the King.) While Orion was away, Sam published a headline in the paper:

TERRIBLE ACCIDENT!
500 MEN KILLED AND MISSING!!!

We had set the above head up, expecting (of course) to use it, but as the accident hasn't yet happened, we'll say

(To be Continued)[12]

Hannibal was a small world, remote from East Coast literature, but as a journeyman printer Sam Clemens could find work elsewhere. In June 1853, at the age of seventeen, he went to St. Louis, where he seems to have stayed with his sister Pamela (by then married to William Moffett), and for two months he worked as a typesetter on St. Louis newspapers. In mid-August, having been unable to find work there, he made his way to New York without telling his mother in advance. He was able to work there as a typesetter and remained for about two months. Two letters he wrote appeared in Orion's newspaper. Sam explains how he traveled to New York in five days, by steamboat and train, with a little sightseeing in Chicago, Rochester, and Syracuse. In New York he saw two "wild men" from Borneo, a magnificent "fruit salon," and the ships of New York harbor. He expressed pride in his type-setting ability. Young Clemens had already developed a literary technique he was to make good use of throughout his career, for instance, as when Huck Finn would relate his story, emphasizing the narrator's response to what he sees. Of the wild men Clemens wrote, "Their faces and eyes are those of the beast, and when they fix their glittering orbs on you with a steady, unflinching gaze, you instinctively draw back a step, and a very unpleasant sensation steals through your veins." In these early letters home, Sam identified himself not as a fledgling writer but as a printer, proud of his ability to set clean proof. He found satisfaction in his discovery that the New York printers had two libraries where he could "spend my evenings most pleasantly." He soon became a lover of books and a lifelong advocate of libraries.

Other letters to his sister Pamela, written in September and October, describe New York sights, including the theater. They were not published until after his death. Soon Sam moved on to Philadelphia, and from there he wrote a series of letters that were published in the *Muscatine (Iowa) Journal*, partly owned by Orion, who had moved 120 miles up the river in September. After printing a portion of a letter dated October 26, 1853, apparently without permission, Orion had invited his brother to write letters for publication, and Sam accepted. The first four letters are somewhat impersonal accounts of Philadelphia and a February 1854 visit to Washington, D.C. With deep respect, the young Clemens described the monuments of American history, the grave of Benjamin Franklin, the Liberty Bell, and objects associated with George Washington. He saw Philadelphia as continuing the European cultural tradition. Some of his reverence was borrowed, for the two Philadelphia letters apparently were written with R. A. Smith's *Philadelphia as It Is in 1852* open in front of him. He had already stumbled upon the borrowing device of innumerable travel writers before him. In writing from Washington, his tone is similar to Smith's as he describes the Capitol, the senators, and the members of the House of Representatives. He saw a printing press used by Benjamin Franklin and was intrigued by the patent office. One letter from Philadelphia reveals Sam's amusement with obituary poetry, a lachrymose subject he would return to in his contributions to the *Galaxy* magazine and in *Huckleberry Finn*.

In the spring of 1854, Clemens was obliged to leave the East because of what he later called "financial stress."[13] He then took his printing skills back "to the Mississippi Valley, sitting upright in the smoking-car for two or three days and nights. When I reached St. Louis I was exhausted. I went to bed on board a steamer that was bound for Muscatine. I fell asleep at once, and didn't wake for thirty-six hours."[14] In Muscatine he worked for his brother, who could pay him no wages, and then to St. Louis, where his mother and sister now lived. Almost a year later, in February and March 1855, four more of Sam's letters appeared in the *Muscatine Journal*. Signed S.L.C., these letters reflect his maturing tastes less apologetically and are perhaps the first strong indication of the writer that was to be. Young Sam reports, for instance, on *The Merchant of Venice:* "I had always thought that this was a comedy, until they made a *farce* of it. The prompters found it hard matter to get the actors on the stage, and when they did get them on, it was harder still to get them *off* again. 'Jessica' was always 'thar' when she wasn't wanted, and never would turn up when her services were required." There is a freshness of diction even in his comments about the weather: "Yesterday and to-day were as bright and pleasant as anyone could wish, and fires were abolished, I hope for the season."

During the following year and a half, when neither Sam nor Orion was connected with a newspaper, he wrote little for publication. By then the brothers both lived in Keokuk, Iowa — between Hannibal and Muscatine. Sam spoke at a printers' banquet celebrating the 150th anniversary of Benjamin Franklin's birth — Franklin the patron saint of American printers — and according to a piece Orion wrote for the *Keokuk Gate City* for January 19, 1856, his speech was "replete with wit and humor" and interrupted by much applause.[15]

Samuel Clemens's interest in humor and in writing arose directly from his pleasure in books. In printers' libraries and later in his own substantial collection, Clemens was an insatiable reader. His early work was influenced by his familiarity with the writings of both English and American literary comedians like Laurence Sterne, Thomas Hood, and George W. Curtis, whose *Potiphar Papers* (1853) satirizes religious hypocrisy and snobbery. In a March 1860 letter to Orion, Clemens identified Oliver Goldsmith's *Citizen of the World* and Cervantes's *Don Quixote* as his *"beau ideals"* of fine writing.[16] Cervantes provided him with a model for expressing both realistic and romantic viewpoints within the same work. Later a different kind of influence upon Clemens, as a young cub pilot, was his reading of Thomas Paine's *Age of Reason* "with fear and hesitation, but marveling at its fearlessness and wonderful power."[17] Paine and Voltaire reinforced his penchant for skepticism.

In the late summer or early fall of 1856, following some eight years of association with printing, Clemens left Keokuk. Once again one can follow his travels from the letters he wrote for publication in the *Keokuk Post*, where he was initially paid $5.00, later increased to $7.50 a letter. He now adopted a pen name and a pen personality. As Thomas Jefferson Snodgrass, he was an innocent ready to be amazed and victimized by his city adventures. The three letters in this series show the strong influence of another of the frontier comic writers, William Tappan Thompson, author of *Major Jones's Sketches of Travel* (1847). Thompson cultivated bad grammar and an outrageous Southern dialect. Clemens's first letter, dated October 18 from St. Louis, is a report from Snodgrass of his visit to a performance of Shakespeare's *Julius Caesar*. This bumpkin's visit is largely predictable, although Snodgrass's quotation from Dickens's *Little Dorrit* comes as rather a surprise.[18] A month later Snodgrass reports again. Just as he had been ejected from the theater in St. Louis because of his ignorance of proper behavior, here his innocence leads to misadventures. He had traveled eastward through Chicago, of which he reports: "When you feel like tellin a feller to go to the devil, tell him to go to Chicago — it'll anser every purpose, and is perhaps, a leetle more expensive."[19]

The third and most ambitious letter, dated Cincinnati, March 14, 1847, explains that the writer had "pooty much quit scribblin" until now when he has at last a "little adventer" to report. The innocent has been taken advantage of again, this time by a young woman who asks him to hold her basket while she goes around the corner. Snodgrass obliges and uses the waiting time to daydream of marrying the woman, whom he supposes is a rich heiress. An hour and a half later, he starts after her, whereupon he hears from the basket the howls of "the ugliest, nastiest, orneriest he-baby I ever seed in all my life." Snodgrass does not know what to do. He keeps the baby for a day, then tries to "poke the dang thing through a hole in the ice" on the river. He is arrested and fined, then released. Such is his tawdry adventure. This sketch was directly inspired by William T. Thompson, who told a similar story in *Major Jones's Sketches of Travel*.[20]

The Snodgrass letters, the last of which was written when Clemens was twenty-one, do not yet show the author-to-be discovering his métier; they simply indicate that Clemens wished to be a humorous writer. He now left journalism for an extended period, and also not surprisingly — for one who had lived in the river towns of Hannibal, St. Louis, Keokuk, Muscatine, and Cincinnati — he was attracted to an occupation on the river. Some fifteen years later, he was to explain his decision in an unpublished autobiographical sketch:

About 1855 [actually April 15, 1857], aged 20, started to New Orleans, with about ten or twelve dollars, after paying steamboat passage, intending in good earnest to take shipping there for the port of Para [Brazil], & explore the river Amazon & open up a commerce in the marvelous herb called coca, which is the concentrated bread & meat of the tribes (when on long, tedious journeys) that inhabit the country lying about the headwaters of the Amazon. Broken-hearted to find that a vessel would not be likely to leave N[ew] O[rleans] for Para during the next generation. Got some little comfort out of the fact that I had at least not arrived too late, if I *had* arrived too soon, for no ship had ever yet left N. O. for Para in preceding generations.

Had made friends with the pilots & learned to steer, on the way down; so they had good-will enough to engage to make a St. Louis & N. O. pilot of me for $500, payable upon graduation. They kept their word, & for 18 months I went up & down, steering & studying the 1275 miles of river day & night, supporting myself meantime by helping the freight clerks on board & the freight watchmen on shore. Then I got my U. S. license to pilot, & a steady berth at $250 a month — which was a princely salary for a youth in those days of low wages for mechanics.[21]

Later he brilliantly described his experiences as apprentice pilot to Horace Bixby, though with some exaggeration, in "Old Times on the Mississippi" (1875).

This piloting phase of his career lasted four years, until Clemens was twenty-five. He learned the river from St. Louis to New Orleans, then served as a steamboat pilot. Very little that he wrote during that time has survived: seventeen letters, one sketch, several pieces of journalism, all slight, and two pieces of fiction that he did not publish. A few letters do give the impression, however, that the pilot was still interested in writing. A letter to Annie Taylor in 1857 describes the French Market of New Orleans and a cemetery of vaults and tombs in the city. Clemens was to have a continuing interest in cemeteries, morgues, and death, as *The Innocents Abroad, Life on the Mississippi, Huckleberry Finn,* and many of his other writings show. To his sister Pamela he wrote a rather literary letter on March 11, 1859, providing a description of the Mardi Gras parade in New Orleans: "The procession was led by a Mounted Knight Crusader in blazing gilt armor from head to foot, and I think one might never tire of looking at the splendid picture."

In "Old Times," Mark Twain described the destruction of the steamer *Pennsylvania* on June 13, 1858. Clemens had made several trips on that boat as an apprentice pilot, including one when it was damaged as a result of a collision with the *Vicksburg,* with which it was racing.[22] Although he was not on the *Pennsylvania* at the time of the "catastrophe," his beloved brother Henry was. After much suffering, he died from inhaled steam. Since Sam had obtained a position for Henry as clerk, the tragedy caused him to feel terrible guilt for many years.[23] Throughout his lifetime Clemens repeatedly experienced guilt; perhaps as a result of this and ensuing disasters, in time he developed a deterministic philosophy that was a means of denying a painful sense of responsibility he felt then and for other events thereafter.

Sam continued to read and enhance his education. His ongoing interest in Charles Dickens is suggested by a quotation in a November 1860 letter to his brother Orion from *Martin Chuzzlewit* concerning Mrs. Gamp's interest in alcohol. Indeed, Clemens regarded Dickens as one of his favorite writers for many years, though eventually he was to claim he found Dickens's sentimentalism unattractive.

These years on the river seem to have been so deeply gratifying to Clemens that he was not tempted to try another career. He obtained his pilot's license on April 9, 1859, and was extremely proud to be working on the *City of Memphis,* "the largest boat in the trade and the hardest to pilot." He was proud, too, of his reputation as a pilot and his acceptance by fellow pilots.

He told Orion, "I derive a *living* pleasure from these things." Throughout his life he referred to his experiences as a pilot, frequently with pleasure but occasionally with gratitude that he had escaped from its demands. In August 1862, he wrote to his sister, "I never have *once* thought of returning home to go on the river again, and I never expect to do any more piloting at any price." But, in January 1866, he wrote to his mother, "I wish I was back there piloting up & down the river again. Verily, all is vanity and little worth — save piloting."

Toward the end of his piloting years, in February 1861, Clemens made a visit to a fortune-teller that piqued his imagination. According to a detailed letter he sent to Orion, she told him, "You have written a great deal; you write well — but you are out of practice; no matter — you will be *in* practice some day." She observed that he enjoyed excellent health but told him, "you use *entirely* too much tobacco; and you must stop it; mind, not moderate, but *stop* the use of it totally." This was only one of many antismoking warnings that Clemens chose to ignore, even though he noted that Madam Caprell's ability to tell the truth about him was remarkable.

"River Intelligence," one of the few known publications of these years, which ended with Clemens's last piloting on the river in 1861, relates to the obscure and muddled history of his pen name. The simplest explanation of the name is the one included in an autobiographical sketch he wrote for his nephew Samuel Moffett in the early part of the twentieth century. It has been unduly neglected. Here he explains, using a third-person voice, that he became the "legislative correspondent" of the *Virginia City Territorial Enterprise*.

> He wrote a weekly letter to the paper; it appeared Sundays, & on Mondays the legislative process was obstructed by the complaints of members as a result. They rose to questions of privilege & answered the criticisms of the correspondent with bitterness, customarily describing him with elaborate & uncomplimentary phrases, for lack of a briefer way. To save their time he presently began to sign the letters, using the Mississippi leadsman's call, "Mark Twain" (2 fathoms = 12 feet) for this purpose.[24]

A few years later, in his autobiography, he explained that while a pilot he composed a "rude and crude satire" of a steamboat man who wrote under the pen name of Mark Twain.[25] In 1874 he was more specific: "Mark Twain was the *nom de plume* of one Capt. Isaiah Sellers, who used to write river news over it for the New Orleans Picayune. He died in 1863, & as he would no longer need that signature I laid violent hands upon it without asking permission of the prophet's remains."[26] But Sellers did not die until a year after Clemens began to call himself "Mark Twain," and no evidence has yet been found that Sellers actually used that pen name. Why Clemens repeatedly asserted that "borrowing" from Sellers is not known.

On the other hand, Clemens did indeed satirize Sellers, whom he called "Sergeant Fathom" in "River Intelligence," a piece he published in the *New Orleans Crescent* in May 1859. He depicted Sellers as reminiscing ludicrously while offering predictions of phenomenally high water. "In the summer of 1763 [ninety-six years before the date of the report] I came down the river on the old *first* 'Jubilee.' She was new, then, however; a singular sort of a single-engine boat, with a Chinese captain and a Choctaw crew." According to the account in Mark Twain's *Life on the Mississippi* (chap. 50), this satire deeply affected Sellers, to the regret of the young Clemens. Another satire that Clemens wrote was a brief "Pilot's Memorandum," which burlesqued the standard reports on river traffic appearing in newspapers. Its humor assumed a good deal of familiarity with the steamboating of that day.

Four other pieces by Clemens the steamboatman were discovered and reprinted in 1982. Three are mere journalism, first published in 1858. More ambitious was "Soleleather Cultivates His Taste for Music," which appeared in the *New Orleans Crescent* in 1859. In it the brash narrator told of his experiences at a St. Louis boardinghouse, where he soothed a sick fellow boarder with his attempts to play first a violin, then a trombone. Soleleather is another version of Snodgrass, but better educated.[27]

Of the two attempts at fiction Clemens made during his years on the river, one is a gothic tale of murder and revenge set in Germany, but with a plot borrowed from Robert Montgomery Bird's *Nick of the Woods* (1837). The other tells of a pilot who returns from the dead to perform an unusually difficult task of piloting. Aside from attesting to Clemens's continuing serious interest in writing, the stories are unmemorable.

With the coming of the Civil War, Clemens left the river, since the war effectively disrupted commercial traffic. In 1899 he described the situation, using the third person: "He was in New Orleans when Louisiana went out of the Union, Jan. 26, 1861, & started North the next day. Every day on the trip a blockade was closed by the boat, & the batteries of Jefferson Barracks (below St Louis) fired two shots through her chimney the last night of her voyage." He returned home and soon joined a group of volunteers who were taking the Confederate side in the conflict, but within two weeks he left them. "'Incapacitated by fatigue' through persistent retreating" is the way he described the volunteers in a statement from the source just quoted.[28] This service was too informal and irregular for it to be said with any truthfulness that he was a deserter, as is sometimes reported. Nearly twenty-five years after the event, he rendered a somewhat fictionalized account of his "war" experiences in "The Private History of a Campaign That Failed."

Sam's next adventure was more crucial than his gesture at combat. In July 1861, he accompanied his brother to the West, where Orion, who had identified himself strongly with the Union side as the great conflict shaped itself, was rewarded with the office of the secretaryship of the territory of Nevada. Sam was eventually hired to be a government clerk at eight dollars a day, but not as Orion's official secretary, as Sam reported in the entertaining account in *Roughing It* (1872).[29]

The trip westward to the territory was long and slow. Leaving on July 18, 1861, they went up the Missouri River to St. Joseph, then travelled by overland stagecoach by way of Salt Lake City. They reached Carson City on August 14. Having finally arrived, Sam found himself in a world that strangely combined ugliness and beauty. He soon undertook some exploring and examined Lake Tahoe, only twenty miles or so from his headquarters in Carson City. He greatly admired the lake, but his negligence there resulted in his starting a forest fire in its tinder-dry terrain. He wrote a vivid account of the lake and the fire to his mother and sister in the early fall. A letter sent a little later, in October 1861, is one of his best early pieces. Testifying to Sam's succumbing to the get-rich-quick fever of the silver miners, it also provides a description of the landscape:

> It never rains here, and the dew never falls. No flowers grow here, and no green thing gladdens the eye. The birds that fly over the land carry their provisions with them. Only the crow and the raven tarry with us. Our city lies in the midst of a desert of the purest, most unadulterated and uncompromising sand — in which infernal soil nothing but that fag-end of vegetable creation, "sage brush," is mean enough to grow. If you will take a liliputian cedar tree for a model, and build a dozen imitations of it with the stiffest article of telegraph wire — set them one foot apart and then try to walk through them — you will understand (provided the floor is covered twelve inches deep with sand) what it is to travel through a sage-brush desert. When crushed, sage-brush emits an odor which isn't exactly magnolia and equally isn't exactly polecat — but a sort of compromise between the two. It looks a good deal like greasewood, and is the ugliest plant that was ever conceived of.

A version of this letter was published in the *Keokuk Gate City* in November. Two subsequent letters, written in January and March 1862 and also addressed to Clemens's mother, seem to have been intended for publication; they also appeared in the *Gate City*. In them Clemens assigns Jane Clemens the role of a worshiping disciple of Fenimore Cooper and admirer of the romantic Noble Savage and portrays himself as a disenchanted old-timer. Later, when he used these same materials in *Roughing It,* he played both roles: he had arrived in the West, he explains, as an innocent tender-foot, full of book learning, but now years later he was writing as a hardened veteran. While the 1872 book version is deservedly better known, these previous letters are a valuable indication of Clemens's development as a writer: he was beginning to assign himself more interesting roles.

The second of these early Nevada letters describes a trip Clemens and three others made to Unionville, Humboldt County, where silver was be-ing discovered and mined. In this letter Clemens mixes information and an-ecdote just as he was to do in his travel books. In a March letter, he responds to an imagined plea from his mother to "tell me all about the lordly sons of the forest." Clemens's response reveals a scornful attitude toward American Indians that would not mellow for decades, unlike his racist views of Afri-can Americans, which dissipated in later years. The description of a repre-sentative Indian, whose name is given as Hoop-dedoodle-do, is thoroughly repulsive. In 1897, Mark Twain wrote that in his youth, "Any young person would have been proud of a 'strain' of Indian blood"; Cooper's great popu-larity was responsible.[30] But on the basis of his experience in Nevada, Clem-ens's advice is, "Now, if you are acquainted with any romantic young ladies or gentlemen who dote on these loves of Indians, send them out here before the disease strikes in."

These long descriptive letters home indicate how thoroughly Clemens was beginning to enjoy playing the skeptic. Chiefly, however, he wanted to get rich quick, and the means was obviously silver. In a letter written to Orion on May 11 and 12, 1862, he reported that he owned a one-eighth interest in a ledge, and "I *know* it to contain our fortune" in gold and silver. The same letter refers to Sam's contributions to the local newspaper; he assumed that Orion was seeing his letters in the *Virginia City Territorial Enterprise*. By June he was thinking seriously of his work as a writer, for he instructs Orion, "Put all of my Josh's letters in my scrap book. I may have use for them some day." (The "Josh" letters written for the *Enterprise* have not survived.) But in the same letter he reports, "I have quit writing for the [Keokuk] 'Gate' [City]. I haven't got time to write." Perhaps it was at this juncture that he was obliged to take on a job that was nothing but manual labor. Ten years later he wrote, "I shoveled quartz in a silver mill at ten dollars a week, for one entire week, & then resigned, with the consent & even the gratitude of the entire mill company."[31] A month later he told

Orion to write to the *Sacramento Union* or to members of its staff to an-nounce that "I'll write as many letters a week as they want, for $10 a week — my board must be paid. Tell them I have corresponded with the N. Orleans Crescent, and other papers — and the Enterprise. California is full of people who have interests here, and its d — d seldom they hear from this country." The explanation for his job hunting is that he was in debt: "The fact is, I must have something to do, and that *shortly,* too."

What happened next is not quite clear, though it turned out to have great consequences. According to his autobiography, Clemens now became so desperate that he "stood on the verge of the ministry or the penitentiary." Fortunately, he recounted, he found occasion to submit to the *Enterprise* for publication a clever burlesque of a speech by the chief justice of Nevada just when his services became necessary: the city editor of the *Enterprise,* Dan De Quille (William E. Wright) was planning a trip home to Iowa. Sam's piece was considered witty, and he was hired.[32] A more probable scenario is that Sam was taken on because of the "Josh" series and because employing Sam might mean that the *Enterprise* printing house would get patronage from Sam's brother, the territorial secretary. In any event, within a short time Clemens was a full-time writer for the *Enterprise,* and the *Enterprise* did obtain the printing contract.[33] Clemens soon adopted the pen name "Mark Twain" for his humorous writings, but probably used his real name for serious news stories. Seemingly he identified in important ways with the adopted name, for now he signed a letter to his mother and sister "Mark." According to one letter he sent to them, "I take great pains to let the public know that 'Mark Twain' hails from there [i.e., Missouri]." For his news-paper work, "They pay me," he wrote home, "six dollars a day, and I make 50 per cent profit by doing only three dollars' worth of work."

The development of Samuel Clemens as a writer cannot be fully docu-mented, since a large portion of what he wrote for publication in Nevada was lost. It has been estimated that he published fifteen hundred to three thousand local items, but there is no file of the *Enterprise,* and one can consult only such sources as the slim collection of clippings in a surviving Clemens notebook and the pieces reprinted in other newspapers. These provide a total of fewer than fifty items, although many of them are notable pieces. The earliest extant pieces signed "Mark Twain" are three letters from Carson City dated January 31 and February 3 and 6, 1863. Written while he was on a week's vacation, they are notable chiefly for their tone: good-natured, confidential, nonchalant. For instance, discussing a wedding he had attended, Mark Twain writes that it was "mighty pleasant, and jolly, and sociable, and I wish to thunder I was married myself. I took a large slab of the bridal cake home with me to dream on, and dreamt that I was still a single man, and likely to remain so, if I live and nothing happens — which has given me a greater confidence in dreams than I ever felt before." The name "Mark Twain" was to be identified with the voice heard here: unpretentious, self-assured, good-natured, accessible.

Another development was taking place within Samuel Clemens. He had gone west after having identified himself, if only briefly, with the Confederate cause. At the same time that he was creating "Mark Twain," Clemens was gradually becoming a Union man, though in Nevada he was largely able to avoid the issue of slavery. He was to confront that issue only after the Civil War.

For the *Enterprise,* Mark Twain wrote local items, unsigned editorials, and reports from San Francisco, Carson City, and the territorial legislature and constitutional convention. (For the convention, he and another reporter provided full and in part verbatim accounts. These are of no literary value, and it is impossible to distinguish Clemens's writing from that of his coworker.)[34] Even routine items frequently have a humorous touch. He suggests in "The Spanish Mine," for instance, that "stout-legged persons with an affinity to darkness" might enjoy an hour-long visit to the mine on which he was reporting. Such unsigned items as the following appeared soon after Clemens joined the *Enterprise* staff. "A beautiful and ably conducted free fight came off in C street yesterday, but as nobody was killed or mortally wounded in manner sufficiently fatal to cause death, no particular interest attaches to the matter, and we shall not publicize the details. We pine for murder — these fist fights are of no consequence to anybody." In this piece — written before the earliest appearance of Clemens's nom de plume — one hears for the first time the voice that was to become famous. Excitement made life tolerable in the dull towns of the West, and Clemens was to celebrate his boyish appreciation of it. As diverting as frontier violence was, if necessary one could always resort to theatrics.

In Nevada, Mark Twain was a successful journalist. Some of his stories were picked up by other papers, especially in California, even though few of the surviving ones give an indication of his later abilities. In the boom-or-bust atmosphere of Nevada, he became especially identified with hoaxes; among other things, these were preparations for Huck Finn's admired imaginative deceptions. One of the earliest hoaxes dates from October 15, 1862. It reports the startling discovery of a "petrified man," found "in a sitting posture" with "the right thumb resting against the side of the nose; the left thumb partially supporting the chin, the fore-finger pressing the inner corner of the left eye and drawing it partly open; the right eye was closed, and the fingers of the right hand spread apart. This strange freak of nature" was examined by a local judge, "Justice Sewell or Sowell, of Humboldt City," who convened a jury to hold an inquest, according to this account. The jury concluded that "deceased came to his death from protracted exposure." Published in the *Enterprise,* the story was picked up by twelve credulous newspapers in Nevada and California. Only the San Francisco publication, headed "A Washoe Joke" (Washoe was a native American name given to Nevada), was appropriately captioned by someone who recognized that the petrified man was winking and thumbing his nose.

At the *Enterprise,* Mark Twain was associated with other stimulating young writers, such as the twenty-four-year-old editor, Joseph Goodman, and Dan De Quille, with whom he roomed. (De Quille had already written up his own effective hoax about a personal portable air-conditioning system.) The new journalist soon discovered that his work was not arduous. Reporters from other journals were ready to swap "regulars," reports from continuing sources of news such as the courts and the registry of bullion. If news was short, it could promptly be invented. For a time Clemens lost his ambition, drank a good deal, and gained a reputation for flippancy, bohemianism, and irreverence. He was proud enough of his direct language to defend it in print: "If I choose to use the language of the vulgar, the low-flung and the sinful, and such as will shock the ears of the highly civilized, I don't want him [a compositor] to appoint himself an editorial critic and proceed to tone me down and save me from the consequences of my conduct; that is, unless I pay him for it, which I won't."[35]

The *Enterprise* phase enabled the writer to discover himself—or, more accurately, allowed Sam Clemens to create "Mark Twain." He learned here about the close connection between the comic and the forbidden—the permissible and those aspects of life not to be mentioned in polite society. He intuited, too, that humor is gratifying because it relaxes a repressive atmosphere. Obviously the raw, blustering frontier environment encouraged his explorations. He was, however, never quite able to determine precisely how far he could go without being offensive, although he sensed that he could amusingly violate inhibiting strictures by satirizing the fastidiousness of the genteel and their attitudes toward romantic love, childhood, grand opera, admiration for the "sublime" in nature, even benevolent humanitarianism. He could offend the pretentiousness of the proper by referring to the unmentionable: sows, nose-picking, vomit, spit, warts, singed cats, body odor. (He was never to outgrow the conviction that bad smells are funny.) A mild specimen of this brand of humor is in a "Letter from Mark Twain" published in August 1863 in which he provides an account of his adventures after taking a tonic called "Wake-up Jake." It affected him for forty-eight hours. "And during all that time, I could not have enjoyed a viler taste in my mouth if I had swallowed a slaughter-house." He almost died, he says, of vomiting and another form of elimination.

This sketch is one of the few in which Mark Twain is a buffoon. More often he asserts in exaggerated form his own superiority. The roles he assigns himself are, in one critic's words, those of the "Social Lion, the Nabob, the Entertainer, and the Ladies' Man."[36] He had determined that his assignment was to be insulting and humiliating to others. It would be some time before he learned how much funnier he could be if he himself were humiliated, especially by becoming, in James Cox's phrase, the fool of his own illusions.[37]

San Francisco was a long 150 miles west from Washoe, through the daunting Sierra Nevada range. The trip took thirty hours. But California was the source of supplies for Nevada, and all the bullion was shipped to San Francisco in bars, with three stages a day in each direction. Clemens visited San Francisco several times during his years in Nevada, and at least three times in 1863. His first trip, which lasted two months, occasioned this parting shot from the May 3 *Enterprise:* "As he assigned no adequate reason for this sudden step, we thought him the pitiable victim of self-conceit and the stock mania. . . . Yes, the poor fellow actually thought he possessed some breeding—that Virginia [City] was too narrow a field for his grace and accomplishments, and in this delusion he has gone to display his ugly person and disgusting manners and wildcat on Montgomery street."[38] In a letter published in September 1863, he describes the trip "Over the Mountains" and in it introduces perhaps the first of his antigenteel narrators. Much of the letter is devoted to Mark Twain's account of the stagecoach driver's conversation. For instance: "I see a poor cuss tumble off along here one night—he was monstrous drowsy, and went to sleep when I'd took my eye off of him for a moment—and he fetched up again a boulder, and in a second there wasn't anything left of him but a promiscuous pile of hash!" The use of such an accomplished yarn-spinning figure became an important part of Mark Twain's literary repertoire.

His narrators, usually veterans of long service in their occupations (including miners, ship captains, and stage drivers), are utterly lacking in self-consciousness. As the man behind the writer became more interested in moving upward in the social scale, he found that when he wished to avoid presenting Mark Twain as too "low" and vulgar a personage, he could introduce a vernacular narrator such as the coach driver to tell his tale. He especially enjoyed relying on characters who were both colorfully profane and profoundly innocent.

Another letter on his adventures in California went to New York, where it was published in the *Sunday Mercury* for February 21, 1864. Artemus Ward, whom Clemens had met when the experienced writer visited Virginia City in late 1863, had suggested that he write occasionally for that Eastern paper. In "Those Blasted Children," Mark Twain describes his suffering at the Lick House in San Francisco, where noisy "young savages" pestered him. "It is a living wonder to me that I haven't scalped some of those children before now," he comments unsentimentally. "I expect I would have done it, but then I hardly felt well enough acquainted with them." The recommended remedies for illnesses in children indicate his studied ignorance: for worms, "Administer a catfish three times a week. Keep the room very quiet; the fish won't bite if there is the least noise."

While visiting San Francisco, Clemens obtained a commission to write a series of letters from Nevada to the *Daily Morning Call*. In the summer of 1863, ten letters as well as half a dozen dispatches from Mark Twain in Nevada appeared in that paper. The *Call* announced that these letters "set forth in his easy, readable style the condition of matters and things in Silverland."[39] Showing journalistic competence and good humor, these pieces helped spread his reputation and prepared the way for a later position on the San Francisco newspaper. In order to emphasize wittily the vast difference between the mild San Francisco climate and that of torrid Virginia City, he reported that "last week the weather was passably cool, but it has moderated a good deal since then. The thermometer stands at a thousand, in the shade, today. It will probably go to a million before night." In another letter he writes that Mr. G. T. Sewall was among those bruised recently in a travel accident; he reminds his readers that Sewall is the man who allegedly held the inquest on the death of the petrified man. An amusing piece published in July 1863 explains that crime is much more common in Nevada than in California. "Nothing that can be stolen is neglected. Watches that would never go in California, generally go fast enough before they have been in the Territory twenty-four hours."[40]

One passage, "A Rich Decision," published in the *Call* in August 1863, is particularly notable because it tells a story that Mark Twain was to return to twice. It appears in "The Facts in the Great Landslide Case" in the *Buffalo Express* for April 12, 1870, and (in only slightly revised form) in chapter 34 of *Roughing It*. The 1863 version informs the reader at the beginning that "some of the boys in Carson" were playing a hoax on old Mr. Bunker, an attorney, who was employed to bring suit for the recovery of Dick Sides's ranch after Tom Rust's ranch slid down the mountain and covered it. In the later versions, the hoax is played on the unwary reader as well, and the story, three times as long, is elaborated and dramatized.

In addition, Mark Twain wrote a few sketches from Nevada for the *San Francisco Golden Era,* a weekly founded to encourage the development of literature in the area. The eminent landscape painter Albert Bierstadt had designed the masthead, and numbered among the local writers were Joaquin Miller, Charles W. Stoddard, and Bret Harte, whose "M'liss" had proven to be the first memorable tale of the California frontier. Mark Twain had the good judgment to learn from his fellows. The editors of the *Enterprise* had been apprentices on the *Golden Era,* and its founder, Rollin M. Daggett, had also founded the *Enterprise.* Many items by Mark Twain appeared in the *Golden Era,* but probably only a few were written especially for it. They include "How to Cure a Cold," published September 20, and "The Lick House Ball," published September 27, both in 1863. The former would be one of the earliest to find a place, in revised form, in *Sketches, New and Old* (1875). It also appeared in 1867 in *The Celebrated Jumping Frog of Calaveras County, and Other Sketches,* Mark Twain's first book. It tells of the author's efforts to get rid of that most common of ailments by adopting various cures offered by well-meaning people: cold showers, drinking a quart of salt water (which caused him, he reports, to throw up everything, including, he believes, his "immortal soul"); then a mixture of molasses, aquafortis, turpentine, and drugs; then gin, then gin and molasses, and gin and onions; then travel; next a mustard plaster, and eventually steam baths. He survives, with difficulty.

During his Nevada years, Mark Twain created his first fully developed character equipped to flout gentility. When a rival reporter, actually a friend named Clement T. Rice, criticized Mark Twain's reports of a session of the Nevada legislature, he replied that Rice's accounts were a "festering mass of misstatements the author of whom should be properly termed the 'Unreliable.' "[41] Thereafter, "the Unreliable" was to make frequent appearances in Mark Twain's writings of the period, both as the butt of his humor and as Clemens's alter ego—his coarser side. The Unreliable borrows, without permission, Mark Twain's most elegant clothes, his boots, his hat, his "white kid gloves," and his "heavy gold repeater." Mark Twain finds him in this garb attending an evening party, where he devours huge quantities of food and drink, including a roast pig, and sings a drunken song. Mark Twain offers to duel with him, "boot-jacks at a hundred yards." The Unreliable swindles a San Francisco hotel when the two visit it. He is constantly obnoxious and boorish. When Mark Twain plans to send back to Nevada "something glowing and poetical" on the San Francisco weather, the Unreliable tells him, "Say it's bully, you tallow-brained idiot! that's enough; anybody can understand that; don't write any of those infernal, sick platitudes about sweet flowers, and joyous butterflies, and worms and things, for people to read before breakfast. You make a fool of yourself that way; everybody gets disgusted with you; stuff! be a man or a mouse." The Unreliable is — as Mark Twain frequently chose to be — the sworn enemy of bombast and sentimentality.

In one letter Mark Twain renders an account of the Unreliable's drunken remarks on his visit to San Jose, "Sarrozay." Rice retaliated when Clemens was ill with a cold and had arranged for Rice to attend to *Enterprise* chores. Over Mark Twain's name, Rice published an apology to all those whom he had ridiculed, especially "the Unreliable," and promised to go "in sackcloth and ashes for the next forty days." The next day, Clemens recovered enough to publish a retraction of "his" apology and a denunciation of Rice as "a reptile" and "jackass-rabbit."[42] Later Mark Twain created a similar fictional character of much fuller dimensions, the outspoken "Mr. Brown." The still-developing author was seeking a means of expressing himself frankly but without sullying himself.

Few of the surviving pieces from the *Enterprise* could justifiably be called sketches. One of these, "Ye Sentimental Law Student," quotes a letter, identified as probably by the Unreliable, effusively expressing the devotion of the writer, "the party of the second part," to "Mary, the peerless party of the first part." "The view from the lonely and segregated mountain peak of this portion of what is called and known as Creation," he avers, "with all and singular the hereditaments and appurtenances thereunto appertaining and belonging, is expressively grand and inspiring." For Mary's benefit he extends his comically legalistic description. Another piece, published in May 1864, provides a learned essay on Washoe in response to an innocent inquiry from a Missourian. He replies, for instance, that it may rain for four to seven days in a row, after which "you may loan out your umbrella for twelve months, with the serene confidence which a Christian feels in four aces."

On July 26, 1863, Clemens lost everything he owned, including mining stocks, when the Virginia City hotel where he lived burned down. He may have felt this was a signal that he should leave Nevada. But he continued to identify himself with the place, though he was unwell for a time. He took advantage of the hot mineral springs at Steamboat Springs, then went to San Francisco, but only for a month.

One of the most famous, even notorious, of Mark Twain's writings of his western years is "A Bloody Massacre near Carson" (October 1863). His purpose, he explained later, was to compose a "reformatory satire" on the "dividend-cooking system" of misleading investors, but he admitted that nobody ever saw the point of the satire.[43] This hoax reported that one

Hopkins, who lived in the old log house between Empire City and Dutch Nick's at the edge of a forest, had been driven to despair by the loss of his savings through financial manipulations in San Francisco. He died after having ridden into town, his throat cut ear to ear, with his wife's bloody scalp in his hand. The husband was discovered to have brutally murdered six of his children. The report included many gruesome details. But Hopkins was, in fact, a bachelor; there was no forest for many miles — and Dutch Nick's and Empire City were one and the same. If the reader did not know this geography, he might have detected the hoax nonetheless: Hopkins's riding four to five miles with his throat cut ear to ear ought to have alerted the wary. But the nearby *Gold Hill Daily News* picked up the story as fact, as did other papers. When Mark Twain wrote in the next issue of the *Enterprise,* "I take it all back," he was widely attacked. California newspapers such as the *Sacramento Daily Union* demanded that he be discharged. Eventually the putative "massacre" became part of the local lore, frequently alluded to in newspapers.

In the spring of 1864, Mark Twain's often obnoxious ways finally crossed the line and brought about his departure from Nevada. He had been feuding fiercely, in print, with the publisher of the *Virginia City Union* when, by chance, a piece he had written — but then held back on advice from Dan De Quille — nevertheless appeared in the *Enterprise.* The story had to do with local efforts to raise money for the Sanitary Fund, a Civil War organization resembling the later Red Cross. It had been stated, Mark Twain wrote, that funds raised for the organization had been misdirected to "a Miscegenation Society somewhere in the East." He then asserted that the charge was "a hoax, but not all a hoax, for an effort is being made to divert these funds from their proper course."[44] The *Union* responded by referring to the writer as having "no gentlemanly sense of professional propriety" and being "a vulgar liar."[45] Clemens demanded "a public retraction" or "satisfaction" from James Laird, the editor of the *Union,* "the satisfaction due to a gentleman," although privately he apologized to the women of the Sanitary Fund. "Satisfaction" meant that Clemens was challenging Laird to a duel. As he explained in 1899, "Dueling was in that day a custom there — a temporary one. The weapons were always Colt's navy revolvers, distance 15 paces; fire, & advance; six shots allowed." Although the duel did not take place, it was illegal to "send a challenge, carry a challenge, or receive one."[46] To escape the law, Clemens wrote his brother, "Steve & I are going to the States." On May 29, accompanied by his friends Steve Gillis, a printer and journalist, and Joe Goodman, Clemens went to California. Partly through his love of mischief, partly as the result of others' malice, partly through mischance, Sam Clemens had become persona non grata in the territory.

The *Gold Hill Daily News* bid good riddance: "Shifting the *locale* of his tales of fiction from the Forest of Dutch Nick's to Carson City; the *dramatis personae* thereof from the Hopkins family to the Ladies of the Sanitary Fair; and the plot thereof from murder to miscegenation—he slopped. The indignation aroused by his enormities has been too crushing to be borne by living man, though sheathed with the brass and triple cheek of Mark Twain." But the *Virginia City Old Piute* was kinder: "We shall miss Mark. . . . To know him was to love him. . . . God bless you, Mark!"[47]

The original and authentic Mark Twain sprang from this Nevada stint. There Samuel Clemens found that he could become a writer by dramatizing a portion of himself and then assuming this identity when he wrote. Who was "Mark Twain"? He was, first of all, a writer who had imbibed deeply in what he would describe in chapter 4 of *Roughing It* as "the vigorous new vernacular of the occidental plains and mountains." His natural style derived from the ways of the old-timers, who had found, before him, that genteel Eastern ways fit badly in the West. Rejecting artificiality, superficiality, and the hypocritical cult of polite conformity, Mark Twain emerged as an irreverent skeptic in religion. In San Francisco, he would soon give proof of his anti-establishment views. But he was by no means an alienated loner, for he had enjoyed and valued his membership in the *Territorial Enterprise* group. More humorous than funny, he grew increasingly fond of burlesquing genteel attitudes. He was not able now or later to create a fully consistent literary personality, but he made his hallmark a self-assured, confidential, unhurried tone. This Mark Twain developed from an appreciation of "characters"—honest, natural, straightforward, manly people—whom he esteemed as "simple-hearted" or characterized by their "simplicity." Although their conversational style and manners are by implication anti-genteel, any words such as *low, common, vulgar,* or even *folk* connote condescension that Mark Twain did not express. Samuel Clemens's signal contribution to the achievement of American literature in the twentieth century lies in his respectful discovery of these vernacular values.[48]

CHAPTER TWO

Journalist and Lecturer

amuel Clemens was now to make California his home for two and a half years. Welcomed by the *Golden Era* as "The Sage-Brush Humorist from Silver Land,"[1] he shortly made his presence felt by speaking at a ceremony at Maguire's Opera House. The occasion was less than extraordinary: the presentation of a cane to a marine engineer who had visited San Francisco in order to resurrect a steamship that had sunk in the bay. The speech, published the next day on the front page of the *San Francisco Alta California* (June 13, 1864), was intended to be amusing; "Mark Twain" was clearly a humorist. He chose to speak on behalf of "your countless friends, the noble sons of the forest," such as the Diggers, the Pi-Utes, the Washoes, and the Shoshones, whom he described as "visibly black from the wear and tear of out door life, from contact with the impurities of the earth, and from absence of soap and their natural indifference to water."

Clemens liked California; he wrote to his mother and sister, "This superb climate agrees with me. And it ought, after living where I was never out of sight of snow-banks 24 hours during 3 years." Later, when he had experienced New England, he was less enthusiastic. In *Roughing It* he complained, "No land with an unvarying climate can be very beautiful" (chap. 56). But while he was there, he expressed great satisfaction with the place. In "'Mark Twain' in the Metropolis," written sometime in June for the *Territorial Enterprise,* he described "the birds, and the flowers, and the Chinamen, and the sunshine, and all things that go to make life happy" in

San Francisco. For a longtime resident of Washoe, he explained, life at San Francisco's Occidental Hotel is "Heaven on the half shell."

In *Roughing It,* Mark Twain remembered this time fondly:

> I lived at the best hotel, exhibited my clothes in the most conspicuous places, infested the opera, and learned to seem enraptured with music which oftener afflicted my ignorant ear than enchanted it, if I had had the vulgar honesty to confess it. . . . I attended private parties in sumptuous evening dress, simpered and aired my graces like a born beau, and polked and schottisched with a step peculiar to myself — and the kan garoo. (chap. 58)

He also wrote two striking pieces for the *Golden Era,* published in June and July, "The Evidence in the Case of Smith vs. Jones" and "Early Rising, as Regards Excursions to the Cliff House." The first of these anticipates "Buck Fanshaw's Funeral" in *Roughing It;* here Mark Twain recounts the absurdly contradictory testimony by witnesses to a fight in language designed to entertain the speaker and outrage the judge, who objects to such expressions as "Busted him in the snoot" and "D—n you old tripe." He insists that they "refrain from the embellishments of metaphor and allegory as far as possible." The effect is to make the judge's formality ridiculous. This sketch seems to have been Mark Twain's longest to date, some seventeen thousand words. It makes heavy use of dialogue, with colorful characters adding to the humor.

"Early Rising, As Regards Excursions to the Cliff House" attacks romanticism. Mark Twain repudiates the maxim "Early to bed, and early to rise, / Makes a man healthy, wealthy, and wise" by contrasting the anticipated pleasures of an early-morning trip to the beach with the actuality of the experience. He joins George Washington, who he finds also stood in disagreement with Benjamin Franklin's maxim. The "gorgeous spectacle of the sun in the dawn of his glory; the fresh perfume of flowers still damp with dew" — Mark Twain is having none of it. The misadventures of his trip were "only just and natural consequences of the absurd experiment of getting up at an hour in the morning when all God-fearing Christians ought to be in bed." The sketch epitomizes the identity that Mark Twain presented in 1864: lazy, skeptical, self-indulgent, open, outspoken, humorous without trying to be funny. If he at this time wished to appear authentic, he was successful; his lack of pretense is charming.

Fortunately, when Clemens arrived in San Francisco after his hasty departure from Nevada, he had a convenient place to head for regular work, the *Daily Morning Call,* a newspaper with a circulation of about ten thousand, largest of the five local newspapers. Employed as a reporter from June to October 1864, he was responsible for reporting on local events, and a file of the paper survives. Because he was not often writing as "Mark Twain," it is not always easy to distinguish his anonymous writings from those of other reporters: Edgar Branch has published a collection of over two hundred pieces.[2] Although Clemens's work on the *Call* did not allow the kind of freedom he had enjoyed in Nevada, he produced many amusing pieces. A particularly playful one explains how the earthquakes of June 23 affected the city. Entertainment was to be welcomed, in his view, even from a near catastrophe.

> There were three distinct shocks, two of which were very heavy, and appeared to have been done on purpose, but the third did not amount to much. Heretofore our earthquakes — as all old citizens experienced in this sort of thing will recollect — have been distinguished by a soothing kind of undulating motion, like the roll of waves on the sea, but we are happy to state that they are shaking her up from below now. The shocks last night came straight up from that direction; and it is sad to reflect, in these spiritual times, that they might possibly have been freighted with urgent messages from some of our departed friends.[3]

Another piece may amuse those who remember Huck Finn's analysis of the loot picked up on the steamboat *Walter Scott.* Here Mark Twain catalogs the contents of a drunkard's pockets:

> Two slabs of old cheese; a double handful of various kinds of crackers; seven peaches; a box of lip-salve, bearing marks of great age; an onion; two dollars and sixty-five cents, in two purses, (the odd money being considered as circumstantial evidence that the defendant had been drinking beer at five-cent houses); a soiled handkerchief; a fine-tooth comb; also one of coarser pattern; a cucumber pickle, in an imperfect state of preservation; a leather string; an eye-glass, such as prospectors use; one buckskin glove; a printed ballad, "Call me pet names"; an apple; part of a dried herring; a copy of the Boston Weekly Journal, and copies of several San Francisco newspapers; and in each and every pocket he had two or three chunks of tobacco, and also one in his mouth of such remarkable size as to render his articulation confused and uncertain.[4]

Among other still-readable items are reports on horse races, theatrical performances, political meetings, and sensational crimes. There are no sketches. The one distinctive development to be noted is that at this time the writer was becoming sensitive to political corruption and the incompetence of public officials. The account of his work on the *Call* in his autobiography tells how he prepared a fiery report on how "some hoodlums chasing and stoning a China-man who was heavily laden with the weekly wash of his Christian customers" were observed by a policeman "with an amused interest—nothing more." His story did not appear, however, because, as the editor explained to Clemens, the *Call* had to respect the prejudices of its readers. But he did manage to criticize, though briefly, the *Call* policy in the *San Francisco Dramatic Chronicle*.[5]

When work for the *Call* became tedious, Clemens hired an assistant. But in October he "retired" "by solicitation. Solicitation of the proprietor," as he put it in his autobiography.[6] Some of his energies at this time were going into the preparation of a book, apparently about his Nevada experiences, since in a letter written to Orion and his wife (dated September 28, 1864) he noted that he expected to ask Orion to send the "files" that he kept of his writings.

Bret Harte had just begun to edit the *Californian*, a rival to the *Golden Era*—Harte being an established California writer who had been there since 1854. In the fall, Clemens began to contribute regularly, and he and Harte began a long association, including, much later, the coauthorship of a play. Later still, Harte provided his biographer with a vivid description of what Clemens looked like when they first met. Harte's account suggests that when Clemens moved to the East, he would want to change his appearance considerably.

> His head was striking. He had the curly hair, the aquiline nose, and even the aquiline eye—an eye so eagle-like that a second lid would not have surprised me—of an unusual and dominant nature. His eyebrows were very thick and bushy. His dress was careless, and his general manner one of supreme indifference to surroundings and circumstances. Barnes [editor of the *Morning Call*] introduced him as Mr. Sam. Clemens, and remarked that he had shown a very unusual talent in a number of newspapers contributed over the signature "Mark Twain." . . . He spoke in a slow, rather satirical drawl, which was itself irresistible.[7]

For a time Clemens enjoyed the relationship, but eventually he came to despise Harte for his insincerity, callousness, and dishonesty, as we shall see.[8]

At the *Call*, Clemens had been paid twenty-five dollars a week. For a weekly article for the *Californian*, which Clemens in a September letter to his mother called "the best weekly literary paper in the United States," he was paid just fifty dollars a month. Although little of what he wrote at this time has lasting interest, it was a crucial period in Clemens's life. At last he could write at length and at leisure, and from October 1 through December 3, each issue of the *Californian* contained a piece by him. In the spring and summer of 1865, he was again writing for the *Californian*. He chose to write accounts of adventures, real and imaginary: visits to the Industrial Fair, to the Cliff House to see a whale on the beach, and to the opera. Several pieces deserve attention. In the *Californian*, one is called "Whereas"; later versions, such as the much-abridged one in *Mark Twain's Sketches, New and Old*, are entitled "Aurelia's Unfortunate Young Man." Here Mark Twain looks askance at the subject of romantic love. Alleging that his advice has been sought by one Aurelia Marie, of San Jose, he recounts her sad story. She is "almost heart-broken by the misfortunes she has undergone." Her fiancé lost first his good looks through smallpox, then a leg by walking into a well, then one arm by "premature discharge of a Fourth-of-July cannon," then the other to a carding machine. Her heart was "almost crushed by these latter calamities." Then her lover lost his eyesight to erysipelas, next his other leg, then his scalp to Indians. What SHOULD she do? Aurelia asks. Mark Twain's advice is that she should furnish "her mutilated lover with wooden arms and wooden legs, and a glass eye and a wig, and give him another show." If he survives ninety days, she should marry him. Her risk will be slight, he notes, since the man will not live long—he is accident-prone.

The amusing account is black comedy. Mark Twain's interest, however, is not in the man but in Aurelia's responses, as is shown by the author's matter-of-factness in describing the young man's experiences. The focus is on Aurelia: "It was a sad day for the poor girl when she saw the surgeons reverently bearing away the sack whose use she had learned by previous experience, and her heart told her the bitter truth that some more of her lover was gone." It is not her lover's suffering that interests Aurelia but her own inner life. The sketch is one of young Mark Twain's freshest and most original.

In "Lucretia Smith's Soldier," Mark Twain aims at a somewhat similar target. It is a burlesque of a popular type of literature of the day, the Civil War romance, in the form of a "condensed novel," a genre then cultivated among San Francisco's literary bohemians. Bret Harte published a volume of such parodies in 1867, and this was Mark Twain's second "novel." (The first is the very brief "Original Novelette," published in the *Call* on July 4, 1864.) The satirist was soon to write several more, such as "The Story of the Bad Little Boy" (1865) and "The Story of the Good Little Boy" (1870). Lucretia's story is by "M. T.," who identifies himself as "an ardent admirer of those nice, sickly war stories in *Harper's Weekly.*" He has now soared "happily into the realms of sentiment and soft emotion," inspired by "the excellent beer manufactured at the New York Brewery." The story tells of how Lucretia Smith, seeking to make up for her earlier rejection of her lover, devotedly tends for a long time in the hospital a wounded soldier she takes to be her man, only to discover the truth when the bandages are removed. "O confound my cats," Lucretia exclaims, "if I haven't gone and fooled away three mortal weeks here, snuffling and slobbering over the wrong soldier!" The sketch was widely reprinted in the East, where it hit its target resoundingly. Toned down, it was included in Mark Twain's first book. Although the piece now seems slight and rather silly, it is another useful indication of the antiromanticism and skeptical frame of mind Clemens had developed.

Now Mark Twain was once again writing for the *Enterprise,* as San Francisco correspondent, and again nearly all of what he wrote is lost. Some of the pieces, it is known, criticized the San Francisco police for corruption, ineptitude, and abuse of Chinese immigrants. These made him unpopular with their chief. When Steve Gillis, for whom Clemens had stood bond after a barroom brawl, fled to Virginia City, Clemens chose to leave town, too, rather than contend with the police. On December 4, 1864, he went to the Sierra foothills, to the Mother Lode country of Calaveras County, California, where he stayed with Steve Gillis's brother Jim at Jackass Hill and Angel's Camp. As he put it in 1872–73, "Got too lazy to live, & too restless & enterprising. Went up to Calaveras County & worked in the surface gold diggings 3 months without result."[9] But there were in fact important results, for there he heard several tales that he was to make much of later. In his autobiography he recalled:

> Every now and then Jim would have an inspiration, and he would stand up before the great log fire, with his back to it and his hands crossed behind him, and deliver himself of an elaborate impromptu lie — a fairy tale, an extravagant romance — with Dick Stoker as the hero of it as a general thing. Jim always soberly pretended that what he was relating was strictly history, veracious history, not romance. Dick Stoker, gray-headed and good-natured, would sit smoking his pipe and listen with a gentle serenity to these monstrous fabrications and never utter a protest.[10]

In the notebook he began to keep on New Year's Day 1865, he recorded several items that were to serve as reminders. Among them are these: "The 'Tragedian' & the Burning Shame. No w*omen* ad*mitted*." "Mountaineers in habit telling same old experiences over & over again in these little back settlements. Like Dan's old Ram, wh[i]ch he always drivels about when drunk." "Coleman with his jumping frog—bet stranger $50—stranger had no frog, & C got him one—in the meantime stranger filled C's frog full of shot & he couldn't jump—the stranger's frog won."[11] The first of these would serve as the basis of one of the Duke and the King's performances in *Huckleberry Finn*, and the story of the old ram would be attributed to Jim Blaine in *Roughing It*. The frog item would see use shortly. The notes also mention Ben Coon, a former steamboat pilot who appeared in his writings almost immediately.

Clemens left the mountains on February 25, 1865, and was back in San Francisco the next day, when in his notebook he recorded: "Home again— home again at the Occidental Hotel—find letters from 'Artemus Ward' asking me to write a sketch for his new book of Nevada Territory travels which is soon to come out. Too late—ought to have got the letters 3 months ago. They are dated early in November."[12] Now Mark Twain wrote fourteen more pieces for the *Californian,* published between March and December. In the first of these, "An Unbiased Criticism," he referred to his experiences in the Big Tree region of Calaveras County, where he had "a very comfortable time." Pretending to be a review of the paintings at the new California Art Union, this sketch is a parody of art criticism, or rather what passed for criticism, for like the targets of his satire, "An Unbiased Criticism" is full of irrelevancies. By far the most engaging is a long comment from Ben Coon, who becomes one of Mark Twain's vernacular narrators. He tells the history of his *Webster's Unabridged,* which has made the rounds of the mining camps: "But what makes me mad, is that for all they are so handy about keeping her sashaying around from shanty to shanty and from camp to camp, none of 'em's ever got a good word for her."

Soon Mark Twain renewed his attack on the genteel in a comic, imaginary "Important Correspondence" concerning the vacancy in the pulpit of San Francisco's Grace Cathedral. The position was in fact open at the time, and each of Mark Twain's "correspondents" had indeed been invited to fill it, as the *San Francisco Evening Bulletin* reported.[13] Mark Twain's letter to Bishop Hawks, D.D., of New York encourages him to take it, despite the terms, for the author argues that he has "a great deal of influence with the clergy here" and "can get them to strike for higher wages any time." The reply concocted for the bishop is full of gratitude. Both writers suggest that they understand the game, with its formalities, pretenses, and hypocrisies. "Hawks" writes:

> I threw up my parish in Baltimore, although it was paying me very
> handsomely, and came to New York to see how things were going in our

line. I have prospered beyond my highest expectations. I selected a lot of my best sermons — old ones that had been forgotten by everybody — and once a week I let one of them off in the Church of the Annunciation here. The spirit of the ancient sermons bubbled forth with a bead on it and permeated the hearts of the congregation with a new life, such as the worn body feels when it is refreshed with rare old wine. It was a great hit. The timely arrival of the "call" from San Francisco insured success to me. The people appreciated my merits at once. A number of gentlemen immediately clubbed together and offered me $10,000 a year and agreed to purchase for me the Church of St. George the Martyr, up town, or to build a new house of worship for me if I preferred it.

Mark Twain manages to create just the right tone for the bishop, with biblical echoes and pious sentiments mixed skillfully with frank expressions of opportunism. Moreover, the satirist had his facts straight about the New York reaction to his "call."

Following a long and witty commentary on the bishop's letter, he promises to publish in the next issue the replies of the Rev. Phillips Brooks of Philadelphia and the Rev. Dr. Cummings of Chicago. But instead he published their telegrams, urging him not to do so and each offering five hundred dollars to discourage him. But now, he reports, he has become overwhelmed by other ambitious clergymen, each seeking his support, some even turning up to be his guests, with good appetites. The combination of affected charity and actual vulgarity makes this whole "correspondence" funny, fresh, and on target, one of the high points of Mark Twain's writing career in California.

In these pieces he was expressing sentiments quite consistent with the values of his other pieces. He had developed a skeptical attitude and a vernacular style to go with it. Making fun of clerical ambition and the associated hypocrisy was part of the same attitude that dismissed romantic love and sentimental views of nature.

In June 1865, the *Californian* announced a new department, "Answers to Correspondents," a parody of the columns featured in many periodicals then as now, though at that time literary advice was sometimes sought as well as more personal kinds of advice. Mark Twain wrote six columns and included parts of them in his 1867 *Jumping Frog* collection. One item is a poem, prefaced by a letter from the poet "Simon Wheeler" of Sonora, California. These demonstrate Mark Twain's continuing interest in vernacular characters, especially narrators, and his increasing skill in rendering their language and their values. Soon Simon Wheeler would achieve wide and lasting fame.

Although some of the pieces written at this time indicate a lack of development, there are two important exceptions, a letter and a story. The letter is Clemens's first real indication of a commitment to writing, to literature. On October 19, 1865, he shared with Orion what he called his life's ambitions. He relates that in his early years he had been interested in becoming a pilot and a preacher; he had achieved the first goal but not the second because he had never had a call. "But I *have* had a 'call' to literature, of a low order—i.e., humorous. It is nothing to be proud of, but it is my strongest suit." The tone of resignation in this letter presumably comes partly because he had now reconciled himself to the fact that the stocks he owned were never going to be worth much, as he had strongly believed, and partly from the fact that humorists did not enjoy a good reputation on the West Coast or elsewhere. If he accepted the role of humorist, he would have to produce a new and distinctive kind of humor—literary burlesque was commonplace—in order to obtain much-needed self-respect. He did recognize that he had talent. As he told Orion, God "did His part by me—for the talent is a mighty engine when supplied with the steam of *education*—which I have not got."

About the time that he wrote this letter, Mark Twain produced the first solid evidence that he had been *called,* nearly a year after he had heard the frog story. Two surviving false starts show that he was being very deliberate in composing this piece; he must have known that he had good materials to care for. One of these early versions, less than one thousand words, is entitled "Angel's Camp Constable." It deals with one of the vernacular narrator Simon Wheeler's pet heroes. The other, too, is only a fragment; it never gets around to its announced topic. Like the version that was at last completed and published, it is a letter addressed to Artemus Ward, who—it will be recalled—had written to Clemens in the fall of 1864 asking for a sketch for his Nevada book. This second fragment, first published in 1981, is entitled "The Only Reliable Account of the Celebrated Jumping Frog of Calaveras County, together with some reference to the decaying city of Boomerang, and a few general remarks concerning Mr. Simon Wheeler, a resident of the said city in the day of its Grandeur." The fact that the story was nine months in gestation suggests that the writer was just beginning to realize what he was to emphasize often in his later years in his comments about literature, notably in "How to Tell a Story," that the "humorous story depends for its effect upon the manner of telling."

The version of Mark Twain's story that was published in the *New York Saturday Press* of November 18, 1865, is entitled "Jim Smiley and His Jumping Frog." (It had arrived too late for publication in *Artemus Ward, His*

Travels.) Told with infinite care, the story is narrated by two tellers, Mark Twain, who introduces his account somewhat pompously, and Simon Wheeler, the garrulous vernacular storyteller, who sets forth his story for Mark Twain's ears. Simon Wheeler, the erstwhile poet, was kin to Ben Coon of Angel's Camp, who (according to Mark Twain's 1897 account) had told him the story.[14] The addition of a second narrator, carefully characterized, enriches the sketch greatly. There is irony in both tellings. The writer pretends that he has had to put up with a preposterous bore as the result of Artemus Ward's request that he look up the Rev. Leonidas W. Smiley; and Simon Wheeler, whom he meets on his search, pretends that there is nothing funny about the story he tells in response. Wheeler possessed "the first virtue of a comedian," the term used in " 'Mark Twain' in the Metropolis" (1864), "which is to do humorous things with grave decorum and without seeming to know that they are funny." Moreover, Wheeler's artfully told story seems endless and pointless. A double irony allows readers to feel superior to the narrator, although an alert one sees the writer is making sport of portraying himself as well.

The story focuses on the narrator as victim, since victimization is also a theme of the story. Jim Smiley, the optimistic and compulsive gambler, always looking for a little excitement, can be fooled by a stranger because he lacks the caution of the experienced Westerner. But before Simon Wheeler reveals Smiley's gullibility in the climax of the yarn, he creates interest in the gambler, as well as in his animals, exaggerated to heroic proportions. The story moves from a catalog of Jim's interests, including chicken fights and straddle-bug races, to a discussion of his horse's surprising abilities and the distinct personality of his dog, the well-named Andrew Jackson. Now Wheeler is ready to tell about Smiley's frog, Dan'l Webster. Wheeler comments, admiringly, "You never see a frog so modest and straightfor'ard as he was, for all he was so gifted."

As the story moves to its climax, the narration moves to drama, and we hear conversations between Jim and the stranger, whose coolness more than matches Jim's studied indifference. Jim thinks he has entrapped the stranger when the latter observes, "I don't see no points about that frog that's any better'n any other frog." Jim's search for a frog for the stranger, to compete with Dan'l, provides the stranger with time to fill what was to become known as the celebrated jumping frog of Calaveras County "pretty near up to his chin" with quail-shot. Thus the stranger's frog is permitted to win, whereupon the winner repeats, again coolly, "I don't see no points about that frog that's any better'n any other frog," and leaves.

It is Mark Twain's control of point of view that makes the story so rich.

We see the narrator's view of Simon Wheeler, and Wheeler's view of Jim Smiley; each is consistent, and subtle. The story gave the writer a new sense of his capabilities. Even before it was published, the *New York Round Table* in an article on "American Humor and Humorists" had called him "foremost" of the "merry gentlemen of the California press." Clemens saw the article, for it was quoted in at least two San Francisco publications. In January, he sent his mother a clipping from the New York correspondent of the *San Francisco Alta California:* "Mark Twain's story in the *Saturday Press* of November 18, called 'Jim Smiley and His Jumping Frog,' has set all New York in a roar, and he may be said to have made his mark. I have been asked fifty times about it and its author, and the papers are copying it far and near. It is voted the best thing of the day. Cannot the *Californian* afford to keep Mark all to itself? It should not let him scintillate so widely without first being filtered through the California Press." The *Californian* of December 16 reprinted the piece.

Mark Twain's Eastern reputation was spread through a series of eight pieces appearing in the *New York Weekly Review* in 1865 and 1866, the first being an account of the October 7 San Francisco earthquake. But there was no sudden change in the author's fortunes. He continued to write for the *Enterprise,* many of his letters being reprinted in the *Golden Era.* In the letter to Orion about his call to humorous literature, he announced that he was beginning work as a reviewer for the *San Francisco Dramatic Chronicle.* Although it was the earliest version of San Francisco's current leading newspaper, it was a poor thing, a four-page advertising handout, in which Mark Twain's work consisted of squibs and fillers in addition to reviews — all anonymous. Only one short sketch appeared there, "Earthquake Almanac." The pages of the *Chronicle* mention Mark Twain frequently during his two months of employment, but usually he is identified as the *Enterprise* correspondent. He also contributed two pieces to the *Examiner* and one piece, ridiculing women's fashions, to the *Evening Bulletin.*

Six new pieces appeared in the *Californian* in late 1865 and early 1866. One deserves mention. "The Christmas Fireside for Good Little Boys and Girls. *By Grandfather Twain,*" subtitled "The Story of the Bad Little Boy That Bore a Charmed Life," appeared on December 23. The story takes all the conventions of the moralistic children's fable and naughtily turns them upside down. This bad little boy has none of the appeal of Tom Sawyer; in fact, he is thoroughly wicked. "And he grew up, and married, and raised a large family, and brained them all with an axe one night, and got wealthy by all manner of cheating and rascality, and now he is the infernalest wickedest scoundrel in his native village, and is universally respected, and belongs to the Legislature." Here Mark Twain presents himself as the satirical outsider.

Such sketches required a fertile imagination; finding something to write about was a constant strain, and he was barely making a living. He was frustrated. In *Roughing It,* he explains that "my interest in my work was gone; for my [*Enterprise*] correspondence being a daily one, without rest or respite, I got unspeakably tired of it. I wanted another change" (chap. 62).[15] Clemens still had in mind the idea of a book, which he mentioned in a letter to his mother and sister on January 20, 1866, but "nobody knows what it is going to be about but just myself." His boredom is reflected in his surviving *Enterprise* letters. After complaining in his January letter that his life was uneventful and that he wished he had accepted an invitation to take a round trip on the *Ajax* to the Sandwich Islands (the Hawaiian Islands), he visited Sacramento, and there the *Daily Union* commissioned him to write twenty or thirty letters from Hawaii. He was to go on the next sailing. This experience was pivotal, for it gave him an opportunity for sustained writing. The experience and observations were a combination that would prove fruitful in his travel books and novels.

Clemens left San Francisco on March 7, 1866, and returned August 13. Concerning this visit he wrote one letter for the *New York Saturday Press,* one for the *New York Weekly Review,* and twenty-five letters to the *Sacramento Union.* He stayed much longer than he expected, as he explained to Will Bowen, an old friend from Hannibal days, in a May 7 letter from Maui.

> I contracted with the Sacramento Union to go wherever they chose & correspond for a few months, & I had a sneaking notion they would start me east — but behold how fallible is human judgment! — they sent me to the Sandwich Islands. I look for a recall by the next mail, though, because I have written them that I cannot go all over the eight inhabited islands of the group in less than five months & do credit to myself & them, & I don't want to spend so much time. I have been here two months, & yet have only "done" the island of Oahu & part of this island of Maui, & it is going to take me two more weeks to finish this one & at least a month to "do" the island of Hawaii & the great volcanoes — & by that time, surely, I can hear from them. But I have had a gorgeous time of it so far.

He visited only those three islands.

Later Clemens edited his Hawaiian letters into a book manuscript, but he was not able to find a publisher. (Subsequently, he revised them for inclusion as chapters 63–77 of *Roughing It.*) While readers of that book usually find the Hawaii chapters weaker than the earlier ones on Nevada and California, the explanation is simply that he was a rapidly maturing writer and that the earlier chapters were written after Clemens's trip to Europe and Middle East and the publication of *The Innocents Abroad*.

Mark Twain's growth from a writer of sketches and news stories, humorous and otherwise, created a change that would lead to severe tensions in his career. Hitherto, in Nevada and California, he had been a critic of the dominant culture. He had chided the clergy, the courts, and the police. He had ridiculed women's fashions. He had even criticized children and romantic young women. He had presented himself as an associate of the disgusting "Unreliable." He was an outsider, a bohemian. In the increasingly sophisticated San Francisco, he was identified as being from Washoe, and he constantly reminded his readers of his origins. He was lazy, a loafer. As a writer he was a hoaxer and a humorist, a man of limited education and uncertain ambition. All this was to change, at least on the surface.

In Hawaii, he discovered, he was a man of importance, on an assignment that gave him prestige. As a result he associated with people of a sort that he would not have known on the mainland. He visited the king; he met the American minister, and he was befriended by Anson Burlingame, who was on his way to an important position in China. When Burlingame asked to see his writings, Clemens provided, as he told his mother in June, "pretty much everything I ever wrote." Soon Burlingame was helping him with a news story about a fire on board the clipper ship *Hornet;* his account was to spread his reputation. Because Clemens was in bed with aggravated boils, Burlingame arranged to have him taken to the hospital on a stretcher to interview the survivors. Then, as he explained many years later in "My Début as a Literary Person," he "spent four hours arranging the notes in their proper order, then wrote all night and beyond it." By nine o'clock the next morning, he was able to get his story on a departing ship; his "scoop" was given space on the front page of the *Sacramento Union*.

Burlingame advised him, "Avoid inferiors. Seek your comradeships among your superiors in intellect and character; always *climb*."[16] The advice was to be heeded, and Samuel Clemens would climb, sometimes leaving Mark Twain far behind, often with unfortunate results for the writer — and perhaps also for the person.

Mark Twain was still a humorist, but the invention of a companion for the traveling writer, Mr. Brown, permitted him to appear much less vulgar himself. To Brown he assigned anything crude or earthy he wished to say. This technique he may have picked up from the English humorist William Combe, who created a sentimental traveler who was accompanied by a servant with a quite different point of view, or, more likely, from Charles Dickens, whose Mr. Pickwick and his servant, Sam Weller, are of the same pattern. (Clemens had read *Pickwick Papers* while in Nevada.)[17] Reporting the adventures of two travelers gave Mark Twain two levels of action: what the travelers saw, and the byplay between Brown and himself. Mark Twain calls Brown "this bitter enemy of sentiment." When Brown is nauseated but unable to find relief, Mark Twain reads him sentimental poetry. "'It is enough,' said Brown, and threw up everything he had eaten for three days." When Mark Twain reports how much he likes the islands, Brown reads the account and proposes that he go on to describe the "cockroaches, and fleas, and lizards, and red ants, and scorpions, and spiders, and mosquitoes, and missionaries."[18]

The best passages are those in which Mark Twain is neither the admiring visitor nor his vulgar companion, but the witty, skeptical, ironic commentator—the writer created by his Western experience. For example, on the subject of the old pagan religion, he observes that there is

> a place where human sacrifices were offered up in those old by-gone days, when the simple child of nature, yielding momentarily to sin when sorely tempted, acknowledged his error when calm reflection had shown it to him, and came forward with noble frankness and offered up his grandmother as an atoning sacrifice—in those old days when the luckless sinner could keep on cleansing his conscience and achieving periodical happiness as long as his relations held out; long, long before the missionaries braved a thousand privations to come and make them permanently miserable by telling them how impossibly beautiful and how blissful a place heaven is, and how nearly impossible it is to get there; and showed the poor native how dreary a place perdition is and what unnecessarily liberal facilities there are for going to it; showed him how, in his ignorance, he had gone and fooled away all his kinfolks to no purpose, showed him what rapture it is to work all day long for fifty cents to buy food for next day with, as compared with fishing for pastime and lolling in the shade through eternal Summer, and eating of the bounty that nobody labored to provide but Nature. How sad it is to think of the multitudes who have gone to their graves in this beautiful island and never knew there was a hell! And it inclines a right thinking man to weep rather than to laugh when he reflects how surprised they must have been when they got there.[19]

Experience in the Pacific islands fed Mark Twain's religious skepticism as it had for Herman Melville before him.

Despite their humor, the Hawaiian letters are now chiefly interesting as historical accounts. They treat geography, the character of the native Hawaiians, politics, industry, and religion. The visitor makes a strong case for San Francisco becoming a whaling center to replace Honolulu. He makes other proposals, such as the use of "coolie" labor in the production of sugar.

While in Hawaii, Mark Twain began a little-known connection with the short-lived *Daily Hawaiian Herald;* from September 5 till December 13 he provided seven contributions, mostly short.[20]

On his way back to California in July 1866, Clemens had the good fortune of finding the surviving captain and two passengers of the *Hornet* and was able to copy their diaries. These, with his account in the *Union,* were the basis of "Forty-three Days in an Open Boat." Clemens was especially proud of this account of the burning of the ship and the survivors' story, as he explained much later in "My Début as a Literary Person," for to qualify for this exalted term, "he must appear in a magazine." His article appeared in what he considered "the most important one in New York," *Harper's New Monthly Magazine.* He proudly called the publication of *this* article (not the "Jumping Frog") his literary debut, and he expected thereby to spread his name "all over the world, now, in this one jump." The article appeared in the December 1866 issue but without a signature; in the index the author was identified as "Mark Swain." The author was indeed a "Literary Person," but "a buried one, buried alive."

In California, Sam Clemens found that he had some money for once: he collected eight hundred dollars from the *Union.* He also had an improved and widened reputation. But he was not sure what to do with himself. In his notebook for August 13 he recorded: "San Francisco — Home again. No — *not* home again — in prison again — and all the wild sense of freedom gone. The city seems so cramped, & so dreary with toil & care & business anxiety. God help me, I wish I were at sea again!"[21] The passage suggests that Clemens had much in common with Tom Sawyer and Huck Finn: a love of freedom and a hatred of routine. He needed excitement and found it where he could. He took advantage of his reputation as an authority on Hawaii to lecture on the subject, and on October 2 he drew a crowd of perhaps eighteen hundred to Maguire's Academy of Music in San Francisco. This was not Clemens's first public lecture, for he had contributed his services to a fund-raising effort for a Carson City church in 1864, but it was the first intended to be profitable to the lecturer. His handbill ominously warned, "The Trouble Begins at 8 O'Clock." Many years later, in 1904, he remembered,

> A true prophecy. The trouble certainly did begin at eight, when I found myself in front of the only audience I had ever faced, for the fright which pervaded me from head to foot was paralyzing. It lasted two minutes and

was as bitter as death; the memory of it is indestructible, but it had its compensations, for it made me immune from timidity before audiences for all time to come.[22]

This lecture was such a success that soon he was speaking on the same topic, with variations, in Sacramento, Marysville, Grass Valley, and eventually in Virginia City, Carson City, and other Nevada towns. Although it contained information, the lecture was full of comic digressions and asides. "It is not safe to come to any important matter in an entirely direct way. When a young gentleman is about to talk to a young woman about matrimony he don't go straight at it. He begins by talking about the weather. I have done that many a time."[23]

Making direct contact with his audience, standing before them not so much as the conveyor of information but as the public personality "Mark Twain," now one of the best known writers in the West, Clemens was rapidly discovering, by trial and error, what it was he could do best. For a good while, lecturing was stimulating, exciting. On December 10 he had the honor of making a special appearance in San Francisco at the request of the governors of California and Nevada, among others. The lecturer was nearly always able to avoid pomposity; it was not difficult for this drawling humorist, for he could control an audience.

The discovery of his talent as a lecturer was to have an important effect on Clemens's life. It focused the writer's attention on how he presented himself but diverted his energies from writing at several points in his career. He became very much in demand as a lecturer, and lecturing was lucrative, a ready source of funds. Eventually he was to switch to reading selections from his writings, as Dickens had done. But in time Clemens's laziness, the enormous success of his 1869 book, and his dislike of routine would keep him from an extended career on the platform.

His Hawaiian experience gave Mark Twain a new role as a lecturer and as a writer, that of mock-serious moralist. In a short piece in the *Californian,* dated August 20, he applied for the editorship of that journal as "The Moral Phenomenon," a title he says he was given by the Sandwich Island missionaries. He had himself served, he declares, as "a missionary to the Sandwich Islands, and I have got the hang of that sort of thing to a fraction." As editor, he would replace sentimental tales, wit, humor, and elevated literature with morality, just what he believes is really called for.[24] If Clemens was now ambitious, ready to undertake the social climbing Burlingame had urged, he was not yet willing to stifle his irreverence. He now added to the cluster of Mark Twain's attributes the pretense of being, sometimes, a moralist.

For five and a half eventful years, Clemens had not been home to Missouri. Tired of the West, he contracted with the *San Francisco Alta California* to supply a weekly letter "on such subjects and from such places as will best suit him," during a trip that would, according to the expectations of the *Alta* proprietors, take Clemens to Europe, India, China, Japan, and back to San Francisco.[24] He left for New York on December 15, 1866. The *Alta* published his farewell the day before his departure. He declared that he was leaving San Francisco "for a season . . . to go back to that common home we all tenderly remember in our waking hours and fondly visit in dreams of the night — a home that is familiar to my recollections but will be an unknown land to my unaccustomed eyes."[25] He wrote to his family that he was "leaving more friends behind . . . than any newspaperman that ever sailed out of the Golden Gate."

In the next eight months, twenty-six letters signed "Mark Twain" appeared in the *Alta*. Although he did nothing more with them, they were collected in 1940 into a book aptly titled *Mark Twain's Travels with Mr. Brown,* since the traveler is accompanied, at least in the early pages, by his vulgar companion. Not as well known as the Hawaiian letters and probably not taken as seriously by their author (who was not now traveling in order to write for a newspaper), these letters are nonetheless attractive and significant in the growth of the writer. Through them one follows Clemens on his trip from San Francisco to Nicaragua, across the isthmus, then up to Key West and on to New York. On the first leg of the journey he met Captain Edgar Wakeman, who was to appear again and again in Mark Twain's works, including *Roughing It,* where he is Captain Ned Blakely, and in "Captain Stormfield's Visit to Heaven," which the writer began in 1868 but did not publish until the end of his life. In his *Alta* letters he had a good deal to say about Wakeman, but the more hearty comment, though incomplete, is in his notebook: "I had rather travel with that portly, hearty, jolly, boisterous, good-natured old sailor, Capt Ned Wakeman than with any other man I ever came across. He never drinks, & never plays cards; he never swears, except in the privacy of his own quarters, with a friend or so, & then his feats of blasphemy are calculated to fill the hearer with awe & admiration. His yarns — " Here he broke off.[26]

Later, long after he found it difficult, if not impossible, to call up his early literary personality, Mark Twain was able to return to the spirit of his earlier self by the use of a vernacular narrator, and a favorite was Captain Wakeman. In one of his *Alta* letters, Mark Twain lets Wakeman tell tall tales of rats. Here Wakeman tells how rats saved his life by indicating that a ship was not safe.

We were going home passengers from the Sandwich Islands in a bran-new brig, on her third voyage, and our trunks were below—he [his friend Josephus] went with me—laid over one vessel to do it—because he warn't no sailor, and he liked to be conveyed by a man that was—felt safer, you understand—and the brig was sliding out between the buoys, and her headline was paying out ashore—there was a woodpile right where it was made fast on the pier—when up come the biggest rat—as big as an ordinary cat, he was, and darted out on that line and cantered for the shore! and up come another! and another! and another! and away they galloped over the hawser, each one treading on t'other's tail, till they were so thick you couldn't see a thread of cable, and there was a procession of 'em three hundred yards long over the levee like a streak of pismires, and the Kanakas [Hawaiians], some throwing sticks from that woodpile and chunks of lava and coral at 'em and knocking 'em endways every shot—but do you suppose it made any difference to them rats?—not a particle—not a particle on earth, bless you!—they'd smelt trouble!—they'd smelt it by their unearthly, supernatural instinct!—they wanted to go, and they never let up till the last rat was ashore out of that bran-new beautiful brig.[27]

Wakeman and his friend wisely followed the rats' example and thereby saved their lives; the ship was never seen again. In the *Alta* letters he is alternately Wakeman and Waxman, though Mark Twain insisted that all the names he used were fictitious.

The trip to New York was by way of Nicaragua, which took two days to cross on "horseback, muleback, and four-mules ambulances," with Clemens traveling by ambulance or "mud wagons."[28] On board the ship that then took them from Nicaragua, cholera broke out among the steerage passengers and soon spread. There were several deaths. Many passengers left the ship when it landed at Key West. On January 12, 1867, the ship reached New York.

What he would do next was not clear to the journalist. Three days after he arrived in New York, Clemens wrote to E. P. Hingston, who had been Artemus Ward's manager, to report that he was planning a lecture tour but needed Hingston to manage him. He wrote to Orion's wife from New York in February that he had been made good offers by newspapermen, and he arranged for the *New York Weekly Review* to publish five of his Sandwich Island letters. By early March he had discovered that "Prominent Brooklyn-ites are getting up a great European pleasure excursion for the coming summer" (p. 111), as he explained to his California readers. His account describes at length how he and a fellow journalist had visited the chief officer of the excursion, with his friend entertaining himself by introducing the Rev. Mark Twain of San Francisco. Playing along, Clemens explained, "I have latterly been in the missionary business." Clemens's friend elaborated on the joke and arranged for him to preach on the vessel while at sea. The next day Clemens went back to book passage for himself and reveal his true identity. The cruise was intended to have a strong religious orientation, with a visit to the Holy Land as a feature. When the letter describing all this appeared in the *Alta,* readers were notified by the editor that Mark Twain's plans had been authorized by his employers. He would leave for Europe in June.

In the interim, in March, Clemens went on to Missouri, where he lectured in St. Louis on the Sandwich Islands and published a series of funny pieces on "Female Suffrage"[29] and then went on to Hannibal, where he also lectured.[30] His visit to his hometown caused him to recall Jimmy Finn and the excitement he brought to Hannibal. Finn was to be portrayed as Huck's "pap." How close to fact the portrait of the town drunkard is in the novel may be suggested by this 1867 account of Finn's reformation and its aftermath.

> Jimmy Finn, the town drunkard, reformed, and that broke up the only saloon in the village. But the temperance people liked it; they were willing enough to sacrifice public prosperity to public morality. And so they made much of Jimmy Finn — dressed him up in new clothes, and had him out to breakfast and to dinner, and so forth, and showed him off as a great living curiosity — a shining example of the power of temperance doctrines when earnestly and eloquently set forth. Which was all very well, you know, and sounded well, and looked well in print but Jimmy Finn couldn't stand it. He got remorseful about the loss of his liberty; and then he got melancholy from thinking about it so much; and after that, he got drunk. He got awfully drunk in the chief citizen's house, and the next morning that house was as if the swine had tarried in it. (p. 214)

Perhaps because of this Hannibal visit Mark Twain soon wrote up another anecdote from his boyhood memories. A request for a contribution to the *New York Sunday Mercury* resulted in "Jim Wolf and the Tom-Cats." While he had some references to boyhood memories in the *Alta* and elsewhere, notably his experience as a "Cadet of Temperance," this is the first extended piece on the subject. The hero, or victim, is Sam's bashful friend Jim, some sixteen years of age, whose efforts one winter night to chase away noisy cats that had awakened him from his sleep leads him on to an icy roof in nothing but his short shirt. He slips and ends up in the midst of a group of girls having a candy pull. The story purports to be, however, not what the author remembers but a story he heard from Simon Wheeler, who had once again caught his visitor and made him listen. In this comic story, the theme is humiliation, but pain and pleasure are artfully mixed. While Wheeler takes pleasure in Jim's acute embarrassment, his humor also helps him to preserve his sense of proportion—and the reader's, too.[31] The story was widely reprinted. Mark Twain liked the story so much that he retold it twice, each time with modifications, in an 1872 speech and in his autobiography.[32]

In the *Alta* letters, the writer reports the limited success of his ambitions to publish a book. When the publishers of Artemus Ward's collection (in which the "Jumping Frog" was to have appeared) rejected his manuscript, Charles Henry Webb, former editor of the *Californian* and now in New York City, arranged to publish *The Celebrated Jumping Frog of Calaveras County, and Other Sketches* in late April. Described as "Edited by John Paul," Webb's pen name, it contains twenty-seven pieces. The author and Webb revised the sketches and stories selected for publication by removing slang, local references, and allusions to gambling, alcohol, sex, and damnation. This first censorship was largely self-inflicted.[33] The prefatory advertisement in the volume explains playfully that "the somewhat fragmentary character of many of the sketches" resulted from "detaching them from serious and moral essays with which they were woven and entangled" in the writings of the man known as "the Moralist of the Main." In his *Alta* letter, Mark Twain praises the "truly gorgeous frog" on the cover, so beautiful that maybe it will be well to "publish the frog and leave the book out" (p. 158).

The writer made nothing from the sales of his first book, to his considerable disappointment. In December 1870, he wrote to F. S. Drake that he had "fully expected the 'Jumping Frog' to sell 50,000 copies & it only sold 4,000." But unbeknownst to him, the publication benefited him considerably. It was pirated by the English publishers George Routledge and Sons and John Camden Hotten, who sold more than 40,000 copies. Moreover, the volume received favorable reviews in England.[34]

Neither from the *Frog* collection nor from the *Alta* letters of the period does one get a strong sense of Mark Twain's identity as a writer. He appears particularly divided on the question of his social standing. Did he want to climb, as Burlingame had urged? He had discreetly cleaned up his earlier pieces for book publication. He was sensitive to the differences between East and West, as his comments in an *Alta* letter show: Sut Lovingood's collection of humorous sketches "will sell well in the West, but the Eastern people will call it coarse and possibly taboo it" (p. 221). Was he to be of the West or of the East? His fortunes seemed to be carrying him east, and his comments in his letters about his New York experience seem to show an increasing liking for it. And New York was where he must succeed. "Make your mark in New York," he wrote to the *Alta*, "and you are a made man. With a New York endorsement you may travel the country over . . . but without it you are speculating on a dangerous issue" (p. 176). On the other hand, he was willing to describe the night he spent in jail as a result of trying to stop a fight: he seems to have enjoyed meeting the prisoners there. He delighted in the conversation of bootblacks; their speech and sentiments are reported appreciatively. He is gladdened that his "old Washoe instincts that have lain asleep in my bosom so long are waking up here in the midst of this late and unaccountable freshet of blood-letting that has broken out in the East." The newspapers are full of violence — murders, suicides, assassinations, fights. "It is a wonderful state of things," he reports (p. 232). The coarseness that he had identified with, even cultivated, in the West — what part was it to have in the continuing development of the literary personality of Mark Twain? Samuel Clemens obviously did not know.

Mr. Brown was disappearing from his *Alta* letters. He appears frequently in the earlier ones, but later he makes appearances only when Mark Twain seems at a loss for something to write about. He is absent from the non-humorous letters written in May, one about a visit to the Bible House of the American Bible Society, one about an asylum for the blind. These institutions could scarcely be treated comically, and the writer had decided to report on more serious subjects. When Mark Twain visits an exhibition at the Academy of Design, he does feel free to make jokes and profess pride in his ignorance: he is "glad the old masters are dead, and I only wish they had died sooner" (p. 239). But his comments are not vulgar or outspoken, as they would be later, when he saw the old masters' paintings in Europe. He was even now working his way to a position that he was to set forth more fully eight years later in "Old Times on the Mississippi." Here he writes:

> It is a gratification to me to know that I am ignorant of art, and ignorant also of surgery. Because people who understand art find nothing in pictures but blemishes, and surgeons and anatomists see no beautiful women in all their lives, but only a ghastly stack of bones with Latin names to them, and a network of nerves and muscles and tissues inflamed by disease. The very point in a picture that fascinates me with its beauty, is to the cultured artist a monstrous crime against the laws of coloring; and the very flush that charms me in a lovely face, is, to the critical surgeon, nothing but a sign hung out to advertise a decaying lung. Accursed be all such knowledge. I want none of it. (p. 238)

Later he would compare the unromantic outlook of the physician and that of the steamboat pilot, who can no longer appreciate the beauty of the river.

This appreciation of the blessings of innocence and ignorance contrasts sharply with another observation, one that shows he had not forgotten that his Western experiences had led him to shed some of his illusions. He writes, "I am waiting patiently to hear that they have ordered General Connor out to polish off those Indians, but the news never comes. He has shown that he knows how to fight the kind of Indians that God made, but I suppose the humanitarians want somebody to fight the Indians that J. Fenimore Cooper made. There is just where the mistake is. The Cooper Indians are dead — died with their creator. The kind that are left are of altogether a different breed, and cannot be successfully fought with poetry, and sentiment, and soft soap, and magnanimity" (p. 266).

Despite uncertainties about his literary identity, Mark Twain tried out a version of his Sandwich Islands lecture. He badly needed the money for the trip he was about to take.[35] In May he appeared at the Cooper Institute, the Athenaeum in Brooklyn, and at Irving Hall in New York, with his friend from the west Frank Fuller as manager. His topic was the Sandwich Islands; the lectures were well received, to the lecturer's great relief. He considered these lectures "a first-rate success"; he "came out handsomely" (pp. 178–79). He had been painfully aware that there were many competing attractions.

Later he would build effectively on this success; now his real interest was the trip he was about to undertake. He wrote to his mother on June 1 of being "wild with impatience to move — move — *move!*" A week later he complained that he had written himself "clear out" in his letters to the *Alta,* "the stupidest letters that were ever written from New York." He had written ten letters in less than three weeks, letters vastly better written than the bulk of his western journalism. He was also writing for the *New York Sunday Mercury,* where five pieces appeared, in addition to "Jim Wolf and the Tom-Cats," and he had written for the *Tribune* and the *Saturday Evening Express.*[36]

Presumably his impatience was chiefly over his dissatisfaction with his career as a writer and his failure to achieve any sense of fulfillment. He was thirty-one years old and had not yet discovered fully his métier. He was growing, intellectually, very fast, even though he considered himself, he wrote his mother, "so worthless that it seems to me I never do anything or accomplish anything that lingers in my mind as a pleasant memory." Meanwhile, his European trip was in his mind not a great opportunity but — as he wrote to his friend Will Bowen — simply an occasion for fun.

CHAPTER THREE

Turning Point

I n 1909, only a year before Sam Clemens's death, *Harper's Bazar* published "The Turning Point of My Life," his last work written for publication. Here he described the composition of *The Innocents Abroad* as "the *last* link" in the chain of events that had made him "a member of the literary guild." All the links he described were no doubt important, but the great good fortune of traveling through the Mediterranean on the *Quaker City,* on assignment, and then having the opportunity to write a book about his experience was crucial. The voyage, which lasted just over five months, from June to November 1867, was the first made by an American ship to the Old World exclusively for pleasure. Clemens was to see the Azores, Gibraltar, Tangiers, Marseilles, Paris, several Italian cities, Athens (just a peek, it turned out, because the ship was quarantined), Constantinople, Sevastopol, Yalta (where he met the czar), Ephesus, Beirut, Damascus, Jerusalem and the Holy Land, Egypt, Spain, and Bermuda (five days), which was to become one of the author's favorite places. He was also to encounter, more frequently than he might have wished, the other seventy-five passengers and the ship's officers. He soon found they were, as he wrote in October to Joseph Goodman back in Virginia City, "the d——dest, rustiest, ignorant, vulgar, slimy, psalm-singing cattle that could be scraped up in seventeen States," and following his return he referred in a letter (to John Russell Young) to "the Quaker City's strange menagerie of ignorance, imbecility, bigotry, & dotage." In truth, however, his associates on ship were probably not very different from the readers he would address when he came to write a book about his experiences; they were just wealthier.

His immediate task, he had been instructed, was "to write at such times and from such places as you deem proper, and in the same style that heretofore secured you the favors of the Alta California."[1] He was expected to produce, according to his later testimony, fifty letters, for which he was to be paid twenty dollars per letter, and in due time the *Alta* published that number.[2] He wrote several others that apparently never arrived. He also had commissions from the *New York Tribune* (for that paper he wrote only seven letters, far fewer than he had planned) and for the *New York Herald* (in which only three unsigned pieces appeared). Half the trip expenses were to come from the fees the *Alta* was to pay him; he expected to profit chiefly from the other assignments, the ones that, as it happened, he could only partially complete. For one thing, it was difficult to write on board ship, as he complained in a letter written from Naples in August, and he could not write on shore because of his continual need to be sightseeing. Thus in his October 1 *Alta* letter he reported that he was on the *Quaker City* for the first time in six weeks but that his "anticipations of quiet are blighted" by "one party of Italian thieves fiddling and singing for pennies on one side of the ship, and a bagpiper, who knows only one tune, on the other."[3]

The letters Mark Twain produced for the *Alta* were written for the audience he had been addressing for years. Not intended to constitute a complete account of the voyage, they focus somewhat erratically on this attraction and that topic. At the end of his sixth letter he is in Paris, though he has surprisingly little to say about that great city; the next is from Genoa, where he announces, "I want to camp here" because of its beautiful women. A few pages later he is inspired to write an account of his companion Brown's French composition to his hotel keeper in Paris. A casual journalistic style permitted movement forward and back in time.

In other respects, these *Alta* letters are like earlier ones about Mark Twain's Hawaiian and American travels and adventures. Brown appears once again, intermittently. There are humorous passages and serious ones, a good deal of irreverence, and a pronounced chauvinism. Few things that the traveler saw struck him as better than what America had to offer. Sometimes he stretched a point to demonstrate to the Old World that America was actually more advanced. When the head of the Russian railroad system told him that he employed ten thousand convicts, Mark Twain topped him: "I said we had eighty thousand convicts employed on the railways in California — all of them under sentence of death for murder in the first degree." "That," he explained, "closed *him* out" (p. 162).

A significant new feature, on the other hand, is the continuing narrative, determined by the prearranged itinerary of the *Quaker City*. What, one wonders, will Mark Twain do and say in Venice or in Jerusalem? There is also the letter writer's running feud with his fellow voyagers, the "pilgrims," who were altogether different in their piety and hypocrisy from his usual associates. In the Holy Land, for example, when he drank at "Ananias's well," he noted that "the water was just as fresh as if the well had been dug only yesterday." He then went on: "I was deeply moved. I mentioned it to the old Doctor, who is the religious enthusiast of our party, and he lifted up his hands and said, 'Oh, how wonderful is prophecy!' . . . I start a bogus astonisher for him every now and then, just to hear him yelp" (p. 202).

Another new characteristic is that Mark Twain begins putting more emphasis on his own reactions, his personal experiences, and less on the places he visited. He knew that he was not the first visitor to write about travels in the Old World; the special nature of his accounts was to come from the responses being *his:* Mark Twain's anticipations and surprises. Since his strength was comedy, he prepared ridiculous expectations so that his actual experiences would unsettle him. Thus in Venice "the fairy boat in which the princely cavaliers of the olden time were wont to cleave the waters of the moonlit canals" turned out to be "an inky, rusty old canoe with a sable hearse-body clopped on to the middle of it" (pp. 97–98). Sometimes the technique is resorted to merely as a throwaway, as when he reports, "After a good deal of worrying and tramping under a roasting Spanish sun, I managed to tree the Barber of Seville, and I was sorry for it afterwards. With all that fellow's reputation, he was the worst barber on earth. If I am not pleased with the Two Gentlemen of Verona when I get there next week, I shall not hunt for any more lions" (p. 55). He put less emphasis on his ridiculous self in the last letters, when the fact that he had few notes and many letters to write caused him to pad his account with biblical stories and even to translate King James version idioms into flat prose. The *Alta* half-seriously apologized for the thirty-fifth letter, marked by the reporter's "strange conduct in presenting . . . information to the public with such a confident air of furnishing news" (p. 229).

Still it should be noted that even while he was traveling, the writer had begun to set higher standards for himself — or rather more genteel ones. On the *Quaker City* he had met a Cleveland, Ohio, woman, Mary Mason Fairbanks, who was also writing newspaper accounts of the voyage, and she served as his critic during the preparation of the last twenty or so letters; his continuing friendship with her and her husband would make him more conscious of genteel values. He refers to her in a revealing letter (the same one quoted previously) to John Russell Young, managing editor of the *New York Tribune,* on his return. "I stopped writing for the Tribune, partly because I seemed to write so awkwardly, & partly because I was apt to betray glaring disrespect for the Holy Land & the Primes and Thompson's [authors of solemn travel books] who had glorified it." But, he explained to Young, "coming home I cramped myself down to at least something like *decency* of expression, & wrote some twenty letters, which have survived the examination of a most fastidious censor on shipboard and are consequently not incendiary documents. There are several among these I think you would probably accept, after reading them. I would so like to write some savage letters about Palestine, but it wouldn't do." He enclosed letters he thought suitable, with the not very encouraging comments that "the letters I have sent you heretofore have been — well, they have been worse, much worse, than those I am sending you now."

Clearly the writer was ambivalent. Exactly what was suitable for an Eastern audience, and how crucial was that literary market? Soon he was to meet a woman who would represent that audience for him; she would serve for many years as the censor he felt he needed. Olivia Langdon's brother, who had been Clemens's shipmate, would provide the necessary introduction. After his trip, however, he returned to New York on November 19, 1867, and went almost immediately to Washington, D.C., to take on for a short time a position he had accepted while still in Europe as secretary to Senator William Stewart of Nevada. Stewart later wrote an account of Clemens's appearance when he arrived in Washington:

> I was seated at my window one morning when a very disreputable-looking person slouched into the room. He was arrayed in a seedy suit, which hung upon his lean frame in bunches with no style worth mentioning. A sheaf of scraggy black [*sic*] hair leaked out of a battered old slouch hat, like stuffing from an ancient Colonial sofa, and an evil-smelling cigar butt, very much frazzled, protruded from the corner of his mouth. He had a very sinister appearance.[4]

Another sketch of a devil-may-care Clemens is provided by a journalist who visited him in his Washington room and later reported in the *New York Evening Post* on "How 'Innocents Abroad' Was Written."

> The little drum stove was full of ashes, running over on the zinc sheet; the bed seemed to be unmade for a week, the slops not having been carried out for a fortnight, the room foul with tobacco smoke, the floor, dirty enough to begin with, was littered with newspapers, from which Twain had cut his letters. . . . And there was tobacco, and tobacco

everywhere. One thing, there were no flies. The smoke killed them, and I am now surprised that the smoke did not kill me too.[5]

Expecting the experience in the nation's capital to be "better than lecturing for $50. a night for a Literary Society in Chicago & paying my own expenses" (as he wrote to his old friend Frank Fuller), he spent the winter in Washington, where in addition to his work as private secretary for Senator Stewart, he gave a lecture on his trip abroad, "The Frozen Truth." His familiarity with the political scene was to prove useful in the writing of a novel. He also gave a humorous account of his Washington activities in "My Late Senatorial Secretaryship."[6] Continuing to act as a journalist, he made the *New York Tribune* office in Washington his headquarters. By December 4 he was writing a new series of letters for the *Virginia City Territorial Enterprise,* eleven letters in all, the last dated March 2, 1868. He identified himself in a letter to Mrs. Fairbanks as a "*Tribune* 'occasional,' *Alta* 'special,'" with "propositions from the *Herald*." For the *Alta* he wrote fourteen letters, the earliest on the day after his arrival in New York, later ones in July 1868, and two in July 1869. He was soon to begin a series of letters for the *Chicago Republican* as well as some for the *New York Herald*.[7] He was open to anything, for he was by now a highly ambitious journalist who could augment his income on the lecture platform. The successful Western journalist was becoming a successful Eastern one. His trip abroad had cured his depression, but it had not yet changed his life.

What he wrote is worth describing as a way of indicating his literary personality at this time, especially his little-known letters to the *Enterprise*. They are much better than the letters written at the same time for the *Alta*. According to his first letter, "To write 'EDS. ENTERPRISE' seems a good deal like coming home again." Mark Twain is full of admiration for Washington, particularly the Capitol, which he has examined several times, "almost to worship it, for surely it must be the most exquisitely beautiful edifice that exists on earth to-day"[8] — this from his vantage point as recent world traveler. He is soon exploring political corruption and problems of poverty in New York. After describing life in a tenement, the struggles of a sixty-year-old ex-circus clown, now a "rag-picker and a searcher after old bones and broken bottles," and the plight of poor little girls who nevertheless enjoy showing off their wretched "rusty rag dolls," he presents the lessons he has learned about the possibilities of political action to redress social injustice.

> In this city, with its scores of millionaires, there are to-day a hundred thousand men out of employment. It is an item of threatening portent. Many apprehend bread riots, and certainly there is a serious danger that

they may occur. If this army of men had a leader, New York would be in an unenviable situation. It has been proposed in the Legislature to appropriate $500,000 to the relief of the New York poor, but of course the thing is cried down by every body — the money would never get further than the pockets of a gang of thieving politicians. They would represent the "poor" to the best of their ability, and there the State's charity would stop.[9]

The longer he made Washington his headquarters, the more disenchanted Clemens became. In particular, he found the Democratic Party thoroughly corrupt, as he reported in a piece he wrote for the *New York Tribune*, "The White House Funeral." Now identifying himself with both the Republican Party and the North, he satirized Andrew Johnson by providing his imagined farewell address: "My great deeds speak for themselves. I vetoed the Reconstruction Acts; I vetoed the Freedman's Bureau; I vetoed civil liberty; . . . I vetoed everything & everybody that the malignant Northern hordes approved; I hugged traitors to my bosom; . . . I smiled upon the Ku-Klux; . . . I rescued the bones of the patriot martyr, Booth."[10]

In the letters that he wrote for the *Chicago Republican* in January and February, Mark Twain worked hard at being funny. Valentine's Day, he explained in one letter, has special meaning for him. "For the last sixty years I have never seen this day approach without emotion." He is moved by the valentines he receives, especially those intended "to conceal the real passion that is consuming the young women who send them." One such reads in part: "SIR: Our metallic burial cases have taken the premium at six State Fairs in this country, and also at the great Paris Exposition. Parties who have used them have been in each instance charmed with them. Not one has yet entered a complaint. . . . Families supplied at reduced rates." Other "valentines" received on February 14 deal with a "patent Cancer-Eradicator," a "double-back action, chronometer-balance, incombustible wooden legs," gravestones, and one "fraught with a world of happiness for me. It — it says: 'SIR: You better pay for your washing. BRIDGET.'"[11]

Two other pieces from Washington, D.C., are sketches. The earlier, published in the *New York Citizen* of December 21, 1867, and entitled "The Facts in the Case of the Senate Doorkeeper," is signed "Mark Twain, Doorkeeper *ad interim*." He tells how as doorkeeper he was "snubbed" every time he attempted to speak on the Senate floor. Eventually he was impeached for a variety of causes, among them charging senators fifty cents admission.[12] Here the writer posed as what can only be termed an inspired lunatic. In "The Facts Concerning the Recent Resignation," published in the *New York Tribune* of December 27, 1867, he tells how as secretary of the Senate Committee on Conchology he never enjoyed the courtesy due him from other members of the cabinet.[13] Again it is the inspired idiot who writes. This persona, in which the writer presented himself as a humorist and nothing more, suggested that "Mark Twain" was at a loss for fresh inspiration.

In late December 1867, Clemens met Olivia Langdon, who was visiting New York with her parents. She was twenty-two, ten years younger than Clemens. Her brother, Charles, had been Clemens's *Quaker City* companion; all five attended a reading by Charles Dickens on December 31. In a letter to the *Alta California* dated January 11, the writer took pleasure in reporting that "there was a beautiful young lady with me — a highly respectable young white woman." Although Clemens was to see his bride-to-be twice more within a few weeks, he did not begin his formal courtship until August, when he visited the Langdons in Elmira. By then his situation had changed significantly.

Just after Clemens arrived in New York following his trip abroad, a man who was to play a crucial role in his life, Elisha Bliss Jr. of the American Publishing Company of Hartford, wrote to ask Clemens for "a work of some kind, perhaps compiled from your letters from the East, &c., with such interesting additions as may be proper."[14] Clemens replied on December 2 that he could "make a volume that would be more acceptable in many respects than any I could now write." He believed that he could revise the letters, "weed them of their chief faults of construction & inelegancies of expression," drop some and write others in their place. He sought more information, especially concerning "what amount of money I might possibly make out of it"; clearly, he was enticed by Bliss's invitation. Early in January 1868, he wrote to his mother and sister to request that they "cut my letters out of the Alta's and send them to me in an envelop."

For a conference with Bliss in late January, Clemens visited Hartford. He stayed with the Hooker family at Nook Farm, where he was later to make his home. (Alice Hooker had been with Olivia Langdon at the Dickens reading.) A few days later, Clemens wrote from New York to accept Bliss's proposition that he furnish "Manuscript properly prepared & written sufficient to make an Octavo volume of at least 500 pages . . . the subject of the same to be the trip of the 'Quaker City' to the Holy Land."[15] The author would have a great deal of revising to do, but he was encouraged by the fact that he was already expecting the book to be highly remunerative, at a time when he had been looking desperately for some project that would pay him well. As he explained to his family in late January, "I wasn't going to touch a book unless there was *money* in it, & a good deal of it." (Bliss had offered him a royalty of 5 percent of sales.) Untroubled by a deadline to deliver the manuscript by "the middle of July," Clemens even continued writing for newspapers.

By January 31, he was writing to Emeline Beach, who had been on the *Quaker City*, asking for names and other information that he had not remembered. He was also consulting the published letters of three other *Quaker City* passengers. But shortly after receiving copies of his own *Alta* letters from his family, he learned that the *Alta* proprietors intended to publish his letters in book form and that they were not willing to let him use them. About the middle of March, he was therefore obliged to head for San Francisco, a trip he described fancifully in a letter to the *Chicago Republican* for May 19. He had "chartered one of the superb vessels of the Pacific Mail Steamship Company for a hundred and eighty thousand dollars." Traveling this time by crossing Panama, Clemens successfully arranged in San Francisco with the *Alta* to publish the *Quaker City* letters in revised form. Although the reason for the long trip was to obtain rights to his *Alta* letters, the author had another enterprise in mind, for he needed money. A celebrity in San Francisco, where Mark Twain's letters to the *Alta*, the *Enterprise*, and eastern papers had been reprinted, he soon had newspapers announcing plans for a lecture.[16] The *Golden Era* was among the many publications that publicized his intentions. Mark Twain was "to enter minutely into the scandal of the *Quaker City*, . . . and how his innate morality was unsuccessfully assailed during his brief but perilous career."[17] He made his presence felt by attending entertainments sponsored by Presbyterian and Methodist churches. The much-publicized lecture, presented on April 14, earned Mark Twain some sixteen hundred dollars and drew such a large audience that it had to be repeated the next day.[18]

The lecturer began by promising to make his performance "somewhat didactic. I don't know what didactic means, but it is a good, high-sounding word, and I wish to use it, meaning no harm whatsoever."[19] After a less-than-triumphant first effort, the *Alta* reported, he "got the hang of the sermon," and thereafter he spoke with "that confidential tone that breaks down . . . barriers between the man on the stage and people occupying the seats."[20] Now he possessed the secret to his continuing success as a speaker. He went on to lecture in Sacramento, Marysville, Nevada City, Grass Valley, and Virginia City, and he reported his experiences to the readers of the *Chicago Republican*.

By May 5, he had returned to San Francisco, where he completed the transformation of his newspaper letters into a book manuscript, a task he had begun earlier in Washington. There was also to be much new matter.

Much of the work consisted simply of pasting newspaper clippings to paper and making revisions in the margins. In his autobiography Mark Twain remembered that he "worked every night from eleven or twelve until broad day in the morning, and as I did 200,000 words in the sixty days the average was 3,000 words a day—nothing for Sir Walter Scott, nothing for Louis Stevenson, nothing for plenty of other people, but quite handsome for me."[21] Then Bret Harte, who was preparing the first issue of the *Overland Monthly,* agreed to review the manuscript. In compensation, Mark Twain let Harte publish four excerpts in his journal. In November 1870, in a letter to C. H. Webb, he reported, "Harte read all of the MS of the 'Innocents' & told me what passages, paragraphs, & *chapters* to leave out—& I followed orders strictly. It was a kind thing for Harte to do, & I think I appreciated it." The cuts were substantial. A surviving manuscript has a few of Harte's notes; one indicates that a description of seasickness should be deleted because it is a hackneyed subject, treated by Dickens, Thackeray, and Jerrold.[22]

After giving a final lecture on Venice in San Francisco, Mark Twain left California for the last time on July 6 to return to New York. He found Captain Edgar Wakeman's ship in the harbor of Panama and was able to record for the Chicagoans a good deal of his colorful talk. This time Wakeman told him a story that he would later develop into one of his very best pieces, "Captain Stormfield's Visit to Heaven." But he reported to the *Republican* simply that "the old gentleman told his remarkable dream."[23] He arrived on July 29 in New York, which was now to serve as his headquarters. Then he went to Hartford to deliver his book manuscript.

While returning to the East, he drafted two sketches in his notebook. One concerns an imagined personage, "Mamie Grant, the Child-Missionary." The complete sketch, preserved in the notebook, is as good an indication of the state of the author's mind and art at this time as one could possibly wish. Mamie is an eager, devoted Sunday school student, just nine years old, deeply read in pious tracts. In her earnest attempts to save the souls of those who call at her uncle's house on business, she manages to stop his newspaper subscription, antagonize the tax collector, and prevent the return of one thousand dollars desperately needed to prevent foreclosure on the mortgage. But she is content. "I have saved a paper carrier, a census bureau, a creditor & a debtor, & they will bless me forever. I have done a noble work to-day. I may yet see my poor little name in a beautiful Sunday School book." Mark Twain's skepticism found do-goodism the target most ready at hand for his satire. The burlesque of moral tracts is truly devastating. In speaking to the census-taker, his Mamie shows a remarkable grasp of "the dreadful game of poker:"

Take these tracts. This one, entitled, "The Doomed Drunkard, or the Wages of Sin," teaches how the insidious monster that lurks in the wine-cup, drags souls to perdition. This one, entitled, "Deuces *and,* or the Gamester's Last Throw," tells how the almost ruined gambler, playing at the dreadful game of poker, made a ten strike & a spare, & thus encouraged, drew two cards & pocketed the deep red; urged on by the demon of destruction, he ordered it up & went alone on a double run of eight, with two for his heels, & then, just as fortune seemed at last to have turned in his favor, his opponent coppered the ace & won. The fated gamester blew his brains out & perished. Ah, poker is a dreadful, dreadful game. You will see in this book how well our theological students are qualified to teach understandingly all classes that come within their reach. Gamblers' souls are worthy to be saved, & so the holy students even acquaint themselves with the science & technicalities of their horrid games in order to be able to talk to them for the saving of their souls in language which they are accustomed to.

The census-taker has had enough and makes a quick departure.[24] But Mark Twain, who saw his own future in the East, already sensed such brazen irreverence was not likely to advance his career: "Mamie Grant" was not offered for publication.

Arriving in New York on July 29, Clemens once again benefited from Anson Burlingame's assistance, and with much help from him and his staff a piece appeared on the front page of the *New York Tribune* of August 4, "The Treaty with China." More significantly, when he visited Olivia Langdon in Elmira, New York, that summer, he promptly fell in love. Very likely Burlingame had something to do with his interest in the Langdons, for it was Burlingame who had told him, "Seek your comradeships among your superiors in intellect and character: always *climb*." If it is not clear that the Langdons were superior in intellect and character, they were certainly superior socially. Clemens extended his visit and was a house guest from August 21 to September 8, during which time he proposed marriage but met discouragement. Olivia's father, Jervis Langdon, had become wealthy chiefly from the coal business. His business, J. Langdon and Company, included as a partner both his son, Charles Langdon, and his son-in-law, Theodore W. Crane, who had married Jervis's adopted daughter, Susan. In antebellum days the Langdons had been dedicated abolitionists and had assisted escaping slaves by means of the "Underground Railroad." Among others, they had assisted Frederick Douglass while he was a fugitive. Clemens now became a frequent visitor to Elmira, a city of some 15,000 people just south of the Finger Lakes area of central New York. The Langdons were in many ways the kind of people whom Mark Twain had been satirizing: distinctly genteel and respectable. They were devout churchgoers whose minister, Thomas Beecher, was a member of the noted Beecher family.

Olivia, twenty-two when she met thirty-two-year-old Samuel Clemens, had formerly been an invalid as the result of severe back pains. She was unable to walk for some time, but by early 1867 she was much improved. It took a great deal of persistence on Clemens's part to persuade her family that he was "respectable" — a very convincing case could have been made that he was not — and to persuade Olivia to accept him.[25] When he could not be in her company, he wrote to her nearly every day, with the result that by the end of November they were "provisionally" engaged. Readers of the letters to Olivia find someone quite different from the person presented heretofore in these pages. Specifically, the letter-writer thought that he needed to become a Christian in order to win Olivia, and after a great deal of mental effort, he was able to write to her mother on February 13, 1869, "I now claim to be a Christian."

Clemens had several occasions to visit Hartford to see his publisher; there he discovered the huckleberry. The little-known passage in which he announces this discovery is in his best humorous style.

> I never saw any place before where morality and huckleberries flourished as they do here. I do not know which has the ascendency. Possibly the huckleberries, in their season, but the morality holds out the longest. The huckleberries are in season now. They are a new beverage to me. This is my first acquaintance with them, and certainly it is a pleasant one. They are excellent. I had always thought a huckleberry was something like a turnip. On the contrary, they are no larger than buckshot. They are better than buckshot, though, and more digestible.[26]

Strange that Mark Twain was to use the name of a berry he discovered in Hartford for a character intimately associated with his boyhood in Missouri and worth noting that from the beginning he linked the berry with moral issues.

In the *Spirit of the Times* for November 7, 1868, one of his funniest pieces yet written made its appearance, though he did not select it for republication in his American collections. It shows his ability to make much of little on the subject of the "Private Habits of Horace Greeley." While expressing admiration for the eminent man, he manages to find a way to make much good-natured fun. He notes, for example, that Greeley "snores awfully." "In a moment of irritation, once, I was rash enough to say I would never sleep with him until he broke himself of the unfortunate habit. I have kept my word with bigoted and unwavering determination."[27]

Suggestive as an indication of how Clemens was sensing his uncertain identity is an amusing sketch he called "A Mystery," published on November 16, 1868, in the *Cleveland Herald* (partly owned by Mary Fairbanks's husband), in which he tells how he has been burdened by a double who runs up costly hotel bills in the name of Mark Twain and then absconds, gets "persistently and eternally drunk," and even imitates Mark Twain in presenting himself as a lecturer, with his topic "The Moral Impossibility of Doughnuts." A few of the double's characteristics suggest that he represents the Mark Twain of the West: "It is a careless, free and easy Double. It is a double which don't care whether school keeps or not, if I may use such an expression." "A Mystery" demonstrates that just ten days before his provisional engagement, and probably while he was a guest in Mother Fairbanks's home, Clemens was expressing sorrow over the demise of his fresher, freer side.[28]

In the fall of 1868, Clemens worked on his book in Hartford, where he was pleased to meet the Rev. Joseph Twichell, who was to have a role in Clemens's marriage and become a longtime friend. Clemens also gave some time to the lecture circuit. He took on the aggressive James Redpath of Boston as his booking agent; Redpath scheduled forty engagements at one hundred dollars each.[29] Mark Twain's topic was announced as "The American Vandal Abroad," permitting him to draw on the whole range of his experiences in Europe and the Holy Land and making use of his book manuscript. He portrayed "that class of traveling Americans who are *not* elaborately educated, cultivated, refined, and gilded and filigreed with the ineffable graces of the first society." When he characterized the vandal as "always self-possessed, always untouched, unabashed — even in the presence of the Sphinx,"[30] it might be said he was making fun of himself. The tour lasted till early March and provided him some "eight or nine thousand dollars," but expenses were so high that in June he told his mother that he had "less than three thousand six hundred dollars in [the] bank." He had been able to visit Elmira from time to time and even to lecture there. The final revisions of *The Innocents Abroad* were made while Clemens was courting Olivia Langdon, who helped with the proofreading and began her long career as his editor. It was for her, for his fellow voyager Mrs. Fairbanks, and for the genteel audience they represented that Mark Twain composed passages of sentimental rhetoric, such as the descriptions of the Sphinx and of the Sea of Galilee at night.

Now Clemens needed to concentrate on establishing his relationship with Olivia and with her parents. By late November 1868, he won a conditional consent that they would be married, but questions remained.

Olivia's mother wrote to Mrs. Fairbanks on December 1: If "a great change had taken place in Mr Clemens," "from what standard of conduct, — from what habitual life, did this change, or improvement, or reformation; commence?"[31] Olivia's father, Jervis Langdon, asked Clemens for the names of people in the West who might serve as references. When Clemens supplied six, Langdon asked a former employee living in San Francisco to interview the six, as well as some others Clemens had not named. Feeling uneasy about what Langdon might hear, Clemens confessed to him, "I think that much of my conduct on the Pacific Coast was not of a character to recommend me to the respectful regard of a high eastern civilization, but it was not considered blameworthy there, perhaps." He then provided the names of additional references. One result of Langdon's inquiry was this comment from a Presbyterian deacon: "I would rather bury a daughter of mine than have her marry such a fellow."[32] Meanwhile, Clemens was assuring Olivia of his transformation: "I am striving & shall still strive to reach the highest altitude of worth, the highest Christian excellence." Ultimately Clemens was able to present himself in a way that both of Olivia's parents found they could accept, and a formal engagement was announced. Clemens told his family, "She said she never could or would love me — but she set herself the task of making a Christian of me. I said she would succeed, but in the meantime she would unwittingly dig a matrimonial pit & end by tumbling into it — & lo! the prophecy is fulfilled."

After finishing proofreading on the *Innocents,* Clemens devoted some attention to the question of where he would settle. "I want to get located in life," he told Olivia in May, 1869. In his thirty-fourth year, he did not have much to show for his years thus far, or so it clearly seemed to the man approaching marriage. For a time Cleveland attracted him; there Mrs. Fairbanks's husband was publisher of the *Herald.* But he decided against it because, as he told them in August, "It just offered *another* apprenticeship — another one, to be tacked on to the tail end of a foolish life *made up* of apprenticeships. I believe I have been apprentice to pretty much everything — & just as I was about to graduate as a journeyman I always had to go apprentice to something else." Instead, with a large loan from Jervis Langdon and with installments to be paid later, Clemens purchased a one-third interest in the *Buffalo Express* and became its associate editor, to "do a little of everything," as he reported to the Fairbankses. For a time Clemens supposed that he was making a real commitment to the paper. In September 1869, he received a letter asking if he would still be lecturing. He replied, "I hope to get out of the lecture-field forever. . . . I mean to make this newspaper support me hereafter."

Finally, in August 1869, *The Innocents Abroad* was published, substantially different from the *Alta* letters from which it was derived. New sections had been added about Paris and Egypt and notably one on the Sphinx. Also inserted were accounts of the narrator's movement from place to place. The changes were made for several reasons. The most obvious resulted from Mark Twain's recognition of the difference between writing for a newspaper and writing a book. In attempting to address a different audience, an eastern one and one that included women such as the woman he was to marry, he dropped local references and eliminated certain coarse expressions, such as "slimy cesspool" and "bawdy house." (The author had warned Olivia not to read *Gulliver's Travels, Don Quixote,* or Shakespeare's plays because they contained "grossness.") He also removed several but by no means all of the irreverent comments that had characterized his treatment of the Holy Land. The character Brown was completely eliminated, never to reappear in Mark Twain's writings, but while dropping Brown's vulgar remarks, Mark Twain retained the merely ignorant comments and assigned them to others. Some he kept for himself, as he sought to flesh out the character of the narrator. Perhaps to compensate for such changes, the writer added to his criticisms of the hypocritical pilgrims. The presence of that theme is underscored by the subtitle he gave his book, *The New Pilgrims' Progress.*

More important, Mark Twain sought to give the account a shape, a sense of design, by developing theme and attitude. He made the account more subjective by placing greater emphasis on the narrator. As he notes in the preface, the book suggests "to the reader how *he* would be likely to see Europe and the East if he looked at them with his own eyes instead of the eyes of those who had travelled in those countries before him." The eyes of Mark Twain were unique, however, for they saw what was funny, what evoked personal memories, and what demonstrated the ways in which reality often differed from expectations. In his Western writings he makes fun of genteel falsehoods and naive tenderfeet and identifies himself as a rugged veteran. Now he himself is often an innocent, and his illusions are stripped away.

What is Europe for the visiting American? Often Mark Twain asserts that it is a misrepresented product, created by years of anticipation. Nothing proves to be as advertised, neither Parisian barbers, Arabian horses, nor the Holy Land itself. Even Jesus Christ, Mark Twain explained, would never visit *there* again, having had the misfortune of seeing it once, which was surely enough. The author is the victim of misleading expectations, though frequently he has no one to blame but his overly gullible self. Nonetheless, he gets revenge by exploding superstitions, myths, and legends; indeed, it is sometimes difficult to distinguish passages of genuine sentiment from burlesque imitation, even though the "genuine" passages were written in a deliberate effort to gratify his new audience. For example, the drafts surviving at Vassar College of the Sphinx description show that he worked hard at this passage, which became a favorite in his lectures. He knew his live audiences liked such purple prose:

> After years of waiting, it was before me at last. The great face was so sad, so earnest, so longing, so patient. There was a dignity not of earth in its mien, and in its countenance a benignity such as never anything human wore. It was stone, but it seemed sentient. If ever image of stone thought, it was thinking. It was looking toward the verge of the landscape, yet looking *at* nothing — nothing but distance and vacancy. It was looking over and beyond everything of the present, and far into the past. It was gazing out over the ocean of Time — over lines of century-waves which, further and further receding, closed nearer and nearer together, and blending at last into one unbroken tide, away toward the horizon of remote antiquity. It was thinking of the wars of departed ages; of the empires it had seen created and destroyed. (chap. 58)

The passage goes on and on.

In *The Innocents Abroad,* Mark Twain adopts an identity, though he does not wear it consistently. He is the honest innocent who is ready to become the skeptic; the iconoclastic democrat; at worst, the ignorant philistine. Usually his good nature and sense of humor ingratiate him with the reader, and his report remains good fun. Indeed, Mark Twain's basic technique was to appear playful.[33]

Again and again, Mark Twain contrasts reality with his own expectations, sometimes by quoting what previous visitors, especially pious ones, had reported. He pretends to be particularly disappointed by the Sea of Galilee, which emerged as "a lake six miles wide and neutral in color; with steep green banks, unrelieved by shrubbery; at one end bare, unsightly rocks, with (almost) invisible holes in them of no consequence to the picture; eastward, 'wild and desolate mountains' (low, desolate hills, he [William C. Grimes, a fictitious author] should have said); in the north, a mountain called Hermon, with snow on it; peculiarity of the picture, 'calmness'; its prominent feature, one tree." To this he adds, "No ingenuity could make such a picture beautiful — to one's actual vision" (chap. 48). Aware that the reality he encountered was not all that his readers wanted, he provided a second account on another level that emphasizes not the actual lake but the people and events it had witnessed.

One of the writer's most difficult problems in transforming his wise-cracking letters into a book acceptable to Middle Americans was coping with his skepticism. He could scoff, imperiously, at Roman Catholic traditions, such as those linked with Veronica's handkerchief, but he obviously could not make fun of Jerusalem's Church of the Holy Sepulchre or the piety of those who visited it. Still he found an outlet, a permissible one, by reporting his ecstasy in being able to visit "Adam's tomb," which he places within the same church. Burlesquing the responses of such visitors as William C. Prime, author of *Tent Life in the Holy Land* (1857), he exclaims:

The tomb of Adam! How touching it was, here in a land of strangers, far away from home, and friends, and all who cared for me, thus to discover the grave of a blood relation. True, a distant one, but still a relation. The unerring instinct of nature thrilled its recognition. The fountain of my filial affection was stirred to its profoundest depth, and I gave way to tumultuous emotion. I leaned upon a pillar and burst into tears. I deem it no shame to have wept over the grave of my poor dead relative. Let him who would sneer at my emotion close this volume here, for he will find little to his taste in my journeyings through Holy Land. (chap. 53)

The passage, only part of which is quoted here, is stressed in the original publication, where a picture shows Mark Twain shedding pious tears. In 1902, a newspaper asked rhetorically, "Who is Mark Twain?" and answered, "The man who visited Adam's tomb, the man who wept over the remains of his first parent. That beautiful act of filial devotion is known in every part of the globe, read by every traveller, translated into every language."[34]

Although often undercut, Mark Twain's dominant intention was to show reality as it is, uncolored by pretense, conventionality, and gentility, his familiar enemies. Here these targets are often specifically *literary,* with Prime's guidebook at the head of the list. The narrator seeks to entertain himself, and thereby he entertains his readers. He finds that there is much fun in being playful, and so he improvises amusement — although doing so in the Holy Land is difficult, since playfulness is too close to irreverence. The author observed to his publisher, Bliss, that "the irreverence of the volume appears to be a tip-top feature of it, diplomatically speaking, though I wish with all my heart that there wasn't an irreverent passage in it." This lament made by the famous "Wild Humorist of the Pacific Slope" presumably came from his desire to please the woman he was courting, who thought "a humorist is something perfectly awful" — as he explained in January 1869 to "Mother Fairbanks." What he would have liked to make fun of was now "forbidden ground," he had reported to this same friend a few months earlier.

Mark Twain's weapon was style. In order to tell the truth, he showed what it is not. Sometimes what it is not is his invention, a kind of exercise in literary absurdity, as in the affectations of the Adam's tomb passage or in the description of a Roman holiday slaughter as it might be described in the *Spirit of the Times*. These experiments are among the high points of the book, reminding readers constantly that it is a piece of writing they are reading, at a significant remove from the ostensible subject. The author in his first *book* — as distinguished from his *Celebrated Jumping Frog* collection — is not the same Mark Twain that readers had encountered earlier. Now he is specifically an author, one who draws attention to his stylistic repertoire.

Mark Twain's iconoclasm is limited, however, as Bret Harte noted when he reviewed the book in the *Overland Monthly*. If Mark Twain rejected the art of the old masters, he shared with many Americans the bad taste that led him to admire such meretricious works of architecture as the Milan cathedral. Sometimes his uncertainty about what he could accept and reject leads to amusing passages, as when he attends a performance of the cancan in Paris. "I placed my hands before my face for very shame. But I looked through my fingers" (chap. 14).

Yet it was passages such as these that helped make *The Innocents Abroad, or The New Pilgrims' Progress* a great success. Published in July 1869, it sold 77,800 copies during its first sixteen months and approximately 125,000 in the United States during its first decade. The advertisements called Mark Twain "the people's author," and indeed he was. Reviews were generally favorable, both American and English, including one by the influential William Dean Howells, who wrote in the December *Atlantic Monthly,* "There is an amount of pure human nature in the book that rarely gets into literature."[35]

In 1870, the English publisher John Camden Hotten published an unauthorized two-volume edition. The first volume was called *The Innocents Abroad . . . The Voyage Out,* and the second *The New Pilgrim's Progress . . . The Voyage Home.* This edition was reprinted several times and also appeared in a one-volume edition. Later, Routledge published an authorized edition, revised by the author, who was paid $250 for it.[36] In time Mark Twain's writings were more widely sold in England than in the United States.

He was acutely conscious that he had written little during the time he was revising the *Innocents,* lecturing, and courting. In a letter to his family written in June 1869, he called this period "the idlest, laziest 14 months I ever spent in my life. . . . I feel ashamed of my idleness, & yet I have had really *no* inclination to do anything but court Livy." Despite the book he had produced, he still thought of himself as a journalist. Among the pieces dating from this time are several sketches: "George Washington's Negro Body-Servant," published in the *Galaxy* in February 1868; "Cannibalism in the Cars," published in the English journal *Broadway* in November, and "Personal Habits of the Siamese Twins" in *Packard's Monthly* in August 1869. The latter two were collected in *Sketches, New and Old* (1875).

One of these sketches was solicited by the American agent of George Routledge and Sons, the English publisher whose pirated *Celebrated Jumping Frog* had sold well. Routledge paid generously for "Cannibalism in the Cars," a fact that the writer was not to forget.[37] Another sketch, "Personal Habits of the Siamese Twins," deserves attention because it is the first evidence of what was to become an abiding interest: the subjects of twins, duality, and the problem of identity, themes to be associated throughout his writing with roleplaying. Actual Siamese twins were being exhibited in the United States when Mark Twain was writing a humorous sketch about the complications of two separate people being physically connected. That the consequences of the actions of each one were the same for both fascinated him: imprisonment and drunkenness for both, though one is blameless. Although not explicitly, the twins are by implication an instance of dual identity.[38] One may presume that the writer's interest in the subject resulted from his attempting, in his thirties, to take on a new identity, that of a candidate for gentility, in Van Wyck Brooks's phrase. Would he be compelled to switch sides in the battle between authenticity and pretentious gentility?

Although he wrote several pieces for the *Buffalo Express* before he took up his responsibilities in that connection, his name appeared on nothing published there until he officially announced his presence on August 21. In his "Salutation" he promised — as if announcing his reformation, somewhat begrudgingly,

> I shall not make use of slang or vulgarity upon any occasion or under any circumstances, and shall never use profanity except when discussing house-rent and taxes. Indeed, upon a second thought, I shall never use it even then, for it is unchristian, inelegant, and degrading — though, to speak truly, I do not see how house rent and taxes are going to be discussed worth a cent without it. I shall not often meddle with politics, because we have a political editor who is already excellent, and only needs a term or two in the penitentiary to be perfect.[39]

Here one can see the old Mark Twain peeking out as well as an interpretation of the new manner of life the writer was entering, uneasily.

During the next thirteen months, Mark Twain published some fifty pieces in the *Express,* mostly in the period through April 1870, including a column of fillers entitled "People and Things" and a later one entitled "Browsing Around." For two months he applied himself diligently. Ten *Express* pieces would make appearances in *Sketches, New and Old.* One that did not appear there, "Rev. Henry Ward Beecher, His Private Habits," suggests a preoccupation with Clemens's need to eliminate his habit of swearing, a frequent topic in his letters to Mrs. Fairbanks. "Mr. Beecher never swears. In all his life a profane expression has never passed his lips. But if he were to take it in his head to try it once, he would make even that disgusting habit beautiful — he would handle it as it was never handled before, and if there was a wholesome moral lesson in it anywhere, he would ferret it out and use it with tremendous effect."[40] "The Legend of the Capitoline Venus," a condensed novel, tells the story of an artist who is denied the hand of the woman he loves until he raises fifty thousand dollars, a story that has autobiographical overtones because it was written while he was under pressure to demonstrate his eligibility for Olivia's hand to her father.

Mark Twain's most ambitious project for the *Express* was a series of letters written on the basis of an idea that engaged him for several years: writing travel letters while staying home by using the reports of an actual traveler as grist for his mill. Charles Langdon, Olivia's brother, was to make another trip, this time a grand tour around the world, accompanied by a tutor, Darius R. Ford, who would send back accounts of their experiences. Mark Twain described his imaginative scheme in the pages of the *Express.* "These letters are [to be] written jointly by Professor D. R. Ford and Mark Twain. The former does the actual travelling, and such facts as escape his notice are supplied by the latter, who remains at home."[41] So Mark Twain announced on February 12. The *Express* built up the series with announcements: "Mark Twain in Saturday's *Express.* A Voyage Around the World by Proxy. First of a Series of Letters." Plans called for at least fifty installments. The trip came to an abrupt halt in Japan when Charles Langdon was summoned home to be with his dying father. But none of the letters published was in any sense by Ford, since none arrived soon enough to serve their purpose. Instead, Mark Twain decided to fill in by recounting his own Western experiences, basing his writings on the lectures on California that he had been preparing. Of the eight pieces he wrote, materials from six later found their way into his next book. Based on his own travels, they are pieces on Mono Lake in California, Silver City nabobs, California mining, and the glorious story of Dick Baker's curious cat, Tom Quartz. The second letter is a wholly fictitious account of Haiti, and the last, on Hawaii, is based on a travel letter Mark Twain had written in 1866.[42] The joint authorship scheme did result in two published letters, appearing in the *Express* on February 12 and March 5, 1869.

If an occasional piece from his pen, in addition to the "Around the World Letters," appeared in the *Express* during the late fall and winter, Mark Twain was largely occupied with another lucrative lecture tour begun on November 1. This time he appeared, with appropriate anxiety, in dubious Boston, where his topic was the one he used throughout the tour, "Our Fellow Savages of the Sandwich Islands." The subject was now a favorite with Mark Twain. He was well received, went on to suburbs of Boston, then to Connecticut, where he made a highly successful appearance in Hartford, and then on to Brooklyn, Philadelphia, and Washington, then back to Pennsylvania, New York, Connecticut, and Massachusetts.[43]

As to his relationship with Olivia, Clemens's reformation even included, if only briefly, abstention from alcohol and, for a somewhat longer time, forswearing smoking. To make sure Olivia understood the enormity of this sacrifice, Clemens explained how content he felt while smoking in bed. He described himself in a letter in January 1869 remaining in bed till 1 P.M., "where he smoked thousands of cigars, & was excessively happy," and in May, he alluded to his intention to read her latest letter to him "in bed, with the added delight of a cigar." Indeed, he found it altogether difficult to avoid smoking when he was a house guest among nonsmokers. (He quite lacked the modern-day awareness that secondhand smoke is distasteful to some people.) Even in an age when smoking was common, Clemens's immoderate smoking was the subject of comment. He once wrote, in self-defense, to his clergyman friend Joseph Twichell, "When they used to tell me I would shorten my life ten years by smoking, they little knew the devotee they were wasting their puerile word upon — they little knew how trivial & valueless I would regard a decade that had no smoking in it!"

Late in 1869, Clemens met William Dean Howells, whose review of *The Innocents Abroad* had just appeared, in the office of James T. Fields, editor of the *Atlantic Monthly,* where Clemens had gone to express his appreciation for the review. Howells was two years younger than Clemens but was already married, the father of two children, and author of two books based on his experiences as American consul in Venice. Then a mere subeditor of the *Atlantic,* Howells began a ten-year stint as editor in 1871. The two men soon became close friends; Howells was frequently able to be of assistance to his highly individualistic associate; he recognized Mark Twain's genius early and was able to encourage him to become a major writer. Clemens fully recognized how valuable Howells was to him; he wrote Howells as early as March 1878, "I owe as much to your training as the rude country printer owes to the city boss who takes him in hand & teaches him the right way to handle his art." Howells provided assistance both before publication by his editing and after by reviewing many of his books, including *Roughing It, The Gilded Age, A Tramp Abroad,* and *Joan of Arc.* He also edited *Tom Sawyer,* and after his friend's death in 1910, Howells wrote a series of pieces that appeared as "My Memories of Mark Twain," later published in book form with his reviews and other pieces on the author as *My Mark Twain* (1910). Here he called his friend a profoundly truthful man, with "a character of high nobility upon a foundation of clear and solid truth."[44] Howells's deeply admiring account of his experiences with his dear friend is a classic appreciation that ought to be better known. A superb edition also exists of the voluminous and articulate correspondence of the two men.

At the end of his lecture tour, on February 2, 1870, Samuel Clemens and Olivia Langdon were married in Elmira. Joseph Twichell and the Langdons' minister, Thomas Beecher, officiated. As planned, the couple settled in Buffalo, to Clemens's surprise not in a boardinghouse but in a large and handsome house of their own, with three servants, a stable, horse and carriage — a generous gift from Jervis Langdon.

Clemens now limited his smoking at home. He wrote to Twichell in December 1870:

> Smoke? I *always* smoke from 3 to 5 on Sunday afternoons — & in New York the other day I smoked a week, day & night. But when Livy is well I smoke only those 2 hours on Sunday. I'm "boss" of the habit. Originally, I quit solely on Livy's account (not that I believed there was the faintest *reason* in the matter, but just as I would deprive myself of sugar in my coffee if she wished it, or quit wearing socks if she thought them immoral), & I stick to it on Livy's account, & shall always continue to do so, without a pang.

He found a plausible excuse to return to regular smoking when he began to write his next book: after suffering from writer's block, "I began to smoke, and I wrote my book."[45] Thereafter till the end of his life he smoked a great deal. According to a letter he wrote in March 1885, he was smoking three hundred cigars a month. Since he especially enjoyed smoking in bed, Olivia was to experience quantities of secondhand smoke for years. The result was, in time, a weakened heart.[46]

For a time after their marriage, the Clemenses read the Bible together and went to church. But soon Sam found difficult the notion that reading the Bible was for the sake of his soul. Moreover, after his experiences in the Holy Land, he found the Bible full of mythology. Judging his practice to be hypocritical, he gave up trying to be a Christian, and in time Olivia gave up her Christianity, too, although she felt obliged on occasion to attend church with her mother.[47]

As to his position at the newspaper, soon Clemens was visiting the *Express* office only twice a week. An indication that he was not much interested in being a newspaperman is that he soon signed up to write a series of pieces to appear in the *Galaxy,* a monthly magazine to which he had already contributed two sketches. On March 11, he wrote to the editor, Francis P. Church, "If I can have entire ownership & disposal of what I write for the *Galaxy,* after it has appeared in the magazine, I will edit your humorous department for two thousand dollars ($2,000) a year." But first he had to meet his obligations to the *Express,* and after his lecture tour he dutifully produced a spate of pieces for the newspaper — ten during February, March, and April, and thereafter an occasional piece, only four during the remainder of his tenure as associate editor.

For the *Galaxy,* Mark Twain had to supply material for ten pages of printed copy a month. Thinking that he might write about his experiences in the West, he wrote to his family in St. Louis to retrieve his files of what he had written for the *Territorial Express.* In a piece called "Introductory," he told his readers what they might expect, noting that he would not limit himself to humor: "I would always prefer to have the privilege of printing a serious and sensible remark, in case one occurred to me, without the reader's feeling obliged to consider himself outraged."[48] In all he produced eighty-seven pieces, many slight, several flimsy, and a number of gems. Certain of the pieces are reminiscences, of "My First Literary Venture" as a contributor to the *Hannibal Journal;* on "A Couple of Sad Experiences," his publication of the petrified man and bloody massacre hoaxes; some memories of Hawaii; and some on his experiences in the San Francisco police courts. In addition, he capitalized on his California memories to write a series of seven "serious and sensible" imaginary letters from "Goldsmith's Friend Abroad Again," in which — following the example of Oliver Goldsmith's "Citizen of the World" letters — he has his letter-writer, a Chinese immigrant to the United States, tell the woeful story of his American experiences. Ah Song Hi's reports, in the face of great expectations, are uniformly painful. He who "wanted to dance, shout, sing, worship the generous Land of the Free and Home of the Brave" is beaten from his very arrival in San Francisco. He is imprisoned, attacked by his fellow prisoners (whose wickedness and crimes he catalogs), then found guilty of disorderly conduct after a farcical trial. Other pieces of social criticism appeared in the *Galaxy.* They include "About Smells," which concerns a Brooklyn clergyman's objections to the odors of common working people in his church, and a critique of a minister who would not officiate at the funeral of an actor. Most of the pieces, however, fulfill his assignment as a humorist, such as his account of how he edited an agricultural paper despite abysmal ignorance. He ludicrously discusses oyster beds under the heading "Landscape Gardening" and recommends the importation of the guano, "a fine bird."

Perhaps the most amusing piece is a putative review of *The Innocents Abroad,* ascribed to the *London Saturday Review* (that journal had reviewed the book favorably with great condescension). Mark Twain fooled many readers into believing that his hoax had actually appeared in England. Mark Twain's mock review finds much exaggeration in the *Innocents* and expresses astonishment at the author's "stupefying simplicity and innocence," "his colossal ignorance." For example, "He did not know, until he got to Rome, that Michael Angelo was dead! And then, instead of crawling away and hiding his shameful ignorance somewhere, he proceeds to express a pious, grateful satisfaction that he is gone and out of his troubles!" The reviewer continues, "The book is absolutely dangerous, considering the magnitude of the misstatements, and the convincing confidence with which they are made. . . . The poor blunderer mouses among the sublime creations of the Old Masters, trying to acquire the elegant proficiency in art-knowledge, which he has a groping sort of comprehension is a proper thing for the travelled man to display." The author of *The Innocents Abroad* proves to be the ideal victim of Mark Twain's irony.

Some thirty-three of the *Express* and *Galaxy* pieces were preserved — mostly in revised form — in *Sketches, New and Old,* the selection from his short pieces that Mark Twain published in 1875. Except for the social criticism, the *Galaxy* and *Express* pieces represent no new development in the writer's career but are rather a continuation of the sketch writing he had begun in the West. To his brother Orion he referred to it as "periodical dancing before the public."

It was the success of the *Innocents* as well as the strain of producing sketches on schedule that would turn Mark Twain to other kinds of writing, although he continued to write a few sketches. He declared to a correspondent on March 3, 1871, that he was determined to write no more for periodicals but instead to write books. He made a similar protest in print, as an introduction to "My First Literary Venture." Accordingly, most of the later short pieces, until the 1890s, are properly stories or essays, such as the damning attack on Commodore Vanderbilt he published in *Packard's Monthly* in March 1869.[49] By the late 1890s, the writer looked back at his early work with distaste. "I find that I cannot *stand* things I wrote a quarter of a century ago. They seem to have two qualities, gush and vulgarity." The pieces are decidedly uneven, but a few, such as "Some Learned Fables" and "Aurelia's Unfortunate Young Man," are still amusing and deserve more attention than they have customarily received.

Strange as it may seem, Mark Twain's writings after he went east had much wider publication in book form in England than in the United States; this was due partly to the activities of literary pirates, who gathered his pieces without authorization from the writer or his American publishers. Two thin volumes, *Eye Openers* and *Screamers,* collected *Express, Galaxy,* and other sketches in 1871. Besides other small volumes, a fat collection of sixty-six pieces was published by Routledge in 1872 as *Mark Twain's Sketches;* this one was, however, authorized. In it a prefatory note from the author states, "This book contains all of my sketches which I feel willing to father." Although he himself prepared this volume for publication, he used the versions of his work that had appeared in England in 1871 as the basis for the printer's copy of a number of the pieces, despite the fact that these versions had been heavily edited by the unauthorized publisher, John Camden Hotten. Hotten himself drew attention to this strange practice of accepting a stranger's unsought editing in a letter to the English journal *Spectator* published June 8, after the 1872 *Sketches* was published. He noted, for example, that he had found a "rather strongly-worded article entitled 'Journalism in Tennessee'" likely to profit from the elimination of "certain forcible expressions," such as "bumming his board" and "animated tank of mendacity, gin, and profanity"; and so he performed the pruning.[50] Now in an authorized edition the same changes had appeared.

Hotten later published a volume of 107 sketches, along with the *Innocents,* combined as *The Choice Humorous Works of Mark Twain* (1873). After Hotten died in June 1873, he was succeeded by the man who was to become Mark Twain's authorized publisher, Andrew Chatto, whose firm became Chatto and Windus. Chatto obligingly gave the American writer the opportunity to revise his work, and he did so, deleting seventeen sketches and making revisions. In 1874, *The Choice Humorous Works* appeared, "Revised and Corrected by the Author." None of these volumes appeared in the uniform edition the writer assembled toward the end of his career. Only *Sketches, New and Old* serves there to represent his early work.

Although Mark Twain was resolved to concentrate on writing books after 1871, just what he would undertake next was not clear to him for a time. In July 1866, he had recorded an idea in his notebook: "Conversation between the carpenters of Noah's Ark, laughing at him for an old visionary."[51] In August 1869, he asked his sister to send him his "account of the

Deluge (it is a diary kept by Shem)," which he described as being of "70 or 80 pages." When he wrote to Elisha Bliss about it in January 1870, he called it a "Noah's Ark" book. He supposed, with hope, that "maybe it will be several years before it is *all* written — but it will be a perfect lightning striker when it *is* done." Although he returned to this work at the end of his life, only partial drafts survive.[52] In 1939, Bernard DeVoto prepared for publication Mark Twain manuscripts he called "Papers of the Adam Family," eventually published in 1962 in the collection *Letters from the Earth.* Rather more to the point is a letter written to Mrs. Fairbanks a little earlier. Here he explained that the success of the *Innocents* had so encouraged him that he intended "to write another book during the summer."

The popularity of the *Innocents* was to have a great effect on Mark Twain's career. In the preface to the second volume of an English edition of the work, he described his modest expectations. "I did not seriously expect anybody to buy the book when it was originally written — and that will account for a good deal of its chirping complacency and freedom from restraint: the idea that nobody is listening, is apt to seduce a body into airing his small thoughts with a rather juvenile frankness."

In March 1870, following his marriage, Clemens was still thinking about a book. He had decided, he wrote the Langdons, that his activities at the *Express* would be limited to writing only "one or two sketches a month"; that chore and his work for the *Galaxy* occupied him "fully only six days every month." He needed time, he explained, "to write a book in." One of his *Express* pieces, published in April, was about the West, "The Facts in the Great Landslide Case," and in May he wrote to Mrs. Fairbanks that since his publishers wanted another book, "I doubt if I could do better than rub up old Pacific memories & put them between covers along with some eloquent pictures." For this purpose he expected to go west with Olivia. But he did not commit himself to a book until July 15, when he signed a contract with Bliss while he was in Elmira, New York, where Jervis Langdon, Olivia's father, was fatally ill. Langdon had accepted Clemens and given him the vital reassurance that it was possible for a wealthy, respectable person to be principled and upright.[53]

He contracted to complete the book in less than six months and immediately began preparation by writing to Orion about their journey to Nevada in 1861. "I propose to do up Nevada & Cal., beginning with the trip across the country in the stage." This time he had no rough draft, similar to his *Alta* letters from Europe, to get him started. But he was excited and optimistic, since he was getting the biggest royalty "ever paid on a subscription book in this country," 7.5 percent.

Like the *Innocents,* the book that Mark Twain was to write about the West belongs to a special class, addressed to a specific readership. The American Publishing Company sold its books not in stores but through agents, who sought subscribers in advance of actual publication by showing a prospectus and sample selections by door-to-door canvassing. The typical buyer lived in a small town and was without access to a bookstore. Such a reader wanted, or it was supposed by such publishers that he wanted, *big* books with many pictures. (*The Innocents Abroad* had 234 illustrations — many not freshly prepared for the book.) Purportedly he did not seek "literature" but information. The typical subscription book therefore was nonfiction, often a first-person narrative with some kind of current appeal. Appearance too was important: several styles of bindings, usually with illustrations on the cover, were offered. William Dean Howells had pointed to the importance of appropriate illustrations in his review of *The Innocents Abroad,* although he had later observed that "no book of quality was made to go by subscription except Mr. Clemens's books, and I think they went because the subscription public never knew what good literature they were."[54] Most authors with literary pretensions had no use for such books. In the city, Howells knew, agents were "a nuisance and a bore," "a proverb of the undesirable."[55] But the success of the *Innocents* not surprisingly prompted Mark Twain to undertake another lengthy subscription book, even though by the time he had finished his first he had complained in June 1869 to Mrs. Fairbanks that he had "lost very nearly all my interest in it long ago." He judged — as he wrote "Uncle Remus," Joel Chandler Harris, in 1881 — "When a book *will* sell by subscription, it will sell two or three times as many copies as it would in the trade; and the profit is bulkier because the retail price is greater."

Mark Twain had come to understand that the appeal of a subscription book did not depend wholly on the author. He told his publisher, Bliss, that he would "write a book that will sell like fury provided you put pictures enough in it." The important role that Bliss played is suggested by the fact that it was Bliss, according to A. B. Paine, who named the book *Roughing It.*[56] The completed book has three hundred illustrations.

The American Publishing Company, which was at this time releasing only two books a year, was distinctly a commercial operation. Although the writer was eventually disenchanted with it because he believed he had been cheated by its officers, he was to prepare most of his books with the memory of the success of the first one before him. As late as 1897, he was still producing sequels. At one point he intended to call the book about his round-the-world tour *The Latest Innocent Abroad* or *The Surviving Innocent Abroad.*

A major consideration for an effective subscription book was its size, which was stipulated in the contract for a new book. The author was to write "a 600-page 8 vo book (like the last) for my publishers," he wrote his family in late July 1870. That would be 240,000 words. But this time the writing did not go as scheduled. Family crises intervened: the death of Olivia's father on August 6; the illness of a house guest who eventually died in the master bedroom of the Clemenses' Buffalo house at the end of September; the premature birth of a child, Langdon — always feeble, on November 7; Olivia's dangerous illness (typhoid) in February 1871. The new father continued to write as best he could under the trying circumstances. But he also let himself become distracted with three other publication ideas. In early December 1870, he proposed that the publishers of the *Galaxy* put out a small work, *Mark Twain's (Burlesque) Autobiography and First Romance,* published in March 1871. (The author sought to circumvent the contract he had with the American Publishing Company by considering this forty-eight-page volume a "pamphlet.") The author's too transparent efforts to be funny resulted in a publication that detracted from Mark Twain's reputation. (Fortunately, it attracted little attention.) Another December project was an ill-fated "diamond book," discussed below. He also decided impulsively that his next book with the American Publishing Company should be a book of his sketches, which he wanted published before the account of his Western adventures. In early January he told Bliss, "Name the Sketch book '*Mark Twain's Sketches*' and go on canvassing like mad." The book was to include "The Jumping Frog," since Clemens now had obtained the rights to the book Webb had published. In addition, he sent Bliss some new sketches and then tried to return to his Western book.

In late January 1871, he wrote to Bliss that he now judged that the volume of sketches should be delayed until the Western book had been published. He would write "night and day" and send him "200 pages of MS. every week" in order to finish by April 15. In exchange, he wanted the book to be published on May 15, since his "popularity is booming now." But he was unable to finish then because of the demands on him from Olivia, who was still very weak. According to what he wrote in 1882, another difficulty was caused by the fact, noted earlier, that he was abstaining from smoking. "I found myself most seriously obstructed. I was three weeks writing six chapters. Then I gave up the fight, resumed my three hundred cigars, burned the six chapters, and wrote the book in three months, without any bother or difficulty."[57]

After writing a good deal, he concluded in March 1871 that he had to undertake a major revision, he told Orion, in order to "alter the whole style of one of my characters & re-write him clear through to where I am now." Probably that "character" was the "hero." As published, the book provides a portrait of a very young and thoroughly innocent young man. His innocence and the adventures it leads to are central in the book. Or perhaps the author was simply offering an excuse for his slow progress.[58]

Before he was finished writing, Clemens found that his trying experiences in Buffalo had soured him on the place, and he had already learned from the success of *The Innocents Abroad* that he did not need to work for a newspaper. He decided that he, his wife, and sickly son, Langdon, should leave Buffalo and that he should dissolve his connection with the *Express*. By March 3, he told J. H. Riley, he had come to "loathe Buffalo so bitterly (always hated it)" that he had advertised his house for sale. He intended to move to Hartford, where in time he expected, he told Riley, to "build a house . . . just like this one." "I want to get clear away from all hamperings, all harassments," he wrote Bliss. A move to Hartford would be made with the assistance of Orion, who had been living in Hartford since late 1870, as a member of Bliss's staff.

In March, the Clemenses moved temporarily to Elmira, where they stayed with Mrs. Langdon. The writer worked productively and without harassments at Quarry Farm, two and a half miles away. In April, his old friend Joe Goodman, his editor when he was a reporter for the *Territorial Enterprise,* arrived for a two-month visit. Goodman's admiration of the manuscript was encouraging, although Mark Twain already had an idea for another book, one that he and Goodman would write jointly. He wrote Orion that it "will wake up the nation." He was more enthusiastic about this new book — which would never be written — than the one he was supposed to be finishing. *Roughing It* was completed by August, although the author himself had digressed from his task during June to prepare lectures he was planning to deliver in the fall, in order to make the money he would need to establish his family with a new home in Hartford. The sale of his interest in the *Buffalo Express* cost him $10,000, but he had $25,000 from the sale of the house his father-in-law had given him.

The last part of *Roughing It* was much the easiest to prepare, since fifteen of the last seventeen chapters were merely revisions of the Sandwich Island letters Mark Twain had written six years earlier. But even when he thought he was through, there was more editing and more revising. To make the book long enough to meet the terms of his contract, he added three long appendixes, one on Mormon history and others well larded with quotations from documents. This device was to prove useful in stretching later subscription books to an adequate length.

Although generally less admired, *Roughing It* is in actuality a distinctly better book than the *Innocents*. Whereas the earlier book was a revision of on-the-spot reports, the new book was based on memories artfully shaped — except for the Sandwich Island chapters, which were composed much as the *Innocents* had been. Autobiographical in outline, *Roughing It* tells the story of Clemens's cross country stagecoach journey, and his life in Nevada, California, and Hawaii, but it is controlled by important shaping concerns as the author looks back nearly ten years to an earlier self. A few years earlier, he had taken a quick look backward, when in November 1868 he had written to Olivia, "I have been through the world's 'mill' — I have traversed its ramifications from end to end — I have searched it, & probed it, & put it under the microscope & *know* it, through & through, & from back to back — its follies, its frauds, & its vanities — all by personal *experience* & not through dainty *theories* culled from nice moral books in luxurious parlors where temptation never comes." Despite his candidacy for gentility, the author presents himself in *Roughing It* as a man of experience. He reminds the reader repeatedly in the early chapters that he has traveled to Europe and to the Holy Land; he suggests that those experiences, as well as the ones he is telling about, made him what he is now. As a result, the reader is encouraged to feel that he is hearing the voice of the authentic Mark Twain, who is providing his autobiography. Here the writer provides answers to some implied questions. How did there come to be this humorist, this skeptical, sometimes cynical character? Who is this frank, confidential, vulnerable, justice-seeking comic writer, whose graceful but firm prose seems to fit him like a glove? The writer's Western experience provides explanations. Chapter 1 begins with the writer mocking his youthful self — the "before" to be contrasted with the present "after." He makes the ex-journeyman printer and experienced ex-pilot of twenty-six sound ten years younger as he describes the jealousy of a younger brother contemplating the older.

> [Brother] was going to travel! I never had been away from home, and that word "travel" had a seductive charm for me. Pretty soon he would be hundreds and hundreds of miles away on the great plains and deserts, and among the mountains of the Far West, and see buffaloes and Indians, and prairie dogs and antelopes, and have all kinds of adventures, and maybe get hanged or scalped, and have ever such a fine time, and write home and tell us about it, and be a hero. . . . What I suffered in contemplating his happiness, pen cannot describe.

This naive youth will go west and there through initiation lose his innocence. *Roughing It* is a retelling of an old familiar story, but in Mark Twain's words it is a fresh and original one. As an exploration of the values that come into existence when the restraints of an ordered life are relaxed, the book is a celebration of freedom. The loss of that innocence, and later that freedom, is recalled with considerable nostalgia, at the same time that Mark Twain implies that the civilization of the East is marked by pretense and vanity.

All the romantic features of the West are here: wild Indians, barren deserts, the buffalo hunt, prospecting, the bucking bronco, the Pony Express rider, the desperado, the tall tale. Early in the book two incidents suggest the ways of the West. Chapter 5 describes the coyote: "not a pretty creature or respectable either," especially to "a dog that has a good opinion of himself." The coyote attracts his attention, leads the dog on, misleading him into thinking that the varmint can be caught, and the dog becomes "more and more incensed to see how shamefully he has been taken in by an entire stranger." At length this coyote "turns and smiles blandly upon him once more," then runs off with a speed that makes the dog's "head swim." Once so taken in, once so humiliated, the dog is unlikely to be victimized again soon. Such lessons were ones that the newcomer had to learn, as in chapter 24, when the narrator is persuaded to buy "a Genuine Mexican Plug" that proves to be unridable. After several painful attempts to master the beast, he meets an "elderly-looking comforter," who informs him, "Stranger, you've been taken in." To emphasize the point he has been making, Mark Twain ends his chapter with this moral: "Now whoever has had the luck to ride a real Mexican plug will recognize the animal depicted in this chapter, and hardly consider him exaggerated — but the uninitiated will feel justified in regarding his portrait as a fancy sketch, perhaps."

Many other stories have a similar point. When in chapter 32 Mark Twain and two companions are lost in a snowstorm, then lose their horses and decide that they cannot survive, each ceremoniously prepares for the end by giving up his dearest vice: the first his bottle of whiskey, the second his playing cards, the third his pipe, each in a spirit of sincere reformation. Then "oblivion comes." But in the morning (in the next chapter), the three wake to discover that they are "not fifteen steps from . . . a stage station." Their situation is "painfully ridiculous and humiliating," and each soon ashamedly gathers up what he has thrown away and vows never to say more about reformation.

Others are taken in, too, in Mark Twain's collection of somewhat imaginative recollections, such as one he had told before of how General Buncombe was humbugged by a practical joke played on him in the landslide case and failed for two months to recognize how he had been victimized.

One of the earliest stories in *Roughing It* shows a victim coping with his situation. In chapter 7, the writer's touring party experiences "disaster and disgrace" in a buffalo hunt. One of their number, Bemis, is thrown from his horse and chased up a tree by a wounded buffalo. He manages to avoid humiliation by resourcefully telling a fanciful tale, full of circumstance. He climbed "the only solitary tree there was in nine counties adjacent," only to find the buffalo climbing after him. So he lassoed him, fired his revolver at the beast, and "shinned down the tree and shot for home," leaving the buffalo "dangling in the air, twenty feet from the ground." Bemis's fantastic tale restores him to comradeship with those who heard it.

Roughing It is dedicated to a friend of Clemens's Western days, Calvin H. Higbie, "In Memory of the Curious Times When We Two WERE MIL-LIONAIRES FOR TEN DAYS." The story of how such riches were obtained, though far from true, is central to Mark Twain's account of a land where great wealth was won and lost overnight. Only a few pages are devoted to Mark Twain's *Enterprise* journalism, with Clement T. Rice, the Unreliable, here being referred to as Boggs. There are memorable and hilarious stories of Scotty Briggs's efforts to communicate with a minister who cannot understand his vernacular, of Ned Blakely (modeled on Captain Wakeman), of Jim Blaine's grandfather's ram and Dick Baker's cat. For the subscription book buyer, there is abundant factual information about that very curious subject, Mormon polygamy; a beautiful description of Lake Tahoe, about which the author had pleasant memories; and a sympathetic analysis of the situation of the Chinese in California. Samuel Clemens's adventures are a good part of the story, but Mark Twain never neglected the maxim "Don't spoil a good story for the truth." Readers who do not have access to an edition with the original illustrations miss a great deal of what both author and publisher intended. Although some of the illustrations had appeared in earlier books, most were drawn for this new one. The chief artist was True W. Williams, who had provided illustrations for *The Innocents Abroad;* his illustrations of *Tom Sawyer* would prove to be a complementary part of that book. Increasingly, the author was to grasp the importance of illustrations; in December 1872, he wrote to the artist Thomas Nast that he recognized the need for "good pictures. They've got to improve on 'Roughing It.'"[59]

In *Roughing It,* victimization and humiliation are constant themes, but the victim is seldom hurt for long, and the tone is good-natured, compassionate, seldom hostile or sadistic. Instead, the book emphasizes the solidarity and community enjoyed by those who have achieved status by being initiated into the fellowship of toughened Western skeptics. As in *The Innocents Abroad,* the narrator is frequently disillusioned, but now he responds with greater cheerfulness. The theme of initiation is lost in the Sandwich Island portion, even though the writer seems to have intended to use it. For those readers who appreciate the accomplishments of the first four-fifths of the book, these last chapters may be left unread, though there is a falling-off even earlier, after the protagonist forsakes the pursuit of wealth for the life of a newspaperman.

Clemens's years in the West had not been financially rewarding. Only two-fifths of the way through the book, in chapter 28, the narrator recognizes that his hopes are never to be realized. "So vanished my dream. So melted my wealth away. So toppled my airy castle to the earth and left me stricken and forlorn." The writing of *Roughing It* brought home to its author, once and for all, the inescapable truth that the West had not rendered him the rewards he had expected and that he had better look elsewhere. He ended his account with what he called the moral of the story: "If you are of any account, stay at home and make your way by faithful diligence; but if you are 'no account,' go away from home, and then you will *have* to work, whether you want to or not." This notion of hard work rather than relocation as a formula for success may have been eagerly embraced as what Clemens feared he had now committed himself to.

When Clemens had first visited Hartford, he was a house guest at the home of John and Isabella Beecher Hooker, the latter a sister of several noted clergymen, including Henry Ward Beecher and Thomas K. Beecher, the Elmira minister who had married the Clemenses. Afterwards he had visited Hartford often to see his publisher. Although it has often been supposed that the Clemenses' move to Hartford was made solely for Clemens's convenience, other factors were important. Olivia enjoyed visiting with the Hookers' daughter Alice. Indeed, Olivia was with Alice when Clemens first met her. Even before the Clemenses were married, Sam and "Livy" had hoped they could live in Hartford.[60]

Thus when, in October 1871 after their summer at Quarry Farm, the Clemenses took up residence in the Hooker house, which they rented, they were moving into a house familiar to both of them. (It still stands today, though much modified.) The Hooker house was part of Nook Farm, a community developed on a tract of a hundred acres to the west of the city. The Clemenses were to become very much a part of it. Among the residents of Nook Farm were Susan and Charles Dudley Warner (the latter would soon become Mark Twain's coauthor), Calvin and Harriet Beecher Stowe, the afore-mentioned Hookers, George and Lilly Warner, General Joseph Hawley (owner of the *Hartford Courant,* governor of Connecticut, U.S. senator), and the Rev. Nathaniel Burton. Harmony and Joseph Twichell lived not far away. William Dean Howells wrote of the enclave, "It seems to me quite an ideal life. They live very near each other, in a sort of suburban grove, and their neighbors . . . go in and out of each other's houses without ringing."[61] The Hartford years were happy ones for the Clemenses, although Mark Twain seldom managed to write very much at his Hartford residence.

Just two weeks after moving to Hartford, he began an unusually extended lecture tour, nearly eighty appearances in Pennsylvania, Delaware, New England, New York, New Jersey, Ohio, Michigan, Indiana, West Virginia, and Maryland. His experiences were interesting enough, he wrote Olivia in January, to be the subject of a book. As his tour ended, his Western book was published in February 1872. Though not so successful as *The Innocents Abroad, Roughing It* sold very well: over 72,000 copies in the first two years. Reviews were favorable, too. One found his genius "characterized by the breadth, and ruggedness, and audacity of the West."[62] In an anonymous review, Howells called it "singularly entertaining," but admitted that the writing was not always marked by "all the literary virtues."[63] Clemens's future neighbor and collaborator, Charles Dudley Warner, opined in the *Hartford Courant,* "It is not mere accident that everybody likes to read this author's stories and sketches; it is not mere accident that they are interesting reading. His style is singularly lucid, unambiguous and strong." A review in the *Boston Evening Transcript* identified as high points of the book Dick Baker's story of his cat, Jim Blaine's account of his grandfather's ram, and Scotty Briggs's conversation with the minister. In England, Routledge published a "Copyright Edition" in 1872; it was entitled *The Innocents at Home.* It was reviewed in the *Manchester Guardian,* which objected to the use of slang and the author's being contented "with dwelling on the outside of things and simply describing manners and customs." The reviewer for the *London Examiner* focused on the author's use of humor.[64] A third publication of the book was that by Tauchnitz of Leipzig, Germany. In an autobiographical sketch, the author wrote with some pleasure, "Baron Tauchnitz proposes to issue my books complete, on the Continent in English."[65]

The American Publishing Company sold 62,000 copies of *Roughing It* during the first four months of publication, more than the author had expected (though soon he learned that it was less successful than *The Innocents Abroad*). Moreover, the English sales of *Roughing It* were also profitable to the author, whereas the pirated publication of *The Innocents Abroad* had not been. With a second success on the heels of the first, Mark Twain was firmly positioned as a solidly productive writer who knew his craft and had found his market.

CHAPTER FOUR

Fumbling, Success, Uncertainty

epeatedly throughout his career, Mark Twain tried to take advantage of an earlier success by producing a sequel. Sometimes he returned to ideas that had proved unsuccessful. Now, even before he had finished *Roughing It,* he was making plans for another book, based on much the same scheme as the one that had failed to work earlier in the preparation of the "Around the World" letters for the *Buffalo Express.* The results this time would be even more disastrous. On December 2, 1870, he wrote to John Henry Riley to propose what he described as "the pet scheme of my life." Just a little earlier he had drawn up an admiring sketch of this same man, "Riley — Newspaper Correspondent," published in the November *Galaxy,* where he explained that Riley wrote on assignment in Washington, D.C., for the *San Francisco Alta.* Now he proposed to send this experienced reporter, a friend of his from his days as a Washington newspaperman, to South Africa, there "to skirmish, prospect, work, travel, & take pretty minute notes, with hand & brain, for 3 months, I paying you a hundred dollars a month for you to live on. (Not more, because sometimes I want you to have to shin like everything for a square meal — for *experiences* are the kind of book-material I want.)" Riley would then write up his adventures, which might, Clemens thought, include getting rich from diamonds, and Clemens would then edit his report, adding parenthetical remarks as well.

On December 4, the compliant Riley replied by wire: "Long letter rec'd. Plan approved. Will get ready to go," and on December 6, Riley wrote a letter confirming his acceptance and making further arrangements with Clemens. On that same day, Clemens signed a contract with Elisha Bliss to prepare a book on the subject of "the Diamond Fields of Africa," based on "notes of adventures &c" prepared by "a proper party," with the manuscript to contain "matter enough to fill at least 600 printed octavo pages." The work was to be delivered by March 1, 1872. A fallback clause permitted substitution of another subject by mutual agreement. The trip was financed to the extent of $2,550 by the American Publishing Company.[1] Clemens had told Bliss in November that the book *"will have a perfectly beautiful sale"* and is "brim-full of fame & fortune for both author [&] publisher."

To meet their agreement, Riley started promptly, and on March 3, 1871, Clemens wrote to him, appreciatively, "Your letters have been just as satisfactory as letters could be, from the day you reached England till you left it." By October 1871, Riley had completed what turned out to be a truly hazardous journey to South Africa and was back in the United States. But Clemens was unable to see him, he declared in a letter, because of illness in the family and lecture-tour obligations. On January 4, Clemens wrote again, naming early March as the time when they would meet. "I shall be ready for you. I shall employ a good, appreciative, genial phonographic reporter who can listen first rate, & enjoy, & even throw in a word, now & then. Then we'll light our cigars every morning, & with your notes before you, we'll talk & yarn & laugh & weep over your adventures, & said reporter shall take it *all* down." Clemens wrote again, on March 27, to describe the qualities needed by the stenographer and to report that he anticipated some thirty thousand words of material from Riley's notes. But the scene so vividly predicted was never to take place. Riley had become ill and could not visit Hartford; he proposed that Clemens visit him in Philadelphia. But they never got together, and in September 1872 Riley died from cancer, reportedly originating from a wound in his mouth caused by a fork while he was eating. Thus ended this unlikely scheme, which had been intended to produce a sequel to *Roughing It*. Mark Twain's next effort at a travel book would be only a little more successful. But the author still pursued a second career, that of lecturer. His manager found that he was in great demand and was eager to start Mark Twain on the road again.

When he agreed to go on the lecture circuit in 1871, Mark Twain was sufficiently experienced that he prepared a list of conditions that he expected his manager, James C. Redpath, to meet. These included all travel on main lines with only short hops (but some of his travel was by slow train, and once he went eleven hours without food), the best hotel in town (but some were quite unsatisfactory and occasionally he had to spend the night in a private house); $125 per lecture for all presentations outside New England (but sometimes he made only $100), and no lectures west of St. Louis. In all he gave seventy-six performances in sixteen weeks, from October till February 1872.

During the summer he prepared three presentations, but since he had been away from the lecture platform for twenty months, his first lectures were far from polished. A major difficulty was with his topics. Some of the ones he had prepared were not well received; consequently, he had to prepare new ones while on the road. The title he gave Redpath to announce was "Reminiscences of Some Uncommonplace Characters I Have Chanced to Meet"; apparently he drew extensively from *The Innocents Abroad*. When this subject failed to please, he devoted a weekend to preparing a lecture on the comic writer and speaker Artemus Ward (whom he had known in Nevada). But again his audiences were dissatisfied, partly because much of what he had to say was already familiar to them. Since he had to read proof on *Roughing It* while touring, he drew on materials from it and as a result was able to perform much more effectively, though to his disgust on two occasions newspapers published long synopses of his lectures. On the road he was often hounded by local residents who felt that they had a right to talk with the lecturer and sometimes made themselves at home in his hotel room. He was expected to enjoy being shown a town's sights, often in cold weather. Even though he made over $10,000 from this tour, he had suffered so much from what he called in a February letter to Mrs. Fairbanks "the most detestable lecture campaign that ever was" that he abandoned the American lecture circuit for more than a decade, till November 1884, when he began a tour with George Washington Cable.[2]

During the 1871–72 tour, Clemens wrote to Olivia frequently, and since his chief enjoyment while on tour was reading, in his letters he tried to provide her with a literary education. The books he recommended had to pass his strict moral sensibility, since for him Olivia's greatest virtue was her purity. Often he marked up the books so that she knew what he wanted her to attend to but sometimes told her *not* to read books, such as *Tristram Shandy* and *Gil Blas* that might, he wrote, "offend your delicacy."

Clemens was back in Hartford for the birth of the second of the Clemens children, Olivia Susan (called Susie and later Susy). But in June the first child, Langdon, died. Eighteen months old, he had never been strong. Later Clemens assumed an unwarranted burden of guilt for his son's death. Perhaps he felt inadequate as a result of his efforts to adapt to the ways of the genteel Langdons, and this feeling was a source of his guilt. Whatever the cause, throughout his life he was to find much to feel guilty about, and being "found out" became a theme in many of his literary works.

Clemens's scientific reading was reinforcing his religious skepticism. He wrote in his notebook, "Geology. Paleontology. destroyed Genesis" and "Is there any word of God except in geology, paleontology, and astronomy?"[3] He was so interested in these subjects that he wrote what he called "A Brace of Brief Lectures on Science," published in 1871, in which he found a way to show his familiarity with modern sciences, specifically geology and paleontology, as well as his abilities as humorist.[4] He began to read with care Charles Darwin's *The Descent of Man* in 1871, the year the book was published.[5]

After a summer on the Connecticut coast without much literary productivity — unless, as is possible, he began *Tom Sawyer* at this time — the writer went to England for his first visit on August 21, 1872. His purposes were twofold. The first was somewhat pressing: to arrange for British publication of his books. He had lost much to pirated editions, and although he had arranged with George Routledge for publication in England of *Roughing It,* he was eager to establish a continuing arrangement for British copyright. Second, he was interested in looking at the possibility of writing a book about England, one like the *Innocents*. (This idea had originated with Routledge's New York agent, Joseph Blamire.) In London he saw the sights and met many famous people, including the writers Charles Reade and Thomas Hood. He was asked to lecture but decided that lecturing should await a return trip, the next year, when he would have Mrs. Clemens with him. "I came here," he wrote in November to his family, "to take notes for a book. But I haven't done much but attend dinners & make speeches." Although he took many notes, he produced little in England and left on November 12. During the winter of 1872–73, he lectured a few times in Hartford and New York and prepared two long articles for the *New York Tribune* on the Sandwich Islands. He wrote up some English sketches and returned to, or began, *Tom Sawyer.* That, however, was to be his second novel.

For some time, Mark Twain had been thinking of writing a novel. As early as April 6, 1871, he had written to the publisher of the *Galaxy,* "I begin to think I can get up quite a respectable novel, & I mean to fool away some of my odd hours in the attempt, anyway." Instead, his first complete novel was begun during the winter of 1872–73 as a "partnership novel" with his Hartford friend and neighbor, Charles Dudley Warner. Working with a more experienced writer was helpful because, as Clemens had explained to Whitelaw Reid, "When a man starts out in a new role, the public always says he is a fool & won't succeed." The collaboration was the result of a conversation about the inadequacy of recent novels. His biographer, Albert Bigelow Paine, describes the origin in this way:

At the dinner-table one night, with the Warners present, criticisms of novels were offered, with the usual freedom and severity of dinner-table talk. The husbands were inclined to treat rather lightly the novels in which their wives were finding entertainment. The wives naturally retorted that the proper thing for the husbands to do was to furnish the American people with better ones. This was regarded in the nature of a challenge and as such was accepted — mutually accepted: that is to say, in partnership. On the spur of the moment Clemens and Warner agreed that they would do a novel together, that they would begin it immediately.[6]

Warner was a newspaperman and essayist; like Clemens, he had never written a novel. But he was very much a member of the Nook Farm society that the Clemenses were seeking to join.

According to Paine, Mark Twain had in mind from the beginning that the book would be about a character modeled after his mother's eccentric cousin, James Lampton. The plan was to hatch "the plot day by day," then each would take a turn in writing. It was, Warner noted, "a novel experiment."[7] Next, as Clemens told Mrs. Fairbanks in April, the writers and their wives gathered nightly "to hear Warner & me read our day's work; & they have done a power of criticizing, but have always been anxious to be on hand at the reading & find out what has happened to the dramatis personae since the previous evening." The role of the wives is shown by Mark Twain's comment in the same letter about a vital part of the plot. "My climax chapter is the one accepted by Livy and Susie, & so my heroine, Laura, remains dead." By the end of April, the book was finished.

The Gilded Age is unduly long (subscription-book length), badly plotted, and uneven. Perhaps the best thing about the book is its title, which supplied a name for the postwar Grant era. Clemens correctly observed in 1883 that the two authors' "ingredients refused to mix, & the book consisted of *two* novels — & remained so, incurably & vexatiously, spite of all we could do to make the contents blend." Because it was a partnership novel, one seldom senses Mark Twain's literary personality in the telling of the story, although incidents and scenes resemble his earlier work. Nonetheless, Mark Twain's portion contains interesting elements of autobiography. Many of the events and characters are based on real people he knew or knew of. The first eleven chapters introduce the subject of the "Tennessee Land" that his father, John M. Clemens, purchased before the family moved to Missouri, and it provides as well a version of the adventures of the Clemens family before Sam's birth. The picture of the fictional Obedstown, Tennessee, and the steamboat scene are effective, but the chief feature of these early chapters is the introduction of Washington Hawkins, a character based on Orion Clemens, and Colonel Sellers, one of the most vivid of Mark Twain's creations, who was modeled after James Lampton.

So vital is the character of Colonel Sellers that he became the inspiration for a dramatization and sequels. He is both a courtly gentleman of the Old South and a true believer in his own fantastic inventions—schemes for getting rich quick. There is an element of self-portrait in the character, for his creator, too, was an inventor and an investor in inventions bound to produce riches. (Clemens had told Riley that their book would "sweep the world like a besom of destruction.") Sellers's wealth would come, he was convinced, from such inventions as his "Infallible Imperial Oriental Liniment and Salvation for Sore Eyes," for which he would soon have factories and warehouses in Cairo, Ispahan, Peking, and other trade centers, with headquarters at Constantinople (chap. 8). Sellers's situation as a result of his outrageous optimism is frequently embarrassing, but despite his foolishness he is presented as a sympathetic character. Mark Twain was to insist to Warner in July 1873 that Sellers is "always genial, always gentle, generous, hospitable, full of sympathy with anything that any creature has at heart." He is, he wrote to another correspondent in September 1874, "a perfectly *sincere,* pure-minded & generous-hearted man."

Sellers's efforts take him to Washington, D.C., where "for the first time in his life his talents had a fair field" (chap. 40). The Washington scene gave Clemens a chance to utilize his knowledge of the capital and its politics. (The reader has been led to expect satire by the ironic comments in the preface, such as "It will be seen that it [the book] deals with an entirely ideal state of society.") The picture of the relationships between speculators, lobbyists, and politicians is memorable, but too often the satire and the plot are at odds with each other, as in the visit in chapter 36 of Laura Hawkins, the femme fatale, to a bookstore, where the clerk's efforts to sell the trash of the day result in his being given a lecture on the subject much more suitable to come from Mark Twain's mouth than from his character's. Because both he and Warner created sets of characters, the novel is heavily populated, but it is Laura Hawkins, an adopted daughter of the fictional version of the Clemens family, who provides the focus of the plot, as distinguished from the theme, in which Sellers is central. Laura is tricked into a false marriage by a Confederate officer and then abandoned. Thereafter she seeks to capitalize on her beauty in Washington's political society and meets with some success until her seducer, now clearly married, reenters the scene only to desert her once again. She follows him to New York and murders him there. Tried on a murder charge, she is acquitted. She then tries to exploit the notoriety that her trial gives her by appearing on the lecture platform, "that final resort of the disappointed of her sex." There she is humiliated by the small crowd gathered to hear her, and she dies humbled.

Subtitled "A Tale of To-day," *The Gilded Age* fails badly as a novel but is valuable as a portrait of its age. It offers no cure for the corruption it depicts and no criticism of President Grant, who was later to become a friend of Clemens. Its angle of vision is that of the genteel society of which Clemens was becoming a member and to which Warner had already been admitted. There is little that is egalitarian or even humanitarian about the book. Yet some passages effectively suggest the spirit of the times.

At first *The Gilded Age* was a great success. That is to say, it outsold *The Innocents Abroad* and *Roughing It* in its first two months. But later sales fell off; only fifty thousand copies were sold during the entire first year. Some reviewers denounced the book. The *Chicago Tribune* reviewer wrote that the authors had "willfully degraded their craft, abused the people's trust, and provoked a strong condemnation."[8] For an English edition published by Routledge, Mark Twain wrote, while in London, a special preface. There he noted that despite his severe criticism of political corruption, he still had "a great strong faith in a noble future" for the United States. Although the book did not sell especially well in England, the *Standard* called it "a book which everyone should read." Several journals compared it to the novels of another American, Henry James.[9]

Even before the book was published, Mark Twain had turned his interest back to his anticipated English book. The partnership novel had served only as brief interruption. In May 1873, the Clemens family left for a five-month visit to England, with side trips to Scotland, Ireland, and France. They were accompanied by a young theological student, S. C. Thompson, who served as shorthand secretary for the English book. (Mark Twain was especially interested in how the English talked.) In June, he contracted with the London office of the *New York Herald* to write a series of papers about a visit of the shah of Persia to London. Thereupon he and Thompson traveled to Ostend, Belgium, to be in a position to describe the shah's entry to England, with Thompson taking notes. (He appears in these letters as Mr. Blank.) After observing the city, they recrossed the channel with the shah, and in London and later at Windsor Castle they witnessed the elaborate receptions given this distinguished visitor.

The accounts Mark Twain wrote, collected by Albert Bigelow Paine into book form in 1923 in *Europe and Elsewhere*, are among his weakest performances. He acts the buffoon, on assignment not to write letters but to deliver the shah. "If I got him over, all right, well. But if I lost him? if he died on my hands? if he drowned?" Then the author asks himself exactly what he is supposed to do and concludes that his task is to impress the shah. Thereafter he constantly questions which of the ceremonies or events will impress the visiting dignitary. Young Prince Arthur greets him, for example, with a "whole broadside of gold and silver medals on his breast — for good behavior, punctuality, accurate spelling, penmanship, etc., I suppose, but I could not see the inscriptions." Despite a few funny touches, these letters are embarrassingly bad — the case of a writer parodying himself, it would seem. For some passages Mark Twain was not guilty; additions were made by a *Herald* employee.[10]

When he began this assignment, he was excited. As he started on the first of his letters, he wrote to Bliss in June that he should "seize them as they appear, & turn them into a 25 cent pamphlet (my royalties 10 per cent) & spread them over the land your own way, but be quick!" After he wrote the last letter, he was more modest. Along with the shah letters he planned to publish, he wrote Bliss in July, he wanted a preface to note that the pamphlet contained "certain sketches of mine which are little known or not known at all in America, to the end that the purchase of the pamphlet may get back a portion of his money & skip the chapters that refer to the Shah altogether." Apologetically he explained, "It is not my desire to republish these New York Herald letters in this form; I only do it to forestall some small pirate or other in the book trade." By August he had decided that the shah pieces as they had appeared were so bad that the whole project should be stopped. When a twenty-five cent pamphlet finally appeared, *Mark Twain's Sketches. Number One,* the shah letters were absent. And despite the implications of the title, there was to be no Number Two.[11]

Finding that he was short of cash, Mark Twain lectured six times in London during October 1873 and once thereafter in Liverpool. A friend from his California days, Charles Warren Stoddard, provides a vivid picture of the writer's lecturing experiences in London:

> There was a first-night such as any author might be proud of. The London *Herald* cheered the American heartily, and the congratulations that followed were sufficient evidence of the lecturer's success. On the second night the house was judiciously "pappered." There were hosts of people who were unaccustomed to the American entertainment, and nothing but skilful management could have drawn them out. The third night, after the *matinée* of the same day, drew a profitable audience; and from that hour the business of the house increased. Extra seats were introduced; the stage was thronged; Mark stood in the centre of the British public and held his own against the infinite attractions of the city. Satur-

day *matinée* and evening saw disappointed people turned from the door; for there was not even standing-room in the hall.[12]

Not surprisingly, Olivia Clemens observed in a letter, "Mr. Clemens can lecture and get money to pay our debts and get us home . . . lecturing is what Mr. C. always speaks of doing when their [*sic*] seems any need for money."[13] Clemens took his family back to Hartford in November, then almost immediately returned, alone, to London for more lectures.

By December 1, he began three weeks of very successful lecturing in London. His topics were the Sandwich Islands and "Roughing It on the Silver Frontier."[14] Parts of these lectures appeared in London newspapers and were soon copied in newspapers all over the United States. A British journalist reported that these lectures "are probably read by a larger number of men and women in America than any public document, the President's message not excepted."[15]

However successful he was now, as the author of two books about his experiences, as a nascent novelist, and as a lecturer with a following on both sides of the Atlantic, Mark Twain was still deeply uncertain of himself. Finding an old friend of California days when he was feeling very much alone, he hired Stoddard as a kind of secretary-companion, and the two lived together "in a kind of gorgeous seclusion that was broken only by our nightly trip to the Lecture Hall," Stoddard remembered. Clemens shared his deepest fear with him, his belief that the time would soon come when he could neither write nor lecture and would therefore be unable to support his family. "I used to go to sleep," Stoddard reported, "night after night with that word of woe in my ears, that Mark would die in the poorhouse."[16]

Perhaps he had more reason to worry at this time than may appear to those with the advantage of knowing how the remainder of his life was to be lived. For one thing, there was to be no English book. At first the writer's problem was that he didn't know enough, he thought. He wrote to his wife in October 1872, "One mustn't tackle England in print with a mere superficial knowledge of it. I am by long odds the most widely known & popular American author among the English & the book will be read by pretty much every Englishman — therefore for my own sake it must not be a poor book." Then, after he had written a few English sketches, he abandoned the notion. He later explained: "I couldn't get any fun out of England. It is too grave a country." He found England "not a good text for hilarious literature."[17] There was another complication: he liked the English, who had received him with enthusiasm. Among the notables that he met were Anthony Trollope, Robert Browning, and Wilkie Collins. Later, in June 1874, he wrote to the *New York Evening Post*, "There may be no serious indelicacy about eating a gentleman's bread & then writing an appreciative & complimentary account of the ways of his family, but still it is a thing which one naturally dislikes to do." Had Mark Twain completed the book on England, it might have been lively and readable but probably not an advance in form or narrative style over his two earlier accounts of his travels and adventures.[18]

When Clemens returned to Hartford in early 1874, he might well have seen that his various literary plans — at least three that he had counted on — had not worked. But he had the satisfaction of seeing that the spectacular house where he and his family would live happily for many years was going up. An expensive construction, designed by architect Edward T. Potter, it would eventually cost — land, building, and furnishings — some $120,000 in the currency of the day. The project was to prove an enormous distraction, for the house required six servants to keep it going, and time and effort were required to entertain the parade of guests that almost constantly filled its rooms. As Clemens complained to Howells in 1875, "My household expenses are something almost ghastly." After the house was finished, the Clemenses undertook extensive renovations. More and more the author found that he had no time to write there.

In April 1874, the Clemenses retreated again to Elmira, where they stayed with Mrs. Langdon until May 5, when the weather was warm enough to go up East Hill to Quarry Farm, above the noise of the city on 250 acres of land. As the author wrote his Edinburgh friend, Dr. John Brown, "It gets fearfully hot here in the summer, so we spend our summers on top of a hill 6 or 700 feet high . . . — it never gets hot there." The Clemenses's second daughter, Clara, was born on the farm on June 8. That year the writer had a new place in which to work, apart from the house, a charming study provided by Susan Crane. Susan, nearly ten years older than Olivia, had been adopted by the Langdons on the death of her natural parents. She and Olivia had attended what was then Elmira Female College, with the younger girl being enrolled in the preparatory class. Later that year Susan married Theodore Crane, and they went to live at Quarry Farm, which Susan had inherited on the death of her mother and stepfather. Ida Langdon, the daughter of Olivia's brother Charles and a playmate of the Clemens children at the farm, described Susan as "gentle, humorous, at times gay, responsive, understanding, tolerant, and lovely to look at." Susan was "entirely able to cope with [Clemens's] teasing, his sallies, his extravagances and explosions; never ruffled or unduly upset by the differences in their philosophies or religious beliefs — devoted to him as he to her."[19]

With these arrangements, Mark Twain spent an unusually productive spring and summer. In May, he had heard of a play being performed in San

Francisco that was derived from *The Gilded Age;* he was able to enjoin the performances and purchase the script of the play from the author, G. B. Densmore, for two hundred dollars, although he himself had intended to write a play based on *The Gilded Age* as early as 1873 and had even copyrighted the idea. By July he had produced a rewriting of Densmore's version. "I don't think much of it, as a drama," he wrote to Howells in July, "but I suppose it will do to hang Col. Sellers on." With John T. Raymond, a skillful and popular actor, performing the part of Sellers, it was a considerable success as a comedy, and Clemens profited to the extent of more than $100,000, although he was never happy with Raymond's vulgarization of Sellers's part.[20] These profits partially compensated Clemens for the two books he had not written, and they unfortunately led him to believe that more gold awaited him in the theater.

Sometime while he was on the American lecture circuit, he wrote a short piece that has attracted special attention. The author explains that while he was on the lecture circuit he had met a hotel servant, a black boy, "the most artless, sociable, and exhaustless talker I ever came across." As he listened to "Jimmy," he wrote, the boy's "talk got the upper hand of my interest," and to preserve the memory, he wrote it down to send in a letter home. "Sociable Jimmy" appeared in the *New York Times* in November 1874. Why he chose to publish it later (along with the explanation above) and so obscurely is not known.

Jimmy's talk anticipates that of Huck Finn in important ways. They have similar speech patterns, including the repetition of words and phrases and the creative use of words. For example, Jimmy likes the noun "buster" and the verb "scoops." Huck features "skreeky" and "smouches." Both use the conjunction "and" freely, and both employ "snake" as a verb.[21] A similar but better-known piece written during the author's 1874 stay at Quarry Farm was to be his first piece published in the *Atlantic Monthly.* "A True Story. Repeated Word for Word as I Heard It" is an account given to the writer by the Quarry Farm cook, Auntie Cord (in the sketch called Aunt Rachel), of her painful experiences as a slave. It is in dialect and, according to Clemens's September letter to Howells, "not altered . . . except to begin at the beginning, instead of the middle, as she did — and traveled both ways." Capturing the language and the personality was made easier because of his experience of recording sociable Jimmy, and in turn transcribing Auntie Cord's talk helped prepare him for his writing work of the summer, since it brought him back to the atmosphere of the pre–Civil War South and memories of his own boyhood. Moreover, his conversations with Auntie Cord would soon provide him with information that he could use in *Huckleberry*

Finn. In an unpublished piece called "A Family Sketch" (1906), he told how the black cook filled the heads of his children with Negro superstitions about spiders, cobwebs, snakes, the weather, the phases of the moon, and the eccentricities of animals.[22]

Back in February 1870, soon after he was married, Clemens had written a letter to Will Bowen, whom he called his first, oldest, and dearest friend. He recalled in it the experiences of his youth, memories of which had suggested to him how far he had come since his Hannibal days. The excitement behind this long, very detailed letter was warranted. Mark Twain was making one of the great discoveries of his career: that he had a highly usable past. Now reminded by Auntie Cord of the old days, he undertook the writing of a novel, solo: *The Adventures of Tom Sawyer*, in which seven incidents recounted in the letter to Will Bowen were retold.[23]

He had, however, never entirely forgotten the literary possibilities latent in his boyhood, as shown by such pieces as "Jim Wolf and the Tom-Cats" (1867); the episode in chapter 18 of *The Innocents Abroad* in which he describes finding a corpse in his father's office; and the pictures of Washington Hawkins and his youthful daydreams in *The Gilded Age*. Not long after writing his letter to Bowen, Mark Twain sketched what has been called the "Boy Manuscript," the diary of Billy Rogers. The story of Billy's romance with eight-year-old Amy suggests that the writer was approaching his boy-hero Tom Sawyer. Much of what Billy does in response to Amy, Tom Sawyer was later to imitate. The "Boy Manuscript" itself is not promising.

Another step toward *Tom Sawyer* was the composition in London in 1872 of the episode in which Tom tricks his friends into whitewashing a fence. The writing of the novel as it is now known was begun after the author's return from London and before he turned to *The Gilded Age*. He wrote about one hundred pages then. In April 1874, he returned to the book, and by September he had written about half, encouraged by the new Quarry Farm study, where he could write without interruption. Early in September, he informed a friend that his new book had been his real concern. He was "wrapped up in it and so dead to anything else." *Tom Sawyer* was not a book produced to meet the demands of a contract, nor was it a sequel to the *Innocents*, as the diamond mine book and the English book were to have been. It was composed readily, from within, as suggested by the author's comment that in creating it he had "pumped" himself "dry" by summer's end. In 1906 he described what had happened. At page 400 of his manuscript, "the story made a sudden and determined halt and refused to proceed another step. . . . I could not understand why I was not able to go on with it. The reason was very simple — my tank had run dry; it was empty."[24]

Perhaps a more specific reason for his inability to continue was that he had to solve a problem concerning Tom's future. When Tom leaves Joe Harper and Huck Finn on Jackson's Island at the end of chapter 15, he prepares a note for Joe. With it he bequeaths "certain school-boy treasures of almost inestimable value." Thereby the author hinted that Tom was about to leave St. Petersburg for greater adventures. But the author was uncertain. On the manuscript at this point, Mark Twain wrote a series of notes about how the story might be continued; they reflect this indecision.

So he put it aside until the following May, when he began it again, in Hartford—for in the previous September the family had moved into their new house and would not go to Elmira during the summer of 1875. Although he told Howells in June that "there is no plot to the thing," he later noted that "there was plenty of material now, and the book went on and finished itself, without any trouble."[25] (With the book behind him, the author and his family vacationed in Newport, Rhode Island.)

The second half of the book was shaped by two decisions: first, to have Tom remain in St. Petersburg (the boys return from Jackson's Island to attend their own funeral), and second, to show Tom in a heroic light. Some of what he wrote in 1875 before the decision showed an immature Tom; these passages, describing the graduation exercises and Tom's joining the Cadets of Temperance (as young Clemens had once done) were now placed *before* Tom's heroic performance at the trial in chapter 23. By July 5, the book was finished, although the author was uncertain whether or not he was right in "closing with him as a boy" instead of continuing Tom's story, as he then told Howells he had planned. His original intention, shown by a note on the manuscript, was to write a four-part novel, of which he had completed only some of the first. "1. Boyhood & youth; 2 Y[outh] & early manh[ood]; 3 the Battle of Life in many lands; 4 (age 37 to 40) return to meet grown babies & toothless old drivelers who were the grandees of his youth. The Adored Unknown a faded old maid & full of rasping puritanical vinegar piety."[26] The "new girl" who becomes Becky Thatcher is identified in chapter 3 as "The Adored Unknown." Much later Mark Twain would attempt to write a version of part 4, but with the "boys" returning as old men.

The Adventures of Tom Sawyer had its origins in several distinct interests of its creator. First, he was still fascinated by the concept of innocence. He had emphasized his own youthfulness and naivete in *Roughing It,* and for him to move backward from young adulthood to boyhood seemed natural. He was also now aware that he could write, without notes or reminders, fiction based on his own childhood. Tom is a version of Sam Clemens the boy, innocent but mischievous and deep-dyed in literary romanticism. Moreover, he was still entertained by the ideas of his early sketches about good boys and bad boys preserved in *Sketches, New and Old* (1875). Furthermore, other writers had begun to write about the "bad" boy — like the hero of *The Story of a Bad Boy* (1869) by Clemens's good friend Thomas Bailey Aldrich. Tom Sawyer differs from most such boys chiefly in that he is brought to a degree of maturity through the initiation process that had interested Mark Twain in *Roughing It.* One final concern was satire.

Tom Sawyer was an enormous breakthrough for Mark Twain. He was not revising an earlier account, working from his brother's notes, editing someone else's reports, or writing with a partner; he was relying on his own memories: of his mother for Tom's Aunt Polly, of the cave where the real "Injun Joe" had been lost (but did not starve), of the schoolhouse.[27] "Most of the adventures recorded in this book really occurred," he stated in the preface; "one or two were experiences of my own, the rest those of boys who were schoolmates of mine." He told an interviewer in 1895, "I knew both those boys [Tom and Huck] so well that it was easy to write what they said."[28] Tom himself is not a single individual, he explained in the preface. He is a combination of three boys "and therefore belongs to the composite order of architecture."

Although autobiographical and highly original, *Tom Sawyer* nevertheless reflects the author's reading. The grave-robbing scene is drawn from *A Tale of Two Cities,* Clemens's favorite Dickens novel. The relationship of Tom and Aunt Polly derives from B. P. Shillaber's books about Mrs. Partington as well as real-life experiences. Like Tom, Mrs. Partington's nephew Ike plays tricks on the cat, steals doughnuts, misbehaves in church, feigns illness to stay home from school, and is inspired by *The Black Avenger* of Ned Buntline (E. Z. C. Judson). The graduation chapter acknowledges his borrowing from Mary Ann Harris Gay's *Pastor's Story and Other Pieces; or, Prose and Poetry.* He used the simple expedient of pasting pages of Gay's collection onto his manuscript. Many other authors influenced the composition: Tennyson, Poe, A. B. Longstreet, George Washington Harris, Carlyle. The cave episode was probably inspired by a news story published in April 1873 about children lost in the Hannibal cave.[29] The chief elements of the plot, such as the love story and the treasure hunt, were widely used in contemporary books about boys. Indeed, in his first solo flight as a novelist, Mark Twain was consciously attempting to write a story after the model of other books about boys. Like Aldrich's boy, Tom Bailey, Tom Sawyer is a bookish boy, and the book as a whole has a bookish, "Eastern" quality, as if the author had chosen to set aside his experiences in Nevada and California.[30] The narrator implies that he is familiar with Mont Blanc and wealthy English gentlemen, and in chapter 25 he observes that "every rightly constructed boy's life" includes a desire to hunt for buried treasure. Mark Twain kept Tom's adventures at a distance so that the reader is continually aware that he is reading a book and that it is modeled on other books. An early reviewer of its sequel, *Huckleberry Finn,* asked whether "the most marked fault" of *Tom Sawyer* "is not its too strong adherence to contemporary literary models." For that reviewer, "the modern novel exercises a very great influence" on *Tom Sawyer.*[31]

The world of *Tom Sawyer* is, however, gratifying to readers, both adults and children. In it wishes — even impossible ones — are granted, and the gratification is greater than in legends and fairy stories because the events in the book are not so greatly removed from daily life. Tom heroically wins Becky Thatcher and is lionized by adults after rescuing her from the cave, a far more delicious achievement than winning the Sunday-school Bible (and afterward suffering humiliation). Tom and his friends escape, run away, and for a time enjoy an idyllic, vastly appealing life on Jackson's Island. This long episode ends with Tom's pleasure at what many have wished for and few achieved — a triumphal return to their own funerals. Even the boys' unhappiness with school discipline leads to wish-fulfillment: the odious father-figure, the schoolmaster Dobbins, is completely defeated at the school ceremonies in chapter 21, when his students display beneath his wig "their master's bald pate," gilded by the sign-painter's boy.

Such antics as these may lead the reader to overlook some of the failings of the book: the variation in point of view from nostalgia to burlesque; the author's occasional abandonment of his role as storyteller to comment on the action and tell his reader what to think, such as does the mock-serious "great and wise philosopher" in chapter 2. The strands of the narrative, though thematically integrated, are only loosely coordinated into a plot. The most successful achievement of *Tom Sawyer* is that it combines Mark Twain's desire to write a popular, appealingly upbeat book and his secret conviction that small-town America actually had little to offer a person who would live both freely and intensely. Tom's search for something better than the restrictive institutions and attitudes of St. Petersburg leads again and again to terror, most fully and climactically in the cave. Tom and Becky learn in its chambers that the unknown is the ultimate threat. There Tom in effect renounces his dreams when he mourns, "I was such a fool! Such a fool! I never thought we might want to come back" (chap. 31). These experiences give him a change of heart, demonstrated at the end of the story when he successfully badgers Huck, the very embodiment of rebelliousness, into accepting respectability. Tom's own submission is a defeat of sorts, since he embraces values that the book as a whole does not recommend.[32] Huck's reluctant abandonment, under pressure, of his comfortable smoking and cursing echoes Clemens's report to Dr. Brown in 1874 that "I was a mighty coarse, unpromising subject when Livy took charge of me 4 years ago. . . . She has made a very creditable job of me." Few readers, however, can be eager for Widow Douglas to take charge of Huck. Inasmuch as Tom has sought adult approval, his eventual acceptance of adult standards is understandable, perhaps inevitable — but not Huck's.

Mark Twain's recent conversations with Auntie Cord may have reminded the author of how much cruelty was associated with slavery, for blacks are almost invisible in the world of *Tom Sawyer.* Only a black boy, little Jim, is introduced briefly in chapter two. It was apparently difficult for Mark Twain to reconcile nostalgia for his lost youth and a recognition of the place of slavery in Missouri. *The Adventures of Tom Sawyer* has always, until recently, been read as a classic children's book — despite a few objections, including one that refers to the book as a "Nightmare Vision of American Boyhood."[33]

The novelist considered publishing *Tom Sawyer* in his friend Howells's magazine, the *Atlantic Monthly,* a most unlikely medium, for he wished to compete with his former friend Bret Harte, whose novel *Gabriel Conroy* was being published by *Scribner's,* with Harte receiving a handsome fee. The fact that he was considering the *Atlantic* shows the author's confusion concerning exactly what he had written. In July he described it to Howells as "*not* a boy's book" but rather one "only written for adults." Only after considering the matter for six months was he able to accept his wife's judgment — and Howells's — and agree that "the book should issue as a book for boys, pure & simple," as he wrote to Howells.

The author's correspondence with Howells concerning *Tom Sawyer* demonstrates one of his limitations as a writer, his inability to discriminate, to judge his own writing. It was for this reason, as well as his eagerness to avoid offending genteel standards, that he submitted his work to his wife and Howells for approval. The experienced *Atlantic* editor's reading led him to propose in July some pruning from the last chapter plus "some corrections and suggestions" in what Howells described as "faltering pencil."[34] Clemens's response in January was simple and forthright. "Instead of *reading* the MS., I simply hunted out the pencil marks & made the emendations which they suggested." Some of these were, however, significant. He shortened the episode in which Becky examines Mr. Dobbins's anatomy book, "tamed the various obscenities," and eliminated from the description of the dog sitting down on a pinch-bug in chapter 5 the phrase "with his tail shut down like a hasp," which Howells described as "awfully good but a little too dirty."[35] Howells later described his friend's responses to his suggestions as "a mush of concessions," although he had supposed that he was merely making "suggestions for improvement" that he hoped would be "never acted on."[36]

While *Tom Sawyer* was written with spontaneity, Clemens had not failed to think of prospective income from the book. He took "a vile, mercenary view of things," he admitted to Howells. He had high expectations. He wrote to a correspondent in April 1876, "I am determined that Tom shall outsell any previous book of mine, and I mean he shall have every possible advantage." But despite its virtues, *Tom Sawyer* did not provide its author what he expected. Because publication by American Publishing Company was delayed, a Canadian pirated edition, selling in the United States for seventy-five cents in paper and one dollar in cloth, took the edge off the market for the American subscription edition.

The original American version of *The Adventures of Tom Sawyer* looks like a children's book. Only 23,638 copies were sold by the publisher during the first year, and less than 29,000 by the end of 1879, and it provided only half the income of *The Gilded Age*. The book was illustrated by True Williams, who had prepared many illustrations for each of Mark Twain's earlier American Publishing Company books. As published, the illustrations are a very important feature, for they were used to make the book feel more substantial: it fills only 275 pages, with large print and wide margins, far less than the usual subscription book. The author did not choose to focus his attention on the 160 illustrations, and perhaps as a result, they are not consistent: the same characters often look different as one turns the pages. The famous fence that Tom has to paint in chapter 2 is not a board fence but a rail fence; Williams apparently based his fence on a prepublication description that the author later changed. Moreover, Williams obviously made use of the illustrations he was preparing for *Sketches, New and Old;* he was preparing the two almost at the same time. Each chapter heading had an elaborate design that occupied much of the page on which each appeared.[37]

The English publication preceded the American edition, which was much delayed. The English reviewers liked it, though they judged that it was addressed to adults, not to children. The *London Athenaeum* began its review, "The name of Mark Twain is known throughout the length and breadth of England. Wherever there is a railroad-station with a bookstall, his jokes are household words."[38] Most American periodicals simply ignored the book, for once again it was a subscription book that was not advertised. Although Howells was enthusiastic, his review appeared too far in advance of the publication to be helpful. Another review, otherwise favorable, protested against the powerful presence of violence in the book: besides "revenge," talk of "slitting women's ears," and "the shadow of the gallows," there is "an ugly murder in the book, over-minutely described and too fully-illustrated, which Tom and Huck see, of course."[39] Mark Twain's penchant for describing violence was far more evident in a children's book than in his Western sketches.

Between stints on *Tom Sawyer*, Mark Twain turned to what is probably his best work of less than book length. Like *Tom*, it was composed from inspiration. In the fall of 1874, Howells had requested a sequel to "A True Story" for the *Atlantic Monthly*. Clemens replied that he had nothing to offer, but that same day he talked with his friend Joseph Twichell during a long walk and, as he reported to Howells, "got to telling him about the old Mississippi days of steam-boating glory & grandeur (during 5 years) *from the pilot house*." He soon decided that he could write not simply a single reminiscence but a whole series on piloting. The satisfaction he could antic-ipate from sharing in that glory and grandeur was a strong motivation. By late November, he had finished one installment. In all, the *Atlantic* would publish seven segments of "Old Times on the Mississippi." Soon after he began, he decided to expand his subject into a book about the Mississippi River, a subscription book, of course. Since the 1860s he had been nursing the general idea, but he had not intended to describe his own experiences until that talk with Twichell. Fortune had again played a major role in shaping the writer's career.

"Old Times" aroused Clemens's enthusiasm. "I am the only man alive that can scribble about the piloting of that day," he wrote Howells in De-cember. "If I were to write fifty articles they would all be about pilots and piloting." "Old Times" became the story of a cub pilot's education and the reality of river currents and sandbars. That Mark Twain conceived of the chapters as specifically for an *Atlantic* audience is confirmed by one of the themes running through the installments. For this educated readership, despite his own limited schooling, he compared the process of learning the river to education from books. The river itself is described in the third installment as if it were a volume in Latin and Greek, "a book that was a dead language to the uneducated passenger." Titles of installments empha-size the point: "Perplexing Lessons," for instance, and "Completing My Education." A humorous account, the narrative maintains an underlying seriousness.[40]

While writing the *Atlantic* installments, he almost longed to return to his former craft. "I am a person who would quit authorizing in a minute to go piloting, if the madame would stand it," he joked in a letter to Howells. A few years later, he was asked, "Would you be a boy again?" He responded, "Certainly I would!" — providing that "I should emerge from boyhood as a 'cub pilot' on a Mississippi boat, & that I should by & by become a pilot & remain one." On the other hand, he endured lifelong nightmares of being "obliged to go back to the river to earn a living. It is never a pleasant dream, either."[41] In his notebook in 1883, he recorded more specifically: "My nightmares, to this day, take the form of running down into an overshadowing bluff, with a steamboat."[42] In "Old Times," his feelings of nostalgia *and* fear undergird the narrative. It was not simply his familiarity with the subject that informs the story. He now was bringing to his writing a newly achieved sensitivity to the large issues of innocence and experience. "Old Times" is as entertaining as *Tom Sawyer,* and up to the last installment, which he told Howells was "odious" and should be left out, the writing went easily.

When Mark Twain wrote "Old Times," the satisfactions of his achievements were tempered by his recent failure to create a suitable sequel to his two successes and by his increasing realization that he was obliged to write what his audience expected. In the sixth installment, he made his predicament explicit: "Writers of all kinds are manacled servants of the public. We write frankly and fearlessly, but then we 'modify' before we print." Unlike writers, kings, parliaments, and editors, the pilot of the 1850s "was the only unfettered and entirely independent human being that lived in earth." He further exaggerated the pilot's authority by portraying the cub pilot as much younger than Clemens really was when he began piloting. Whereas in reality he was twenty-one, he appears in the first installment to be only about sixteen. Indeed, this youth is pleased even to be sunburned: "I wished that the boys and girls at home could see me now." The comedy of "Old Times" results from the repeated revelation of the young cub's ignorance and innocence and from his consequent embarrassment and humiliation. The humor is often on the verge of being painful, as when the cub is tricked by a practical joke before an audience assembled to watch, but the author is obviously enjoying the telling of his story, and the reader suspects that the writer is deliberately emphasizing the cub's naivete.

"Old Times" gives as much attention to the master as to the apprentice. Horace Bixby is perhaps the most powerful authority figure in Mark Twain's writings. While he is a strict, demanding teacher, he is preparing the cub to be like him. Early in young Sam's education, they work together on a "big New Orleans boat," "a grand affair" where the boy is respectfully "sir'd" by "the regiment of natty servants." This experience encourages him to anticipate the day when he too will be a Bixby, whose prowess is demonstrated early in the sequence in a virtuoso performance Mark Twain entitled "A Daring Deed." The recognition that Bixby received for his achievement is not lost on the cub. In the third installment, the cub learns "The face of the water, in time, became a wonderful book" that he successfully "mastered." The author does not describe his experience as a licensed pilot, since the basis of the humor concerns his failures and his embarrassment. Instead, he suggests what it means to belong to the community of river men, with their solidarity and tradition.[43] He implies, too, that the process by which he learned to be a pilot was essential to his becoming an effective writer.[44]

Yet before the comedy of "Old Times" is over, it is qualified. After all, the cub's task results in his losing his ignorance and thereby his innocence. "I had made a valuable acquisition," he attests. "But I had lost something too. I had lost something which could never be restored to me while I lived. All the grace, the beauty, the poetry, had gone out of the majestic river! . . . All the value any feature of it had for me now was the amount of usefulness it could furnish toward compassing the safe piloting of a steamboat." Unlike the passenger who sees "all manner of pretty pictures" as he looks at the river, the pilot sees "the grimmest and most dead earnest of reading matter."[45] Of course, Mark Twain was mistaken if he supposed that he had lost the ability to respond to the poetry of nature, as *Tom Sawyer* and *Huckleberry Finn* and "Old Times" itself demonstrate. But his portrayal of youthful innocence paralleled his view of the "rough, coarse, unpromising subject" that Livy had taken charge of. Tellingly, the passage about the difference between the pilot's perception and the passenger's is clothed in the most genteel rhetoric.[46]

Soon after he began the "Old Times" installments, Clemens sought to persuade Howells to travel with him to New Orleans to gather materials for the book he planned to make about the river. In January he informed Howells, "The piloting material has been uncovering itself by degrees, until it has exposed such a huge hoard to my view that a whole book will be required to contain it if I use it. So I have agreed to write a book for Bliss." That same day he described his intention more specifically: he would "stop in September with the ninth chapter [i.e., installment] & then add fifty chapters more & bring the whole out in book form in November." This proved to be a highly optimistic forecast. Neither the trip to New Orleans nor the continuation beyond the *Atlantic* installments would materialize for several years.

At the end of 1874, while beginning "Old Times," Mark Twain began to put into shape a substantial collection of his sketches for an American audience. He called the book *Sketches, New and Old,* but in reality most were old, though he continued the revising process by eliminating coarseness as he had in preparing his sketches for English readers. Some of the new pieces are slight, such as an after-dinner speech he had delivered in London. The longest of the new pieces, "Some Learned Fables, for Good Old Boys and Girls," had been rejected by Howells when Clemens had sent it to him in September. It is a beasts' fable, with a few pleasant touches. Several of the creatures in the story are scientists, and the expedition of these geologists, paleontologists, and archaeologists is strongly satirized. The hero of the piece is Tumble Bug, who seems to have just arrived from the West to insult the pompous Dr. Bull Frog (who has been identified as O. C. Marsh of Yale), Professor Snail, and other dignitaries. Although too long and unfocused, the sketch suggests that Mark Twain still had a good word to say for the vernacular values he had adopted in the West and remained dubious about book-learning.[47] Altogether different is another piece, "Experience of the McWilliamses with Membranous Croup," the first of several McWilliams stories, which provide an oblique look at life in the Clemens household. The Olivia figure of the story, extremely solicitous for the welfare of her child, makes heavy demands on her husband, usually in the most delicate and indirect way. The family picture is amusing, but the sketch may be read as the author's subtle revenge, for in both this and other "McWilliams" sketches, a long-suffering husband has to cope with a silly wife. Howells thought that it "must read like an abuse of confidence to every husband and father."[48]

In the preparation of this collection of sixty-five pieces, the writer explained to Howells in September, "I destroyed a mass of sketches, & now heartily wish I had destroyed some more of them." As a whole, *Sketches, New and Old* represented his past, about which he had become thoroughly ambivalent. He could already see that he had become a better writer and that his earlier work was that of an apprentice. "Every man," he told his brother in 1878, "must *learn* his trade — not pick it up. God requires that he learn it by slow and painful processes." But he could find merit in some of his older pieces, such as "The Scriptural Panoramist," written for the *Californian* in 1864. Therein a brief tale is told of a showman who hires a pianist, "a wooden-headed old slab," to provide a suitable musical accompaniment to both a showing of religious pictures and the showman's own pious rhetoric. But again and again the pianist undercuts him. A picture of the Prodigal Son, for instance, is introduced with comments about "the ecstasy beaming from the uplifted countenance of the aged father, and the joy that sparkles in the eyes of the excited group of youths and maidens, and seems ready to burst into the welcoming chorus from their lips. The lesson, my friends, is as solemn and instructive as the story is tender and beautiful." Thereupon the pianist bangs out the song "Oh we'll all get blind drunk / When Johnny comes marching home!" After the third such juxtaposition, "all the solemn old flats got up in a huff to go — and everybody else laughed till the windows rattled." The showman thereupon "grabbed the orchestra and shook him" and ordered him to "vamose the ranch." Mark Twain's sympathies are clearly with the pianist and his unintentional deflation of the showman's pretentious genteel rhetoric.

As usual, Howells befriended Clemens by publishing a review of the volume, and what he found was quite different from what Clemens had any reason to suppose he would: "a growing seriousness of meaning in the apparently unmoralized drolling" of a *subtile* humorist." He objected to nothing and even listed "The Scriptural Panoramist" as a familiar favorite.[49] Olivia Clemens expressed her deep gratitude to Howells, with her husband explaining that "the thing that gravels her is that I am *so* persistently glorified as a mere buffoon" by other commentators. He told Howells in October that his friend was "heroically trampling the truth under foot in order to praise" him. Despite the kind words, the subscription book sold poorly, fewer than twenty-four thousand copies by the end of 1879 — even worse than *Tom Sawyer.*

The "growing seriousness" of Mark Twain that Howells thought he detected in October 1875 may have been a response less to the *Sketches* than to a piece that Howells had published that month — anonymously, at the author's request. "The Curious Republic of Gondour" was prompted by Clemens's sense that he now belonged to an elite class. In the political utopia that he describes, universal suffrage "had seemed to deliver all power into the hands of the ignorant and non-tax-paying classes," with unhappy results. The imagined remedy was to give additional votes beyond the basic one to those possessing wealth or education — the more money or learning, the more votes. But "learning being more prevalent and more easily acquired than riches, educated men became a wholesome check upon wealthy men, since they could outvote them."[50] This brief piece would presumably have appealed especially to readers of the *Atlantic,* and if they did not know the author's identity, the editor did. Howells asked in August for "some more accounts of the same country."[51] None, however, were forthcoming.

Perhaps the "Gondour" essay is the one Clemens read to the Monday Evening Club of Hartford in the previous February under the title "Universal Suffrage." Other club members included the learned J. Hammond Trumbull, who had contributed the polyglot chapter headings for *The Gilded Age,* the lawyer William Hamersley, who would later invest in the Paige typesetting machine, General J. R. Hawley, and Joseph Twichell. The man from Missouri who had little formal education had been clearly accepted into the inner sanctum of Hartford's intellectual establishment.[52]

After sending Howells the lightweight "Literary Nightmare," later called "Punch, Brothers, Punch!" — which was, Howells reported in January 1876, "an immense success"[53] — Mark Twain submitted something far better. In January 1876, he drafted "The Facts Concerning the Recent Carnival of Crime in Connecticut." It was inspired both by the author's experiences and the treatment of morality and conscience he found in a book he had been reading, William E. H. Lecky's *History of European Morals* (1869), which became one of his favorites. Deliberately distinguishing his narrator from himself (the narrator, for instance, is the father of sons), Mark Twain tells a revealing story about his double, "a shriveled, shabby dwarf . . . not more than two feet high," forty years old, a distorted figure but with "a sort of remote and ill-defined resemblance" to himself. This figure has Samuel Clemens's famous drawl, a resemblance underscored by being noted three times. The narrator, a prosperous and successful writer, lives comfortably and well. But his conscience, the dwarf, will not leave him alone and catalogs his misdeeds. "It is my *business* — and my joy," his conscience announces, "to make you repent of *every*thing you do." The narrator thereupon tells how he finally found relief from his conscience's tormentings — he rose up, tore apart, and killed his conscience, a deed that freed him to undertake an ensuing "carnival of crime in Connecticut."

If in "Gondour" Mark Twain had indicated his embracing of the cultural values of his respectable New England community, the "Carnival of Crime" hints that he was not happy about submitting to the self-discipline and social demands being made of him, though he chose to disguise his protest in humor. To get the pleasure out of the "Carnival," he read it to his Hartford club, and according to Joseph Twichell, he made it "vastly funny," although Twichell also recognized its implications.[54] Huck Finn too would have problems with his conscience, and indeed the subject is brought up repeatedly in Mark Twain's writings, including his letters, at times associated with feelings of humiliation.

He wrote a friend in 1903, for instance, about a torturing self-doubt: "I was afraid I had blundered into an offense in some way and had forfeited your friendship — a kind of blunder I have made so many times in my life that I am always standing in a waiting and morbid dread of its occurrence." More humorously, he could joke with Mary Rogers, daughter-in-law of his financial adviser, in November 1906: "I've had an awful accident. I have coughed up my conscience. I wouldn't have taken $40 for her, she was just out of the repair shops and had fresh paint on and new rubber tyres." His fullest and bitterest complaint occurred in a letter to Howells written in April 1882:

> Oh, hell, there is no hope for a person who is built like me; — because there is no cure, no cure. If I could only *know* when I have committed a crime: then I could conceal it & not go stupidly dribbling it out, circumstance by circumstance, into the ears of a person who will give no sign till the confession is complete; & then the sudden damnation drops on a body like the released pile-driver, & he finds himself in the earth down to his chin. When he supposed he was merely being entertaining.

The nature of the offense is unknown but can be presumed to have been trivial.

In "Carnival of Crime," then, Mark Twain created a funny but serious and personal work — not a spoof but a small domestic masterpiece. In it Mark Twain's authentic voice is discernible. He is a victim, his own victim, and society's, too. He is being confidential, even perhaps confessional, but not embarrassingly so. His almost violent impulses find an irreverent but acceptable outlet. From the curious title onward, the work exhibits masterful control. The fascinating theme links the sketch with other *doppelgänger* stories such as Conrad's "The Secret Sharer" and Dostoevski's "The Double."

Another, quite different means by which Mark Twain released himself from his sense of being "manacled" took the form of a piece he wrote later in the same year, 1876, at Quarry Farm, where he once again retreated for the summer. "[Date, 1601] Conversation, As It Was by the Social Fireside, in the Time of the Tudors," was written, according to the author's later remembrance, while he was reading "ancient English books" preparatory to writing *The Prince and the Pauper.* He noted that "frank indelicacies of speech" were "permissible among ladies and gentlemen in that ancient time." The excerpt of conversation he wrote, somewhat masked by attempts at archaic English, makes much of farts and codpieces in an arch, somewhat adolescent way. Queen Elizabeth asks, "O' God's naym, who hath favoured us? Hath it come to pass yᵗ a fart shall fart *itselfe*? Not soche a one as this, I trow. Young Master Beaumont; but no, 'twould have wafted him to Heav'n like down of goose's boddy. 'Twas not yᵉ little Lady Helen, — nay, ne'er blush, my child; thou'lt tickle thy tender maidêhedde with many a mousie-squeak before thou learnest to blow a hurricane like this. Was't you, my learned & ingenious Jonson?" The fact that royalty, the nobility, and the great writers of the age might have talked in such a way that was so "picturesque and lurid and scandalous" was what amused the author,[55] who sent the piece to Twichell—partly because he thought he would enjoy it and partly because Twichell was a clergyman and thus a symbol of gentility. (There seems to be no record of his showing it to Mrs. Clemens.) Later, according to his notebook, he sent it anonymously to a magazine editor who had claimed he was looking for a "new Rabelais." "How the editor abused it & the sender," noted the author.[56] Others, such as John Hay, called it a masterpiece, a classic.[57] By 1879 the author felt, according to a letter to his sister, that "it should only be shown to people who are learned enough to appreciate it as a very able piece of literary art." After a few copies were printed in 1880, the author himself arranged for the clandestine printing of fifty more copies in 1882 by the press of the U.S. Military Academy at West Point. Many other editions have since appeared, though "1601" does not appear in any collections of Mark Twain's works—except the Oxford Mark Twain. It is too self-conscious, too much the work of a naughty boy playing hooky, to be of general interest.

During the summer of 1876, Mark Twain's chief literary activity was to begin a sequel to *Tom Sawyer*, which he had finished the year before. He had thought when finishing *Tom* of writing about another boy, this time in the first person. By the end of the summer, he had come to a stopping point in what he was calling "Huck Finn's Autobiography," having already reached the place where Huck and Jim's raft is destroyed by a steamboat. He liked what he had written "only tolerably well," he told Howells in August, and now put the project aside for three years. Two months later he accepted a fatal proposal from Bret Harte, who visited him in Hartford, to write a play together and "divide the swag," as Clemens told Howells. (Harte's *Two Men of Sandy Bar* had been unsuccessfully produced only a month or so earlier.) The two writers put together a play set in the Mother Lode mining country of California, with a plot about a Chinese laundryman, miners, and a snob, centering on an apparent murder, disguises, and mistaken identity. Mark Twain's chief contribution was to translate Harte's stilted dialogue into the vernacular; the broken English imposed on the actor who played a stereotyped Ah Sin was Harte's responsibility. The two hoped to capitalize on Harte's immensely popular "Plain Language from Truthful James," a doggerel poem in which the famous "Heathen Chinee" is named Ah Sin. Other characters in the play had also appeared in Harte's earlier writings.[58] Once again the author showed little grasp of the nature of his talent, writing to Moncure D. Conway in December 1876, "If I can make a living out of plays, I shall never write another book."

By February 1877, the two had finished the work, such as it was, and in May it was performed in Washington, D.C., and then at the end of July in

New York. Charles T. Parsloe was admired for his broadly comic performance as Ah Sin, but the play had nothing else to recommend it and soon closed in New York. Later it was revised in St. Louis and in upstate New York, but it left the stage finally and permanently in October. Although Mark Twain's part in the composition was not great, he took responsibility for it when Harte stepped in front of the curtain before the first performance. Soon after, in a letter to Mollie Fairbanks, the co-author alluded to it as "that dreadful play." (By then he had manufactured an even worse one, *Simon Wheeler*, single-handed.) Now he broke, permanently and vehemently, with Harte. Although there had been much friction between the two during the composition, the determining factor seems to have been Harte's criticism of Mrs. Clemens while he was a guest in the Hartford house.[59]

Mark Twain was even less productive during the three-year period after the fall of 1876 than in the three years after the completion of *Roughing It*. During the earlier period he had at least the profitable *Gilded Age* and *Colonel Sellers* to show; this time he had even less. He had begun an unlikely story — perhaps it was to have been a novel — that he called "The Mysterious Chamber," the personal narrative of a bridegroom trapped for years in a room where he must improvise ingeniously to survive.[60] Whether or not the work has autobiographical overtones, its literary sources include *Robinson Crusoe* and the novels of Dumas *père*.

A second aborted effort resulted when Mark Twain and Howells concocted a plan by which each of twelve writers was to produce a work from the same plot. But only Mark Twain composed one, and he was pleased with the results. He wrote to Howells that his wife said it was "good." He added, "Pretty strong language — for her." Later he tried unsuccessfully to simplify the plot, but gave up the task. The 8,500-word story that Mark Twain wrote, "A Murder, a Mystery, and a Marriage," was derived from a balloon story that he had begun in 1868 and recorded in his notebook. At that time he had given it up; according to his notebook entry, "While this was being written, Jules Verne's 'Five Weeks in a Balloon' came out, & consequently this sketch wasn't finished."[61] The story, set in a small Missouri village, focuses on Jean Mercier, who is found in a snow-covered field, injured, but alive. There are no tracks in the snow. How did he get there? In time he turns out to have been Jules Verne's assistant: when the two set off together on a balloon voyage, Mercier in a fit of anger pushed Verne overboard. Eventually he ends up in Deer Lick, Missouri. The story focuses on a *mystery* — how this Frenchman ended up in Missouri — and a *murder* — committed by the same Frenchman — and would have culminated in a *mar-*

riage, but the identification of the murderer prevents it. The story lacks real characters, and the plot is obviously far-fetched. It has never been published, but a version was privately printed in 1945. Perhaps the most entertaining feature of the story is that Mercier, Jules Verne's former hired hand, is said to have had a task very much like the one Mark Twain had chosen J. H. Riley to undertake: he embarked on adventures "in all sorts of disagreeable vehicles" in order to provide Verne with fodder for his books.[62]

Equally lacking is the story of a transcontinental and transoceanic telephone romance, "The Loves of Alonzo Fitz Clarence and Rosannah Ethelton," which appeared in the *Atlantic Monthly.* More ambitious than any of these is "Orion's Autobiography," begun in late March 1877 before the first rehearsals of *Ah Sin.* Clemens's brother Orion had changed careers and religions frequently, each time with the utmost conviction, always full of hope that all would now be well. Sam had watched in amusement and exasperation. He had been assisting Orion financially for some time. Eventually he would encourage Orion to write his own autobiography, but now Mark Twain began one for him. He introduced him, he wrote Howells as he began, "at 18, printer's apprentice, soft and sappy, full of fine intentions, & shifting religions, & not aware that he is a shining ass." The piece, which provided the author with some psychological relief, was given up after a few weeks; the surviving fragment, entitled "Autobiography of a Damned Fool," was first published in 1967. What its narrator attempts and what he suffers as a result of his ridiculous projects — such as trying to start a harem of middle-aged women — makes cruel fun of his sibling. Twenty years later, Mark Twain would again become obsessed with fictional characters modeled on Orion, introducing versions of him into a whole series of story fragments, most effectively and sympathetically as Hotchkiss in "Schoolhouse Hill," published in 1969 in *The Mysterious Stranger Manuscripts.*

There are other indications of the failure of Mark Twain's creativity at this time, such as the series of four papers he wrote as the result of a nineday trip to Bermuda with Joseph Twichell in May 1877. "Some Rambling Notes of an Idle Excursion" first appeared in the *Atlantic Monthly.* He soon had reservations, too late, about the first two pieces, and his Quarry Farm listeners did not like the second two.[63] The trip had been made, Clemens told his sister-in-law before he left, "to get the world & the devil out of my head so that I can start fresh at the farm early in July." But because he had kept full notes of his voyage and experiences, such as they were, and since he had enjoyed himself, he decided to go ahead and write up an account. The pieces make agreeable reading, with some entertaining conversation recorded, but what is remarkable is that they are not by "Mark Twain" but by

Samuel Clemens. That is, the literary personality of the earlier personal writings is almost completely stifled. These "Notes" are recorded by an observant, curious, rather dignified man of forty-two, who mentions, for example:

> The next day, in New York, was a hot one. Still we managed to get more or less entertainment out of it. Toward the middle of the afternoon we arrived on board the staunch steamship Bermuda, with bag and baggage, and hunted for a shady place. It was blazing summer weather, until we were half way down the harbor. Then I buttoned my coat closely; half an hour later I put on a spring overcoat and buttoned that. As we passed the light-ship I added an ulster and tied a handkerchief around the collar to hold it snug against my neck. So rapidly had the summer gone and winter come again!

The striking disappearance of Mark Twain requires consideration. Was it Clemens's choice? He was writing for the *Atlantic* readership, "the only audience that I sit down before in perfect serenity," he had told Howells in December 1874, because they do not "require a 'humorist' to paint himself striped & stand on his head every fifteen minutes." Perhaps the title "Some Rambling Notes" was intended to prepare the reader not to expect much humor, but one could surely expect what was signed "Mark Twain" and purported to tell his adventures to have qualities of the genuine article. Mark Twain would reappear in several works after 1877, but only when the subject encouraged the writer to be in character.

The Clemenses' large and ostentatious Hartford house was home for three daughters who required various nursemaids and governesses, a wife who made most of the family decisions, and an author who seldom wrote there. It was staffed by maids, a butler, a coachman, cooks, and more. Olivia saw her role as requiring that she "keep up with all the current literature, . . . know all about art, . . . help in one or two benevolent societies." Women like her "must be perfect mothers — they must be perfect housekeepers & graceful, gracious hostesses, they must know how to give perfect dinners, they must go and visit all the people in the town where they live, they must always be ready to receive their acquaintances — they must dress themselves & their children becomingly and above all they must make their houses 'charming' & so on without end."[64] Mark Twain's familiar literary personality appeared distinctly out of place in such a setting.

In the account of his Bermuda trip, the author manages to introduce into his rather stolid account one lively talker, and his words give the account a little of the earthiness and stylistic authenticity one identifies with Mark

Twain. The ship's captain, a dull fellow, has the one function of providing the occasion for some reminiscences of Captain Ned Wakeman, this time sailing under the name "Hurricane Jones." His biblical "interpretations" brighten the piece up for a brief space before it subsides to commonplaces. This time the reminiscence was at second hand; Joseph Twichell, with whom he traveled to Bermuda, told him the story. Twichell had met Wakeman after Clemens had alerted him to what a great talker the seaman was, and Wakeman had told Twichell how to interpret miracles.

After the "Notes," Mark Twain began a manuscript that pleased him so much he wrote fifty-four pages the first day in a rush and finished it within a week. He was encouraged by Chandos Fulton, a New York theater impresario, who had written him in March that he wanted a piece for two comedians and thought the plot Clemens had outlined to him six months earlier had in it "the germ of a good acting play."[65] *Captain Simon Wheeler, The Amateur Detective. A Light Tragedy* was written as a satire of Allan Pinkerton's methods and as a burlesque of his books, such as *The Expressman and the Detectives, Mississippi Outlaws and the Detectives,* and *Poisoner and the Detectives.* Simon Wheeler shares the name of the memorable narrator of the "Jumping Frog," but he had little else to recommend him. The plot, very much like that of *Ah Sin,* revolves around a murder that did not take place. Three New York detectives, as well as Wheeler, seek to identify the murderer. Each has his own outlandish theory. One believes that the murder weapon was a hymnbook, and he collects all the hymnals he can find. Like Tom Sawyer, Hugh Burnside, the central figure, attends his own funeral, though in disguise; he is thought to be the murdered man. There has in fact been a killing, an accidental one; the murdered man proves to be the desperate "pirate" Jack Belford — a member of the Canadian publishing firm that had profited from the unauthorized publication of *Tom Sawyer.* In addition to a ridiculous plot, the play suffers from long passages of absurd dialogue.

After finishing his play, which the author decided was not a comedy but a farce, he diligently altered, amended, and rewrote it. Then he went to New York to arrange for performance, as well as to see the production there of *Ah Sin.* He told Howells in August that Dion Boucicault, a leading figure in the New York theater, had described *Simon Wheeler* as a much better play than *Ah Sin.* But to the surprise of no one who has read the play, he could find no producer.[66]

Howells imprudently encouraged Mark Twain to rewrite the work as a novel, and in the fall and winter of 1877–78 the latter began the task, but he gave it up before he was half through. The novel fragment is far more interesting than the play, both because Mark Twain was a much more skilled writer of prose fiction than of drama and because he added several new elements to his story. There is now a vividly realized setting: a little Missouri town where the two leading families, from Kentucky and Virginia, have inherited a feud that foreshadows the Grangerford-Shepherdson feud of *Huckleberry Finn*. Judge Griswold resembles Colonel Grangerford, as well as Judge John Marshall Clemens. Hugh Burnside is now a poet, of the same sentimental school as Emmeline Grangerford. Captain Wheeler tells of a dream, an early version of "Captain Stormfield's Visit to Heaven," perhaps because Howells suggested in October that his amateur detective "ought to be as like Captain Wakeman as you can make him." Marred by the continuing effort to satirize detectives, the novel is at least readable. It differs from most of Mark Twain's longer efforts at fiction in that it has a love interest.[67]

On December 17, 1877, while still working on the novelization of his play, Clemens attended an *Atlantic Monthly* dinner in Boston honoring John Greenleaf Whittier. Such dinners were the occasion of much speech making, and Clemens had participated in a good many. He was now a regular contributor to the pages of the *Atlantic*, sixteen of his pieces having appeared there. Still, as a Western humorist he was much less admired in Boston than in the rest of the United States or in England. In the speech he delivered, he reverted to the character of Mark Twain — quite naturally, since he was aware of how much he differed in background and in literary interests from the genteel writers of New England, many of whom were present that evening. He chose to "drop lightly into history," to tell a tale of his Western days, when he was "callow and conceited," just establishing himself as a writer, and ready to "try the virtue of my *nom de plume*." He spoke of being in the Mother Lode country, at nightfall, when he identified himself as he sought to gain admittance to a miner's cabin. Inside, the miner was soon telling him how he had been visited just the night before by "a rough lot," men who identified themselves as Henry Wadsworth Longfellow, Ralph Waldo Emerson, and Oliver Wendell Holmes. (The three august writers were among the guests before whom Mark Twain spoke.) These freeloaders had eaten the miner's food and drunk his whiskey and stolen his boots and recited their poetry. They had threatened him when he protested. Now that another noted writer had arrived, the miner judged that he'd have to move. "I ain't suited to a littery atmosphere."

> I said to the miner, "Why, my dear sir, *These* were not the gracious singers to whom we and the world pay loving reverence and homage; these were imposters."

The miner investigated me with a calm eye for a while, then said he, "Ah—imposters, were they?—are *you?*" I did not pursue the subject; and since then I haven't traveled on my *nom de plume* enough to hurt. Such is the reminiscence I was moved to contribute, Mr. Chairman. In my enthusiasm I may have exaggerated the details a little, but you will easily forgive that fault, since I believe it is the first time I have ever deflected from perpendicular fact on an occasion like this.[68]

The speech is masterful and, delivered in Mark Twain's inimitable manner, must have been delicious. No doubt there was an element of hostility behind the speech, an implication that the writers' gentility had an element of phoniness in it, but most of the audience was entertained. The *Boston Globe* reported on December 18, "This eccentric story was told in Mr. Clemens's characteristic drawling, stammering way, and produced the most violent bursts of hilarity. Mr. Emerson seemed a little puzzled by it, but Mr. Long-fellow laughed and shook, and Mr. Whittier seemed to enjoy it keenly." The same day the *Boston Journal* reported that the speech "aroused uproarious merriment." The only initial complaints about the speech appeared in the *Boston Herald,* which protested the use of wine, and the *Boston Advertiser,* which decried the absence from the celebration of women such as Harriet Beecher Stowe.[69]

William Dean Howells, who had introduced the speaker, was not at all pleased, however; he believed the performance was offensive and was convinced that others thought so, too. Certain out-of-town newspaper reports took highly critical stances. Soon Mark Twain was apologizing to the three writers, and even years later he was still smarting from what Howells called, after Clemens's death, "the amazing mistake, the bewildering blunder, the cruel catastrophe." The "awful speech," in Howells's opinion, came "near being the death of us all."[70] Howells also had come from the "West," and one suspects he was afraid that his generous friendship with Clemens would lead to his own elite status being challenged.

Such an experience was not to be forgotten. Clemens felt humiliated. Toward the end of his life, he looked at the speech again. He found that there was not "a suggestion of coarseness or vulgarity in it anywhere." But only a few days later he called it "gross, coarse." After another four months, he gave it what he called "a final and vigorous reading-aloud—and dropped straight back to my former admiration of it."[71] The Whittier birthday speech demonstrates how challenging it sometimes was for Samuel Clemens to be Mark Twain. He was in a bind. His highly profitable success as a writer and as a lecturer rested on the brash literary personality he had created, and on that success he had built a life, complete with family, servants, and an elegant home in a cultured New England city. Some members of the Hartford community always regarded him as a vulgarian who did not belong, a tramp printer and a Civil War deserter (from the Confederate side at that).[72] By the end of 1877 he had good cause to question how solid his standing was. How, one wonders, would he himself have truthfully answered the miner's query? Was "Mark Twain" an impostor? His future was uncertain. He had quite as many failures as successes: two disastrously bad plays and at least five books that he had not been able to complete: "English Notes," "Orion's Auto-biography," "The Mysterious Chamber," "Old Times," "Huck Finn's Auto-biography," and soon the novel version of *Simon Wheeler, Detective*. His one complete novel, *Tom Sawyer,* had brought him only thin profits. His most recent book publication was very slight, a little book containing "A True Story" and "The Carnival of Crime"; and in 1878 there was to be only a pamphlet collecting the "Rambling Notes" and seven other pieces. His income and Olivia's from her inheritance had been reduced by the national financial problems of the 1870s.

Clemens wrote to Howells a week after the Whittier dinner, "I feel that my misfortune has injured me all over the country; therefore it will be best that I retire from before the public at present." In 1900 he recorded in his notebook, "Howells tried to comfort me, but cried & laughed all the time. Said it was the ghastliest funeral since the Crucifixion."[73] As late as 1906, he remembered that for "the first year or two after it happened, I could not bear to think of it. My pain and shame were so intense, and my sense of having been an imbecile so settled, established and confirmed, that I drove the episode entirely from my mind."[74] He was not crushed, but he needed an opportunity to reorganize his career, even if it meant leaving his Hart-ford home for a time. Fortunately he had contemplated such a sojourn (though not so extensive) even before the Whittier speech, for he had written to Mrs. Fairbanks in September: "Our plan for the spring is this: to leave, the 1st of May, & settle down in some good old city in Germany & never stir again for 6 months." Living in Europe would reduce living ex-penses. The trip would in fact last seventeen months, and the author was to produce very little work that he could publish during that time.

How did Clemens feel about himself and his career at this time? He wrote, revealingly, to his mother in February 1878: "Life has come to be a very serious matter with me. I have a badgered, harassed feeling, a good part of my time." His "projects" had gotten nowhere. "I have about made up my mind to take my tribe & fly to some little corner of Europe & budge no more until I shall have completed one of the half dozen books that lie begun, up stairs." His feeling of intimidation showed publicly when he could not deliver the speech he had prepared for a dinner in April honoring Bayard Taylor, who was going to Germany to serve as U.S. minister. The speech itself survives, and though it was intended to be amusing, this time the speaker does not appear as Mark Twain.[75] For several years after the publication of *Tom Sawyer,* that persona was not often in evidence on the American scene and was soon for a time to disappear.

CHAPTER FIVE

Contracts, Inspirations, Obligations

ark Twain was ready to take on a sequel. Leaving behind his many incomplete manuscripts, including that of "Huck Finn's Autobiography," to collect dust for a good while, on March 8, 1878, he signed a contract to write a sequel to *The Innocents Abroad,* a subscription book about new European travels. The composition of that book now became the justification for his trip to Germany. A secondary purpose was to make purchases to enhance the ornate splendor of the Clemenses' Hartford house. Along with a friend and a nursemaid, the family left New York in early April. In May they were settled in Heidelberg, with a room away from the family rented specifically for the writer's task. Clemens made notes of the trip for the book he had in mind, but at first he had no plan other than to compose a travel diary of what he and his family were doing, as his notebook entries suggest. At the end of May, he wrote to Howells that he was about to go to work. Olivia, too, was informed that the great day was about to arrive; she wrote to her mother, "Tomorrow Mr. Clemens goes to work[;] he has been making notes since we left home, so he has a great deal of material to work from."[1] Clemens kept up his notebook, in which he recorded comments on the opera, current events, the family's dealings with their landlord, and other small adventures. The first drafts, made from these notes but later discarded from the book, do not stray far into fiction. Even more than with *Roughing It,* creating what became *A Tramp Abroad* gave Mark Twain enormous grief, as would *Life on the Mississippi.* Clearly his motivation was commercial, not creative. In

each instance, creating a subscription book meant producing a substantial manuscript.

By mid-July he had written about fifty thousand words, but, as he wrote to Frank Bliss, "it is in disconnected form and cannot be used until joined together by the writing of a dozen intermediate chapters," which he did not think he could produce until fall. In early August, however, an event occurred that made a significant difference: his Bermuda traveling companion, Joseph Twichell, arrived for a five-week visit. The two men rambled together, then took two longer excursions. The writer was shaken out of his lethargy. He drafted more usable notes and even discovered a plan for the book. He later wrote to Twichell that whereas he had feared "his interest in the tour" was "so slender that I couldn't gouge matter enough out of it to make a book," he now realized that it wasn't materials he needed but the right mood: "The mood is everything."[2] The plan, which he told Frank Bliss was "new and better" (better, apparently, than nothing), was to "appear, — casually and without stress, — that I am over here to make the tour of Europe *on foot*. I am in pedestrian costume, as a general thing," he explained to Howells in January 1879, "& *start* on pedestrian tours, but mount the first conveyance that offers, making but slight explanation or excuse, & endeavoring to seem unconscious that this is not legitimate pedestrianizing." He thought that assigning himself such a comic role, a kind of innocent, would prove enough to hang the book on. The "joke" was to be kept secret but was to be underscored by a preface (later discarded). Traces of this unifying joke remain at the beginning of the first chapter in the published version, where the author explains that he had decided to furnish mankind with "the spectacle of a man adventurous enough to undertake a journey through Europe on foot." Either way, the invented "joke" is so slight as to be insufficient to provide a focal point for the book.

Twichell's visit provided another idea to the still-struggling author. After he wrote to Twichell in November that he had not "gathered any matter before or since your visit worth writing up," he began to collect notes on an imaginary traveling companion, based on Twichell but without much personality — nothing like the outrageous Mr. Brown of former days. His notebook records attitudes and adventures with this character, first called Hagerty, then Harris. When in early January Clemens had a frustrating adventure, trying to find a sock in the dark, he wrote up an elaborate account of it, first in his journal, and assigned it to the time of his travels with Twichell, or rather Harris. This new character is introduced at the beginning of the book, but his presence is insignificant — usually he is invisible — until halfway through, at the point corresponding to the time when

Twichell arrived in Europe. Harris acts as the author's "agent" and takes on such unpleasant tasks as attending a church service. Though he is unimportant as a character, the pages in which Harris appears are more entertaining than the early ones, which describe mostly commonplace travel adventures.

Continuing to search for materials after Twichell's visit, Clemens led his family to Italy, then settled down in Munich for three months. In January 1879, he wrote Twichell that he had produced 1,300 pages of manuscript, 400 of which he had torn up, leaving "about 900 which need no tearing." By this time he knew that the book would lack unity and that there would be only some good "spots." Perhaps because he needed to salvage something from his German experiences, he now identified two additional purposes for his trip: to learn German and to understand art, even to try his hand at pen-and-ink sketches. He would have liked, he wrote regretfully, to follow a suggestion from Howells that he write "sharp satires on European life," but he was not, he told his friend, "in a good enough humor with ANYthing to *satirize* it: no, I want to stand up before it & *curse* it, & foam at the mouth, — or take a club & pound it to rags & pulp." He was clearly in no state of mind to be the easygoing Mark Twain. At the end of February, the entourage moved to Paris, where Clemens intended at last to finish his book. Perhaps because he was ill there, he developed a strong dislike of France and the French and was even more unable to write the book he intended. He prepared several chapters highly critical of the French, including their habits of courtship and marriage (based not on personal knowledge but on a book), but he included none of this material in the final version, although some pages were published elsewhere.[3] In Paris, Clemens finally decided to finish the book after his return to the United States. They remained in Paris for five months, during which they received visits from many American friends. In an interview, Clemens said his new book was "a gossipy volume of travel, and will be similar to the *Innocents Abroad* in size, and similarly illustrated."[4] The Clemenses thereafter traveled through Belgium and Holland and then spent a month in England. Almost predictably, the writer now found England less satisfactory than he had previously. He wrote, prophetically, in his notebook:

> For some years a custom has been growing up in our literature to praise everything English, & do it affectionately. This is not met half-way & so it will cease. English individuals like & respect American individuals; but the English nation despises America & the Americans. But this does not sting us as it did when we were smaller. We shall presently be indifferent

to being looked down upon by a nation no bigger & no better than our own.[5]

Early in September, the Clemenses arrived back in New York. At Quarry Farm he continued his writing efforts. In all he wrote an immense amount, nearly half again as much as he needed, but he was not satisfied with its quality — and for good reason. We can see what he rejected, for he saved most of the unused pages, even though he frequently referred to having thrown out or torn up quantities of material.[6] In October, Clemens wrote to Twichell, "I have been knocking out early chapters for more than a year, now — not because they had no merit, but merely because they hindered the flow of the narrative." During the autumn, despite interruptions (such as a visit to a Civil War reunion in Chicago, where Ulysses S. Grant was the honored guest), he continued to write on what he now referred to, in a letter to Thomas Bailey Aldrich, as "that most lagging and hated book." Finally he decided in January that he had done enough. As an account of his trip, the book ends abruptly (though few readers would wish the book longer) with a telescoped account of the visit to France and England by way of Holland and Belgium. Before he had finished the last part, the early part of the book was already set in type, and in March 1880, *A Tramp Abroad* was published. As with *Roughing It,* completing the book was a painful, exhausting experience.

The title *A Tramp Abroad* was intended to recall *The Innocents Abroad.* The "tramp" refers to a series of chapters about the author's experiences while traveling with Mr. Harris in Germany, Switzerland, and — more briefly — Italy, but the narrative is frequently interrupted by digressions. Although nothing holds the book together except the binding, three themes provide some unity: the journey through Europe on foot, the tramp's intention to study art, and his desire to learn the German language. The three motifs are identified in the first chapter, but even there one finds a digression, the first of many retellings of German legends that fill the initial nineteen chapters. Perhaps this attention to legends should be considered a subtext, an indication of the writer's attitude toward the legendary past and thus preparation for the writing of *A Connecticut Yankee in King Arthur's Court.* Material that could not be worked in, even as digressions, appears in six appendixes.

In the first chapter, Mark Twain tells of having "the luck to stumble upon a book which has charmed me nearly to death. It is entitled 'The Legends of the Rhine from Basle to Rotterdam' by F. J. Kiefer; Translated by L. W. Garnham, B. A.," and it has "fed me in a very hungry place." Thereafter Kiefer's book is cited repeatedly, as well as legends of the Neckar River; in all, these embellish seven chapters of the book. But it is in the invented

"Legend of the 'Spectacular Ruin'" of Sir Wissenschaft (chap. 17) that we meet a predecessor of the Connecticut Yankee. Back in the Middle Ages, a "fire-breathing dragon" had been wreaking havoc with such dreadful results that the German emperor promised anyone who could destroy the monster "any one solitary thing he might ask for." "At last Sir Wissenschaft, a poor and obscure knight, out of a far country, arrived to do battle with the monster." Told of the failed knights before him, he asked, "'Were any of these heroes men of science?' This raised a laugh, of course, for science was despised in those days." Offered a spear, he refused it. He carried with him what proved to be "the common fire-extinguisher known to modern times." It put out the dragon's fires, and "the dragon curled up and died." Sir Wissenschaft then asked for "the monopoly of the manufacture and sale of spectacles in Germany." The wish was granted, and to it the emperor added a decree that everyone buy "this benefactor's spectacles and wear them, whether they needed them or no. So originated the widespread custom of wearing spectacles in Germany." Sir Wissenschaft's commercial and technological abilities make him a forerunner of Hank Morgan, Mark Twain's Connecticut Yankee.

Neither the narrative account nor the digressions of *A Tramp Abroad* are spontaneously funny. Instead, the author seems to recall, with a start, every few chapters that he has a reputation as a humorist. For example, in chapter 44 he and Harris "climb" Mont Blanc by telescope and observe the view: "the grand processional summits of the Cisalpine Cordillera, drowned in a sensuous haze; to the east loomed the colossal masses of the Yodelhorn, the Fuddlehorn, and the Dinnerhorn." The passage continues too long. The author's attitude toward what he had written is shown by his comment, in June, to Twichell: "I have made the burlesque of Alp-climbing prodigiously loud, but I guess I will leave it so."

Even his idolizing biographer, Albert Bigelow Paine, granted that in *A Tramp Abroad* "very often he [Mark Twain] does not laugh heartily and sincerely at all, but finds his humor in extravagant burlesque."[7] Several of the best parts are unrelated to the account of the tour: the futile efforts to torment Nicodemus Dodge, Clemens's fellow apprentice back in the Hannibal printshop — even by placing Jimmy Finn's skeleton in his bed; a reminiscence of the winter of 1867, when Clemens and Riley were Washington newspaper correspondents; Mark Twain's forty-seven-mile tour of his bedroom floor in the dark to find a missing sock. As Twichell's journal shows, some of Harris's comments came directly from the clergyman.

The last part of the book leans heavily on the writings of the English alpinist Edward Whymper; indeed, he — not Mark Twain — wrote chapter

41. Those who read an early printing, with 328 illustrations, may find the book more appealing. But the self-assured, often victimized Mark Twain is too seldom present.

On the other hand, appendix D, "The Awful German Language," proved that Mark Twain was still alive and conscious. As a student of the language, he is regularly defeated. He is sympathetic with the Californian who said that "he would rather decline two drinks than one German adjective" and with the student who found "the only word in the whole language whose sound was sweet and precious to his ear and healing to his lacerated spirit": *damit*. But when "he learned that the emphasis was not on the first syllable, his only stay and support was gone, and he faded away and died." Mark Twain heroically volunteers to reform the language, to trim it down and repair it, though he is satisfied that a gifted person *could* learn the language — in thirty years.

The high point of the book is the blue jay yarn, which has been ranked a masterpiece of the same order as *Huckleberry Finn*. As in that novel and in the jumping frog story, Mark Twain employs a meandering narrator. The story had been told by Clemens's friend Jim Gillis, but it is now assigned to one Jim Baker, a lonely California miner. Baker has a respect for blue jays, their vocabulary, and their grammar, but he also notes less appealing aspects of their "humanity": their lack of principles, their deviousness, and their interest in gossip. What Baker has to say on behalf of the jays' grammar is qualified by his own occasional lapses, and his appreciation of their "out and out book-talk" is diminished by his own remoteness from literature. He proves, however, to be an excellent storyteller, fond of wonderfully concrete details. He focuses on one particular blue jay who tries to fill a hole with acorns — dropping "enough in there to keep the family for years."

Jim understands this jay. It was, the bird judges, a "perfectly elegant hole," and the anticipation of hearing a nut fall, hearing it *hit,* puts the "heavenliest smile" on his face. The jay's frustration when that sound is denied him makes him determined to fill the hole. The nub of the story is the exposure of the absurdity of this effort, when his fellow jays discover that he's been trying to fill a *house* with acorns by dropping them through a knothole in the roof. The spectator jays are vastly amused. Every summer for three years thereafter, jays flock to the site of his folly. The story is skillfully told, with the stress shifting from the jay's humiliation, which is merely implied, to the other jays' glorious sense of humor. Jim Baker's blue jay yarn amounts to an unintentional practical joke, played on the joker, and his own naive gratifications. It is the perfect story for Mark Twain to tell because his earlier stories gave him and the jay much in common.

Despite its amorphous shape and the silliness of many of its burlesques, *A Tramp Abroad* sold well: sixty-two thousand copies in the first year in America, and in England, where he was very popular, it remained the best selling of all Mark Twain's books during his lifetime. William Ernest Henley, who reviewed it, called the *Tramp* "a worthy sequel" to *Roughing It* and judged that many parts are "equal to the funniest of those that have gone before."[8] The reviewer in the *British Quarterly Review* wrote that "Mr. Mark Twain is delightful," and the reviewer for the *Graphic* of London noted that the author's "charm is that he puts things so unexpectedly — says the very thing which nobody would ever think of saying."[9] Howells wrote admiringly of the book for the *Atlantic Monthly*. As he often did, Howells saw the serious side of his friend's writing: "His humor springs from a certain intensity of common sense, a passionate love of justice, and a generous scorn of what is petty and mean."[10] But the book is probably best seen as a break, though not a clean one, with Mark Twain's past and an indication of what kind of writer he conceived himself to be as he moved toward *The Prince and the Pauper.* The young Sam Clemens had much in common with Mark Twain, but the middle-aged celebrity was someone quite different. Nearly two years in Europe and ten years in Buffalo, Elmira, and Hartford were having their effect, as was Olivia Langdon Clemens.

In 1877, the writer was deeply gratified when an arrangement was made with the German publisher Tauchnitz to issue *Tom Sawyer,* and later works, to European purchasers. In time Mark Twain was to become a great favorite on the European continent, especially in Germany. But because he had suffered substantial losses from both Canadian and British pirates, he devoted himself for many years to the creation of a proper copyright law. In 1875, he drew up a copyright petition to submit to Congress; later he went to Washington to lobby Congress and to speak before congressional committees. In 1900, he spoke in London before a committee of the House of Lords on the subject. Even in his last years he was still seeking adoption of a properly binding international law, one that was finally enacted in 1909.[11]

The difficult gestation of the *Tramp* was in striking contrast to the composition of its successor. *The Prince and the Pauper* had its origins in Samuel Clemens's reading, not in his experience. He read, probably in 1874, William E. H. Lecky's *History of European Morals from Augustus to Charlemagne,* a book that aroused his interest both in early European history and in the sources of morality. (Its influence on "The Carnival of Crime" has already been noted.) In a copy of Lecky's history, Clemens wrote, "It is so noble a book, & so beautiful, that I don't wish to have even trivial faults in it."[12] His thinking about his next project was consequently shaped in 1876 by his reading, with great interest, Charlotte M. Yonge's *The Little Duke* (1854), which tells of how Richard, duke of Normandy, profits from his experiences at the corrupt court of Louis IV to become a just and merciful ruler. The influence of this book on his final product was strong.[13] Now his latent interest in history was heightened. It came to include the history of the English language, especially early modern English, and in the summer of 1876 he compiled "Middle Age phrases for a historical study" and wrote "1601." During the next summer, he read books on England in the sixteenth century: James Anthony Froude's *History of England,* and the portion of David Hume's history on Henry VII and Henry VIII. He read widely in French history and historical fiction. Especially influential was Hippolyte Taine's *The Ancient Regime,* which describes France in precise detail as it was before the Revolution.

The French historical readings had many consequences. First, some of the "history" in *The Prince and the Pauper* is derived not from English history but from French; specifically, chapter 7 is based on Taine. Second, noting that Taine had recognized the value of "the characteristic detail, the animating fact, the specific circumstance, the significant, convincing, and complete example,"[14] Mark Twain followed Taine's directions in assisting the reader's imagination by loading his novel with details about architecture, costume, the setting of a nobleman's estate, and the furnishings of the hermit's hut, where one sees "a bed of rushes and a ragged blanket or two; near it was a pail, a cup, a basin, and three pots and pans; there was a short bench and a three-legged stool"—and the detailed description continues (chap. 20). (Taine had written that Louis XIV had 383 "officers of the table." Mark Twain increased the number to 384!) Like Taine, the writer described society as being polarized between the privileged and the deprived. Finally, because of his deep interest in the French Revolution, especially as presented in one of his favorite books, Thomas Carlyle's *The French Revolution,* that subject would become a subtext in his novel about life along the Mississippi, *Huckleberry Finn.*[15]

In the summer of 1877, he selected a title for his historical fiction but, still interested in the theater, what he planned was a play. He recorded in his notebook in July, "Write Prince and Pauper in 4 acts and eight changes."[16] Before the summer was over, however, according to Albert Bigelow Paine, he had composed four hundred pages before laying it aside.[17] The earliest version of his plot took place in Victorian England, with Albert Edward, heir to the throne, exchanging identities with a London slum dweller. Then the author decided that his purposes would be better served by moving further back into English history. In November 1877, he sketched in his notebook the basic plot: "Edward VI & a little pauper exchange places by accident a day or so before Henry VIII' death. The prince wanders in rags & hardships & the pauper suffers the (to him) horrible miseries of princedom, up to the moment of crowning, in Westminster Abbey, when proof is brought & the mistake rectified."[18]

Mark Twain returned in February 1878 to what he now called "a historical tale, of 300 years ago," and unlike the *Tramp*, which was soon to occupy him, he was writing "simply for the love of it." In a letter to Mrs. Fairbanks, he called his work "grave & stately" and thus "considered by the world to be above my proper level." Enough had already been written to permit Clemens to read portions to the "Young Girls' Club" he had founded earlier, hardly the audience Mark Twain had been accustomed to addressing. But then hastily made plans for his European trip intervened, and he seems not to have touched the manuscript for about two years. He returned to it with "jubilant delight" early in 1880. His interest amounted to "intemperance," he told his brother in February. In a letter to Howells, he implied a strong distinction between his current book and the one he had been preparing. His pleasure was so great, he explained to Howells, that he was not concerned (for once) with whether the book sold or not. He was enjoying the act of creation and trying not to rush for fear he would end his pleasure. "I have even fascinated Mrs. Clemens with this yarn for youth," he wrote Howells. "My stuff generally gets considerable damning with faint praise out of her, but this time it is all the other way." In mid-September he thought he had completed the book, or so he wrote Thomas Bailey Aldrich, and by early December Howells had read and admired it, calling parts "incomparable," although he had some substantial suggestions for revision. Mark Twain agreed to drop the "whipping-boy story," to which Howells objected, despite its already having been published in the *Hartford Bazar Budget* for July 4, 1880.[19] Before the book was finally completed, the author "added over 130 new pages of MS to the prince's adventures in the rural districts." These additions were made at least in part to give the novel the proper heft for a subscription book. "The number of pages before," the author explained to his publisher in January 1881, "was 734 — the number is 870, now — fully as bulky a book as Tom Sawyer, I think." (But numerous buyers had judged *Tom Sawyer* not big enough.) After a few final revisions on February 1, 1881, the book was finished. The author expressed his pleasure in a letter to Annie Lucas: "I like this tale better than *Tom Sawyer* — because I haven't put any fun in it. I *think* that is why I like it better. You know a body always enjoys seeing himself attempting something out of his line." Mrs. Clemens was eager to have the book "elegantly gotten up,"[20] and it was lavishly produced.

Elisha Bliss had died in October 1880. Even before his death, Clemens had decided that he should have made more money from his books than he had obtained from Bliss's American Publishing Company. Now he decided that he needed to have full control of the publishing of his books. James R. Osgood, an established Boston publisher and former partner in Ticknor and Fields, had published *A True Story, and the Recent Carnival of Crime* as a trade book in 1877. Since Clemens was eager for the publication of *The Prince and the Pauper* to make a statement about his more versatile literary identity, he made a contract with Osgood for the publication of his novel by subscription, although Osgood knew next to nothing about the subscription business. The unusual arrangement called for Clemens to pay the production costs, with Osgood receiving royalties — 7.5 percent, on books sold.

F. T. Merrill, the artist who had prepared the illustrations for Louisa May Alcott's *Little Women,* was selected to prepare most of the illustrations. Mark Twain liked his work very much. He told Benjamin Ticknor, Osgood's partner, that Merrill's illustrations "clear surpass my highest expectations"; he was "enchanted." "Merrill probably thinks he originated his exquisite boys himself, but I was ahead of him there." The pictures of the boys "look and dress exactly as I used to see them in my mind's eye." Howells both read proof and reviewed the novel, anonymously, well before its publication in December 1881, when it appeared simultaneously in England, Canada, and the United States.

As its author recognized, *The Prince and the Pauper* was out of Mark Twain's line, and his friend Joe Goodman from the Virginia City days told him so unflinchingly: "What could have sent you groping among the driftwood of the Deluge for a topic when you could have been so much more at home in the wash of today?"[21] What sent him was a need to write a book of the sort that Mrs. Clemens and his daughters (a third, Jean, was born in July 1880) would approve. And there were others pushing, too. Mrs. Fairbanks had urged him to write "another book in an entirely different style." "The time has come for your *best book,* your best contribution to American Literature."[22] The Hartford clergyman Edwin P. Parker had asked him to do himself "vast honor" and his friends "vast pleasure" by writing a book with "a sober character."[23] Clemens did exactly as he had been encouraged to do. Dedicated to "those good-mannered and amiable children Susie and Clara Clemens," and subtitled "A Tale for Young People of All Ages," *The Prince and the Pauper* is well mannered and amiable. Susy was delighted. She recorded in her biography of her father (much of which years later Clemens inserted into his autobiography) that it was "unquestionably the best book he has ever written." She objected to people thinking of him as "a humorist joking at every thing." She has wanted her father "to write a book that would reveal something of his kind and sympathetic nature." In her eyes, the new book was "perfect."[24] Mrs. Fairbanks rewarded her child — Clemens always addressed her as "Mother" — with the highest compliments. "The book is your masterpiece in fineness."[25] The December 28 *Hartford Courant* congratulated the author for "writing a book which has other and higher merits than can possibly belong to the most artistic expression of mere humor." His neighbor, Harriet Beecher Stowe, told him it was "the best book for young folks that was ever written."[26] Only Joe Goodman is recorded as thinking the book a mistake.[27]

In what ways *The Prince and the Pauper* satisfied the genteel readers of Hartford and elsewhere is not hard to perceive. A historical tale set in England, laden with learning about the past, it appealed to those burdened by a need to learn from a novel as well as be entertained, especially Americans whose model was English gentility. Clemens himself was well acquainted with England and had broken bread with many of its aristocrats. Having dredged up historical material for the book, he was able to show off, like Tom Sawyer, even if some of his erudition was precariously balanced and some of it derived from reading in French history. He proudly sent copies of his book to over seventy people, among them Holmes, Emerson, Whittier, and Longfellow, whom it must have been particularly gratifying to address after the negative fall-out of his Whittier birthday dinner performance; the Scottish clergyman-poet George MacDonald; Charlotte M. Yonge, whose *Little Duke* had contributed to his book; and American author Rose Terry Cooke. Specially printed and bound copies went to the "amiable" Susy and Clara. He had assuredly done something out of his line — and he wanted the world to know of this development.

Compared with Mark Twain's other books, fictional and otherwise, *The Prince and the Pauper* is well plotted and unmarred by tangential or uncontrolled burlesques. The experiences of the prince and the pauper after they exchange roles are neatly parallel: each boy finds that his new "father" believes him to be mad; each is befriended by his "sister," and each wakes from sleep thinking that his trying experiences have been just a bad dream. But the novel lacks nearly every quality that one customarily associates with Mark Twain. There is little humor. With a setting in the mid-sixteenth century, the time of Henry VIII and Edward VI, so remote from Clemens's own experience that he documents it with footnotes citing authorities, the book achieves no illusion of being present at the events it describes. The master of the colloquial style here writes dialogue in a labored imitation of Tudor English. "Searched you well—but it boots not to ask that. It doth seem passing strange." A few metaphors echo the writer's background. The guardians of Tom Canty, the pauper who by mischance becomes the prince, "felt much as if they were piloting a great ship through a dangerous channel." For Tom himself, according to chapter 6, "Time wore on pleasantly, and likewise smoothly, on the whole. Snags and sand bars grew less and less frequent."

Nevertheless, much about the romance reflects the author's longtime as well as recent interests and concerns. The westerner who had come east for renown was much interested in the notion of role exchanging, which was now to become a dominant theme in his writings. The courtly ceremonies of Europe had attracted him as early as his first visit in 1867, when he saw Napoleon III and met the czar of Russia, as well as later when he covered the Persian shah's tour. Increased financial pressures on Clemens are reflected in Tom's worried comments in chapter 14 on royal expenditures: "We be going to the dogs, 'tis plain. 'Tis meet and necessary that we take a smaller house and set the servants at large." Like Tom Sawyer (and Samuel Clemens), Tom Canty yearns for excitement and is bored by routine, and— like the hero of the earlier novel—both boys are basically good-hearted and innocent. Their goodness is underscored by the cruelty of the society in which they live, soon to become for Clemens a preoccupation. He had often been sensitive to suffering, as his writings about the Chinese in California show. He was moreover disenchanted with monarchy if not with its trappings. What the prince learns of suffering and oppression makes him a merciful king (during his brief reign) after the two boys change places a second time. The education that the prince undergoes is more than an indictment of a system of government or a historical epoch. Unlike *The Little Duke, The Prince and the Pauper* depicts man's cruelty as an enduring part of his nature. Although a book for children, it is the first of its author's works to castigate the entire human race. Like Mark Twain's Huck and later his King Arthur, the prince learns the facts of life through his travels, and like them he is aided by a companion, one Miles Hendon.

Mistakes and mysteries of identity are important themes in *The Prince and the Pauper,* problems to which the author would often return. The switch of roles that forms the basis of the plot permitted Clemens to demonstrate what was becoming one of his pet ideas, later set forth simply: "Training is everything." The differences between the prince and the pauper are only skin-deep, for they are still young. The pauper quickly learns to play the role of prince as a result of his on-the-job training. Later Clemens would perform a more fundamental experiment by switching a "black" slave and the son of a white aristocrat while they are still babies. But *The Prince and the Pauper* looks backward, too. Like the tenderfoot narrator in *Roughing It*, both boys at the beginning of their adventures have their vision distorted by romanticism; their experiences serve as educational correctives.

Because of Clemens's ambitions, encouraged by Mrs. Clemens, production costs of the book were high. These expenses were borne by the author, who thought he could thus increase his profits. But inasmuch as his regular readers did not expect him to write such a work and owing to Osgood's lack of subscription-publishing knowledge, *The Prince and the Pauper* turned out to be a financial failure. As might be expected, the book received bad reviews in England — one writer called it "a ponderous fantasia on English history" and noticed that "the absurd description of the young King's levee" must have been derived from the author's reading "about the ceremonies of the bedchamber introduced by Louis XIV"[28] (as indeed it had). It fared better among American reviewers. Joel Chandler Harris welcomed its author as a "true literary artist."[29] What Howells wrote was doubtless most important, for it contributed to Clemens's view of himself as a writer: Howells called the new novel "a manual of republicanism which might fitly be introduced into the schools."[30] Both the *Atlantic* and *Harper's* published distinctly favorable reviews. While Mark Twain could not exactly become the polite littérateur his Hartford friends sought, he had made a bold gesture in pursuit of their approval. And hereafter he would steadily move in the direction of serious social criticism.

Mark Twain's reliance on his reading in *The Prince and the Pauper* demonstrated that he was indeed a reader. His Hartford neighbor, Charles H. Clark, wrote in 1885:

> For years past he has been an industrious and extensive reader and student in the broad field of general culture. He has a large library and a real familiarity with it, extending beyond our own language into the literatures of Germany and France. He seems to have been fully conscious of the obligations which the successful opening of his literary career laid upon him, and to have lived up to its opportunities by a conscientious and continuous course of reading and study which supplements the large knowledge of human nature that the vicissitudes of his early life brought with them.[31]

By the early 1880s, Clemens was involved in a whole series of investments. Back in 1872, he had arranged for the manufacture of "Mark Twain's Patent Self-Pasting Scrap Book," a moderately remunerative device, with the business end run by his friend from the *Quaker City,* Dan Slote. In addition to it and a typesetting machine (of which more is to be said), he owned over 150,000 shares of stock in twenty-three companies.[32] In February 1880, he purchased the patent on an engraving process called Kaolatype, originally also in the hands of Slote. (The procedure, ultimately unsatisfactory, formed stereotype plates by engraving on a steel plate through a layer of kaolin—a kind of china clay.) Clemens arranged for his nephew (by marriage) Charles Webster to look into the matter, the beginning of a relationship that would have extensive consequences. When Webster reported that Slote was cheating him, Clemens appointed Webster to manage the business. Before long, Webster was acting in various ways as Clemens's business manager.[33] The immediate consequences, other than financial losses for Clemens, were the use of Kaolatype in engraving the cover of *The Prince and the Pauper* and the facilitation of Clemens's further entry into business.

During the fall of 1881, when he had finished a version of *The Prince and the Pauper,* Clemens wrote to his old friend Charles W. Stoddard, who was then living in Hawaii. With "the house full of carpenters and decorators," he complained that he got little done in Hartford, not even adding a chapter to one of his incomplete books. He kept "three or four in the stocks all the time," he wrote; this was to be his usual practice hereafter. He explained that the only time he had for work was during his summer "vacation," but he recognized, as he wrote to Mrs. Fairbanks, that "a nine months' vacation is too burdensome." With few exceptions, he wrote only during his summer stay at Quarry Farm, despite the fact that his style of living in Hartford was very costly. In 1882 Clemens drew up a list of his investments and domestic expenditures since January 1, 1881. They included:

Greenhouse lot	$12,000
Improving and grading, say	700
Kaolatype expenses	3,900
New kitchen &c.	9,000
Plumbing	1,500
My new book	10,000
Fredonia Watch Co. [investment]	3,500
Engineering Co. [investment]	14,500
New carriage	650
Crown Pt. Iron Co. [investment]	10,000
Stocks	4,500
Amer. Ex. in Europe	5,000

Decorating	5,000
Law expenses	2,000
Rugs	1,625[34]

This list, totaling $83,875, does not include the salaries of six full-time servants and part-time maids, secretaries, governesses, and nurses for the children, amounting to some $1,650 per year, and such routine expenses as food, heating, and clothing.[35]

What did he do with his days in Hartford? He devoted much time to correspondence; he often received books from unknown authors and took time to offer advice.[36] Since he frequently lacked inspiration or ideas for his own writing, there were countless temptations for socializing. Joseph Twichell wrote in 1896 that for twenty years "the list of people of high distinction, in this and other lands, statesmen, divines, authors, artists, who have counted it fortunate to be his private guests, has been a very numerous one."[37] Olivia Clemens suggests the atmosphere in an undated letter: "The house has been full of company, and I have been 'whirled around.' How can a body help it? Oh, I cannot help sighing for the peace and quiet of the farm. . . . Sometimes it seems as if the very sight of people would drive me *mad*."[38] Investments, business, editing, even seeing a book through press seemed to be activities that Clemens's daily regimen could accommodate; what it could *not* accommodate was the daily application required for literary composition.

One project that Mark Twain kept in the stocks for many years, adding to it as ideas occurred to him, was "Captain Stormfield's Visit to Heaven." Originating in what Captain Ned Wakeman told him in 1868 about a dream, the story had its inception soon after. As he told his brother, in a letter of March 23, 1878, he was at first unhappy with the results, tried again later, and talked it over with Howells. He continued to make notes about what he might include, then returned to it in the fall of 1881, about the time he was protesting that he could not write in Hartford. In 1905 or 1906, he would devise an introduction and two beginning chapters. But in the 1880s he judged that what he had written could never be published, apparently because of Mrs. Clemens's objections. Since he liked the piece very much, he was, he explained in 1906, "never willing to destroy it."[39]

Even in his last years, he added to it from time to time. Eventually he published an "Extract" from it in *Harper's* in 1907 and 1908, and after further editing, he brought that portion out in book form in 1909. But it was never finished. A version with two chapters that precede the 1907 extract appeared in 1952, and other editions with added materials were published in 1970 and 1995.[40]

Despite its fragmentary character, "Captain Stormfield's Visit to Heaven" is one of Mark Twain's most ingenious pieces. It had several sources: Wakeman's story, whatever it was; an 1868 novel about heaven that Clemens had read; a joke he seems to have found in a collection such as *Old Abe's Jokes* (1864); his desire to make fun of some conventional Christian notions, especially the concept of heaven; and his continuing pleasure in satirizing human nature, especially its pretensions.[41] Because of the ongoing circumstances of composition, the story cannot be readily placed in Clemens's literary career. The author himself said he wrote it "a month or two" after he heard the story in 1868, but that comment was made nearly forty years later, in 1906.[42] Its themes are those that he was drawn to in the 1870s, and in a few respects it anticipates *Huckleberry Finn*.

One version has a title page, in Albert Bigelow Paine's hand, which reads: "Travels of Capt. Eli Stormfield, Mariner, in Heaven / Taken from his own Lips by / Rev. George H. Peters, of Marysville, Calif."[43] The Reverend Mr. Peters, to whom the story is told, is the name given to Joseph Twichell in "Rambling Notes," and, in a portion of his autobiography composed in 1906, Clemens refers to Twichell as "(alias Peters)."[44] Clemens had met Twichell in 1868, but it is doubtful that he would have introduced the Congregational minister, however indirectly, into the story until a good deal later. The early chapters that Clemens did not publish tell of Stormfield's death and subsequent immense trip through space to his unknown destination. As much as anything else, the character of the narrator Stormfield resembles Mark Twain's early literary personality. He is frank, forthright, irrepressible, authentic — though at times fooled by his own expectations. Speaking a slangy, colloquial English, he tells his story with obvious relish. During his thirty-year journey, Stormfield meets several people, much as Huck does in his trip down the river. His experiences with Solomon Goldstein cause him to lose his anti-Semitism. He has already learned a good deal about blacks, for when he meets one named Sam he notes, "He was a good chap, and like his race: I have seen but few niggers that hadn't their hearts in the right place" (p. 147).

After the trip, which includes a steamboatlike race between Stormfield and a comet, he arrives in a heaven quite different from the traditional Christian one. In it creatures from all over the universe gather, including those from miniscule Earth, known in heaven as "the Wart." In the Christian corner of this vast place, men and women of the *Quaker City* variety of Christians discover that their vision of heaven is a bore and that human nature remains what it always was — to Stormfield's great relief. While the story has some of the appeal of fantasy, with a little science fiction added, it is also a thoughtful exploration of the essential human condition. For instance, the dead soon know how undesirable it is to reexperience the "awkward, diffident, sentimental immaturities of nineteen" (p. 161). People are granted their wishes in heaven, such as to be young again, only to discover, to their discomfort, how vain they then are. (In one of his very last works, Mark Twain would have more to say about what joys in heaven are most satisfying.) Those with ability, such as the unknown poet Billings from Tennessee, are royally received, for heaven is a natural aristocracy where talent is justly recognized. "Captain Stormfield" is a joyful satire, one of the author's most successful.[45]

The fact that he was unable to complete the work deserves comment. His method of composition rested heavily on the unpredictable nature of inspiration: he supposed that he *might* be able to finish a work if he found just the right moment to return to it. As a consequence, many novels and stories remained unfinished, and some that were finished, such as *Tom Sawyer, Huckleberry Finn,* and *A Connecticut Yankee in King Arthur's Court,* have endings that are unsatisfactory to many readers. Chopping off the beginning and breaking off without supplying an ending, Mark Twain called his published Stormfield story an "extract." The technique works beautifully, and one wonders if some similar method could be found to make palatable to more readers other attractive fragments, especially from the writer's last years. The publication of "Captain Stormfield's Visit" in 1907–8 was remunerative enough to provide Clemens with the money for the loggia of his last house, at Redding, Connecticut, and after trying other names, the owner chose "Stormfield" for his cold and remote hilltop dwelling.

Olivia Clemens had kept the story from being published during her lifetime; she was her husband's censor, appointed by him. When she was too ill to edit his work, he wrote to Frederick Duneka of Harper, "I have been — in literary matters — helpless all these weeks. I have no editor — no censor." After her death, in 1905, he commented in a letter, "She edited all my manuscripts, beginning the labor of love before we were married, continuing it 36 years." He told Archibald Henderson a more candid version: "After my marriage, she edited everything I wrote, And what is more — she not only edited my works, she edited me."[46] Because his designated editor epitomized the genteel society of her time, Van Wyck Brooks identified her as the chief culprit in what he called the tragic "ordeal of Mark Twain." In 1920, Brooks lamented that "Mark Twain had thrown himself into the hands of his wife; she, in turn, was merely the echo of her environment."[47]

Mrs. Clemens was in a position of power and authority for several reasons. In a letter to Thomas Lounsbury written in 1904, Clemens described his attitude as "a reverent & conscious worship. Perhaps it was nearly like a subject's feeling for his sovereign." Clemens often distrusted his own taste and so sought her judgment. His daughter Susy tells of his leaving parts of a manuscript with Mrs. Clemens for her to "expergate."[48] Sometimes, however, he gained momentary confidence in his own judgment. Beside a speech he had written for Jim in *Huckleberry Finn,* he noted emphatically, "This expression shall not be changed."[49] What Mrs. Clemens did to her husband's manuscripts seems to have been on a considerably smaller scale than what Howells did. Also she was an expert proofreader, though a very bad speller.

Olivia Clemens's potentially important influence lay in her requests that her husband write more books of the sort she approved, such as *The Prince and the Pauper.* Therein she was not often successful. Her recurrent attitude is shown in an undated note probably of about 1902: "Think of the side I know, the sweet, dear tender side — that I love so. Why not show this more to the world?"[50] She was especially concerned about her husband's public image. He wrote in 1899 to Samuel Moffett, "Oh, yes, write as many articles about me as you please. I am not afraid of you." Mrs. Clemens added, "It is better however to submit the articles," to her or to Clemens. Howells, who knew both husband and wife, probably had the most advantageous position for understanding the relationship. He told Paine that he greatly admired Mrs. Clemens's "wonderful tact with a man who was in some respects, and wished to be, the most outrageous creature that ever breathed."[51] But there were major losses for "Mark Twain" when Clemens sought gentility by marrying Olivia. Annie Fields, who was a houseguest of the Clemenses, recorded in her diary during an 1876 visit that her host "was always bringing the blood to his wife's face by his bad behavior. . . . His whole life was one long apology. His wife had told him how well we behaved (poor we!) and he knew he had everything to learn."[52] Olivia Clemens undoubtedly revised the man far more drastically than she ever edited the author.

One of the outlets that Mark Twain found for dealing with Olivia took the form of three stories about the fictional McWilliamses, written between 1875 and 1882. These remarkably intimate reflections of the disagreements between husband and wife are presented from the husband's point of view. The stories are good-tempered, with the emphasis on the wife's inclination to worry, usually in a needless fashion.

Olivia was not alone in her role as censor, however; the whole family was involved. For some years the author read each day what he had written to his family gathered together for that purpose. After Susy's death, he was to recall:

My first book, *The Innocents Abroad,* was edited & revised in proof by my prospective wife. Several later books were criticised & edited in manuscript before going to the press, by my wife & Mr. Howells. About 1880 Susy joined the staff and helped to edit *The Prince and the Pauper.* She was eight years old, then. In 1884, Clara, aged ten, joined the staff, & helped the others edit *Huckleberry Finn.* The children were a valuable reinforcement for my side. . . . They remained on the staff continuously thence forward, & helped as well as they could to edit all the subsequent books chapter by chapter nightly, as each day's work was completed.[53]

Knowing that he would soon read aloud to his wife and children what he had just written had an immensely consequential effect on what Mark Twain wrote.

The long-delayed "Captain Stormfield's Visit" occupied the writer for only a few days in 1881. It is instructive to see what else he wrote during that year, following the completion of *A Tramp Abroad* and *The Prince and the Pauper.* In March, Howells encouraged him to write a small "burlesque book of etiquette." "Think what a chance to satirize the greed, solemn selfishness, and cruel dullness of society!"[54] Pleased with the idea, Clemens gathered a collection of etiquette books and began his satire. Perhaps Howells, and Clemens, thought of the project as a way for the author to express his reservations about genteel manners. Before he gave up the project, he had completed nearly a hundred pages, some few passages of which were published posthumously. He devoted three days of hard work to another burlesque that he was much taken with: a version of *Hamlet* with a new character added to the script, Basil Stockmar, a subscription-book agent. Stockmar finds the characters of the play to be "the oddest lot of lunatics outside the asylum."[55] The adapter did not return to this project after he reached act II, scene 2. In May he sold "A Curious Experience" to the *Century.* This longish piece, over ten thousand words, is simply Clemens's retelling, without much personality or art, of a Civil War story that had been related to him. It wholly lacks originality.

Instead of his usual practice of heading for Quarry Farm and a summer of creativity, Clemens vacationed during June and July on the Connecticut coast, at Branford. Toward the end of June, he described himself as "having a luxuriously lazy & comfortable time." Only in August did the Clemenses visit Elmira. There the author was ill in bed for a time with lumbago. He was not even up to writing letters. With some determination he notified a correspondent, "I'm going to lay this pen entirely aside for a week or more." Thereafter Clemens was to be ill with some frequency, but whether his illnesses prevented his writing or whether they in effect protected him from the knowledge that he could not write is unclear. He was able to complete an essay on "Mental Telegraphy" that he had begun in 1878, but he was unable to find a publisher who would accept something quite so out of his line, and the essay was pigeonholed until 1891, when it was published. In the fall he read some volumes of Francis Parkman's histories, which provided information useful to him in his next major project. On a visit to Montreal in November to secure British copyright for *The Prince and the Pauper,* he made quantities of notes for a sketch on Canada. He considered making a burlesque of Jacob Abbott's moralistic *Rollo's Tour of Europe,* but nothing came of the idea. Both would seem to have been unpromising, but the writer needed to find *something* to do. Instead of writing, Clemens was devoting much of his time to investments, mostly unremunerative, and to editing books, such as a "Cyclopedia of Humor," not to the writing of them.

The year 1881, according to Paine, saw Clemens's expenditures soar over the $100,000 mark, with some $41,000 being poured into bad investments, and $30,000 spent on his house and the purchase of additional adjacent land.[56] The investments were distractions, as were arrangements for publishing with Osgood. He told a St. Louis newspaper that he could not attend a St. Louis "River Convention" in the fall of 1881 because he was "putting a book through the press, and this sort of work requires not merely daily but hourly attention." The publication of *The Prince and the Pauper* was a major preoccupation during much of 1881. At the end of this highly uncreative year and into 1882, he devoted weeks to preparing a "biography" of Whitelaw Reid, a project that came to nothing. He had mistakenly supposed that Reid, editor of the *New York Tribune,* had been attacking him; a slashing biography was to have been revenge.

The next year, 1882, did see the publication of a book by Mark Twain, though one that took little effort on his part. In March he asked his publisher Osgood to look over the files of the *Atlantic Monthly* and combine what he found by the author there with selections, to be made in consultation with Howells, from some unpublished pieces he had collected—the writer abdicating any responsibility for either selection or ordering. The result was *The Stolen White Elephant, Etc.* Much of the volume merely reprints the contents of *Punch, Brothers, Punch! and Other Sketches,* which had been published in 1878 by Clemens's onetime friend and business partner, Dan Slote, with advertising in the book for Clemens's self-pasting scrapbook, while Slote's company was producing. The other eight pieces first published here are very slight. Of all Mark Twain's books, it is the least distinguished. The most interesting pieces are the brilliant "Carnival of

Crime" and two more "McWilliams" pieces derived from the Clemens family's experiences with lightning and the burglar alarm.

Something better was soon to come for the author. In the back of Clemens's mind was the long-delayed trip to the Mississippi River to find materials for a book. In July 1881, he had written to the Louisiana novelist George Washington Cable, "Howells is still in the mind to go to New Orleans with me in November for the Mississippi trip." But Howells was not to go, and by December the plan was for Osgood to accompany Clemens instead. In February, Clemens began to make notes on steamboating. Very much aware of his ignorance, he recorded: "I am so indolent, & all forms of study are so hateful to me, that although I was several years living constantly on steamboats, I never learned all the parts of a steamboat. Names of parts were in my ear daily whose office & locality I was ignorant of, & I never inquired the meaning of those names. For instance, I think I never saw the day that I could describe the marks on a lead line. I never knew what 'in the run' meant — I couldn't find the run in a boat to-day, & be *sure* I was right."[57] These notes suggest that he was planning — not more of the kind of personal story he told in "Old Times," but an augmentation of his earlier pieces with an authoritative, factual account of the river, introducing personalities and anecdotes to enliven the account. Pages and pages of his notebook bristle with ideas about what to put into his book. He reminds himself: " 'Harris' is along, as usual. And I use false name because it is mysterious & stylish." "At Memphis get facts about the pilot who stood at wheel & was burned." "Get notable steamer explosions." "Find Ab Grimes" (whom he had known in his piloting days).[58]

On April 10, Clemens signed a contract for a Mississippi book with Osgood, with the same cost-sharing that had been involved in the production and sales of *The Prince and the Pauper;* he agreed to have the book finished by October 1, 1882, less than seven months from then. On April 17, well prepared, Clemens left for the river. Besides Osgood, Roswell Phelps made the trip. A Hartford stenographer and former schoolteacher, Phelps kept notes for the writer. The three took the train to St. Louis, then a steamboat to New Orleans. On April 22, Clemens wrote to his wife, "We are having a powerful good time & picking up & setting down volumes of literary stuff." Two sets of notes survive: Phelps's full collection, transcriptions he made of his shorthand, and some notes by Clemens. Unlike the obligatory notes made for *A Tramp Abroad,* these show the writer's excited interest in returning to what he had known long ago. In New Orleans he visited George Washington Cable and Joel Chandler Harris; the latter had come from Atlanta for the meeting. On a ten-mile harbor tour, the former pilot was permitted to steer. Then Osgood, Phelps, and Clemens traveled back up the river on the boat of the master pilot, Horace Bixby, who had been celebrated in "Old Times." After reaching St. Louis, Clemens went to Hannibal for a three-day visit. He had been away from Hannibal since 1867. He recorded in his notebook: "Alas! everything was changed in Hannibal—but when I reached third or fourth sts the tears burst forth, for I recognize the mud. *It,* at least, was the same — the same old mud."[59] Ending his trip, Clemens went up the river and finally reached St. Paul. He was so tired that he went directly home on May 22. The trip had lasted a little more than a month.

The visit was not a success for Clemens, since he had managed to collect far less information than he had anticipated. In his book he admitted that "the main purpose of my visit [to New Orleans was] but lamely accomplished. I had hoped to hunt up and talk with a hundred steamboatmen, but got so pleasantly involved in the social life of the town that I got nothing more than mere five-minute talks with a couple of dozen of the craft" (chap. 51).

In Hartford the writer began the book as he intended, by adding to the account of his days as a cub pilot the story of his experiences with the pilot Brown and the death of his brother Henry. He next built his contrasting account around his 1882 trip, which begins with chapter 22, where Osgood is playfully described as a "poet." At first he planned to use his two companions, whom he dubbed Thompson and Rogers, much as he had used Brown and Harris earlier. Thompson and Rogers are introduced, but only casually, in chapter 22; they are not really significant until chapter 32, where they serve to integrate Karl Ritter's narrative, which Mark Twain had drafted years before, into the story. Thereafter the two companions are nearly forgotten, except for an occasional reference to the "poet."

In returning to his old haunts, Clemens seems to have planned to make use of himself as the innocent victim once more. Since he had much experience as a pilot, this time he would have to use an assumed name. He tried the name of C. L. Samuels of New York. This ruse soon evaporated, for Clemens was immediately recognized just as soon as he arrived in St. Louis, according to chapter 22, and recognized again just six hours below St. Louis soon after he induced the pilot to invent tall tales of the river to entertain his pretended innocence. "Thus ended the fictitious-name business." The explosion of his incognito, as he called it, meant the abandonment of a fictional narrator and therefore the simplification of the book.

The Clemens family's trip to Quarry Farm for the summer was delayed by the illnesses of Jean and Susy, and the writer was prevented for a time from writing. Before they left in mid-July, he had nonetheless composed more than fourteen chapters. As these were to be augmented by "Old Times on the Mississippi," he had therefore finished nearly half the book. Soon after he arrived in Elmira, Clemens wrote to Osgood, "I wish you would set a cheap expert to work to collect local histories of Mississippi towns & a lot of other books relating to the river to me. Meantime all those people who promised to send such things to us ain't doing it, dern them." Another indication that this book was to reflect his reading as well as his experiences was his subscribing to the *New Orleans Times-Democrat,* which he had been receiving in Hartford and now had sent to Elmira. He also borrowed books from George Washington Cable.

At Quarry Farm, Mark Twain next composed the famous chapter "The House Beautiful," extrapolated from his own description of the Granger-fords' parlor in the incomplete manuscript of *Huckleberry Finn,* as well as several bits from Clarence C. Cooke's *The House Beautiful: Essays on Beds and Tables, Stools and Candlesticks* (1877), and something from Charles Dickens's *American Notes.* (He refers to Dickens by name.) The borrowings are well integrated in this chapter into a powerful piece of satire. He also lifted most of a chapter from his unfinished *Huckleberry Finn* manuscript for insertion into chapter 3, in which he told of the "mighty rafts that used to glide by Hannibal." Soon the books from Osgood's agent arrived, twenty-five volumes in all. He then requisitioned additional books, this time by name. Later he was supplied with a series of magazine articles about New Orleans, the Mississippi, and St. Louis, and he based chapters 27 and 29 specifically on them. In addition, he devoted two more chapters to a picture of "departed America" as it had been seen by English travel writers of the early nineteenth century that he called "a most strange and unreal-seeming world."[60] Intended to follow chapter 40, these chapters about early-day travelers were later dropped at Osgood's suggestion and were not published until 1944. At the end of the two deleted chapters, Mark Twain wrote disgustedly, "I dredged through all those old books, mainly to find out what the procession of foreign tourists thought of the river towns of the Mississippi. But as a general thing, they forgot to say" (p. 300).

In the deleted chapters, especially the second, the writer found much to criticize in the America of the past: the severity of its laws, its chauvinism, the vulgarity of its newspapers. Of the disappearance of such features, he observes, "We mourn, of course, as filial duty requires — yet it was good rotten material for burial." But, he finds, "The most noticeable features of that departed America are not *all* gone from us. A few remain; some as bulkily prominent as ever, others more or less reduced in size and significance" (p. 295).

When he returned from the historical report to the contemporary narrative of his Mississippi trip, he began to introduce this new concern with social criticism. Such a theme was encouraged by a chain of events as well as by his reading in travel books. In June, Howells had shown Clemens his essay "Mark Twain," which was to be published in the September issue of *Century*. There Howells warns the reader that if "he leaves out of the account an indignant sense of right and wrong, a scorn of all affectation and pretense, an ardent hate of meanness and injustice, he will come infinitely short of knowing Mark Twain." Howells's essay in turn prompted a *Century* editor, Robert Underwood Johnson, to write to Clemens on August 9 to request that he undertake a series of articles on "Permanent Sources of Corruption in Our Government," "the lobbying, logrolling, running primaries and conventions, R.R. pass system, establishment of newspapers to form public opinion, &c., &c., &c. We mean a serious exposition of the ways that are dark."[61] Although Clemens did not accept the proposed assignment, he now had reason to think that America was ready to listen to what he might write about its social imperfections. Specifically, he began to organize his Mississippi book around the principle of change, so much so that the work has been called a hymn to progress. "From St. Louis northward," he observed, "there are all the enlivening signs of the presence of active, energetic, intelligent, prosperous practical nineteenth-century populations" (chap. 57). By contrast, he made much of the South's backwardness. The problem, he asserted, was that the region was tied to outdated ideas, as symbolized by the Louisiana state capitol in Baton Rouge, a ridiculous "imitation castle," and by Sir Walter Scott's brand of medievalism, still popular in the South. Mark Twain hyperbolically argues that Scott was "in great measure responsible" for the Civil War because he had provided the models for systems of rank and caste so revered by the South. In his mind, evidently Mark Twain assumed the mission of a modern-day Cervantes on a crusade to rescue the South from decadent romanticism. (He would assume the same role, and define it more satisfactorily, in *A Connecticut Yankee*.)

The manuscript was taking shape, but there were delays nonetheless; the writer's poor health was one hindrance. On September 19, he wrote to Charles Webster that he was "not well yet, & my book drags like the very devil. Some days I cannot write a line." But by the end of his stay at Quarry Farm, he had added to his manuscript twenty-three chapters. He had incorporated "The Professor's Yarn," left over from *A Tramp Abroad*, although he admitted to readers, "I insert it in this place merely because it is a good

story, not because it belongs here — for it doesn't." He had written an introduction based largely on Francis Parkman's history, and he had definitely
decided to illustrate "keelboat talk and manners" in chapter 3 with the
aforementioned chapter from his *Huckleberry Finn* manuscript. He was
thus about five-sixths done. He was, however, unable for several reasons to
meet the October 1 date for completion named in the contract with Osgood. He had given himself too little time, he and his family had been ill,
and he had not found all that he had expected in the books he had been sent.

Sometime in the fall, Clemens sent Osgood what he had written and
asked him to edit it, since Howells was in Switzerland. Osgood's memo
survives, with Clemens's responses. Once again he was docile, ready to
accept uncritically whatever was proposed.[62] The consequences of Osgood's
editing, and of the writer's acquiescence, were of real import. Among the
parts dropped are some in which Mark Twain's literary personality was most
in evidence. Without them, the familiar narrator — irreverent, spontaneous,
and humorous — and the vernacular narrators he introduced were largely
absent, although the colorful Uncle Mumford survives. Omitted, for example, is a passage at the point where Rob Styles is questioned by the sup-
posedly ignorant narrator in chapter 24.

> "Have you ever been blown up on a steamboat?
>
> "Nine times."
>
> "It is a large experience."
>
> "Yes. I was flung through the roof of the same cabin in Walnut Bend
> three times in five years."
>
> "That seems very remarkable."
>
> "It was considered so. Yes, three times through the same roof. The
> third time, the man moved away."
>
> "He moved away?"
>
> "Yes. He was a nervous, sedentary, student-sort of a man, trying to
> cipher out the Development business, and Survival of the Fittest, and
> one thing or another, and he said he would rather move than be always
> being interrupted and bothered so. Repairs took a good deal of time,
> too."
>
> "Yes, and expense, of course."
>
> "Well, no; not expense; I paid that. I always do. But this third time I
> fetched the cook along; and I reckon if the truth was told, he didn't
> altogether like it. He never said so; but I judged, from his coolish way,
> that he thought I was making too free. He had always been cordial
> before. I may be wrong; but you know you can always tell a good deal by
> the way a man acts. He appeared constrained — that was the thing that

struck my notice, not anything that he said. He never once looked at the cook, and he didn't ask me to sit down—he had always asked me to sit down, before. Well, it was a pretty chilly atmosphere, take it by and large, and we didn't stay long. When we were leaving, he did make shift to ask me to drop in again when I was passing—nothing very hearty about it, though—but I just gave him a stiff bow, and remarked in just about as cutting a style of cold politeness as I knew how to handle, that I wasn't in the habit of shoving in where I couldn't fetch a friend along who was going my way and there wasn't time to organize and put the thing through according to the gilt-edged requirements of Walnut Bend society. I had him, there! He couldn't say a word. So I just shouldered my wheel and meandered away."

"You had your wheel along, too?"

"Happened to have it that time—didn't usually take it. But you don't take *anything*, purposely, you know. You don't *think* of anything. There isn't time." (pp. 181–82)

The story is assuredly Mark Twain's invention, not Styles's; in his notebook the author had simply recorded: "Had a great deal of talk about the river and the steam boat men, most of whom are dead now. He [the pilot] located a dozen for me who were still alive."[63]

Another tall tale, one of Mark Twain's most inventive, was deleted from chapter 34, "Tough Yarns." It is told by a resident of Arkansas City, "an austere man" with "the reputation of being singularly unworldly, for a river man." In addition to his comments about remarkable mosquitoes, he tells a wild yarn about a balloonist who reaches a belt of dead air and is stranded there. Eventually he is joined by a fleet of other balloons, inhabited by an international gathering of fifty-four corpses "and a lot of dried animals of one sort and another," a kind of Sargasso Sea of the air (p. 255). Had this tale been published in 1883 instead of appearing for the first time as an appendix to a Limited Editions Club book sixty years later, it might well be celebrated. (Fortunately, it now appears in a Penguin edition.)

A good measure of the old Mark Twain is present in yet another deleted passage about a group of California miners who were criticized by a San Francisco religious paper for giving "the sublimest mountain gateway up-reared by the hand of the Creator in all that majestic region" the profane name of "The Devil's Gorge." The humiliated and disgraced miners "hadn't meant the least harm," and to make amends they renamed the spot "Jehovah Gap." As the author comments, "A religious editor must be hard to please, indeed, who could find a flaw with that" (pp. 186–87).

That Mark Twain should reappear in a book about a revisit to the Mississippi is hardly surprising, especially since he had traveled without his wife and family. The narrator, however, provides constant reminders of the passing of time from 1857, when he became a steamboat man, to the present, 1882. He had described the change movingly in a May 1882 letter to Olivia Clemens, written while he was on his trip: "That world which I knew in its blossoming youth is old and bowed and melancholy, now; its soft cheeks are leathery & wrinkled, the fire is gone out in its eyes, & the spring from its step. It will be dust and ashes when I come again." Samuel Clemens too had changed: for one thing, he was a celebrity. Once in a while his account recalls the attitude of the earlier writer, as in chapter 22, where he explains with feigned innocence, "The first time I ever saw St. Louis, I could have bought it for six million dollars, and it was the mistake of my life that I did not do it." In a deleted passage, he continued, "I was young and heedless, and naturally more given to pleasure-seeking than to providing for the future; it was impossible to foresee that out of that smutty village would grow the imperial city of today; and besides, I had only thirty-five dollars, anyway. Still, if I had known then what I know now, I would have borrowed" (p. 171). Here, fleetingly, is the familiar voice.

Finishing *Life on the Mississippi* was difficult for Mark Twain. In November and December, he wrote the last chapters, but he was still revising in mid-January. Then he wrote to Osgood, "*No I don't want to read proof of the old Atlantic matter* — but I want it read *almighty carefully* in Boston, and *no* improvements attempted." He was much less particular about new material: "There will be 20 to 25,000 more words than necessary; so the scissors can be freely used." Despite his resolve, the author appears to have read proof of "Old Times," for a comparison reveals that he made forty-five changes in these fourteen chapters, and while all were small, many are improvements.[64]

Life on the Mississippi looks like other subscription books, only more elegant and better illustrated; it occupies 624 pages and has, as the title page notes, "more than 300 illustrations," many of them full-page and excellent. The representations of Clemens as a cub pilot show him as a boy, not as the young man he in fact was. Most of the illustrations are by John Harley, who had provided some of the ones in *The Prince and the Pauper*.[65] On the back of the title page of the books appear the words "By S. L. Clemens / Mark Twain," and both below and at the sides appear the words "Trade Mark." In 1873 Mark Twain's attorney had had some success in court in attacking a publisher who had published something by the author without his permission "under the rule, that a man has a trademark in his articles published under a *nom de plume*." Subsequently, he had recommended that Osgood undertake a suit based on the same principle: he wanted to sue a person who had been "*violating my trademark* — copyright not to be mentioned."[66] Mark Twain's inclusion of his "trade mark" in the book, he must have thought, might provide protection from piracy — but he had no further success using this approach. Toward the end of his life he would create the Mark Twain Company to look out for his literary property — and his precious pen name.

Life on the Mississippi became a classic largely because of the *Atlantic* papers, crucial chapters in "Mark Twain's autobiography." The rest of the book, despite what seems like padding and some dullish sections, is what Mark Twain was aiming for: a memorable study of the great river and of the dramatic nature of change in American life. It disappoints those who look for Mark Twain in it. The recent edition that restores the deleted passages to the place where they belong gives the book increased appeal, but Osgood's cuts do not make him the chief culprit. The author himself, it may be argued, misconceived the book. His original plan of 1871 was to "spend 2 months on the river & take notes," and, he told his wife, "I bet you I will make a standard work." This nebulous conception led to his wide reading and to his neglect of the fictionalizing that had gone into *The Innocents Abroad* and *Roughing It*. The arduous experience of writing *A Tramp Abroad,* not long before, also affected the Mississippi book. Having slaved over the *Tramp* for a long time, the author was quite ready to flesh out his new book by citing authorities.

In spite of Clemens's intimate familiarity with his subject, *Life on the Mississippi* was not commercially successful, at least from his point of view. The failing, he believed, lay with the publisher, Osgood. His company was still not an experienced subscription publisher. After three disappointing books, Clemens elected to leave Osgood, whose firm failed in 1885.

The reviewers expressed quite different attitudes toward *Life on the Mississippi*. One found passages in it "equal to anything" Mark Twain had written and "the purely descriptive parts of his narrative . . . marked by even more than his customary sprightliness and spirit."[67] Lafcadio Hearn called it "in some respects . . . the most solid book that Mark Twain has written."[68] An English reviewer described the second half of the book as "mere reportage."[69] There seems to have been no reviewer to protest the disappearance of Mark Twain from the last thirty-eight chapters.

CHAPTER SIX

A New Voice

ark Twain's penchant for sequels finally paid off handsomely when he recognized that the story told in *The Adventures of Tom Sawyer* could be continued. When he finished that novel, he recalled that his first intention had been to continue the story into Tom's adulthood, but he had thought better of it. In July 1875, he wrote to Howells, "By & by I shall take a boy of twelve & run him on through life (in the first person) but not Tom Sawyer — he would not be a good character for it." When Howells read *Tom Sawyer*, he recommended dropping the last chapter; a revised version of it may well have developed as chapter 1 of the new novel, in which Huckleberry Finn introduces himself by explaining, "You don't know about me, without you have read a book by the name of 'The Adventures of Tom Sawyer,' but that ain't no matter. That book was made by Mr. Mark Twain, and he told the truth, mainly."

As he approached the ending of *Tom Sawyer*, the writer may have seen the possibilities that would be open to him if he made Huck his narrator. In chapter 30, he let Huck speak at some length, and immediately the story comes alive, for Mark Twain endows what Huck tells with a most distinctive personality. As was to become his habit, Huck invents a story to get himself out of a tight spot.

Well, you see, I'm a kind of a hard lot, — least everybody says so, and I don't see nothing agin it — and sometimes I can't sleep much, on accounts of thinking about it and sort of trying to strike out a new way of doing.

That was the way of it last night. I couldn't sleep, and so I come along up street 'bout midnight, a-turning it all over, and when I got to that old shackly brick store by the Temperance Tavern, I backed up agin the wall to have another think. Well, just then along comes these two chaps slipping along close by me, with something under their arm and I reckoned they'd stole it. One was a-smoking, and t'other wanted a light; so they stopped right before me and the cigars lit up their faces and I see that the big one was the deef and dumb Spaniard, by his white whiskers and the patch on his eye, and t'other one was a rusty, ragged looking devil.[1]

In the new book, Huck's voice is even stronger and clearer, and he is now far more of a rebel than Tom had been. Thus Mark Twain's decision to adopt Huck as his narrator had important implications. Any discomfort, resistance, or resentment that Samuel Clemens felt from the "civilizing" he had been undergoing could be readily expressed in Huck's attitude. Telling the story with Huck's voice released quantities of pent-up psychic energy.

By the time he began *Huckleberry Finn,* Mark Twain was experienced in using vernacular narrators, such as Simon Wheeler of the jumping frog story, and between 1876, when he began the new novel, and 1884, when he finished it, he continued to make use of such storytellers: Jim Baker, who tells the blue jay yarn, Rob Styles, and Uncle Mumford of *Life on the Mississippi*. But he was now using less and less frequently the voice of Mark Twain of the West, presumably because he himself was now a different person. Employing Huckleberry Finn as a narrator permitted him to return to old values and attitudes: irreverence, skepticism, outspokenness. Samuel Clemens's entrance into polite eastern society had inhibited him for a time from writing as the Mark Twain he had been before his marriage. In fact, writing with Huck's pen, he achieved more complete liberation from the conventions than writing as "Mark Twain" had ever permitted him. His literary personality in *The Prince and the Pauper, A Tramp Abroad,* and the 1882 portions of *Life on the Mississippi* had most of the time been restrained, even tame. Huck's quite distinctive voice — he differs from Mark Twain in essentially lacking a sense of humor and even being melancholy in temperament — permitted the writer to celebrate what he still valued, or at least what one side of him still craved: freedom, self-indulgence, the pleasure principle, laziness, skepticism, but now tempered by charity (caring) and decency, too.

Because new information concerning the stages of the composition of *Huckleberry Finn* has become available since the 1990 discovery of the first part of the manuscript, the complex story behind Mark Twain's masterpiece can now be fully told. He began *Adventures of Huckleberry Finn* even before

Tom Sawyer was published. In the summer of 1876, he wrote chapters 1–17 and part of chapter 18, except for a substantial insert, written later, about the steamboat *Walter Scott;* it would constitute the bulk of chapter 12 and the whole of chapters 13 and 14. The new book begins exactly where the previous one had stopped; it is therefore helpful, if not necessary, to read the sequel with Tom's story in mind. Huck is now enmeshed in the Widow Douglas's attempts to give him what he has never known: discipline, manners, life on a regular schedule. He sees it all as a restriction of his freedom, and he struggles against the regimen that Clemens himself had sought when he married Olivia. (Clemens had pleaded with her in January 1869, "You will break up all my irregularities when we are married, & *civilize* me . . . won't you?") Huck cherishes his liberty so much that he cannot take very seriously the widow's warnings that his resistance will send him to hell. At first he turns almost desperately to Tom Sawyer for relief. But in chapter 2, Tom proves to be virtually as rigid in his way as the widow is in hers. He insists that everything be done "regular." Tom tells him, "Don't you reckon that the people that made the books knows what's the correct thing to do? Do you reckon *you* can learn 'em anything? Not by a good deal." At this point Huck does not object, though the reader suspects that he is sympathetic with Ben Rogers, who pronounces Tom's plan "a fool way." As Huck might, Ben qualifies his acceptance of Tom's plan by proclaiming, "I don't take no stock in it."

The boys do agree that they cannot desecrate Sundays with their games, and in the next chapter Huck explores his own religious attitude. Prayer, he finds from a cursory survey of his experience, doesn't work—at least not efficaciously enough to suit a boy. Huck's pragmatic skepticism permits the author to express his own amused attitude toward conventional religion—and one thinks of how "Livy" had prohibited her husband's publishing "Captain Stormfield's Visit." Perhaps Huck's philosophizing is intended to suggest the growth of a questioning spirit, for soon he shows little respect for Tom's schemes; he describes them simply as "lies."

The early chapters of the book consistently show St. Petersburg to be a false, dishonest, hypocritical community. Restrictive, rigid, regulated by arbitrary rules, the town is an uncomfortable place for a free spirit such as Huck. Tom is thoroughly identified with this conventional, respectable society of St. Petersburg, and to underscore the orientation of his sequel, the writer characterizes him from the very beginning as a much less appealing figure. In *Tom Sawyer* the author had described approvingly Tom's gradual socialization; now Tom has sold out, and as an instrument of conformity he explains to Huck what *must* be done. In the former book, Tom

1858: *Clemens at age twenty-two, when he was a "cub" (apprentice) to the steamboat pilot Horace Bixby. After receiving his license on April 9, 1859, Clemens made many trips between St. Louis and New Orleans until the Civil War ended his career in spring 1861. He published a series of articles in 1875 about his experiences on the river, "Old Times on the Mississippi." (Courtesy of Special Collections, Vassar College, Poughkeepsie, N.Y.)*

Mark Twain

1863: *Clemens at age twenty-seven, during his first visit to San Francisco in May. After brief service in June 1861 in the Missouri Marion Rangers (Confederate volunteers), he had accompanied his brother Orion, newly appointed secretary of the Nevada Territory, to Carson City as Orion's assistant, but he soon began prospecting and then writing for newspapers nearby. (Courtesy of the Mark Twain Papers, University of California, Berkeley)*

Three of the suspected men still in confinement at Aurora.

1864: *Mark Twain (center) at age twenty-eight, with Nevada legislators William H. Clagett and Speaker A. J. Simmons. Clemens worked as a reporter for the* Virginia City Territorial Enterprise *and covered the Nevada state constitutional convention in 1863. As a humorist now calling himself "Mark Twain," he was invited by his fellow reporters (the "Third House") to give in January 1864 the "Governor's message," which drew a full house and was called by "good judges" "the best thing of the kind they had ever listened to." (Courtesy of the Mark Twain Papers, Tufts Collection, University of California, Berkeley)*

1874: *Mark Twain at age thirty-eight in his summer study in Elmira. After a year in Buffalo, the Clemenses moved to Hartford, Connecticut. Clemens initially divided his time between lecturing and writing, but he gradually focused on writing, mostly in this study during the summers, when the family resided at Quarry Farm, the home of Olivia's adopted sister and brother-in-law, Susan and Theodore Crane. (Courtesy of the Mark Twain House, Hartford)*

(Opposite) 1870: *Mark Twain at age thirty-four, associate editor of the* Buffalo Express. *In 1867, he had traveled to the Mediterranean and the Holy Land on assignment for the* San Francisco Alta California. *Thereafter he revised his reports into a book,* The Innocents Abroad *(1869). Its success permitted him to marry Olivia Langdon of Elmira, New York, on February 2, 1870. (Courtesy of the Mark Twain House, Hartford)*

1884: *The Clemens family, Livy (thirty-nine), Clara (ten), Jean (four), Sam (forty-nine), and Susy (twelve) at the house built for them in Hartford. They resided here from 1874 until 1891, when they began a long residence in Europe. Of this whole family, only Clara outlived Sam. The house still attracts many visitors. (Courtesy of the Mark Twain Papers, University of California, Berkeley)*

(Opposite) 1890: *Mark Twain at age fifty-four, in Onteora in the Catskills of New York State, the family's summer residence that year. Since 1884, the author had written only one major work,* A Connecticut Yankee in King Arthur's Court *(1889), and had devoted much of his time to his publishing company, Charles L. Webster and Company, and to raising funds for the Paige typesetting machine, in which he was unwisely investing. (Courtesy of the Mark Twain Papers, University of California, Berkeley)*

1895: *Mark Twain at age fifty-nine at the beginning of a round-the-world lecture tour, taken in the summer somewhere during his trip across America. In 1891, unable to afford the maintenance of their Hartford house, the Clemenses had moved to Europe. In 1894, Webster and Company went bankrupt. To pay the company's debts, Clemens felt obliged to undertake this demanding tour. (Courtesy of the Mark Twain Archive and the Center for Mark Twain Studies, Elmira College)*

had looked at Huck's freedom with envy; now he calls Huck a numskull, a "perfect sap-head." Tom is now cruel and aggressive; he has had to develop techniques for controlling others, since he has nothing of value to offer. He is an egotist and a hypocrite. The characterization of Tom ensures that Huck will have to go his own way.[2]

Whereas slavery is not a significant element in the world of *Tom Sawyer*, it is now at the heart of the society and is symbolic of what is wrong with it. In what is to become a serious world, Huck is to have an adult to accompany him, the slave Jim, who makes two separate appearances in these early chapters. On both occasions he is seen rather comically, full of African-American superstitions of the sort Clemens had learned from a former slave at Quarry Farm and from Uncle Daniel back at the Quarles farm, but Jim is also shrewd enough to take advantage of both of the two situations in which he finds himself. Mark Twain's brilliant method for setting forth his attitudes toward slavery and its basis in racism was, in one black critic's words, to "focus on a number of commonplaces associated with 'the Negro' and then systematically dramatize their inadequacy." His "strategy with racial stereotypes is to elaborate them in order to undermine them." On the raft with Jim, Huck discovers, and the reader along with him, that his racist beliefs, his prejudices, about African Americans simply do not correspond to his experiences with Jim.[3] Among several astute decisions, Mark Twain had the good sense to omit from his published text the buffoonlike, racist portrayal of Jim in a dissecting room found in the recently discovered opening half of the manuscript.[4]

The first real indication that the story is to have a serious aspect comes not with Jim's appearance but through the introduction of Huck's Pap, an immensely threatening figure in Huck's consciousness. With the entrance of Pap, the writer begins his demonstration of the ridiculousness of racism. Pap tells of being outraged by his encounter with a black man who doesn't act like a black man — or, rather, does not fit Pap's racist stereotype. A college professor, the black man wears fine clothes, and he votes. By contrast, Pap himself is repulsive: he wears rags, has no education, and on election day is probably too drunk to vote. Soon this terrible man almost kills his own son, after taking full advantage of him.

Although Mark Twain may not have yet known it, Pap's mistreatment of Huck is the occasion for the action of the book: Huck's flight and his instructive adventures on the river. At this point Pap serves chiefly as a means of defining Huck's vulnerability. If the boy is an outsider, he is not a leech or an aggressively antisocial outcast like his father. The existence of African Americans at the bottom rung of society gives poor white trash like

Pap some sense of dignity. Although there is a comic side to Pap, his attempt to kill Huck in a fit of delirium tremens is anything but funny.

Huck's subsequent ingenious escape and his teaming up with Jim, who has fled slavery to avoid being sold down the river, lead to their journey southward by raft to the Ohio River at Cairo, whence Jim intends to head northward to the free states. They cannot simply cross to free territory, since Pap has obtained money from Judge Thatcher to hunt Jim "all over Illinois." What the writer had in mind to develop as a plot while he was writing this part is not clear. Perhaps he merely hoped something would occur to him. Perhaps it was to be a burlesque murder-detective story, like *Simon Wheeler, Detective,* with Jim put on trial for murdering Huck, who had covered his own tracks by creating the impression that he had been killed. In any event, in chapter 16 Huck and Jim discover that they have passed Cairo, Illinois, where the Ohio River joins the Mississippi. Jim had envisioned the Ohio as his route to freedom, but the writer, who — typically — was improvising his story, did not know the Ohio: the destruction of the raft at the end of the chapter was simply a way of stopping the trip down the river, but it also denied Jim access to freedom.

This initial installment of the book that Mark Twain wrote in 1876 originally included the "Raft Passage," which he later "stole" for inclusion in *Life on the Mississippi.*[5] Coming after the second paragraph of chapter 16, it was included in the completed manuscript of *Huckleberry Finn* that the author submitted in 1884 to his nephew, Charles Webster, who — as explained below — had been given the task of running a new subscription publishing house created by the writer. Webster wrote to Mark Twain, "The book is so *much* larger than Tom Sawyer, would i[t] not be better to omit that old Mississippi matter? I think it would improve it." The author casually agreed.[6] Dropped only for reasons of space, the passage assuredly should be restored, as it has been in the University of California text, within "The Works of Mark Twain" series. Without the passage, a gap occurs in the novel and crucial information is omitted — not to mention an alteration of the pace of the novel. In this episode Huck swims to a big raft to learn where he and Jim are in relation to Cairo. There he overhears remarkable conversations and learns how Cairo can be located. Where the Mississippi is joined by the Ohio, the water of the latter is distinguishable as "a wide band of clear water all the way down the east side of the Mississippi for a hundred miles or more." Huck soon relies on this information in chapter 16, when he sees "the clear Ohio water in shore, sure enough, and outside was the old regular Muddy!" That observation causes him to acknowledge glumly that "it was all up with Cairo."

There are other good reasons to include the discarded passage. Above all, it contains some of the most colorful writing in the book in the fighting challenges of "the Child of Calamity" and "Bob." More specifically, Huck overhears the raftsmen discussing "what a king has to do, and how much he got," information the reader needs to understand that Huck knows when the "king" comes aboard his raft. The episode also includes a tale about a dead child's pursuit of his murderous father, thematically related to Huck's escape from *his* father. Throughout the novel, Huck repeatedly invents stories about the troubles of his family. This time he identifies himself as a child killed by his father.[7]

Two episodes in the 1876 portion of the book show Huck's growing recognition of Jim's worth. Both episodes begin with Huck playing practical jokes on Jim. After the first badly misfires, Huck guiltily hides the evidence that would show Jim to have been bitten by a rattlesnake as a result of "some fun" Huck has attempted. In the second, Huck makes a dramatic apology for the trick he has played on Jim in having pretended that their separation in the fog was only something Jim has dreamed.

After Huck and Jim pass Cairo in the night, apparently all that the author could think of was to have a steamboat smash "straight through the raft," separating Huck and Jim. Jim now being absent, movement in the story is suspended. Huck finds his way to the Grangerford house. The 1876 portion of *Huckleberry Finn* ends with Huck asking Buck Grangerford to tell him what a feud is.

When he left off writing this first section of the book, Mark Twain was at an impasse and did not yet value the manuscript highly. He returned to it in mid-November 1879 and continued till mid-June 1880. During this time he completed chapter 18 and wrote chapters 19, 20, and 21, for he saw a way to continue his story, which now became far more serious. In the Grangerfords, courtly southern aristocrats, Huck all but finds himself a family — until he discovers the violence of their feud with the Shepherdsons and then witnesses the death of his friend Buck. Whereas Emmeline Grangerford had gushily sentimentalized her poetic accounts of death, in chapter 18 Huck tells of the grisly deaths he observes with terse restraint. He explains how he felt, "so sick I most fell out of the tree," then adds, "I ain't agoing to tell *all* that happened — it would make me sick again if I was to do that. I wished I hadn't ever come ashore that night, to see such things. I ain't ever going to get shut of them — lots of times I dream about them."

While writing chapter 18, the writer decided that he should continue Huck's adventures by raft and wrote himself a note: "Back a little. CHANGE — raft only *crippled* by steamer."[8] But instead of revising, he merely has Jim inform Huck that the raft had only been damaged. He apparently wanted to continue his story of Huck and Jim together on the raft, if he could ever decide what his book was truly going to be about. At this time, presumably, he drew up a long list of possible activities for the two. They include

Negro campmeeting and sermon — "See dat sinner how he run."
The scow with theatre aboard
A house-raising
Village school — they haze Huck, the first day
The country cotillions
The horse trade
Candy-pulling
Dinner manners at the tavern with a crowd.[9]

What he wrote next determined what he would *not* take up: Jim's escape to freedom.

Having passed Cairo, Huck and Jim had decided in chapter 16 that they must continue south until they find "a chance to buy a canoe to go back in." The two return to the raft after the feud episode and after Jim has got their floating home "all fixed up agin mos' as good as new, en we's got a new lot o' stuff, too, in de place o' what 'uz los'." They do not now discuss their need for a canoe, probably because the writer has forgotten about it, and when Huck locates one in chapter 19, instead of planning how to transfer their stuff to it from the raft, preparatory to heading north, he uses it merely to try to pick some berries. To replace the motivation furnished by Jim's search for freedom, with Huck assisting, the author introduces two new characters who provide a plausible rationale for a journey southward into the area he had known as a pilot. The Duke and the King become uninvited guests on the raft. When in chapter 20 they ask if Jim is a runaway slave, Huck quick-wittedly asks, "Goodness sakes, would a runaway nigger run *south?*" With the Duke and the King aboard, Jim and Huck are necessarily more con-cerned about Jim being sold or seized as a runaway than with heading northward in a canoe. The writer accordingly has an excuse to describe life in the river towns as the four stop periodically for the two charlatans to pick up a few dishonest dollars. These con artists know how to take advantage of the gullible townsmen they meet, who seem almost eager to be deceived. The author's familiarity with their kind goes back at least as far as the stranger who loaded Jim Smiley's jumping frog with shot. The grandiose roles the two assume on the raft — "the rightful Duke of Bridgewater" (which soon becomes Bilgewater) and "the wanderin', exiled, trampled-on and sufferin' rightful King of France" — allow the writer to make *Huckleberry Finn* a kind of international novel.

Mark Twain had been fascinated by pretenders to European titles and estates, including two of his own relatives, one claiming to be the rightful earl of Durham; later the author would write *The American Claimant* on the subject. (He would read much about the lost dauphin, Louis XVII, in a book purchased in 1882, Horace Fuller's *Noted French Trials: Impostors and Adventurers*.)

The portion of *Huck Finn* written in 1879–80 extends to the end of chapter 21. Colonel Sherburn has murdered the drunken Boggs, and an impulsive crowd of citizens is on their way to lynch him. Sherburn is presented unsympathetically. The writer was still not sure where the story was headed.

In the summer of 1883, with the effort of writing *Life on the Mississippi* behind him, the writer indulged himself by returning to the Huck Finn manuscript, and by August 22 he would judge that he had finally reached the end. He may have been encouraged by a sense that his story was topical, for much attention was being given at the time to the "Southern Question," and books realistically describing the South were in demand. The writer had read George Washington Cable's books, and on his Mississippi tour he had talked with Cable at length in New Orleans. Cable's enlightened view of the black race found expression in essays such as "The Freedman's Case in Equity" and "The Silent South," both of which appeared the same year as *Huckleberry Finn*. Indeed, when Mark Twain's book appeared, it would be read as another contribution to the nation's understanding of the South.[10]

Whatever led to the release, Mark Twain suddenly was able to write freely, as he reported to Howells in July from Elmira.

> I haven't piled up MS so in years as I have done since we came here to the farm three weeks & a half ago. Why, it's like old times, to step straight into the study, damp from the breakfast table, & sail right in & sail right on, the whole day long, without thought of running short of stuff or words. I wrote 4000 words to-day & touch 3000 & upwards pretty often, & don't fall below 2600 on any working day. And when I get fagged out, I lie abed a couple of days & read & smoke, & then go at it again for 6 or 7 days.

Because he had not particularly valued the book, he had not discussed this story with Howells recently, and he went on to write, "And *I* shall *like* it, whether anybody else does or not. It's a kind of companion to Tom Sawyer." By late August he could say to Howells, "I've done two seasons' work in one, & haven't anything left to do, now, but revise." These revisions were to be unusually extensive, however, and the book was not completely done until well into 1884.

The fact that the book was written at several times resulted in various inconsistencies, such as resurrecting Huck and Jim's raft after the reader had been told that a steamboat had "come smashing straight through the raft," and the portrayal of Colonel Sherburn, first seen as the murderer of "the best-naturedest old fool in Arkansaw," then converted into a spokesman for the author, expressing sentiments like those that Mark Twain himself had set forth in *Life on the Mississippi*.[11] In the last phase of composition, thoroughly confident in depicting the Mississippi River and its environs since he benefited from the revivifying 1882 trip, Mark Twain took Huck and Jim southward to Arkansas and Louisiana. But the book does not purport to present what Clemens had seen the year before. On its title page, *Adventures of Huckleberry Finn* is dated "Forty to Fifty Years Ago," or 1835–45. The writer could comment on the ugliness of "civilization" in America's heartland at that former time because of his familiarity with the travelers' accounts he had recently read for *Life on the Mississippi*. He had written admiringly of Mrs. Trollope's account, of her justifiable indignation at "slavery, rowdyism, 'chivalrous' assassinations, sham godliness, and several other devilishnesses."[12] The civilization that Huck observes in this earlier epoch is similarly disgusting; the latter part of the book suggests the author's disenchantment with the South and its backwardness forty to fifty years previously. Yet it also implies a disgust with certain features Mark Twain had observed during his 1882 Mississippi River visit.

Likewise he drew on the reading he had done in preparing himself to write *The Prince and the Pauper* (1881). Those history lessons, for example, give Huck the opportunity in chapter 23 to make an assessment based on *his* reading and experience.

Look at Henry the Eight; this'n 's a Sunday-School Superintendent to *him*. And look at Charles Second, and Louis Fourteen, and Louis Fifteen, and James Second, and Edward Second, and Richard Third, and forty more; besides all them Saxon heptarchies that used to rip around so in old times and raise Cain. My, you ought to seen old Henry the Eight when he was in bloom. He *was* a blossom. He used to marry a new wife every day, and chop off her head next morning. And he would do it just as indifferent as if he was ordering up eggs. "Fetch up Nell Gwynn," he says. They fetch her up. Next morning, "Chop off her head!" And they chop it off. "Fetch up Jane Shore," he says; and up she comes. Next morning "Chop off her head" — and they chop it off. "Ring up Fair

Rosamun." Fair Rosamun answers the bell. Next morning, "Chop off her head."

As Brander Matthews marveled in his 1885 review, the observations are so telling because Mark Twain's use of young Huck as narrator permits the author to "set down, without any comment at all, scenes which would have afforded the ordinary writer matter for endless moral and political and sociological disquisition."[13] Huck the storyteller cannot serve the author as a satirist: this boy doesn't know enough to denounce what he sees, although he can be appalled. Still, the general satiric technique of the book, subtly ironic, is far more effective than comparable sections of *Life on the Mississippi*.

The last part of the book includes some of its best passages — and some of the worst. The most admirable feature is an exploration of the concepts of liberation and subjection. As Huck and Jim travel down the river in the company of the Duke and the King, the reader is reminded of earlier events that now take on new meaning. When Jim and Huck are on the river by themselves, they are "free and easy and comfortable," as Huck points out in chapter 18. At the end of chapter 29, the two mistakenly believe that they are "free again and all by ourselves on the river and nobody to bother us." This image of Huck and Jim's earlier freedom seems more and more attractive as the Duke and the King successfully hoodwink the people along the shore. The behavior of the gullible victims becomes discouragingly predictable, as in their response to the "Thrilling Tragedy of THE KING'S CAMELOPARD or THE ROYAL NONESUCH" with its tag line "Ladies and children not admitted." The Duke observes astutely that "if that line don't fetch them, I don't know Arkansaw!" In the Tennessee town of the Wilkses, only two people are skeptical enough to escape the King and the Duke's victimization. Significantly, the writer had observed the "decay of independent thought" in the South on his *Life on the Mississippi* trip. During the 1880s, freedom from society and its conformist pressures apparently loomed as a more preoccupying theme to the author than the historical one of freedom from slavery that had provided the focal concern in earlier chapters on the river.

Huckleberry Finn is far and away Mark Twain's greatest book because the writing was a liberating experience for its author, freeing for a time the man whose "whole life was one long apology" from both the inhibitions of the culture he had chosen to embrace as well as the inexorable requirements of the subscription book. Now he spoke neither as Samuel L. Clemens nor as the almost relinquished Mark Twain, but as an outsider, Huck Finn. Through the amateur storyteller Huck, the celebrated novelist Mark Twain, who has been subjected to civilization, flees for a time to the river of his youth, escaping more completely and out of greater need than young Sam Clemens ever had. The exhilaration that the author felt provides the otherwise inexplicable energy behind the book, a display of originality and artistry seldom sustained in the writer's other books.

As Mark Twain's most richly conceived fictional creation, Huckleberry Finn exhibits a complex set of traits. He is an innocent, but with the exception of a few blind spots he is instinctively shrewd and far from naive. His resourceful imagination helps him to survive even though he has as his companion an escaping slave. He has fundamental convictions, which deepen as the book continues, in opposition to those of the society in which he is placed. His most meaningful attitudes are based on an acute moral apprehension. Because Huck is intelligent, quick, and inventive, he is able to survive, but because he is lower-class, without education or status, he is powerless to accomplish much. (Mark Twain's later hero, the Connecticut Yankee, shows what a hero *with* power could do, but most readers in our time have been appalled by what the Yankee awesomely accomplishes.) Huck's age is, as the author might say, slippery. He is fourteen but prepubescent; sometimes capable beyond his years, he seems often much younger than fourteen. He has no family — or worse than none, since his father is at best a parasite, at worst a sinister and sadistic alcoholic. But Huck's imagination conjures up sentimental stories in which he joins a close-knit family. He is ungrammatical, but he can spell — after a fashion. Most readers do not find themselves reading a book but listening to a skillful talker. Like his creator, who relished amateur playacting, Huck can assume a role with finesse and satisfaction. He is a nonconformist, partly by inclination and partly by ignorance. At the opening of the book, he is just starting to grasp, and largely to dislike, the ways of civilization. A pleasure-seeker, he nevertheless makes tough moral decisions. He has wide-open eyes; he is always alert, aware. Perhaps most magnetically, he is oblivious to his own worth — not modest or self-effacing but simply profoundly obtuse. As a narrator, Huck makes extensive use of a technique Mark Twain had developed early: telling not so much what happens as what was experienced, by the ear, the eye, all the senses. Occasionally Huck addresses the reader intimately, telling him almost privately what his senses make him feel.

Huck's reliability as a narrator and his appealing personality establish the central conflict of the book, which is not so much between Huck and his society as between Huck and himself. Throughout his adventures, Huck has an excruciating struggle that recalls the more amusing and more physical one between Mark Twain and his conscience in "The Carnival of Crime in Connecticut" (1876). Huck has been brought up in a slaveholding society that reinforced the basis of its peculiar institution by appeals to religious authority, especially that of the Bible. Victimized by this thorough indoctrination, Huck is able to help his friend Jim escape from slavery only by believing himself to be depraved. In chapter 31, Huck states his belief that "if I was to ever see anybody from that town [St. Petersburg] again, I'd be ready to get down and lick his boots for shame." In a notebook entry of 1895, Mark Twain refers to *Huckleberry Finn* in such a way as to suggest the centrality of Huck's struggle, writing of his belief in "the proposition that in a crucial moral emergency a sound heart is a safer guide than an ill-trained conscience. I sh'd support this doctrine from a book of mine where a sound heart & a deformed conscience come into collision & conscience suffers defeat. Two persons figure in this chapter: Jim, a middle-aged slave, & Huck Finn, a boy of 14, son of the town drunkard. These two are close friends, bosom friends, drawn together by community of misfortune."[14]

Huck Finn is not Mark Twain, but he nonetheless resembles the writer's identification of himself as both the innocent *and* the veteran. Huck displays his innocence when he himself is hoodwinked. He visits a circus and is taken in by a horseback rider whose cavortings give him a real scare. But mostly through Huck the writer was able to explore two intertwined themes that engaged him fully: the relationship of the individual to society, and the meaning of freedom. (In a late fragment, "Indiantown" [1899], Mark Twain was to suggest strongly that he had a bad conscience over his having won a shaky place in eastern society—by becoming a hypocrite.) Although Huck (like Melville's Confidence Man) wears a variety of masks and identities in order to survive, he never sacrifices his fundamental honesty. He skillfully copes with society, even that of the feudal and feuding Grangerfords, without losing his humanity; in fact, he becomes more human and achieves a stronger individualistic identity. He and Jim are most fully themselves on the raft, away from society's oppressions, as Huck insists at the end of chapter 18: "Other places do seem so cramped up and smothery, but a raft don't. You feel mighty free and easy and comfortable on a raft."

The writer and most readers approve of Huck's being an outsider, apart from a society dominated by sentimentalism, vulgarity, cruelty, and dying religion. The fact that Huck feels obliged to look up to Tom as an authority figure is powerfully ironic, since Huck's innate attitudes and actions provide a severe judgment on Tom. The best parts of the book are devoted to Huck's disenchantment with Tom and his artificial ways, Huck and Jim's comradeship on the raft, and Huck's celebration of freedom and nature. The reader and the writer know that one day the raft will have to tie up, that

Huck will have to return to a less isolated condition. Although he fantasizes about how he will "light out for the Territory," in none of the sequels can the author show Huck exercising his freedom: he ends up back again with Tom, once more looking up to him. There is no way for him to achieve self-fulfillment, for his creator was unable to conceive a setting that would permit the expansion of his consciousness. Huck is free, but has no place to go. He cannot grow up. Thus it has been argued that Huck's "function . . . is to demonstrate the absolute incompatibility of the sort of self he is and the sort of world in which he tries so hard to live."[15] Although Huck is a fully realized character whose tale is masterfully told, the seriousness of his continuing debate with his conscience concerning what to do with Jim is undercut by the fact that the writer used Huck simultaneously as a deadpan comic mask, as in the circus episode. Moreover, if Huck is to be understood as an innocent hero confronting evil, then his inner life is too simple for him to play a truly tragic role.[16]

Mark Twain drew on his personal experiences and his reading. The shooting of Boggs by Sherburn, for instance, is based on an incident of Clemens's boyhood in Hannibal. He recounted the story on four separate occasions in addition to the incident appearing in *Huckleberry Finn*. In his autobiography he described the event this way: "The shooting down of poor old Smarr in the main street at noonday supplied me with some more dreams: and in them I always saw again the grotesque closing picture — the great family Bible spread open on the profane old man's breast by some thoughtful idiot, and rising and sinking to the labored breathings, and adding the torture of its leaden weight to the dying struggles."[17] Colonel Sherburn's melodramatic address to the lynch mob that comes after him seems specifically to illustrate an idea that the writer had picked up from Thomas Carlyle's *French Revolution,* where after describing scenes involving Mirabeau, Marat, Robespierre, and Danton, Carlyle comments, "Is it not miraculous how one man moves hundreds of thousands?"[18] What is most remarkable is the author's skill in translating into the Mississippi River valley events that he had encountered only in books. Also contributing to the mob scene is the author's distress at southern violence and the tendency to resort to lynch mobs, as he indicated in a chapter written for *Life on the Mississippi* but deleted from the published version.[19]

The book also reflects several of the author's many ambivalences. These are especially evident — and troublesome — in the ending. The much-discussed "evasion" chapters at the end of the book are the result of the writer's dilemma. What could he do to resolve the conflicts of the plot? Were Huck to succeed in his plans, almost forgotten during the episodes with the Duke and the King, he would assuredly be a social outcast. To prevent that outcome, Mark Twain made elaborate plans to restore Huck to the community, even though earlier he had shown Huck to be superior to its values. He reintroduces Tom, then has Huck abandon the identity he has achieved by resubordinating himself to Tom. By Miss Watson's freeing Jim, society is transformed into a more decent-seeming institution. Now Huck does not have to face ostracism or life as an outlaw, and his earlier decisions to help the slave escape are proved to be without meaning. Jim, loyal to Tom as well as to Huck, receives compensation for the suffering inflicted on him in the form of forty dollars that Tom gives him, an act that might be read as symbolic of the author's own monetary terms of submission to social pressures. In the end, Huck does not celebrate Jim's freedom; oddly, nothing whatever is said about Jim's returning to his family. The book ends, not with Huck's return to Hannibal, but rather with Huck's determination to refuse to go back to his "home." Few readers find that they can accept what happens in the story after Tom reenters it. Mark Twain concluded his book by returning to a work of fantasy. John Seelye's *True Adventures of Huckleberry Finn* provides an intelligent if grim alternative with Jim's death and Huck's profound depression.

Mark Twain still believed that his books should be sold by subscription, but not with Osgood, who had failed to find many subscribers to *The Prince and the Pauper* and *Life on the Mississippi*. Enter Charles L. Webster, who was already acting as the author's business manager and had worked with Osgood on the sales of *Life on the Mississippi*. In May 1884, Mark Twain created "Charles L. Webster & Company," a new subscription publishing house, with Webster, who was married to the daughter of Clemens's sister Pamela, in charge. Although the firm was to have some successes, eventually it created enormous financial problems for the writer.

Mark Twain took unusual care to revise his manuscript instead of giving it to Howells for editing or shipping it right off to be published. The manuscript and surviving notes by the author show the attention he gave the work. For example, he wrote, "Back yonder, Huck reads & tells about monarchy & kings &c. So Jim stares when he learns the rank of these 2."[20] Jim needs to know something about royalty and nobility before the Duke and the King arrive. So Mark Twain wrote a long insert consisting of most of chapter 12 and all of chapters 13 and 14. Here Huck goes aboard the wrecked steamboat *Walter Scott* and obtains the loot, including books, that a group of thieves have collected so that he can "read considerable to Jim about kings and dukes, and earls, and such, how gaudy they dressed, and how much style they put on, and called each other your majesty, and your grace, and your lordship, and so on, 'stead of mister." The writer also took this opportunity to identify the poet-novelist Scott as the guilty purveyor of corrupt romanticism, as he had in *Life on the Mississippi*. The *Walter Scott* episode also helped emphasize Huck's charity and the contrast between the good life on the raft and the pervasive rascality of life on the land.

A full-dress scholarly edition of *Huckleberry Finn* would issue in 1988; in its preparation, the editors made use of the then-known three-fifths of the manuscript. Since then, the remainder has been discovered, and in 1996 what was described on the dust jacket as "The Only Comprehensive Edition" appeared; it included previously unknown passages found in the newly located manuscript. These are of very doubtful authority, since the author clearly did not choose to include them in the work published in England in 1884 and in the United States in 1885. Indeed, the longest addition, Jim's comical account of a visit to a dissecting room, is quite at odds with the sympathetic portrayal of Jim in the novel as the author ultimately chose to characterize him. The anticipated revision of the 1988 text will introduce no important changes.

The portion of manuscript available during preparation of the 1988 edition (at the Buffalo and Erie County Public Library) confirms the scope of the author's revisions. He made more than nine hundred textual changes, including deleting and adding whole paragraphs, and he rewrote extensively, especially his account of Huck's final struggles with his conscience. One telling change is the transfer of the speech of the King over Peter Wilks's coffin in chapter 25 from direct quotation to indirect reporting; Huck's reaction to the hypocrisy now becomes as significant as what the King said, although most of the King's words are preserved. The original version reads:

> Friends — good friends of the diseased, & ourn too, I trust — it's indeed a sore trial to lose him, & a sore trial to miss seeing of him alive, after the wearisome long journey of four thousand mile; but it's a trial that's sweetened & sanctified to us by this dear sympathy & these holy tears; & so, out of our hearts we thank you, for out of our mouths we cannot, words being too weak & cold. May you find sech friends & sech sympathy yourselves, when your own time of trial comes, & may the affliction be softened to you as ourn is to-day, by the soothing ba'm of earthly love & the healing of heavenly grace. Amen."[21]

This version is almost too good for the King. In the published version, Huck renders what the King said in a boy's language, which has no place for sentimentality.

Well, by-and-by the king he gets up and comes forward a little, and works himself up and slobbers out a speech, all full of tears and flapdoodle about its being a sore trial for him and his poor brother to lose the diseased, and to miss seeing diseased alive, after the long journey of four thousand mile, but it's a trial that's sweetened and sanctified to us by this dear sympathy and these holy tears, and so he thanks them out of his heart and out of his brother's heart, because out of their mouths they can't, words being too weak and cold, and all that kind of rot and slush, till it was just sickening; and then he blubbers out a pious goody-goody Amen, and turns himself loose and goes to crying fit to bust.

Like this one, most of the changes result in a distinct improvement; few are really softenings of the sort usually identified with Mrs. Clemens and Howells.[22]

Since at first the book was to be sold by subscription, time was required to set up an organization. Later, additional copies would be "dumped" — sold to retailers. Between completion and publication, extensive publicity was lavished on the book. Chapters appeared in the *Century* in December, January, and February — dutifully revised to suit the genteel taste of its editor, Richard Watson Gilder. Clemens read portions of *Huckleberry Finn* on a reading tour he made with George Washington Cable from November to February (a tour made necessary by the poor book sales of the volumes that Osgood had published). Parts were published in February in New York and Chicago newspapers. The writer made himself available to reporters to talk about the book. His onetime employer, the *Alta California,* noted that it was "probably the best advertised book of the present age."[23]

Several features of the book are often ignored by modern readers. The high-culture frontispiece is a heliotype of a solemn-looking bust of the author, based on a sculpture by Karl Gerhardt, who had just returned from three years of study in Paris, paid for by Mark Twain. Drawing attention to the bust would, the author hoped, give Gerhardt's career a boost and increase the value of the book. The bust showed the author in profile, looking like a Roman dignitary. His serious expression suggests that despite the "Notice" at the front of the novel warning readers to look for neither a motive nor a moral, the author knew that he had written an important book.[24]

The illustrations merit attention; they have been available to many readers through the several facsimiles of the first edition, the text published by the Mark Twain Project through the University of California Press, and the Oxford Mark Twain. Since the book was to be published by the author's own company, for the first time he could select the artist. He chose Edward

W. Kemble, an illustrator for the new magazine *Life* who also had made drawings for the *New York Daily Graphic*. Kemble was only twenty-three years old. Selecting the artist was only one step toward the author's full control of the appearance of the book that became his masterpiece; he intended to edit Kemble's drawings. As Albert Bigelow Paine was to explain, he "decided to have the *Huckleberry Finn* book illustrated after his own ideas."[25] His chief concern was to make the book as acceptable as possible to middle-class readers, even if the illustrations undercut its emphasis on violence. He told Webster that he did not want the artist to follow the book "too literally." Of special importance for Mark Twain was the portrayal of Huck, since the boy would not describe himself in his first-person narrative. In the author's imagination, Huck "is an exceedingly good-hearted boy, & should carry a good & good-looking face," he told Webster. True Williams's sketch of Huck in *Tom Sawyer* had not been flattering; Huck wore a full-length ragged coat and carried a large dead cat by a hind leg. Kemble's Huck — on the cover of the book — is better dressed and smiling, a person whom readers could readily accept. The author insisted that the characters not be "ugly" or "forbidding and repulsive," and he was pleased when Kemble chose to "modify his violences."[26] To avoid the unpleasant, Kemble even provided pictures that have no real basis in the text, such as "Henry the Eighth in Boston Harbor" and "Solomon and His Million Wives." Probably the most unfortunate aspect of the illustration is that Jim is shown as a comic, stereotypical black, never the kindly and humane person Huck discovers him to be. Mark Twain did not object. Kemble would eventually gain recognition as an artist whose specialty was the comic depiction of Negroes. He became noted for his openly derogatory if nonthreatening presentations of blacks, as is suggested by his own comment much later: "My coons caught the public fancy."[27] Twain chose a different artist for his next book; in 1889 he called Kemble's illustrations "tiresome" and said if they were handed to him today, "I would put them promptly in the fire."[28]

Adventures of Huckleberry Finn was "officially" published in the United States in December 1884 but was not actually available until the following February. (One reason for the delay is famous; in November, Webster learned that an obscene illustration had been included in the subscription agents' prospectus. Someone in the press room had maliciously tampered with an engraving of Silas Phelps; he was shown with his genitals exposed.[29] The printer so thoroughly corrected the book that not a single copy has been found that contains the offending illustration.) Canadian and English editions came out before Christmas.

There were favorable reviews in the *British Quarterly Review* and the *Westminster Review,* which found an "abundance of American humour of the best sort,"[30] and the aforementioned enthusiastic one in the *Saturday Review* by the American Brander Matthews. Contrary to what once was thought, the American press widely reviewed the book. The Hartford papers pointed to the "many pleasant episodes, innumerable original characters," the "extraordinary power" of the presentation of life along the Mississippi, and its "living pictures." Some reviewers recognized the author's strong moral sense. Thomas Sargeant Perry wrote in the *Century,* "Life teaches its lessons by implication, not by didactic preaching; and literature is at its best when it is an imitation of life and not an excuse for instruction." On the other hand, the book was condemned by the Concord, Massachusetts, library. One library committee member called it "the veriest trash." More striking than the negative reviews were the scattered negative, even hostile, comments that appeared here and there registering the extent to which the genteel were offended by the language and irreverence. The *Boston Advertiser* was one such; the *Springfield Republican* referred to the author's "low" moral level; and even the *Arkansaw Traveler* found the "vulgar humor" out of date.[31] The book nonetheless sold well: 51,000 copies in the first fourteen months.

How Clemens regarded the book is uncertain; perhaps he basically *felt* uncertain. He brashly told Webster that its rejection by the Concord public library was "a rattling tip-top puff" that would "sell 25,000 copies sure." He wrote to his sister, "Those idiots in Concord are not a court of last resort, and I am not disturbed by their moral gymnastics." When the Concord Free Trade Club made him a member, he amused himself by responding:

> A committee of the public library of your town have condemned and excommunicated my last book and doubled its sale. This generous action of theirs must necessarily benefit me in one or two additional ways. For instance, it will deter other libraries from buying the book; and you are doubtless aware that one book in a public library prevents the sale of a sure ten and a possible hundred of its mates. And, secondly, it will cause the purchasers of the book to read it, out of curiosity, instead of merely intending to do so, after the usual way of the world and library committees; and then they will discover, to my great advantage and their own indignant disappointment, that there is nothing objectionable in the book after all.[32]

The author must have found it harder to ignore his family's opinion. Daughter Susy complained that it was a reversion to her father's "old style" after *The Prince and the Pauper,* which she found much more satisfactory.[33] Yet the best evidence of what the author was thinking may well be the fact that he promptly returned to Huck when next he reached Quarry Farm.

Over the years, *Huckleberry Finn* became immensely popular all over the world, with 696 foreign editions already published by 1976 and translations into more than fifty languages. Among the many who have identified the contribution that *Huckleberry Finn* has made to the development of American literature are Ernest Hemingway and Ralph Ellison. Hemingway wrote memorably in *Green Hills of Africa* (1935), "All modern American literature comes from one book by Mark Twain called *Huckleberry Finn.* If you read it you must stop where Nigger Jim is stolen from the boys. That is the real end. The rest is just cheating. But it's the best book we've had." Ellison, noting that both black and white authors were able to employ the vernacular because of the example of *Huckleberry Finn,* asserted that Mark Twain "transformed elements of regional vernacular expression into a medium of uniquely American literary expression and thus taught us how to capture that which is essentially American in our folkways and manners. For indeed the vernacular process is a way of establishing and discovering our national identity." Among the other admiring American writers are William Faulkner and Sherwood Anderson.[34]

The evolution of Clemens's personal attitudes about race relations left behind a notable proof of his enlightenment. In the year when *Huckleberry Finn* was published in the United States, on the day before Christmas 1885, Clemens wrote to the dean of the Yale Law School offering to pay the boarding expenses of a black man, Thomas McGuinn. He offered as justification for what he was doing this explanation: "We have ground the manhood out of them [blacks] & the shame is ours, not theirs, & we should pay for it."[35]

But now business became a major distraction from writing; sadly, it would continue to interfere for many years. Not only publishing but inventions and investments took time, even with helpers such as Webster and his assistant, Fred J. Hall. By far the most important was James Paige's typesetting machine, to which he was drawn because he knew from experience how labor-intensive typesetting was. As early as 1881, Clemens had begun to put money into the machine, which was to be the disappointment of his life. Even while he was writing *Huckleberry Finn,* he invented a game to teach his children history, taking time out, he told Howells in July 1883, because he had "struck a dull place," where he did not know how to proceed. Soon the game and variations of it, along with their commercial possibilities, became a preoccupation that lasted into the next year.

In the summer of 1883, Mark Twain completed another story besides *Huckleberry Finn*. This one, "1002d Arabian Night," he intended to bring out anonymously, but Howells, who read it for him, reported in September that he felt "bound to say that I think this burlesque falls short of being amusing."[36] The long tale, only recently published, is intriguing chiefly because of its theme of switched identities. Two babies, one the child of the sultan of the Indies, the other the child of the grand vizier, are exchanged: the boy is brought up as "Fatima" and the girl as "Selim." The comic possibilities fascinated the author, but more tragic ones were to occur to him a few years later when the theme was revamped along the lines of race and the setting changed to Missouri, where it took shape as *Pudd'nhead Wilson*. Although his 1883 tale burlesques Scheherazade's tales, Mark Twain was in fact a great admirer of the *Arabian Nights*. He drew from this work more than any other except the Bible and Shakespeare. Nearly fifty references to it have been identified. Tom and Huck, for instance, both have read it.[37]

The fact that these three undertakings — the completion of his masterpiece *Huckleberry Finn,* the invention of a history game, and the composition of a farcical burlesque — all occupied Twain's mind at the same time is a frightening demonstration of how the pressures on him to be genteel and to make money caused him to resist and almost to betray his genius. His perspective is apparent in a report he sent his former publisher, James R. Osgood, who remained his friend. "The thing I am grinding at, now," he wrote on September 1, "is my long series of history games, the which I *caveated* in the patent office the other day. *They'll go,* I judge." He mainly valued the games for the dollars they might produce. Then, to complete his account of his activities, the inventor-author casually added, "I've finished '1002' (Arabian Nights Tale) & likewise 'the Adventures of Huckleberry Finn'; had written 50,000 words on it before; & this summer it took 70,000 to complete it."

Another work proved to be useful only when doctored into a play. In September 1881, Clemens had proposed to Howells that the latter write a play entitled "Col. Mulberry Sellers in Age." It would feature the colorful character from *The Gilded Age* and the successful drama that emerged from the novel, with Sellers now depicted at seventy-five and Lafayette Hawkins (based on Orion Clemens) at fifty. The plot would focus on Sellers's delusion that he was the rightful earl of Durham (much as the Duke pretends that he is the rightful heir in *Huckleberry Finn*), as well as on Sellers's "Impossible Inventions." Clemens wanted Howells to draft the plot and dialogue, though he himself intended to "re-write the Colonel's speeches &

make him properly vulgar & extravagant." In due time Howells explored the possibilities of producing such a play with several New York theater men, who encouraged him. Finally, in the fall of 1883, Howells and Clemens fell to work and collaborated on the project. Later they returned to it again and again. "No dramatists ever got greater joy out of their creation," Howells later wrote.[38] In their hands, the protagonist of *The American Claimant; or, Colonel Sellers as a Scientist* evolved into a near-lunatic. After being given several trial performances, the play died in 1887.[39]

The next thing the writer tried was equally unsuccessful. In January 1884, he began a novel about Bill Ragsdale, a half-caste interpreter he had met in the Hawaiian Islands. This was to be a serious work, and for it the author "saturated" himself "with knowledge of that unimaginably beautiful land & that most strange & fascinating people," as he wrote to Howells. The story was to begin "3 months before the arrival of the missionaries." Ragsdale's successful career had ended with the discovery that he had contracted leprosy; he then exiled himself to the leper colony on Molokai, where he died. Presumably the timelessness of the paradise that Hawaii had been was to be contrasted with what it became with the coming of "civilization" and the introduction of suffering and death from leprosy. That the writer chose to undertake such a politically sensitive story was possibly an act of atonement for having produced the most ungenteel *Huckleberry Finn*. So much is suggested by his comment to Mrs. Fairbanks, whom he especially wanted to see what he was doing. On January 24, 1884, he wrote to her: "I finished a book last week, & am shirking all other duties in order to give the whole remnant of my mind to a most painstaking revision of it— for this work is not a humorous but a serious work, & may damn me, tho' Livy says *No*. I do wish you would come & read it in MS & judge it, before it goes to the printers. Will you? You shall have till March 1st — 5 weeks." A few days later he wrote again, emphasizing the gravity of the novel. Very little survives of what he wrote that January, only a few pages of description, although he had referred to it as finished. Nothing more was said about the manuscript.[40]

The play and the lost novel were only two of many literary activities that occupied Clemens during the year following the completion of *Huck Finn*. In January he finished a dramatization of *Tom Sawyer* that he had begun in 1875, and in February he wrote to Charles Webster that it was "a *good* play, a good *acting* play." But it has nothing of the atmosphere of the novel, no Jackson's Island episode, and Tom is only sketchily characterized. Instead, the dramatist emphasized comedy. Not as bad as *Colonel Sellers as a Scientist*, its chief interest is a scene he told Eustace Conway he forgot to include in the novel: a school session with lessons on history, grammar, arithmetic, and spelling. The whole of act 4 takes place in the cave, where in this arrangement Tom and Huck save Amy and Becky from a threatening Injun Joe. Tom shows no signs of maturation. Told by Aunt Polly to kneel in repentance for his outrageous behavior, instead he stands on his head. Obviously written only for money, the play was rejected on the grounds that adults could not represent the dozens of children required for the cast.[41] Another effort at dramatization, this time of *The Prince and the Pauper*, likewise found no producer. Its text does not survive. (Later, in 1890, a version of the story was produced in New York, concerning which Clemens was soon engaged in a protracted lawsuit.)[42] The thrust of Clemens's motives was clear from his early 1884 letters to Howells, filled with calculations of potential dramatic royalties.

When Clemens and his friend Joseph Twichell attempted to learn to ride the bicycle in the spring of 1884, the author was soon setting down his experiences. He was following, as he had not always, a doctrine set forth a few months later in a letter to Olivia: "Whatever you have *lived,* you can write — & by hard work & genuine apprenticeship, you can learn to write well; but what you have not lived you cannot write, you can only pretend to write it." The bicycle essay is characterized by a return to Mark Twain's breezy earlier manner, reporting with good humor his disasters and catastrophes. The so-called expert who teaches him notes anxiously that he is not in proper physical condition: he describes Mark Twain's biceps as "pulpy, and soft, and yielding, and rounded; it evades pressure, and glides from under the fingers; in the dark a body might think it was an oyster in a rag." The finished essay is the result of much labor; the writer informed Webster that he "revised, & doctored, & worked at the bicycle article," but ended by not liking it. Paine, on the other hand, would enjoy "Taming the Bicycle" and place it in a collection published in 1917. Another misadventure, this time with a dentist, led the author to write "Happy Memories of the Dental Chair," incomplete and eventually published only in part.

The work of the summer of 1884 at Quarry Farm began with proofreading *Huck Finn,* with help from Howells. He commenced another project, an ambitious one, although it was to lead nowhere. Early in July, Clemens sent to Webster for copies of Richard Dodge's *Plains of the Great West* and "several other *personal narratives* of life & adventure out yonder in the Plains & in the Mountains . . . especially life *among the Indians.*" He needed these books because he intended "to take Huck Finn out there." He had promised as much at the end of Huck's initial story. For this sequel the author made extensive use of Dodge's book on the plains and also his *Our Wild Indians,* as well as numerous other sources — along with his own experience, for he had Huck and Tom follow the Oregon Trail through Nebraska to Wyoming, the route he and Orion had taken in 1861. Jim starts out with them, for he is eager to see the Indians.

What he accomplished is an informed account of the plains experience, but the treatment of the Native Americans, against whom Clemens had a long-standing prejudice, degenerates into stereotypes. Before he stopped, he had composed most of nine chapters. Then he put the work aside and (unlike Huck's first story) did not return to it. The fragment, "Huck Finn and Tom Sawyer Among the Indians," was first published in *Life* magazine in 1968, then in a 1969 collection.[43]

The opening sentences try to capitalize on the popularity of *Huckleberry Finn:* "That other book which I made before, was named 'Adventures of Huckleberry Finn.' Maybe you remember about it. But if you don't, it don't make no difference, because it ain't got nothing to do with this one." This fragment explored new territory, both literally and figuratively. The boys leave civilization behind and head west. Although Tom Sawyer's adventuresome spirit dominates the first chapter and part of the second, the book soon becomes more sober. Huck's experience on the prairie in chapter 4 is a discovery of his need for people, for civilization. "It was the biggest, widest, levelest world — and all dead; dead and still; not a sound. The lonesomest place that ever was; enough to break a body's heart, just to listen to the awful stillness of it. We [Tom is with Huck] talked a little sometimes — once an hour, maybe; but mostly we took up the time thinking, and looking, because it was hard to talk against such solemnness." Even Tom becomes relatively somber in the face of the immensity of the land. Huck has much to learn, for after the Indians attack a family of emigrants that the boys have joined, he gradually understands that the pretty girl the Indians have taken with them is apparently the helpless object of their sexual lust. The fragment breaks off with the boys and the girl's sweetheart still looking for her, but fully aware of what she has suffered, a painful knowledge. This time the author's inability to continue the story was not simply that his tank had run dry; rather, he seemed unable to make headway after Huck's loss of innocence. Despite what he had learned about human nature in his first book of adventures, Huck had at least preserved his basic innocence.

Twelve months after completing *Huckleberry Finn,* then, he had nothing to show except the revised manuscript. Otherwise there was only a series of misdirections and fragments. Probably during this period he drafted three statements of religious belief. Not published until 1973, these few sheets suggest that in the face of misfortune his attitudes could readily turn into bitter pessimism. The writer of these private documents acknowledges the existence of God but not in terms of providential intervention in man's world. The Scriptures, he states, were "imagined and written by man," the moral laws created by human experience. There is no system of divine reward or punishment. Whether there is life after death he is uncertain and "wholly indifferent." He finds biblical injunctions frequently wrongheaded and inconsistent. He levels most of his criticism at man's hypocrisy and tendency to be cruel. The Bible he calls "the strongly worded authority for all the religious atrocities of the Middle Ages."[44]

Clemens's skepticism about traditional Christianity had dated at least from his San Francisco days and had been amplified by his *Quaker City* experiences. For a while it was reined in as he joined a bourgeois society that embraced a liberal Protestantism — the society of the Langdons, Olivia Clemens, Hartford, and Joseph Twichell. He had adopted an innocuous kind of deism, accepting a belief in a God whose "beneficent, exact, and changeless ordering of the machinery of his colossal universe is proof that he is at least steadfast in his purposes."[45] The harsher, more misanthropic views now expressed in his statements of the early 1880s turned into an explosive diatribe in 1885, which was later inserted into his autobiography; here he attacked man's cruelty, malice, nastiness; any mortal is "the buzzing, busy, trivial enemy of his race."[46]

The writer who had established himself as a humorist was increasingly becoming a creature of moods. His anger was cloaked only by his fear of exposure, which would be detrimental to his standing as a successful commercial author. He resembled a businessman who wanted merely to protect the value of his reputation. Yet he became more and more convinced of the validity of his opinions, and as he repeatedly rehearsed their outlines, they rose closer to the surface of his consciousness when he wrote what he hoped would sell. This mixture of motives would make it more and more difficult for him to produce popular books of the sort that he had produced at an earlier stage. Indeed, after *Huckleberry Finn* he was never again to find a wholly satisfactory vehicle for the expression of his heartfelt concerns with freedom and authenticity.

CHAPTER SEVEN

Retirement Thwarted

espite his literary genius, Mark Twain usually thought of his writing chiefly as his means of making a living. But now he judged that other ways of making money looked easier and more effective. Paine quotes him as having said in his fiftieth year, "I am frightened at the proportions of my prosperity. It seems to me that whatever I touch turns to gold."[1] To a correspondent he confided, in July 1885, that the world might well view him as "the shrewdest, craftiest, and most unscrupulous business-sharp in the country." Later he had reason for greater modesty.

In February 1885, General Ulysses S. Grant, long one of Clemens's heroes, accepted a publication offer for his memoirs from author-turned-publisher Mark Twain, on behalf of Charles L. Webster and Company. From then until Grant's death the following July, Clemens was much occupied with Grant's progress and health. Clemens's daughter Susy recorded, "Mamma and I have both been very much troubled of late because papa, since he has been publishing Gen. Grant's book, has seemed to forget his own books and works entirely. . . . He said that he had written more than he ever expected to, and the only book that he had been pertickularly anxious to write was one locked up in the safe down stairs, not yet published."[2] (That work was presumably "Captain Stormfield's Visit to Heaven.")

The period from the end of the summer of 1884 to February 1891, better than six years, was the least productive in Mark Twain's writing career. During those years he actually thought of himself as being on the verge of retirement. His output can be summarized: several essays on copyright, now his favorite public cause; one slim story — a retelling, without much art or personality; two plays, one little more than a jeu d'esprit in English and German, a second that does not survive; two sketches, commendable but slight; a reminiscence / sketch; and a long novel. In 1906, the author had an explanation for such niggardly use of his talents in the middle of his career: "It was quite natural that I should think I had written myself out when I was only fifty years old, for everybody who has ever written has been smitten with that superstition at about that age."[3]

In a lengthy account of his dealings with Grant in the autobiography, Clemens blandly (and unrepentantly) reported that the general told him "he had stopped smoking because of the trouble in his throat," and was told by physicians that the quickest way to cure the problem was to stop smoking. Later Grant was diagnosed to have contracted throat cancer. "I am an excessive smoker," wrote Clemens, "and I said to the general that some of the rest of us must take warning by his case." Grant's doctor then said that excessive smoking was probably the "origin" of Grant's cancer, but that depression was "more than likely the real reason."[4] At any rate, Clemens stubbornly did not "take warning" and continued on his course as "an excessive smoker."

Following Grant's painfully slow death, Clemens busied himself over his funeral, the question of where the ex-president was to be buried, and the posthumous publication of Grant's *Memoirs*. The two-volume work proved to be a spectacular best-seller, with Grant's family receiving some $430,000 from its sales. In subsequent years the work received favorable critical recognition and appears, for example, in the Library of America series. An indication of Clemens's involvement in the project is the listing he provided a correspondent in February 1887:

> sold 610,000 single volumes at an average of $4.00 each;
> used 906 tons of paper,
> and in the binding 35,261 sheep, goat, and calf skins;
> 25 ¼ miles of cloth a yard wide;
> 275 barrels of binderpaste,
> $21,639.50 worth of goldleaf.

Although the project was highly profitable, Clemens chose to invest his earnings with Webster and Company. Unfortunately, Clemens made serious errors in judgment. Other difficulties included an embezzling bookkeeper and Charles Webster's limited business abilities. The result was that Clemens never thereafter profited from the company he had created.

The year 1885 thus held little time for literary work at Quarry Farm, and the summer of 1886 was similarly unproductive, though by then Mark Twain had finally begun a novel. He described it in November 1886, in a letter to Mrs. Fairbanks, as his "holiday amusement for six days every summer the rest of my life" and said that he did not intend to publish it "nor indeed any other book." He did plan, he said, to write two other books, only two, one of which would be his autobiography. The summers of 1889 and 1890 yielded nothing, for he had by then finished his "holiday amusement." Significantly, he was domiciled for only a month at his favorite writing location, in Elmira, in 1889, and in 1890 the family summered in the Catskills. (One reason for the change in 1890 was the death of Theodore Crane, who, with his wife, Susan, owned Quarry Farm.)

Clemens still expected that he would become wealthy from the Paige typesetting machine; he had begun investing in it in 1881. In 1885 he told Charles Webster, distinctly prematurely, "*Now* the dam typesetter is in lucrative shape at last. . . . It is in perfect working order (the machine is,) & stands ready & willing to submit itself to any test an expert chooses to apply." He was to be disappointed, but not until the machine required additional large quantities of both Clemens's money and his time over many more years. His patience (or foolish tenacity) was remarkable. He wrote to Orion in January 1888, "Everything promises that the typesetter will be finished & exhibiting its powers or its lack of them April 1st. Then my expenses on it will suddenly shrink to $300 a week & I shall be glad."[5] When his own funds for the machine were inadequate, he went on the road to find additional investors. The fiendishly complicated machine, now on exhibit in the basement of Clemens's Hartford home, left him convinced time and again that it was perfected or on the brink. Even when the rival Mergenthaler Linotype machine was a proven success, the investor's confidence continued. By Clemens's estimate, the Paige machine should have paid him $55 million a year! After pouring in nearly $200,000, he was chagrined at his inability to raise enough funds to buy all rights to the machine and its manufacture; yet in February 1891 he had nothing to show for his investments.

Several literary plans also failed to come to fruition. His notebook for April through August 1885 shows that he was thinking about an essay on wit and humor as well as a book on "Picturesque Incidents in History and Tradition." In the summer of 1888, he made notes for a play on the Franco-Prussian War of 1870–71, based on Alphonse Daudet's "Le Siège de Berlin." This he seems to have finished and intended to publish in the *Century* magazine.[6] But the play was not published and does not survive. Another effort, a dramatization of *The Prince and the Pauper* to which he contributed, produced no money for him, only frustration.[7]

Back in October 1877, Mark Twain had given a speech in Hartford at a dinner commemorating the anniversary of a military company. He drolly told the Civil War veterans, "I, too, am a soldier! I am inured to war. I have a military history." Then in an entertaining speech he related how at the onset of the war he had joined a Confederate company in which he served as "Second Lieutenant and Chief Mogul of a company of eleven men." After frequent moves to avoid the enemy for "a week or ten days," this unruly band complained of an insufficient supply of umbrellas and Worcestershire sauce and of being pestered by the enemy even before breakfast. Thereupon Mark Twain sought instructions from the brigadier under whose command they were supposed to be. He replied, "Stay where you are at this time, or I will court-martial and hang the whole lot of you." In response, the detachment (also referred to as a regiment and a brigade) "disbanded itself and tramped off home, with me at the tail of it."[8]

Perhaps because he had already dealt with them in a humorous way, he was receptive later to a request for his war experiences. Accordingly, his first fully realized work of these years was one proposed by Robert Underwood Johnson of the *Century*, which had published excerpts from *Huckleberry Finn*. In October 1884, the magazine had begun publishing a notable series of papers on "Battles and Leaders of the Civil War" with leaders such as Grant, McClellan, Longstreet, and Beauregard among the contributors. In a letter of May 11, 1885, Johnson described what he wanted as a "little article on your experiences in the Rebel Army, making it, as far as possible, characteristic of the state of things in Missouri early in the war. We have some difficulty, in covering that part of the field." Since Clemens was conferring with Grant at the time, he was able to talk with the general about "his and my first Missouri campaign in 1861."

In November 1885, Mark Twain completed "The Private History of a Campaign That Failed" and submitted it to Johnson, who accepted it enthusiastically. He called it "excellent — uproarious."[9] The piece promptly appeared in the December *Century*. Besides providing a humorous sketch, the writer judged that he would provide a socially acceptable answer to the embarrassing question, What did you do during the war? He had already told the rest of the story of his early years in his books: what his boyhood had been like, how he became a pilot, went west, then visited Europe. To answer the war question without embarrassment was not easy.

"The Private History" consciously fits the prescription that Johnson had provided, "the state of things in Missouri early in the war." Thus at the end of the essay the author dutifully describes his piece as a not unfair picture of what went on in many and many a militia camp in the first months of the rebellion, when the green recruits were without discipline, without the steadying and heartening influence of trained leaders; when all their circumstances were new and strange, and charged with exaggerated terrors, and before the invaluable experience of actual collision in the field had turned them from rabbits into soldiers. If this side of the picture of that early day has not before been put into history, then history has been to that degree incomplete, for it had and has its rightful place there.

Likewise, the humorous beginning of the essay makes clear that the author expected it to be read in the context of the larger *Century* series: "You have heard from a great many people who did something in the war; is it not fair and right that you listen a little moment to one who started out to do something in it, but didn't?" Thereafter Mark Twain purports to tell of his experiences of June and July 1861 with the Marion County, Missouri, Rangers, a small group of increasingly demoralized and disorganized volunteers.

In his account of the Marion Rangers Mark Twain makes use of two techniques that mitigate any charges that might have been made against him. The events of the war, *his* war, are treated in burlesque fashion; he makes them into a joke. Then he exaggerates his own youth and innocence. In the narrative he appears to be closer to sixteen than to his actual age of twenty-five. In addition, he uses the occasion to attack the very concept of war. In "The Private History," some men haphazardly became identified with the Confederacy, some with the Union, neither for very sound reasons. The one man killed in Mark Twain's war is Everyman, his death meaningless.[10]

Encouraged by the success of Grant's *Memoirs,* Clemens and Webster undertook several books on celebrities. Perhaps the most notable was Father Bernard O'Reilly's *Life of Pope Leo XIII.* Clemens was exceptionally enthusiastic. Joseph Twichell recorded in his diary that, according to Clemens, the publication would be "the greatest event in the way of book publishing that ever occurred; and it seems certain, M. T. will make a vast amount of money by it."[11] Howells records that his friend "had no words in which to paint the magnificence of the project, or to forecast its colossal success."[12] Something of the dimension of the undertaking is suggested by the fact that Mark Twain's publisher-envoy, Webster, accompanied by his wife, Annie, journeyed to Rome, where he gained an audience with the pope and was made a papal knight, complete with fancy uniform. The trip seems to have been designed to provide publicity for the book. Webster brought back a rosary for the Clemenses. In October, Clemens wrote to

Annie that the gift had "created such another stir in this household as was before utterly unimaginable." Olivia sought three more rosaries for the Catholic maids they employed. But the book was a monumental dud. Later Howells recalled, "The failure was incredible to Clemens; his sanguine soul was utterly confounded."[13]

The writer's high expectations for the Pope Leo book did not prevent him from tackling a book of his own. In December 1885, he had informed Webster, "I am plotting out a new book, & am full of it." The project was inspired by Clemens's encounter with Sir Thomas Malory's *Morte d'Arthur* in late 1884. During his lecture tour with George Washington Cable, he had written to his daughter Susy full of excitement at the book that Cable had encouraged him to pick up. "When I get home, you must take my Morte Arthur and read it. It is the quaintest and sweetest of all books. And is full of the absolute English of 400 years ago."[14] Soon he had made notes on the comic situation of a "knight errant in armor in the middle ages."[15] Listing the problems of such an armored knight — the inability to scratch, to blow his nose, to dress or undress — he seems to have thought of a burlesque. The next step was to envision the knight as a "Hartford man waking up in King Arthur's time," as Howells phrased it in January 1886 when commending the idea. This Yankee was to combine impressive mechanical abilities as well as the characteristics of both Clemens's current hero, General Grant, and the author himself.

Another contribution to the development of the novel was the author's careful review during the summer of 1885 of two chapters of W. E. H. Lecky's *History of the Rise and Influence of the Spirit of Rationalism in Europe* (1865), chapters that dealt with "The Declining Sense of the Miraculous." From this source Mark Twain derived a contrast in his story between the scientifically based "miracles" that his hero performs and the bogus "magic" of the hero's enemy, Merlin.[16]

Notes that the author made hardly suggest the pacifism implied in his recent "Private History," an inconsistency that seemed not to bother him in the least. An early entry in his notebook suggests violence on a scale that he had not previously depicted in his fiction: "Have a battle between a modern army, with gatling guns — (automatic) 600 shots a minute, (with one pulling of the trigger,) torpedos, balloons, 100-ton cannon, iron-clad fleet, &c & Prince de Joinville's Middle Age Crusaders." Another reads: "He mourns his lost land — has come to England & revisited it, but it is all changed & become old, so old! — & it was so fresh & new, so virgin before." This memorandum means that the author already planned for his Hartford man to revisit England in modern times. Another indicates that from very early the writer anticipated his misplaced Yankee's ultimate defeat: "Country placed under an interdict."[17]

Although Mark Twain seldom committed himself to writing while he was in Hartford, in February 1886, he told Webster that he had now "begun a book, whose scene is laid far back in the twilight of tradition: I have saturated myself with the atmosphere of the day & the subject, & got myself into the swing of the work. If I peg away for some weeks without a break, I am safe; if I stop now for a day I am unsafe, & may never get started right again." Ten days later Susy recorded, "Yesterday evening [February 21] papa read to us the beginning of his new book, in manuscript, and we enjoyed it very much, it was founded on a New Englanders visit to England in the time of King Arthur and his round table."[18] Since the author soon put the work aside, he must have thought himself "safe." He did not even take the manuscript with him to Elmira in the summer. At Quarry Farm he told an interviewer, "I made up my mind that I would loaf all summer," even though "the three summer months which I spend here are usually my working months."[19] Yet he had not discarded the work, for in November 1886 he read parts of it, "A Word of Explanation" and the first four chapters of what he called "The Autobiography of Sir Robert Smith of Camelot," to the members of the Military Service Institute and their guests at Governor's Island, New York. He briefly described how the rest of the work would develop the story, as he then anticipated. He even let reporters copy and quote parts of his manuscript. At this point, two plot elements were in reverse order from the form they would assume in the final version: the protagonist kills the king's opponents with gatling guns, then runs the kingdom himself, with the Knights of the Round Table thereafter becoming members of a stock exchange. The writer made the whole story sound amusing; later, he would shape a more sinister ending for serious purposes.[20]

These early portions of the story provide the frame, including the introduction of a Hartford man now temporarily named Sir Robert Smith but soon to be described as a Connecticut Yankee with expert knowledge from his experience as foreman in an arms factory. This Yankee wakes up in King Arthur's Britain and logically supposes, when he sees a medieval fortress, that he must be in Bridgeport, where showman P. T. Barnum had built a house resembling a castle.[21] An authorial voice begins "The Tale of the Lost Land," which is then told by the Hartford man who awakened on June 19, 528. An adventure story with much borrowing from Malory,[22] the narration dwells on the frankness of the spoken language in a prior day, an interest of Mark Twain's in his earlier "1601." This part of the story heads toward an event scheduled for noon on June 21, the narrator's execution.

His means of avoiding death had been suggested by Lecky's *Rationalism,* which related the frightening effect of an eclipse in prescientific times. When a selection from the manuscript appeared in the *Century,* the author provided an explanation that his Yankee's "escape from death at the stake [was] by means of a 'miracle'—at least he passed the thing off on those simple and superstitious people as a miracle."[23]

In the summer of 1887, after more than a year's neglect, Mark Twain returned to his *Connecticut Yankee* manuscript at Quarry Farm. There he described himself in a letter to Webster as working seven hours a day "in such a taut-strung and excitable condition that everything that *can* worry me, does it." His book reflected his tense, irritated mental state. He found himself, he wrote Webster, no longer writing a comedy; the work had "slumped into funereal seriousness." Among other distractions he found himself discouraged by a series of difficulties at his publishing house. Taking satisfaction from the wicked new tone of his narrative, he began to see potential advantages for sales. In a letter to Webster and his assistant, Fred Hall, he called it "an uncommonly bully book," "a 100,000-copy book, if Huck Finn was a 50,000-copy book." The portion written in 1887 *before* the tonal "slump" seems to have been chapters 5–12, with the exception of chapter 10, written later. In the brighter passages, the Yankee escapes execution by capitalizing on his knowledge that an eclipse of the sun is due. He threatens in chapter 5 that he "will blot out the sun, and he shall never shine again; the fruits of the earth shall rot for lack of light and warmth, and the peoples of the earth shall famish and die, to the last man!" Consequently becoming "the second personage in the Kingdom" next to Arthur and winning the title of "the Boss," he begins to flex his nineteenth-century inclinations.

Presumably the Yankee's defeat at the end of the book was already in the author's plan, for in chapter 8 he wrote, echoing Lecky's *Rationalism:* "Yes, in power I was equal to the king. At the same time there was another power that was a trifle stronger than both of us put together. That was the Church. I do not wish to disguise that fact. I couldn't, if I wanted to. But never mind about that, now; it will show up, in its proper place, later on. It didn't cause me any trouble in the beginning—at least any of consequence." Mostly the early part of the book is good-humoredly entertaining. The author cannot resist burlesquing tales of knighthood and chivalry in chapter 11 when the Yankee agrees to rescue the occupants of "a vast and gloomy castle," but such burlesque is in keeping with the creation of comedy. Troubles with consistency are evident in the language, which teeters between the genteel and the vernacular. The Yankee describes in chapter 11 his rescue mission with Alisande (Sandy), the damsel in distress. Everyone was respectful, except some shabby little boys on the outskirts. They said: "Oh, what a guy!" And hove clods at us. In my experience boys are the same in all ages. They don't respect anything, they don't care for anything or anybody. They say, "Go up, baldhead" to the prophet, going his unoffending way in the gray of antiquity [see 2 Kings 2:23]; they sass me in the holy gloom of the Middle Ages; and I have seen them act the same way in Buchanan's administration; I remember, because I was there and helped.

What kind of tone his Yankee was to employ was already problematic.

The discomforts that first attracted Mark Twain to the idea of writing a story about a knight in armor make their appearance in chapter 13. Trying to sleep without undressing before a lady, the knight is tormented by bugs, ants, and worms; he is frozen and "crippled with rheumatism." These discomforts are not truly amusing, however. Then the Yankee and Sandy meet a group of men repairing a road. The author pauses to provide a long, critical analysis of feudalism, hierarchy, monarchy, and the established church — once again reflecting discussions in Lecky's *Rationalism.* Hereafter the Yankee's adventures frequently serve as the occasion for such analyses, with this head superintendent of a Connecticut arms factory recalling "the ever memorable and blessed [French] Revolution" as part of the context from which he passes judgment on ancient English institutions.

In *Huckleberry Finn,* some of these same concerns had been explored but with less intensity and in better humor. There they were nearly always subordinated to the story: Huck's character and limitations rendered impossible any extended philosophizing. Moreover, whereas the earlier novel had been flavored by Clemens's reading in historians who wrote with a moral purpose, notably Carlyle and Lecky, now the author was aroused by a historian who was a polemicist. In 1886 and 1887, he had been reading *The People's History of the English Aristocracy,* by George Standring, an English radical thinker. This book moved the creator of the Yankee, since it was in keeping with private sentiments that he had been cultivating. Thus supplied with ammunition he was eager for his fictional spokesman to use, he echoed Standring's discussions of the evils of primogeniture and entail and the British devotion to nobility.[24] It was his old favorite, Lecky, however, who taught him to believe that the chief villain behind medieval society's ills was the Church.[25] Such reading now eroded his love affair with England, which had begun to fail with his 1879 visit. The shift in direction of the Yankee's story came about when Mark Twain transformed his hero into a crusader for modern liberal causes.

Before he left Elmira, the author had reached chapter 20, in which the Yankee completes his mission with Sandy — or supposes it is completed.

This section includes their extended stay at Morgan le Fay's castle, where the Yankee is exposed to an exhibition of inhumanity in the queen's dungeon. Touches of realistic humor implicate the narrator — or the author — in sadism, as when in chapter 17 he lightly gives Morgan le Fay permission to hang the band that repeatedly plays "In the Sweet By-and-By" — whereas the queen had ordered only the composer hung. Extravagant burlesque hardly blends well with his new, serious purposefulness.

Another influence was to be felt before the author returned to his manuscript. During the spring of 1888, Mark Twain was asked by L. S. Metcalf, editor of *Forum* magazine, to defend the United States against Matthew Arnold's condescending criticism in "Civilization in the United States." In the previous spring, Mark Twain had felt offended by Arnold's passing criticism of Grant's English in the latter's *Memoirs* and had delivered a patriotic speech defending the general. Now he was eager to write what Metcalf wanted, but found that he could not produce a satisfactory manuscript. Since Arnold soon died, he could not direct a reply specifically to the Englishman. Instead, Mark Twain planned to write a book on "English Critics on America: Letters to an English Friend," and in 1890 he did deliver a speech "On Foreign Critics."[26] But his more immediate task in 1888 was to finish his Yankee book. Some of what he drafted in response to Metcalf's request went into the novel when he did return to the book in the summer of 1888, back in Elmira. Getting a late start, he wrote only chapters 21–24, although he made notes then on how to finish the story.

In these chapters the Yankee shows off by the use of gunpowder and fireworks. He sounds like Tom Sawyer when in chapter 23 he explains, "You can't throw too much style into a miracle." Throughout this episode and the next, the Yankee keeps "his trademark current," improving his reputation for possessing supernatural powers. Clemens's notebook suggests that he identified himself with the Yankee in such comments as these: "I make a *peaceful* revolution & introduce advanced civilization." "The first thing I want to teach is *disloyalty* till they get used to disusing that word *loyalty* as representing a virtue."[27]

In October, after his short summer of writing in Elmira, Mark Twain took up his book again at Joseph Twichell's house in Hartford, where he went to avoid the interruptions he often complained of at home. He now composed chapter 10, "Beginnings of Civilization," which was necessary to explain introductions of the telephone, the telegraph, and other modern inventions. His treatment of slaves in chapters 24 and 25 is chiefly derived from a book on American slavery, *Slavery in the United States: A Narrative of the Life and Adventures of Charles Ball, a Black Man* (1837), although both

Lecky's *European Morals* and his *Rationalism* are other sources.[28] The presence of slavery here implies that the novel is at one level a continuation of the author's critique of the antebellum South in *Life on the Mississippi,* with the Yankee out to reform a world that Samuel Clemens had known in his youth. Chapters 27–33, more than one-quarter of the book, describe the Yankee's adventures while traveling with King Arthur, the story being carried on by travels, as in *The Prince and the Pauper,* in which Edward and Miles Hendon have a similar tour, and in *Huckleberry Finn,* in which Huck and Jim's voyage on the river is central to the plot. In all three books, the adventures — and calamities — provide an education.

The remainder of the book hastily disposes of several of the author's earlier ideas for the plot, with the Yankee killing off nine knights by revolver and transforming the remaining knights into railway conductors, sewing-machine salesmen, and the like. Without any previous hint to prepare for the event, the reader is abruptly confronted with the fact of Sandy's marriage to Hank Morgan, the Yankee having been given a full name at last in chapter 39. Their marriage permits the author to remove Morgan from the country so that in his absence a whole series of events can take place. Consequently, in chapter 42, Morgan and the reader are provided with a telescoped account of the developments, so rapid as to cause Morgan to exclaim, "What changes! and in such a short while. It is inconceivable. What next, I wonder?" The reader's sentiments exactly. The Church's interdict against the Yankee and the complete destruction of the advanced civilization he had created leave him with just fifty-two boys as his loyal followers. The holocaust that the Yankee and his boys then create is Mark Twain's most terrific use of violence, shocking and disturbing even to modern readers practically inured to mass destruction. The postscript returns the story to the nineteenth century, in a final interview between the reader of the Yankee's manuscript, who had been introduced in the preliminary "A Word of Explanation" (but now all but forgotten) and the dying Yankee. In March 1889, three years after Mark Twain had begun it in earnest, the novel was completed.[29]

A Connecticut Yankee in King Arthur's Court was published on December 10, 1889. But before it appeared, on November 4, the *New York World* published a damaging story headlined "Mark Twain Accused of Plagiarism." It explained that "the plot and many of the incidents [in *Yankee*] coincide with those of 'The Fortunate Island,' a story written by Max Adeler (pen name of Charles Heber Clark) and published in a collection in 1881." (The *World,* where the plagiarism charge originated, had a satiric and humorous column called "Personal and Pertinent," in which Mark Twain had frequently been treated with hostility. The once-honored humorist and satirist now was vilified as a capitalist and entrepreneur.)[30]

In point of fact, "Professor Baffin's Adventures," later entitled "The Fortunate Island," just may have inspired *A Connecticut Yankee in King Arthur's Court*. In Adeler's story, Baffin finds himself on an island where the inhabitants live much the way people did in the days of King Arthur. Like the Yankee, the professor shows off his nineteenth-century knowledge; both Baffin and Hank Morgan barely escape execution, and throughout both works, science is opposed to superstition. Adeler's islanders treat the past with reverence. Though the tone of Adeler's story is far lighter than Mark Twain's, and Adeler's story is much shorter, many other parallels can be noticed.[31]

In an interview he gave on January 12, 1890, Clemens said that he had heard about the charge, and in Howells's company he had purchased Adeler's book. He found it "very funny and brief, and I confess I not only enjoyed it, but was much relieved in mind when I had finished." His relief was quite possibly based on the fact that the story he read was not "The Fortunate Island" but another work by Adeler, "An Old Fogy"; both appear in the same 1882 Boston publication. During the interview, however, he acknowledged and advanced one of his pet theories — that there is such a thing as unconscious plagiarism.[32] When *A Connecticut Yankee* was about to appear, he was so troubled by the attack on his originality that he asked Sylvester Baxter, who had agreed to review his book favorably before publication, to "stand by to defend the Yankee from Plagiarism. . . . Come, protect the Yank from that cheapest & easiest of all charges — plagiarism."[33]

A second defense tactic was to relate the concerns of the Yankee to such contemporary events as the overthrow of the emperor and proclamation of a republic in Brazil, reports of the atrocities of the czar of Russia, and scandalous behavior by aristocratic Englishmen. In November, he wrote to Howells, "These are immense days! Republics & rumors of republics, from everywhere in the earth." He wanted his "book to speak now when there's a listening audience, alert & curious to hear — & try to make that audience hear with profit." He wanted his readers to see that what was original about the *Yankee* was the timelessness of its democratic tendencies, which he now conceived to be the central purpose of his book.[34]

In our own day, some readers find that the Yankee's destructiveness was prophetic of what technology would permit man to do against humanity, with Morgan an authoritarian villain, and some see the book as an indictment of industrial progress. The writer intended to signal something different. To his English publisher he wrote, "I wanted to say a Yankee mechanic's say against monarchy and its several natural props." When he selected chapters for magazine publication, he applied a summary of parts of the story, to which he supplied an interpretation. "Meantime the Yankee is very busy; for he has privately set himself the task of introducing the great and beneficent civilization of the nineteenth century, and of peacefully replacing the twin despotisms of royalty and aristocratic privilege with a 'Republic on the American plan' when Arthur shall have passed to his rest."[35] The ultimate defeat of the Yankee should not be read, therefore, as an indication of the author's growing pessimism, for the ending was in Twain's plans from the beginning, and of course there was no valid way he could end the book with historical integrity except by the complete destruction of the "beneficent civilization" that the Yankee created. Yet the defeat of the hero does not imply that his creator no longer believed in him or in progress. The mood of the "Final PS by MT" is indeed one of loss and even tragedy, as the dying Yankee grieves over his separation from his wife and child; such responses to domestic tragedy are only fitting and without broad implication. The author's own comment was: "If any are inclined to rail at our present civilization, why—there is no hindering him; but he ought to sometimes contrast it with what went before, and take comfort— and hope, too."[36] As an eminent Mark Twain authority has put it, the author of *A Connecticut Yankee* "assumed progress as a booming fact."[37]

After the unfavorable comments on *Huckleberry Finn* and its creator, the writer was determined that there should be nothing in his new book that could give offense. He first submitted his already revised manuscript to Edmund Clarence Stedman, a distinctly genteel poet and critic, who wrote a long critique. Stedman found only a few objectionable passages, including some reversions to what he chastisingly called the "peculiar early-manner-of Mark-Twain-ish exaggeration . . . *out of keeping* & mars the *vraisemblance*." He admired what his friend had done; he told Clemens, in sum, "You have let your whole nature loose in it, at the prime of your powers."[38] Still, Olivia Clemens, who was unable to read the manuscript because of an eye problem, was afraid that there remained "coarseness which ought to be rooted out, & blasts of opinion which are so strongly worded as to repel instead of persuade," Samuel Clemens told Howells in August, while assuring him that the book had been scrubbed clean.

Among passages deleted were some that are indeed coarse—the coarsest, probably, ever to appear in a manuscript Mark Twain was writing for publication, as well as passages that reflected the author's growing pessimism. For example, pronounced vulgarity appears in a description of the priest at Morgan le Fay's castle in chapter 17.

He was the private chaplain, and the royal family were devoted to him, could not do too much for him, although they tried. That is, they married him to a comely young girl, one of the chambermaids, who enriched him with a ready-made family of royal origin, natives of the castle — a pleasant way of providing for the private chaplains of noble families which was to retain its popularity in England for eleven or twelve centuries yet — barring an interval between the abolition of Catholic priest-marriages and erection of the Protestant Established Church.[39]

Another deletion shows the writer's unfolding misanthropy. In chapter 20, after Sandy flings herself upon hogs she believes are distressed damsels, a long passage, absent from the published version, recounts the Yankee's reaction. It reads, in part:

> Yes, we are just as pitiful and shabby as we can be, we human beings, in some of our aspects, but it is seldom that we are confronted with the fact and forced to recognize it. All Beliefs that are not our Beliefs, are Superstitions; all Superstitions are Grotesque Absurdities. Why certainly — of course. It is a truism.
>
> I despised Sandy for hugging the hogs, for it showed that she was the slave of a grotesque and absurd superstition that the apparent hogs were not hogs, but ladies. But I presently remembered that I had only recently sloughed off the Roman-Catholic-Presbyterian belief that a baby that dies without some ecclesiastical mummeries over it, is burned in hellfire forever and ever because of that omission. So Sandy was but the mirrored reflection of my very recent self, after all — and of course no longer despicable. (pp. 668–69)

The elimination of such opinions as these was partially motivated by the author's assumption that he was at the end of his career. In August 1889, he told Howells that the book was "my swan-song, my retirement from literature permanently," and he used a self-dramatizing metaphor to represent his determination to end his career in a way that would not distress his wife. "I wish to pass to the cemetery unclodded." Howells's efforts to purify the text further gave "peace to Mrs. Clemens's soul," her husband declared. As it turned out, however, Mark Twain was to be far more heavily clodded for his Yankee than for the errant Huck.

A Connecticut Yankee is Mark Twain's only major work of a period when he was seeing himself in a new light. He was older; he had read much, especially in historical writings; he had traveled; he had entered the world of business and for a time experienced considerable success. In an America whose dominant values were shaped by the free enterprise system, he could think of himself as positioned in the mainstream. For example, his opinions were being sought, respectfully, by journal editors; he was in effect being asked to speak for America. In 1886 he had shown the breadth of his concerns by delivering an address advocating respect for the American wage earner, a tribute to the Knights of Labor.[40] While finishing his new book, he drafted a series of prefaces that indicate his belief that he had written a book with major implications. His first concerns, he wrote, were the "odious laws which have had vogue in the Christian countries within the past eight or ten centuries," and these he had illustrated "by the incidents of a story." His second concern was "human liberty," which he described as being just a hundred years old and even now reserved just "for white people."[41] Profoundly influenced by Lecky, he saw Christianity — or rather the powerful established church — as the opponent of humane laws and of liberty, for the church inculcated qualities of submission, passivity, and respect for the status quo. Consequently, the people of Arthur's England, from lowest to highest, could see the Yankee as a human being deserving respect and dignity. Thus the church's training was the source of all that was wrong with the society that Mark Twain's time traveler visited, and in chapter 18 the author's philosophy bursts forth didactically:

> Training — training is everything; training is all there is *to* a person. We speak of nature; it is folly; there is no such thing as nature; what we call by that misleading name is merely heredity and training. We have no thoughts of our own, no opinions of our own: they are transmitted to us, trained into us. All that is original in us, and therefore fairly creditable or discreditable to us, can be covered up and hidden by the point of a cambric needle, all the rest being atoms contributed by, and inherited from, a procession of ancestors that stretches back a billion years to the Adam-clam or grasshopper or monkey from whom our race has been so tediously and ostentatiously and unprofitably developed.

The idea came right from Lecky — and out of another book, Charles Darwin's *The Descent of Man*.[42]

A "laboratory novel," *A Connecticut Yankee* considers the question of whether men can be trained to become participants in responsible self-government. The answer is a qualified affirmative. King Arthur shows that retraining can work, but the credulity, irrationality, and conformity of many of the king's subjects are too deeply dyed for reformation. The thesis suggested by the conclusion is derived from Lecky, who developed the concept of reversion. Arthur's subjects have been so victimized by their earlier training that they revert to being mere animals when terrorized by the church's interdict.

How the writer felt about his book as an expression of his feelings and his thoughts, derivative or not, is suggested by a letter written in August 1889 to Howells, who had just sent the author a favorable report on his manuscript. Now, perhaps with a sigh, Clemens wrote: "Well, my book is written — let it go. But if it were only to write over again there wouldn't be so many things left out. They burn in me; & they keep multiplying & multiplying; but now they can't ever be said. And besides, they would require a library — & a pen warmed up in hell."

He was, however, very much aware of what he wanted the illustrations being prepared by Daniel Carter Beard to provide. "I have aimed," he wrote Beard, "to put all the crudeness and vulgarity necessary in the book, and I depend on you for the refinement and scintillating humor for which you are so famous." When he saw Beard's illustrations, he was delighted. He termed them "charming & beautiful," and he called Beard's sense of humor "delicious." Later he wrote to Beard, "Hold me under permanent obligations. What luck it was to find you!" Beard's illustrations appeared in both the American edition and the English, the latter being entitled *A Yankee at the Court of King Arthur.* Beard's satirical drawing of the slave driver as a version of Jay Gould gave the book a sense of contemporaneity.[43]

Webster and Company was of continuing concern for Clemens. Its financial condition was now so unsound that some kind of change in management was mandatory. In April 1888, Webster was given what was referred to as a year's leave of absence, although he realized that in actuality he was being given a polite dismissal.[44] Fred Hall took over, but the company was in hopeless condition. The only hope was that the *Yankee* would restore the company's health.

The *Connecticut Yankee* was intended to appeal to both English and American readers, although to his English publisher Clemens had written that "the book was not written for America; it was written for England." But English readers were likely to find that the Yankee confirmed Matthew Arnold's view that Americans were materialists who lacked culture. For American readers, prospective purchasers of another subscription book, the *Yankee* was described as an answer to "the Godly slurs that have been cast at us for generations by the titled gentry of England. . . . Without knowing it the Yankee is constantly answering modern English criticism of America, and pointing out the weaknesses and injustice of government by a privileged class."[45]

A Connecticut Yankee was widely reviewed: eleven American reviews, eleven British, and one Australian review have been identified. The range of reaction was considerable, from laurels to clods. The book was called offensive, laborious, vulgar and delightful, clever, and delicious. One extreme, perhaps, was the admiring reviewer who found it "impossible to read . . . without seeing that the great American humorist has been moved by the spirit of democracy." He identified as themes of the book "human equality, natural rights, unjust laws, class snobbery, the power of the rich and the dependence and oppression of the poor."[46] Howells had similar comments in his January 1890 review in *Harper's*. At the other end of the critical spectrum was the British reviewer who found that Mark Twain "has turned didactic, and being ignorant is also misleading and offensive."[47] English readers were also offended because Twain was dealing with Arthurian legends that Lord Tennyson had all but sanctified in his *Idylls of the King*. They might, moreover, have detected that Daniel Beard had depicted Merlin to resemble Tennyson.

Much to the author's disappointment, the book sold only 32,000 copies in the United States during the first year. Despite Fred Hall's efforts, the Webster Company was in such bad condition that it was unable to pay Clemens anything at all, and the British response was so negative that sales of all of the author's books were hurt.[48]

With two books in a row being described in some quarters as vulgar, Clemens wrote to an English friend and admirer, Andrew Lang. A surviving draft shows it to have been a long letter in which the author defends himself from critics. These people judge, he complains, by "the cultivated-class standard," while writers, such as himself, might choose to address "the mighty mass of the uncultivated," the class that, he contends, he had merely sought to entertain, since he was "not qualified" to "help cultivate the cultivated classes." He asked Lang for help in persuading critics to value what is written for "the Belly and the Members" as well as what is "written for the Head." Written in an excess of modesty, the letter is not to be taken as reflecting the author's final view of himself, but it does suggest that he was painfully hurt by objections to his two most recent novels. He was all the more sensitive because he had thought of them as marking the end of his illustrious career.

During much of his career, Mark Twain had traded on his standing as a writer from the West, distinctly not part of the genteel establishment, and not as a bookish person. But in fact the author was a great reader. When he was asked in 1890 the Desert Island Question—What books would he select if he were limited to just a few? — his answer indicated that he had not separated himself from the literary tradition he gave the impression of having rejected. His choices were the works of Shakespeare, the poems of Robert Browning, Thomas Carlyle's *French Revolution,* Sir Thomas Malory's *Morte d'Arthur,* the historical writings of Francis Parkman (which he had read while preparing *Life on the Mississippi*), *The Thousand and One Nights* (better known as *The Arabian Nights*), James Boswell's biography of Samuel Johnson; the dialogues of Plato, and Samuel Pepys's diary.[49] Although the list is that of an autodidact, it is hardly eccentric.[50] Later he was to add to this list of favorites the *Memoirs* of the duke of Saint-Simon (1675–1755), Suetonius's *Lives of the Twelve Caesars,* and the Rubáiyát of Omar Khayyám, to which he was to add verses of his own.[51]

Other writings of the *Connecticut Yankee* years are slight. For "English as She Is Taught," Mark Twain provided simply a framework and running commentary on schoolchildren's boners, most in the matter of vocabulary. He published it in the *Century* for April 1887; it appears in the "Definitive Edition." "Meisterschaft," a play in English and German, was written for the young people who laboriously studied German at the Clemenses' home.[52] It was published in the *Century* in January 1888.[53] In "A Majestic Literary Fossil," a slight piece of journalism, composed in 1889 and published in *Harper's,* Mark Twain unearths a medical dictionary of 1745 and provides a commentary on quoted passages. Like the play, it helped fill the pages of the "Definitive Edition." In the midst of these quite forgettable pieces, another is considerably more original: "A Petition to the Queen of England," written in the fall of 1887 and published in *Harper's.* Informed that he owes income tax on his British royalties, Mark Twain petitions the queen, since the tax in question was granted to "Her Majesty." "My idea had been that it was for the Government, and so I wrote *to* the Government, but now I saw that it was a private matter, a family matter, and that the proceeds went to yourself, not the Government." Spinning the piece out with reminiscences of seeing the prince of Wales, irrelevant details, and citations from the official document he has received, the writer adopts a version of his early manner, playing the sublime fool, a naive, simpleminded man from the country. The chief difference is that the author has now become a personage, a fact that he reflects in his petition, though with the utmost modesty. Whereas in the *Yankee* Mark Twain is frequently angry, here he is calmly self-assured. He presents himself as altogether well meaning but not very bright. He avoids several possible lapses into familiar comedy routines to maintain a consistent and charming personality. The sketch, though slight, is a milestone worthy of attention, since the appearance of the original "Mark Twain" was a rare phenomenon in the late 1880s.

Sometime after the completion of the *Yankee,* perhaps late in 1890, the writer began two articles, and while he finished neither, they suggest that he had reached another turning point, not in technique but in attitude. The earlier is entitled "Letters from a Dog to Another Dog Explaining and Accounting for Man: Translated from the Original Doggerel"; it anticipates one of Mark Twain's last works, "Letters from the Earth." The letter-writer tries to explain that human beings are ridiculous, selfish, and cruel only because of their environment. All man's foibles, including his belief that he ascended from lower animals and his invention of heaven (which excludes all animals except himself), are explored. But the dog-narrator asks for generosity: "Give a man freedom of conscience, freedom of speech, freedom of action, and he is a Dog."[54] Although the piece is playful, it is Mark Twain's most severe indictment of humanity to date, more sweeping than the one inspired by Sandy's embracing of the hogs. But before he abandoned the "Letters," he began a kind of sequel, "A Defense of Royalty and Nobility." Here the author of the *Yankee* reverses the position he took in the novel by arguing that Americans who condemn monarchy and nobility are hypocritical, since they revere millionaires and those whose membership in the Four Hundred results from having the right ancestors: "ancient Dutch peddlers & barkeeps of the region." He then cites chapter 6 on kingship and nobility in his own Dog Letters in order to argue that it is not environment but human nature that makes man both seize privileges and admire reverentially those who hold them.[55] This is a striking about-face. *A Connecticut Yankee* implies that real progress is possible for man, that he deserves better than he gets. In other words, training is everything. But here he argues that human nature itself is the important *given*. These ideas would turn up in his next novel, and for many years the writer would dwell on this low estimate of human nature, as he had in the comments about Sandy and the hogs. Personal misfortunes would only intensify this attitude later. The most obvious sources of his pessimism at this time were his financial disappointments and the various physical ailments that more and more frequently incapacitated him.

During the late 1880s, Clemens found many occasions to visit New York City. In January 1888, he had the good fortune of being identified with the creation of the Players Club, organized by the actor Edwin Booth and the producer Augustine Day. When the Players Club acquired a house on Gramercy Park, Clemens thereafter had a pleasant and familiar place to stay in New York, and he often stayed there, especially in the 1890s.

In February 1891, Clemens realized that he could no longer devote thousands of dollars a month and much of his energies to the typesetting machine and that he would have to return to the pen as a means of making a living. (How much he invested is not clear. He had written Howells fifteen months earlier than he had spent "more than $3,000 a month for 33 consecutive months." But the total was probably close to $300,000.) His investments and his heavy living expenses required that he make certain changes immediately. Already he had borrowed $10,000 from his mother-in-law. "He dug out from his pigeonholes," according to Paine, "such material as he had in stock"[56] and arranged for the publication of "Mental Telegraphy," written fourteen years earlier, and "Luck," a thin and unoriginal story composed in 1886. Both were published in *Harper's*. Sometime in 1891, again according to Paine, he drafted a statement, perhaps a letter, in which he examined his life and his career, with emphasis on what he had learned from the varieties of work he had done, as printer, pilot, soldier, prospector, reporter, platform lecturer, financier, publisher, and author. He concluded, wisely, that "as the most valuable capital or culture or education usable in the building of novels is personal experience, I ought to be well equipped for that trade" (p. 916). The author seemingly was endeavoring to rededicate himself to his true career, although he had wandered into sixth-century England and King Arthur's court and would again wander very far from his personal experience. How could he believe, one wonders, what he wrote when he declared in a letter published by Paine, "I confine myself to life with which I am familiar when pretending to portray life"?

As he returned to his career as a writer, his first effort began as a salvaging operation. He novelized the play on Colonel Sellers to which he and Howells had once devoted so much time and affection. (The idea of making a novel out of it dates from as early as 1884.) The new book was begun on February 20, 1891, and a few days later Clemens announced to Howells that his title was "Colonel Mulberry Sellers, American Claimant of the Great Earldom of Rossmore in the Peerage of Great Britain."

At the outset of the task, the author was unusually elated. He wrote to his brother in February 1891, "I think it will simply howl with fun. I wake up in the night laughing at its ridiculous situations." He wrote to Fred Hall, "I have written 10,000 words on a book whose canvass [for orders] is to begin *September 1*, and issue Dec. 10 with 75,000 orders — and not a single one short of that." In other words, he was requiring Hall to find 75,000 readers who would buy his book.

Soon crippled by rheumatism, he tried dictating into a phonograph, only to find, as he told Howells in April, that the device "hasn't any ideas & it hasn't any gift for elaboration, or smartness of talk, or vigor of action, or felicity of expression, but it is just matter-of-fact, compressive, unornamental, & as grave & unsmiling as the devil." The manuscript contains the author's note at the end of chapter 11: "Here follows 6,000 or 8,000 words done on the phonograph. The cylinders will be found (uncorrected &

execrably worded) in my billiard room, if wanted."[57] Presumably these words were later transcribed and typed for the author. More likely the phonograph had something to do with the glaring faults of the novel. Maybe the explanation was what he told Joe Goodman: "I am at work again — on a book. Not with a great deal of spirit," then, bolstering himself, "but with enough — yes, plenty." The novel was completed just seventy-one days after it was begun, and shortly thereafter the author sold the rights to periodical publication for $12,000 to the McClure syndicate, which published it in various American newspapers and, in England, in the *Idler* magazine. The book was published in 1892 in the United States by Charles L. Webster and Company, with illustrations by Daniel Beard, and in Great Britain by Chatto and Windus.

Clemens wrote Howells in May that in writing the novel he had salvaged only half a day's writing from the script of the play. Because his inspiration to begin with was the play, he told his story largely by means of dialogue, with only a few comments from the author, mostly about the distinctively English characteristics of one of his two central characters. The story begins with two of the secondary elements of the play, Colonel Sellers's eagerness to become an earl and his conviction that the rightful heir, who falls in love with his daughter, is in reality his "materialization" of a dead man. The basic idea of the claimant in both the play and the novel stemmed from the belief of Clemens's distant cousin, Jesse M. Leathers, that he was the rightful earl of Durham. Leathers had even sought out Clemens as a financial backer and had promised to split the profits if the author would provide him with legal expenses. The idea fascinated Clemens, who himself daydreamed of discovering that he might be the earl of Durham. Mark Twain's original claimant has a name like Clemens's cousin — Simon Lathers, whose death, just before the action of the novel begins, permits Colonel Sellers to take his place as the American Claimant. What had dominated the play, Sellers's preposterous scientific inventions, figure as well in the novel. The only dialogue that Mark Twain borrowed from the play concerned Sellers's invention of a cursing phonograph for timid sea captains.[58]

Outwardly Lord Berkeley, who travels to America, resembles some of Mark Twain's earlier innocents who learn from their experience, but this time there is little opportunity for humorous adventures. Except for a few scenes in which he is introduced to the horrors of the boardinghouse (scenes that echo the experience of Dickens's Martin Chuzzlewit), much of Berkeley's initiation is by way of lecture and discussion, not incident. All that remains of Mark Twain's optimism in *The American Claimant* is the ridiculous figure of Colonel Sellers, who is "always keeping breast to breast with the drum-major in the great work of material civilization" (chap. 8). The novel ends with his describing his latest project: furnishing climates, for a fee, by controlling sunspots. It is as if Sellers is Mark Twain's Yankee with nothing left but demented dreams.

The American Claimant is Mark Twain's response to his own *Yankee*. But whereas the earlier novel, despite its preachiness and muddled thinking, had strong imaginative appeal, its successor is the writer's weakest novel— crowded with plot, theses, ideas, and heavy-handed satire. Writing quickly, he used his own serious social analysis of only a few years earlier as the object of his attack, for then he had been guilty, according to his newest spokesman, of leaving out "the factor of human nature" (chap. 14). This tendency toward pessimism had been observable for some time, but the collapse of his dreams of great wealth and his other disappointments were contributory. Now he no longer had faith in progress or democratic reform.[59]

The reviews of *The American Claimant* were better than the book de-served. The *Academy* of London found the book "quite up to the author's usual standard" but noted that the humor is "somewhat monotonous." Another London journal was less generous, noting that "extravagance and exaggeration are no longer wholesome farce, but wearisome and fatuous, occasionally something worse." The *Spectator* singled out Mark Twain's treatment of Colonel Sellers as "one of the most characteristic pieces of American humor of extravagance that we have ever seen."[60] The American press was largely silent.

The most striking of several changes in the author's life and writings at this time was an obligatory mobility. On June 6, 1891, the Clemenses went to Europe again, chiefly because of Mrs. Clemens's health — but because of her husband's, too. They would soon discover another reason to live abroad: with a diminished income, they could escape the enormous costs of their Hartford home. They did not suspect they would never live in their beloved house again. What began as a trip intended to last six months was to become a ten-year odyssey. During these years Clemens visited America frequently on business; in 1893–94, one stay lasted nine months. But his residence was in Europe, in Aix-les-Bains, Marienbad, Berlin, Bad Nauheim, Florence, Munich, Paris, London, Lucerne, Vienna, and elsewhere, with a full year occupied with a round-the-world lecture tour. The retreat was symbolic of his state of mind. He was an American writer who had virtually lost his once inimitable voice and was groping now even for his identity.

CHAPTER EIGHT

Searching

Although the Clemenses needed money badly, for a time what Mark Twain managed to produce was of little value. Encouraged to take himself seriously, he had grown intellectually as the result of his reading, his interest in political liberalism, and his religious and philosophical questioning. But if *The American Claimant* botch was taken as representative of all that he could now produce, his literary career appeared to be over. At any rate, in Europe he turned away from imaginative writing to journalism while he awaited a likely literary idea. If none came, he could once again try a sequel to something he had created previously. But he no longer had the luxury of abandoning tasks that proved disappointing, as he had with the English book of the early 1870s. He was obliged to cash in, if at all possible, on what he could produce. He kept especially alert for novelties and current fads. Being across the sea from editors with whom he had to transact business probably would prove an added difficulty.

Olivia's health was increasingly a serious concern. As early as 1891, before the Clemenses began almost a decade of residence in Europe, Olivia experienced disturbances of the heart, and, according to her husband's autobiography, doctors had repeatedly warned that she might have only two years to live.[1] She was often obliged to spend extended periods in bed and was sometimes a semi-invalid; her shortness of breath would amount to a nagging reminder of her limitations.

In Europe during the summer of 1891, Clemens tried to combine health cures for his wife and himself—he suffered from rheumatism in his arm—

with writing for much-needed money. For the McClure syndicate and the *New York Sun,* he had contracted to send six letters from Europe at $1,000 apiece, and by the end of August he had produced four. The family's first stop was Aix-les-Bains, which Olivia had been ordered to visit. Thus Mark Twain's first letter was "Aix — The Paradise of the Rheumatics," a pleasant piece of ephemeral journalism — as they all turned out to be. Two passages are worth attention. The buildings of Aix alerted the author to the drift of time, especially to passing belief systems. He was most interested in changes in human conceptions of the deity. It was chiefly the vastness of the universe and the insignificance of man's planet that engaged Mark Twain. "To-day He is a Master of a universe made up of myriads of gigantic suns, and among them, lost in that limitless sea of light, floats that atom," the earth, "a mere cork adrift in the waters of a shoreless Atlantic." The writer's imaginative grasp of the dimensions of the universe had the effect of increasing his pessimism, for in comparison with an immense cosmos, man seemed very insignificant.

Another side of his discouragement comes into focus in this essay: his perception of man as an incubator of diseases, a theme he would explore fully in "Letters from the Earth." Here, however, his attitude is humorous. He reports meeting a man who came to the baths to learn if he had any ailments. If he did have any, he was told, the baths would make them appear. The doctor's prognosis proves valid as each day the baths cause more and more illnesses to be apparent, until after the fourth treatment he becomes "one vast, diversified, undulating continental kind of pain, with horizons to it, and zones, and parallels of latitude, and meridians of longitude, and isothermal belts, and variations of the compass — oh, everything tidy, and right up to the latest developments, you know. The doctor said it was inflammation of the soul, and just the very thing." Except for this facetious anecdote, there is no fictionalizing, just description and report.

From Aix the Clemenses went to Bayreuth for ten days, "At the Shrine of St. Wagner," as he called his account. His attempt to arrange for the journey there provided him with material for an account of a traveler's ineptitude, "Playing Courier," which was good-natured but slight. The letter on Bayreuth mixes appreciation of Richard Wagner's operas with amazement at the reverence with which they are treated; it is on the whole a sober account. Next comes "Marienbad — A Health Factory," which describes the Clemenses' trip to Bohemia and the health treatments, all briskly but unremarkably described. One might have hoped that in getting his body in order, Clemens might have put his writing arm back into shape, but the evidence shows no such thing. Another humdrum essay resulted from the Clemens family's trip to "Switzerland, the Cradle of Liberty" in September.

To prepare for more ambitious travel writing, Clemens left his family to make a ten-day trip down the Rhône. Eventually he drafted 174 pages of "The Innocents Adrift," but though he was optimistic for several years about the results, he finally gave up the project. A version heavily edited by Paine would appear in *Europe and Elsewhere* (1923). In the fall the Clemenses settled in Berlin, where the writer devoted three days and nights to the translation of *Der Struwwelpeter*, which he called "the most celebrated child's book in Europe." In October, he told Fred J. Hall, who had succeeded Charles Webster on his retirement, that he expected the Webster Company, as well as Chatto and Windus of London, to publish the translation, illustrated. But the book did not appear until 1935, when Harper and Brothers published it as *Slovenly Peter*, a collection of verses about the fates of naughty children, with a preface by Clara Clemens, the translator's surviving daughter.

In Berlin the family lived for a time at an unsavory location, innocently selected, with the writer composing a sketch on the subject, "Koernerstrasse," which his family persuaded him not to publish. Instead, he supplied a sixth and final letter on "The German Chicago," full of admiration for Berlin, written while he was recovering from pneumonia. Another piece written at this time, "Postal Service," exists only as an unpublished fragment. Both pieces repeatedly compare American and European ways.

Mark Twain was already a noted literary figure in Germany. Many of his works had been translated into German, including *The Innocents Abroad, Tom Sawyer, Life on the Mississippi,* and *Huckleberry Finn.* In Berlin, Mark Twain was much sought after by journalists, who interviewed him, and he met intellectuals through the American ambassador, William Walter Phelps. Through his cousin Mollie Clemens von Versen, wife of a Prussian general, he met Emperor Wilhelm II and members of his court, an occasion he remembered in a December 6, 1906, autobiographical dictation. He was "greatly pleased that his Majesty was familiar with my books," he recalled.[2] But he also had to take to his bed for most of a month, suffering from "congestion of the lungs," as he told Fred Hall. (Probably the illness was a consequence of his heavy smoking.)

The old, original Mark Twain was still alive, although he had become shy about making public appearances. During that Berlin winter he appeared privately, a fact well hidden for almost eighty years. In a sketch initially entitled "A Singular Episode" but later referred to by the author as "The Late Reverend Sam Jones's Reception in Heaven," Mark Twain — who identifies himself by name in the sketch — manages to obtain entrance into Heaven by exchanging passes with the sleeping archbishop of Canterbury on the train to New Jerusalem and Sheol. This furtive exchange leaves the archbishop with the damnable reputation of "a professional humorist," a person of "frivolous nature and profane instincts." Yet the archbishop turns out to be satisfied to go on to Sheol when he learns that a fellow passenger, the Texas evangelist Sam Jones, has won admission to heaven. Despite his "special, illuminated, gilt-edged personal pass," Mark Twain is soon in trouble for being what he describes as "a light speaker" — in other words, a blasphemer. The brief sketch ends quickly when all the inhabitants of heaven rush for the underworld after getting an earful of Jones's preaching.

In this unpretentious and charming story, Mark Twain takes obvious satisfaction in seeing himself as a highly questionable personage amid the genteel circles of heaven. The manuscript bears this annotation: "Not published — forbidden by Mrs. Clemens. — S.L.C." But the author could read the story as after-dinner entertainment, as he also read "Captain Stormfield's Visit," and he reported to Mrs. Clemens the pleasure he took from an 1894 reading. In November 1907, he commented,

> I was ever so fond of the "Reception" article, and dearly wanted to print it, but it was hilarious and extravagant to the very verge of impropriety, and I could not beguile my wife into consenting to its publication. In that day Sam Jones was sweeping the South like a cyclone with his revival meetings, and converting the unconverted here and there and everywhere with his thundering torrents of piety and slang. I represented him as approaching the New Jerusalem in the through express, and in the same pullman in which he and his feet together were occupying two chairs, sat his grace the Archbishop of Canterbury (Mr. Tait) and I.[3]

The sketch was finally published, inconspicuously, in 1970.

Meanwhile, Hall published through the Webster Company a thin collection of Mark Twain's writings entitled *Merry Tales,* consisting of "The Private History," "Luck," "Meisterschaft," "Playing Courier," and two older pieces, "A Curious Experience" and "Mrs. McWilliams and the Lightning." Much more important was the fact that the Webster Company continued to publish books that did not sell and that its debts were constantly increasing. But at this time Clemens did not pay much attention. He had other matters on his mind, such as his health and that of his wife. In March they sought a milder climate and so headed south, to France and Italy, before returning to Berlin.

"Sam Jones's Reception" was truly "a singular episode." Because of his poor health, Clemens wrote to Hall in April 1892, "I do not expect to write any literature this year. The moment I take up a pen my rheumatism returns." Very likely his lack of inspiration had something to do with his physical problems. At any rate, soon his pen would be as busy as ever. The beginning of the deliverance seems to have followed a two-week visit to the United States on business in June. (This was the first of six visits, totaling over twelve months, that Clemens made between his departure with his family in June 1891 and their return in May 1895.) On the way back, he drafted "About All Kinds of Ships," a formless piece that compares his 1892 ship with ones he has traveled in before; it provides an imaginary interview in which Noah is questioned by a German ship inspector and a description of what sailing on Columbus's ship might have been like — and whatever else occurred to the writer. (The essay appears in the Definitive Edition.)

In August 1892, Mark Twain finally found something that engaged him, a story that at first he called "Huck Finn in Africa." The basic idea of the story had come to him back in 1868, when he recorded in his notebook, "Trip of a man in a balloon from Paris over India, China, Pacific Ocean, the Plains, to a prairie in Illinois, in a balloon." Soon he began writing this sketch in his notebook, but before he had finished it, he noted, "Jules Verne's 'Five Weeks in a Balloon' came out," and he dropped it.[4] Later, in 1876, he used a version of the plot idea to take a man mysteriously to the prairie in "A Murder, a Mystery, and a Marriage," which is still unpublished, and in a deleted portion of *Life on the Mississippi* there is a tall tale of a balloon adventure.

In 1892 a new idea inspired Mark Twain to return to a balloon story, but although the idea does not appear in what he wrote, it excited his creativity. Only five days after he had begun what had been "Huck Finn in Africa," he reported to Fred Hall that he had written half, or 26,000 words, of a book he was now calling "Huckleberry Finn and Tom Sawyer Abroad" or "Huckleberry Finn Abroad." He thought of it as the first of a series, with the serviceable Huck as narrator in each. The two boys and Jim would visit Germany, England, and other locales. By finding a way to stop the story and then start it up again, he thought he could write a novel (really a novella) in two parts. In this fashion he could soon have the first part ready for serial publication.[5] He did find a way, although an obviously contrived one, to stop the story, and this part, some 30,000 words, was published as "Tom Sawyer Abroad" in *St. Nicholas,* a children's monthly magazine, since the Clemens family insisted it was a story for girls and boys.

The plot idea that had started Mark Twain on *Tom Sawyer Abroad* was not employed in the first half. But the first half was all there was to be; the author held back from writing more to see if the first numbers should prove popular, then failed to return to it. Although *Tom Sawyer Abroad* is a sequel to *Tom Sawyer,* not *Huckleberry Finn,* in that it lacks any real seriousness, it deserved better than it received at the hands of the editor of the magazine in which it appeared, Mary Mapes Dodge, to whom the author sold the story for $4,000. He thought he knew what the editor of a children's magazine expected, for he told Hall, "I tried to leave the improprieties all out; if I didn't, Mrs. Dodge can scissor them out." Scissor she did. She made Huck's language more genteel and reduced references to bodily functions, alcohol, and death, to African Americans, and even to church groups that might have been offended. In Mrs. Dodge's version, "scabs" became "scars," "sore places" are "tender spots," and Jim becomes a "darky," not a "nigger." A long preposterous passage — some eight hundred words — was cut from chapter 8, about the place of swearing in the Catholic church, based presumably on the anathema. Huck asks Tom, "Can a bishop cuss, now, the way they useter?" To which Tom replies, "Yes, they learn it, because it's part of the polite learning that belongs to his lay-out — kind of bells letters as you may say — and although he ain't got no more use for it than Missouri girls has for French, he's got to learn it, same as they do, because a Missouri girl that can't polly-voo and a bishop that can't cuss ain't got no business in society" (chap. 8). Presumably the writer learned of Mrs. Dodge's alterations, for he wrote to Hall that he should use the original version, not the bowdlerized *St. Nicholas* printing, as the basis for *Tom Sawyer Abroad* in book form. Perhaps the letter arrived too late. At any rate, when the Webster Company published the story as a book in 1894, the edited *St. Nicholas* text was used as the basis of chapters 1–9 of the publication and the authoritative typescript only for the remainder. To read what Mark Twain had written for publication — presumably after the work had been censored by Mrs. Clemens — one must go either to the English text, which seems to have been based on a copy of the original, or to the recent Iowa–California edition, published in the same volume as *Tom Sawyer* and based on the holograph manuscript. There the author is identified (as in the first edition) as Huck Finn, with Mark Twain indicated as the editor. (Unfortunately, the Oxford Mark Twain, using only American first editions, includes the Webster and Company text of *Tom Sawyer Abroad.*)

Tom Sawyer Abroad begins as the boys' next adventure after *Huckleberry Finn,* its mood being that of the final chapters of *Huck.* Huck asks, "Do you reckon Tom Sawyer was satisfied with all them adventures? I mean the adventures we had down the river, and the time we set the nigger Jim free and Tom got shot in the leg. No, he wasn't." (In *Huckleberry Finn* Jim is never called "nigger Jim.") The story takes Huck, Tom, and Jim in a navigable balloon from St. Louis to Africa. There they have a series of adventures, beginning in the Sahara, where they rescue a kidnapped child and experience a sandstorm. They discuss the possibility of importing Sahara sand to America, but decide against it when Tom shows a sophisticated familiarity with import duties. After Jim and a guide picked up in Egypt return to Missouri to fetch a corncob pipe for Tom, they come back with word that Aunt Polly insists on Tom's return. Upon Tom's getting his pipe, the story abruptly breaks off with this sentence: "So then we shoved for home, and not feeling very gay, neither." Mark Twain wrote to Hall that the story, although he could have continued it, "doesn't need another finish." Few readers would agree.

This first published sequel to *Huckleberry Finn* places the three familiar characters—or rather feeble imitations of them—very far from the reality that Mark Twain knew, lofted above in a balloon to have adventures that never truly take place. Was this story written by the Mark Twain who satirized Tom Sawyer's romantic notions and showed us Huck facing the grim facts of poverty and ignorance on the river? Huck does express pleasure at being away from civilization, but he refers not to the reality we have seen him meet but the "reality" introduced by letters in the mail and newspapers that "fetches you the troubles of everybody all over the world, and keeps you down-hearted and dismal most all the time, and it's such a heavy load for a person" (chap. 7). The Huck who traveled by Mississippi raft is largely absent.[6]

Huck tells the story—but not nearly so well as he had told about his experiences on the river. The air through which the balloonists travel is, like the river in *Huckleberry Finn,* essentially a place of safety, and Mark Twain shows skill in picturing what they see in the desert below. But the focus is on Tom, whose aggressive leadership again makes Huck and Jim into his straight men. This Huck is less innocent than ignorant and far too full of admiration of Tom, and this Jim is simpleminded and quite lacking in dignity. The story—if it can indeed be said that there is a story—is disappointing, despite some amusing touches, for nothing is made of the trip; it is purposeless. One conjectures about what it might have been had Mark Twain delivered the episode that served as the genesis of the story: "Somewhere after that great voyage," he wrote Hall, Huck "will work in the said episode and then nobody will suspect that a whole book has been written and the globe circumnavigated merely to get that episode in an effective (and at the same time apparently unintentional) way." The absence of this "said" episode or any other excuse for the balloon trip, except as a pleasant celebration of ballooning, severely limits the story.

Daniel Beard prepared the illustrations for publication in the *Saint Nich-*

olas printing, and they appeared in the book; Mark Twain liked them. *Tom Sawyer Abroad* was published as Charles L. Webster & Company's last book, with copies arriving in Washington, D.C., for copyright on the very day of the company's failure. Only the English edition received the attention of reviewers. Critics found it a disappointment to admirers of both Tom and Huck. Needless to say, the book publication was not remunerative to Clemens. The author, the manuscript, and the germ of the story—whatever it was—all deserved better results than they got.

While still revising *Tom Sawyer Abroad,* Mark Twain went on to a novel he had begun earlier in the summer of 1892. The story of the composition of *Pudd'nhead Wilson,* which is now one of the most frequently read of Mark Twain's works, provides valuable insights into Mark Twain's weaknesses as a writer and consequences of his commercial motivation. To express his ideas on racism, identity, and dualism, Mark Twain returned to antebellum Missouri. Although inspired by several original devices, ultimately he was unable to create a unified work and, in order to salvage his writing efforts, he chopped his story into two, neither part of which is satisfactory.

Mark Twain began the work upon hearing about the Tocci twins, who had one body, two heads, and two distinct personalities. (He may have read about them in the December 12, 1891, issue of *Scientific American.* The frontispiece of "Those Extraordinary Twins" shows the author looking at a poster about "Wonderful Twins.") He conceived of it as a "howling farce" and was supremely gratified by his achievement. "I think all sorts of folks will read it," he told Hall. "It is clear out of the common order—it is a fresh idea—I don't think it resembles anything in literature." Since 1869, when he had written about Chang and Eng, twins joined by a ligature, he had been fascinated by Siamese twins. Later he would refer to this "crude attempt to work out the duality idea, which has puzzled and interested the world during so many ages."[7] The twins he now wrote about, Angelo and Luigi, like the Toccis, were connected: "conglomerate twins," he called them, whose comic possibilities vastly stimulated the writer.

Count Luigi and Count Angelo create a great sensation when they arrive in a small Missouri town. They are soon found to disagree about everything: the use of intoxicants, religion, politics. There is romance, with Angelo finding that he has a rival not in his brother but in Tom Driscoll, "nephew" of a local judge.

The writer became interested in a plot for determining the responsibility of an act by one of the twins, with some "scientific" method, perhaps palmistry, put to use. Soon he saw that the amusing questions raised by the twins concerning responsibility were potentially parallel to similar questions about race. To create an analogy, he would have Tom Driscoll's mother, a light-skinned member of the black community, identify herself to her adult son and explain that she had switched him while he was a baby with a white child who had been brought up as a slave, one Chambers. The mother, Roxana, would then use her information to blackmail Tom into stealing from Judge Driscoll, who was Tom's father — a fact he had kept from Tom. During the robbery, Tom kills the judge, who first identifies himself in an attempt to prevent his murder. So much, at least, seems to be suggested by two manuscript notes in the Mark Twain Papers. One reads, in part:

> "Spare me! — I am your father!" (He was hesitating — had concluded that he couldn't do it.)
> "Now for *that,* you shall die."
> (Kills him) Tom (Chambers) is to be pardoned — he is glad — but when he finds he is a valuable slave, he commits suicide.

The second in its entirety reads:

> Shall we have baby foot-marks of Tom and Chambers taken at 10 months to prove legitimacy of Chambers after Tom's suicide & declaration of what Roxy told him?
> *Yes.*[8]

When Mark Twain reached approximately this point, the Clemenses moved to Florence, where they arrived in September for a nine-month stay. In the winter of 1892–93, Olivia was, according to Susan Crane, "very far from strong & well, being obliged to live in seclusion, & be free from all extra care, & all excitement. . . . Her difficulty is of the heart, which necessitates a quiet life."[9] In mid-November, the writer picked up his story again, excited by a new possibility regarding identification. He had been reading Sir Francis Galton's just-published book, *Finger Prints,* and was fascinated by this newly discovered technique for crime detection. Its pages suggested to him a climactic murder trial. Moreover, a secondary character, assigned the hobby of collecting fingerprints, would now become a major character. As Mark Twain put it in a letter to Fred Hall, "The minor character will now become the chiefest, and I will name the story after him, 'Pudd'nhead Wilson.'" Later (in June 1895) he told a correspondent that the accident of hitting on Galton's book "changed the whole plot & plan of my book." Working long and hard now, as much as thirteen hours a day, he completed a story of 60,000 to 80,000 words by December 20. What had seized his imagination was a sensational courtroom scene in which Wilson would reveal by means of fingerprints the true identity of the men who had been switched as babies. After completing this big scene, he filled in the early episodes in which Wilson fingerprints the babies, Roxy exchanges them, and then, after the passing of time, Tom torments the white boy, now considered black, with whom he had reversed roles. The Italian twins remain the focus of much attention, although they are not present in the most suspenseful scenes.

This version of the story, which survives in manuscript form at the Morgan Library in New York, suffered from three weaknesses. First, because Mark Twain wrote the ending before he composed many of the scenes for which it was intended to be the denouement, he gave too much attention to the showman Wilson and too little attention to those most affected by the revelation, Tom and his mother, whose roles are slight in the manuscript. Second, since he not only created new scenes that involve Tom but also retained ones from his earlier version, Tom is inconsistently portrayed. The original Tom was white; the revised one is partly black. Thus in the published version in chapter 10 Tom is haunted by the discovery that he is, by Southern racial standards, black; in chapter 11 that obsession does not appear, the chapter having been written before chapter 10 — before the author had decided to give Tom black blood. Third, the book still contained farcical scenes involving the Siamese twins, quite out of keeping with the grimmer elements. But despite these flaws, the author decided that he had finished. The introduction of the fingerprint notion had been exhausting. He explained to Hall that he had "to entirely re-cast and re-write the first two-thirds," and although the original composition "didn't cost me any fatigue," "revising it nearly killed me," he wrote to Laurence Hutton. "Revising books is a mistake."

In February 1893, he sent his manuscript, which he considered complete and good, to Fred Hall, "type-writered and ready for print." About a month later, Clemens himself headed for America, and there Hall apparently discouraged him from publishing the story in its present form. Once again the author showed himself to be a poor judge of his work, for the manuscript was at this time a botch. After a brief visit, he returned to Italy with his manuscript. By late July, he was in Germany, having again revised the novel. In the new version he had subordinated but not eliminated the twins and had separated them; they are no longer "conglomerate." But he failed to revise his manuscript thoroughly, and vestigial remains of the twins' former nature remain. For example, Angelo describes in chapter 6 how they had been "placed among the attractions of a cheap museum in Berlin," obviously in their status as freaks. Second, he pruned the story to focus it on the murder and the trial. He gave this emphasis because, as he explained to Hall, the fingerprints idea was "virgin ground — absolutely *fresh,* and mighty curious and interesting to everybody." He did little rewriting, too little; mainly he deleted. Novelty and sensationalism would presumably sell books; a serious, probing study of race relations would not.

The condensing made the story acceptable; it was sold to the *Century* for $6,500 and was published in seven installments from December 1893 to June 1894. At least on the basis of timing, the book can be said to make a contribution to an understanding of the cultural basis of race, since it was published during the decade when "Jim Crow" laws were defining the place of the African American in American life. *Plessy v. Ferguson,* in which the Supreme Court legalized segregation based on the principle of "separate but equal" facilities, had originated in a case involving a light-skinned man.

A year after Mark Twain had finished the final revision, he salvaged what he had discarded about the twins to make it into a separate story; the twins return to their conglomerate state. He added some connecting, summarizing links without even troubling to hide them (he put them within brackets in reduced type), and wrote a self-denigrating preface in which he described the history of the tales. Because of the impatience with which the writer performed the "literary Caesarean operation," as he graphically called it in his preface, the more important of the two, *Pudd'nhead Wilson,* is not a satisfactory story.

Since Webster and Company was no longer in business, the author arranged for publication of both stories together by his old publisher, the American Publishing Company of Hartford. The two parts of *The Tragedy of Pudd'nhead Wilson and the Comedy of Those Extraordinary Twins* were illustrated by F. M. Senior and C. H. Warren. (Senior alone did the illustrations for *Twins.*) The illustrations fill the margins and available white space. Here blacks are pictured as wholly black, with stereotypical thick lips and smiling faces, but Roxana, Tom, and Chambers are white. But once Tom is identified as a slave, he is thereupon pictured as black. The twins of *Pudd'n-head Wilson* have been separated, whereas in the illustrations of *Twins,* they are humorously depicted with four arms that function in an ill-coordinated manner when the twins try to eat. Yet the two stories seem almost as fully connected as Angelo and Luigi remain in the second story. All parts of the book should be read together, including the preliminary "Whisper to the Reader" and the author's preface to *Twins.* These latter two items in fact link the stories. Moreover, there are thematic relationships: the relationship of

Angelo to Luigi, the conglomerate twins, is analogous to Mark Twain's characterization of the relationship of blacks to whites under slavery; the efforts to determine individual responsibility by legal classifications defining the status of Siamese twins is analogous to efforts to determine the status of racially mixed offspring.[10]

The presentation of ideas about the influence of training, the problem of identity, and the effect of role exchange are blurred. Specifically, the book appears to argue that race is insignificant and training all-important. The notion is set forth as a generalization in "Pudd'nhead Wilson's Calendar" at the beginning of chapter 5: "Training is everything. The peach was once a bitter almond; cauliflower is nothing but cabbage with a college education." This thesis is persuasively demonstrated by the "white" Tom Driscoll, brought up as a slave and permanently damaged by the experience. But what of the false, "black" Tom, brought up as an aristocrat? His mother says in chapter 14 that his weakness, his cowardice, is a result of his black blood: "It's de nigger in you, dat's what it is." Her comment is to be understood as the author's irony: slavery has made black people despise their own race — but not altogether ironic, for the false Tom seems truly bad by nature. If the source is not his blood, perhaps it is his training as a slave master. But aristocrats are paradoxically characterized as honorable men, especially the most prominent, Judge Driscoll.

What Mark Twain wrote originally — and presumably what he meant to convey — was clear enough. In the chapter now designated chapter 10, just after Tom's recognition that because he is partly black he can be sold like a dog, the author provided the following explanation, later unfortunately deleted.

In his broodings in the solitudes, he searched himself for the reasons of certain things, & in toil & pain he worked out the answers:

Why was he a coward? It was the "nigger" in him. The nigger *blood?* Yes, the nigger blood degraded from original courage to cowardice by decades & generations of insult & outrage inflicted in circumstances which forbade reprisals, & made mute & meek endurance the only refuge & defence.

Whence came that in him which was high, & whence that which was base? That which was high came from either blood, & was the monopoly of neither color, but that which was base was the *white* blood in him debased by the brutalizing effects of a long-drawn heredity of slaveowning, with the habit of abuse which the possession of irresponsible power always creates & perpetuates, by a law of human nature. So he argued.[11]

In other words, training has ruined Tom—inherited training. It is not his black blood, which is insignificant (one part in thirty-two), but his inborn submissiveness (from his one slave parent) that determines his character. This Lamarckian doctrine is what Mark Twain had offered as an explanation of Tom's behavior, although he chose to have Tom see it for himself, since the author restrained himself from comment. The passage was dropped, presumably, to give the story added focus. As revised, the author asserted in a July 1893 letter to Hall, "*This* time 'Pudd'nhead Wilson' is a success! . . . The whole story is centered on the murder and the trial; from the first chapter the movement is straight ahead without divergence or side-play to the murder and the trial; everything that is done or said or happens is a preparation for these events." But another more intriguing explanation is that perhaps Mark Twain made his deletions because he did not want to face, or to have his readers face, the full implications of his story. Such an explanation is supported by the ending, in which Tom is sentenced to life imprisonment, then when it is recognized that this sentence would be unjust since by it his owners would lose a slave's commercial value, Tom is pardoned and then sold down the river. Like the deletions, this ending disregards the serious issues that the story has raised and appears to put Mark Twain on the racist side of the issues of the book.[12] A simpler explanation is that expediency disturbed the story, since the author was determined to get something published to sustain himself in a difficult financial pinch.

Recently, however, *Pudd'nhead Wilson* has been extensively examined, with some readers finding the story to characterize "racial differences" as defined by "culture." Such differences thus have nothing to do with the kind of identities demonstrated by fingerprints, for the distinctions derive, in Mark Twain's words, from "a fiction of law and custom" (chap. 11), nothing more.[13]

An obvious characteristic of *Pudd'nhead Wilson* is the author's air of detachment, underscored by a consistently ironic vision of life. External and internal forces seem to be manipulating the characters and their lives, with Wilson himself—according to what the author wrote to his wife in January 1894—not a character but "only a piece of machinery—a button or a crank or a lever, with a useful function to perform in a machine, but with no dignity above that." Among the manifold ironies are those in the entries created for "Pudd'nhead Wilson's Calendar": "Why is it that we rejoice at a birth and grieve at a funeral? It is because we are not the person involved." Even if many of Wilson's calendar entries sound suspiciously like Mark Twain, they contribute to the caustic tone of the book without outright authorial intrusion. The ironies rise from the underlying philosophy of determinism, which is much more fully developed here than it was when the author wrote the *Yankee*. In accord with Clemens's recent personal experience, commercial values dominate, with powerful consequences. From Wilson's joke about dog ownership, which opens the book, to Roxy's suffering from the failure of a bank and her blackmailing of Tom, the book stresses the dire results of the institution of slave ownership.[14] In the world of the novel, each person rigidly occupies a place in the hierarchical structure; each person's behavior is thus predetermined. The lives of the aristocrats, such as Judge Driscoll, are controlled by laws that "could not be relaxed to accommodate religions or anything else. Honor stood first; and the laws defined what it was and wherein it differs in certain details from honor as defined by church creeds and by the social laws and customs" (chap. 12). When Roxy attempts to tamper with the social structure by removing her son from his place at the bottom of the ladder, her effort almost immediately creates unexpected results: her son, now her master, takes pleasure in abusing her. Wilson, an inexorable instrument of doom, returns the switched identities to their original places.[15]

Those interested in the writer's fascination with duality should attend to "The Comedy of Those Extraordinary Twins," in which the twins are conglomerate. In later works, two personalities in "conglomerate" twins are superseded by multiple personalities within one individual. Here Luigi tells Aunt Betsy that since both he and Angelo have "utter and indisputable command" of their joint body during alternate periods, *"We are no more twins than you are."* Aunt Betsy, who has no more idea of what to make of the remark than the reader, replies, "Now that I know you ain't you you don't *seem* so." Just as Mark Twain had discovered his story of the Yankee becoming serious despite his wishes, so here the "Twins" became serious enough that an operation was necessary. Had the writer kept to one of his earlier plans, the conglomerate "Twins" and *Wilson* story would have had an added dimension, for Tom and Chambers were to have been half-brothers, both sons of Judge Driscoll.

Only a few reviews appeared in America when the book was published. The *New York Times* of January 20, 1895, referred to "the fun and drollery and the comedy and tragedy of two of Mark Twain's most interesting stories." A Chatto and Windus version of the book appeared without the "Twins." Several British reviewers singled out for praise the portrayal of Roxana, one of the few women in Mark Twain's writings whose sexuality is fully developed. The reviewer in the *Idler* of August 1894 wrote admiringly of the construction of the book and found fault only with "the two alleged Italian noblemen." In the *Athenaeum* of January 19, 1895, a reviewer praised

"Pudd'nhead Wilson's Calendar," but not the character. The *Critic* offered a mixed judgment: "admirable in atmosphere, local color and dialect, a drama in its way, full of powerful situations, thrilling even, but it cannot be called in any sense *literature.*"[16]

At the end of August 1893, not long after completing the final version of *Pudd'nhead Wilson,* the author headed for America again, the second time that year. Now he would make an extended stay, with business and financial troubles keeping him too uneasy to permit him to return to his family until the following spring. The stock market had crashed in June, and with it went the chances of the Webster Company's survival. The specific occasion of the downfall of the company was the fact that it had taken on a highly expensive, multivolume work, *The Library of American Literature,* a vast anthology, handsomely illustrated with portraits of the authors. Fortunately for Clemens, during this visit he met Henry H. Rogers, a Standard Oil executive, who urged Clemens to let him handle his affairs. Rogers soon became his financial adviser and later his agent and friend, roles he was to play for sixteen years. In late 1893, Rogers arranged for the sale of the *Library* to his son-in-law, William E. Benjamin, for $50,000. This stop-gap measure provided the company with wherewithal to pay some of its bills.

Earlier, during the summer of 1892, Mark Twain had been in the midst of a period of intense literary activity. Nearly everything was written to keep the pot boiling. Besides *Pudd'nhead Wilson* and other pieces already mentioned, he produced five short stories, nine essays, and possibly a brief reminiscence, "Macfarlane," which Paine included in his edition of the autobiography. "A Cure for the Blues" is an essay that the writer puffed in a November 1892 letter to Hall as "the most delicious that has been offered to a magazine in thirty years." He wrote it as the mocking introduction to a grandiloquent short story, *The Enemy Conquered; or, Love Triumphant* (1843), by one Samuel W. Royster. Mark Twain expresses profound delight in the story of Major Elfonzo's love for Ambulinia Valeer, told by Royster with exquisite artlessness. After *Harper's* magazine turned them down, the introduction and story were then published in the *Century.*

A little better is "The £1,000,000 Bank-Note," a tale probably inspired by the author's need for credit as he faced bankruptcy. It tells of an experiment. Armed with a borrowed million-pound bank note, the narrator is able to rise to prosperity as well as marriage with a wealthy heiress, merely by impressing people with the uncashed note. The story was published in a collection issued by the Webster Company in 1893 (before *Tom Sawyer Abroad*): *The £1,000,000 Bank-Note and Other New Stories,* which was misleadingly named, since the fictional piece about the bank note was actually the *only* "story" in the collection. The others, essays or sketches, consist of "A Cure for the Blues" (with *The Enemy Conquered* to fatten the collection); two newspaper letters, "Playing Courier" and "The German Chicago"; the sketches on ships and the old medical book; and "Mental Telegraphy" and "A Petition to the Queen," in all a lightweight collection.

Two other stories of this period show Mark Twain even more out of his element, as he attempted to write the kind of story he once satirized. "The Californian's Tale" is another of the pieces that the writer had ready for Fred Hall to place in the fall of 1892. Before it could appear in one of the collections the two were trying to make, the author lent it to Arthur Stedman for *The First Book of the Authors Club, Liber Scriptorum*, in 1893. Despite its name, "The Californian's Tale" is not told by one of Mark Twain's superb vernacular narrators, although it is a first-person narrative; it is a sentimental tearjerker in the manner of Bret Harte's earlier California stories. The germ of the story is an experience the writer had in his California days. The narrator wanders into the cabin of a relic of the played-out gold country and uncovers the aftermath of a tragic Indian depredation.[17]

During the years 1892–94, the Clemenses traveled extensively in Europe, although frequently the writer was obliged to be in the United States —including the extended period from September 1893 to May 1894. Increasingly the family's movements were determined by Olivia's health. (It presumably benefited, too, from the fact that she was frequently separated from her husband during the years when she lived chiefly in Europe and he was in the United States. During their separations, she was protected from his thick and constant tobacco smoke.) In June 1893, the family traveled to Munich and various spas, where Olivia took curative baths. There Olivia's heart condition was misdiagnosed; according to a letter that Clemens wrote to his brother and sister-in-law in July, "the highest authority in Europe has just decided that there is nothing serious the matter with Livy." In 1894, the Clemenses' residences were in France, including La Bourboule-les-Bains, which they visited for Susy's health.

"The Esquimau Maiden's Romance," published in *Cosmopolitan* at the end of 1893, reports the narrator's Arctic companion's tale of her disappointment at the loss of her lover, exiled for having stolen one of her father's highly prestigious fishhooks. The hook is eventually found in the girl's hair—but it is too late. While the narrator was having a bit of fun at the expense of the girl's highly provincial sense of wealth, he and the author seem unable to decide whether the story is sentimental or satiric. Perhaps the story served its purpose when it provided the author with eight hundred dollars, which he used for living expenses during a New York stay at the Players Club. More consistently satirical, but not funny, "Is He Living or Is He Dead?" tells of a group of starving artists who boost the prices of the works of one of their number, François Millet, by arranging for him to be "dead" and commemorated by a funeral. It was also published in *Cosmopolitan*. Later the writer used the plot for a full-length play.

Why was Mark Twain writing such stuff? He needed the money. The soon-to-be-defunct Webster Company was more and more a liability. His manager, Fred Hall, found it "absolutely impossible" to send him money "with any regularity."[18] The pieces he published in *Cosmopolitan,* the Eskimo and artists stories, were not very remunerative; the editor had offered him only five thousand dollars for *twelve* such pieces. One good story of uncertain date was published at this time, "Adam's Diary," although it had been turned down by *Cosmopolitan*.

"Adam's Diary" appears to have been composed sometime before the spring of 1893. At that time, the writer was approached by two acquaintances, Charles and Irving Underhill, who sought from him something amusing for a collection they were preparing concerning Niagara Falls. At first he protested that he could not think of anything funny to write on the topic, but then he realized that his unpublished "Adam's Diary" could be adapted merely by transplanting the Garden of Eden to Niagara Falls. He is said to have become so enthusiastic that he declared, "Where else could it have been? Wasn't Niagara just made for the Garden of Eden? Of course it was the Garden of Eden."[19] By April 14, 1893, he was ready to mail off the revised version, as he then told a correspondent, inasmuch as he had "worked at the Adam Diary until I have got it to suit me." It then appeared in *The Niagara Book,* published in Buffalo by Underhill and Nichols in 1893, which contained ten essays, including one by William Dean Howells and "The Earliest Authentic Mention of Niagara Falls. Extracts from Adam's Diary. Translated from the Original Ms. By Mark Twain." Although he was promised a thousand dollars for the contribution, the author received only five hundred dollars, for the book was not a success, and the Underhills lost money.[20]

The "Diary" made its next appearance in *Tom Sawyer, Detective, As Told by Huck Finn, and Other Stories,* published in London by Chatto and Windus in 1897. This text appears to be the pre–*Niagara Book* version, for it has no references to Niagara Falls. Previously, in 1895, the writer had sent to Harper's a copy of *The Niagara Book* with this comment on the first page: "[Revised for use in Harper edition of my books. It is revised enough now I think, but Alden can revise it some more if he likes. S.L.C.]" This text *is* heavily revised, with all the Niagara references removed. On the envelope is a comment from Frederick A. Duneka of Harper's: "J. 27/4 On finding that we had set Adam's Diary for book-form I brought this out. It was learned, however, that Mr. Clemens had sent a later copy than this condensed for the mag."[21]

The next publication, and the first by Harper, took place in 1904, a separate edition of *Extracts from Adam's Diary,* with many illustrations. This text, however, is the same as that in *The Niagara Book.* In the summer of 1905, Mark Twain prepared, once more, a revision, this time by marking up the 1904 publication. He wrote to Duneka on July 16, 1905, to report what he was doing and to request "another Adam's Diary, so that I can make 2 revised copies." Clemens's own copy of the 1904 publication, annotated, is now in the C. Waller Barrett Collection at the University of Virginia. The other is from a copy of the 1904 volume that belonged to Duneka. The former has corrections in Mark Twain's hand; the latter has the same corrections in Duneka's. Moreover, Duneka's copy includes a typescript of four pages that reproduces the five manuscript pages of additions with a note as to their proper location in the revised work.[22] The revised version of "Adam's Diary" appeared at last in 1995 in *The Bible According to Mark Twain.*[23]

When "Eve's Diary" was published in *Harper's Magazine* in December 1905, it did not include any part of "Adam's Diary." Nor did the publication in *Their Husbands' Wives,* edited by William Dean Howells and Henry Mills Alden (New York: Harper and Brothers, 1906). The 1905 addition to "Adam's Diary" first appeared in *Eve's Diary* (1906), and this text appeared in subsequent American printings.

The essays of this period are far more rewarding than the stories. Four are witty, self-assured, and good-natured. The longest is "In Defense of Harriet Shelley," written in Italy in the fall of 1892 and published in the prestigious *North American Review* in July 1894. (Publication had been delayed because the author had mislaid the manuscript.) An attack on Edward Dowden's life of Percy Bysshe Shelley, "a literary cake walk," the essay has sometimes been dismissed as the writer's defense of the moral purity of Victorian woman. But another reading could see in it a hard-hitting and fair-minded critique, with Mark Twain writing as an admirer of Shelley, an admirer too of good prose, and a detester of overwriting and of unwarranted calumny. Mark Twain's description of Dowden's book berates its method as much as its style:

> This is perhaps the strangest book that has seen the light since Franken-stein. Indeed, it is a Frankenstein itself; a Frankenstein with the original infirmity supplemented by a new one; a Frankenstein with the reasoning

faculty wanting. Yet it believes it can reason, and is always trying. It is not content to leave a mountain of fact standing in the clear sunshine, where the simplest reader can perceive its form, its details, and its relation to the rest of the landscape, but thinks it must help him examine it and understand it; so its drifting mind settles upon it with that intent, but always with one and the same result: there is a change of temperature and the mountain is hid in a fog. Every time it sets up a premise and starts to reason from it, there is a surprise in store for the reader. It is strangely near-sighted, cross-eyed, and purblind. Sometimes when a mastodon walks across the field of its vision it takes it for a rat; at other times it does not see it at all.

After this elaborate metaphor, Mark Twain conducts an extended analysis of the relationship between Shelley and his first wife, Harriet. This time a love of exaggeration and digression did not get the best of him; he provides a strong, persuasive discussion.

The other essays were written in the United States under less than auspicious circumstances. Clemens had not yet abandoned the Paige typesetter. He predicted in his notebook on April 23, 1893, that his forthcoming profits would provide "much more [money] than I ever shall need," and nine months later he was celebrating: "*Jan. 15, 1894*. This is a great date in my history—a date which I said on the 5th would see Paige strike his colors. A telegram from Stone says he has done it. Yesterday we were paupers, with 3 months' ration of cash left & $160,000 in debt, but this telegram makes us wealthy."[24] A few days later he noted that "the great Paige compositor Scheme [is] consummated," and on February 2, he wired Olivia," *Our ship is safe in port.*"[25] Once again, however, Clemens was to be frustrated.

In April 1894, Webster and Company collapsed, and Clemens assumed his share of the firm's massive debts. Certain creditors perceived that Mark Twain's copyrights were the most valuable thing he owned. But when Rogers, to whom Clemens had given power of attorney over his affairs, supervised Webster and Company's entry into voluntary bankruptcy proceedings, he shrewdly arranged that Olivia Clemens, who had invested her own money in the publishing company, should be awarded her husband's copyrights and royalties as a preferred creditor.[26] Rogers did more than lend astute financial assistance. He gave Clemens good advice: "A literary man's reputation is his life; he can afford to be money poor, but he cannot afford to be character poor; you must earn the cent per cent and pay it."[27] In the campaign to protect Mark Twain's public image, he apparently went so far as to retain a press agent who planted stories about the author's social activities and his courage in raising money to pay his debts. (Later, as noted below, Rogers would arrange for Harper and Brothers to become Mark Twain's publisher.)

Finally, in May 1894, Clemens was able to settle down in Europe again; it was not until the following January that the author-turned-businessman saw *all* his optimistic expectations disappointed; until then he still hoped to generate income from the Paige typesetter. He wrote to Rogers that it was "difficult for me to soberly realize that my ten-year dream is actually dissolved." (Actually it had lasted even longer.) Why had he so persisted? Since Clemens had once been a typesetter himself, the lure of The Machine was enormous. Then, too, the financial losses he had already suffered made him more and more determined to return to his vanished Hartford lifestyle. Moreover, he, and more especially his wife, were determined to pay off all the outstanding debts of Webster (he owed about $80,000). Still, the analysis of that possibility was not hopeful. From Olivia Clemens's inheritance, the family could expect $4,000 a year; from American Publishing Company royalties, an additional $1,500; and from Chatto and Windus, his English publisher, about $2,000. From new writings he calculated he earned $5,000 a year. With so little coming in, it would be years before he could be debt-free. Nevertheless, he resolved to reimburse the friends who had invested in the machine at his prompting; in time, for example, he repaid both the actor Henry Irving and Bram Stoker, Irving's manager.

Mark Twain composed three essays during the winter of 1893–94, while living at the Players Club in New York City, despite the understandable fact that he was "so tuckered out with 5 months of daily and nightly fussing with business, that I shall not feel any interest in literature or anything else until I have had a half-year of rest and idleness to compensate that account." So he wrote to Arthur Hardy in February. "The Private History of the Jumping Frog Story" was written at the request of William H. Rideing, who was associated with the *North American Review,* where it appeared in April 1894. Mark Twain recounts his astonishment at learning that his frog story could be found in ancient Greek, with a wily Athenian as the stranger and a Boeotian in Jim Smiley's role. (He did not know that the Greek text was actually based on his own story, and that the editor of the anthology had prepared it.) Mark Twain explained how the story was told to him many years before in California. This interest in narrative art became the focus of another essay, "How to Tell a Story," written on February 8, 1894, and first published in the *Youth's Companion* in October 1895. Here he dissected the technique of the humorous story, as distinguished from those behind the funny story and the witty story. The humorous story, which he identifies as American, depends upon oral delivery. Told gravely, it benefits from the teller's concealing the fact that his story is at all amusing. For Mark Twain, the most important feature was the pause, and he demonstrates his technique by telling an African American ghost story, "The Golden Arm."

The third essay of the New York winter was "Fenimore Cooper's Literary Offenses." Unlike "A Cure for the Blues," this criticism is gloriously funny, possibly the author's funniest essay. He sets forth eighteen "rules governing literary art" that he contends Cooper violated in *The Deerslayer*. Number seven, for instance, stipulates that "when a personage talks like an illustrated, gilt-edged, tree-calf, hand-tooled, seven dollar Friendship's Offering in the beginning of a paragraph, he shall not talk like a negro minstrel in the end of it." Some of the "rules" Mark Twain had regularly violated in his own fiction; others, however, point up principles to which he was seriously devoted, such as these. "12. *Say* what he [the author] is proposing to say, not merely come close to it. 13. Use the right word, not its second cousin." "17. Use good grammar. 18. Employ a simple and straightforward style." In any event, Mark Twain's analysis of the plot and representative episodes of Cooper's novel is often inaccurate and unfair, although written with such assurance and wit that many readers have found it difficult to take Cooper seriously after reading this tour de force. *The North American Review* published it in July 1895. Fifty years later, Bernard DeVoto published Mark Twain's sequel, "Cooper's Prose Style," which is less funny but still amusing. The author of the two, according to the manuscript, is "Mark Twain, M.A., Professor of Belles Lettres in the Veterinary College of Arizona." This sequel begins as an appreciation of a passage from *The Last of the Mohicans*, although the professor soon finds blemishes. One alleged deficiency, of course, is his longtime target, Cooper's Indians. "A Cooper Indian who has been washed is a poor thing, and commonplace; it is the Cooper Indian in his paint that thrills. Cooper's extra words are Cooper's paint — his paint, his feathers, his tomahawk, his warwhoop."[28]

Mark Twain also wrote at this time two much slighter essays. "Traveling with a Reformer" was derived from trips Clemens had made to Chicago with James R. Osgood in 1882 and with Fred Hall more recently to investigate the typesetter. Having discussed petty irritations that afflicted travelers, the author imagined vividly how such annoyances might be eliminated by a reformer with a talent for invention. *Cosmopolitan* ran this piece in December 1893. "Mental Telegraphy Again" appeared in *Harper's Magazine* in September 1895. Mark Twain's need for money from journalism and an increasing breadth of interests were leading him to the role of a sage, a wise old man.

After his long stay in the United States during 1893 and 1894, very nearly a year, Clemens joined his family in Paris. They summered in the south of France and later at Etretat in Normandy. Although the author made another six-week trip to America that summer, he managed to do a little writing, some of it on shipboard, during what had formerly been his intensive writing season. Besides work on a major novel that he had begun early in 1893, Mark Twain wrote "What Paul Bourget Thinks of Us," published in the *North American Review* in January 1895. The essay began as a means of putting some "odd time" to use, with the author "laughing," enjoying himself. He wrote three "malicious chapters" that contrast "America's contributions to modern civilization with France's," as he reported to Rogers in October 1894. After three more weeks he mailed off the essay. When Paul Blouet (under his pen name of Max O'Rell) attacked the essay, also in the pages of the *Review*, Mark Twain wrote "A Little Note to M. Paul Bourget," mistakenly supposing that Bourget had replied through Blouet. Bourget's *Outre Mer*, a journal he had kept during a visit to the United States, had been critical of America, although hardly as severe as Mark Twain had been on several European countries in *The Innocents Abroad* or on France in pages he had written for *A Tramp Abroad*. In "What Paul Bourget Thinks of Us," he scoffed at the idea that a Frenchman could understand the "American soul."

> There is only one expert who is qualified to examine the souls and the life of a people and make a valuable report — the native novelist. This expert is so rare that the most populous country can never have fifteen conspicuously and confessedly competent ones in stock at one time. This native specialist is not qualified to begin work until he has been absorbing during twenty-five years. How much of this competency is derived from conscious "observation"? The amount is so slight that it counts for next to nothing in the equipment. Almost the whole capital for the novelist is the slow accumulation of *un*conscious observation — absorption. . . . [The native novelist] lays plainly before you the ways and speech and life of a few people grouped in a certain place — his own place — and that is one book. . . .
>
> And when a thousand able novels have been written, *there* you have the soul of the people, the life of the people, the speech of the people, and not anywhere else can they be had.

Seldom had Mark Twain been so obtuse and pretentious.

Mark Twain, the "native novelist," had himself long been fascinated by a figure from Bourget's homeland, Joan of Arc. According to his later account, as a boy Clemens had picked up in a Hannibal street a single leaf from a biography; he remembered that it dealt with Joan in prison, insulted and mistreated.[29] This chance event began a lifelong interest. In the early 1880s he had someone compile a reading list, and by the time he reached Europe in 1891 he had read with care several accounts of France's saintly liberator, such as Janet Tuckey's romantic and popular *Joan of Arc*. Soon he made preliminary plans for a book. A notebook entry of September 1891 reads, "Chatto send me — Joan of Arc books / Sieur de Joinville's Louis IX," and one written later that fall reads, "Only one Burgundian in Domremy [Joan's village]. She would have liked to have him beheaded 'if it would please God.'"[30] The writer's interest in Joan was not unusual, for in his time she was the subject of cults in France, Germany, and England as well as in America. Susy Clemens and her mother, for instance, had read Schiller's *Jungfrau von Orleans* in 1885; both were delighted.[31] In the midst of a long period devoted to potboilers, Mark Twain's book on Joan was his one serious effort.

The book was begun in Italy, three miles from Florence in the Villa Viviani, on August 1, 1892, after the completion of *Pudd'nhead Wilson* but before its revision. Paine suggests that the ancient villa may have been an influence on the composition; at any rate, the family lived there contentedly for nine months.[32] At first Mark Twain labeled the book — as he had the *Yankee* — as "private & not for print." It was written, he wrote to Mrs. Fairbanks, "for love, & not for lucre, & to entertain the family with, around the lamp by the fire (the day's chapter of the tale, the day's product of 'work' as this sort of literary daydreaming has been miscalled)." He wrote tellingly to Hall that he thought of the book as "a companion to the Prince and the Pauper." In his notebook he referred to Joan as a unique person: "Only one human being has lived in this world whose merits are beyond the reach of over-praise — Joan of Arc. . . . And when we consider this child's age, & origin, and upbringing & environment, & remember what thoughts she thought, what words she said, what undertakings she conceived & what achievements she wrought, we are forced to grant that no other heroic career is comparable to hers."[33] At first he wrote very rapidly and found himself well along in the story by early February. Then he was quite ready to see the book published, but only, he told Hall, "in handsome style, with many illustrations." At this point, for once thinking more about the dignity of his craft than of money, he supposed that his work would appear only as a book; he was not interested in magazine serialization.

Interruption came in March, when Clemens returned to America. By that time he had reached Joan's raising of the Siege of Orleans in book 1, chapter 22, and he was uncertain whether he would continue the story beyond that point.[34] A year later he had written no more, although he still expressed eagerness, in a letter to Olivia, to "get to work at that book once more." His readiness was not merely the result of his admiration for Joan; thoughts of commercial benefits had begun to manifest themselves. To his wife he confided in April: "All the signs of the times show that by a year hence Joan of Arc will be *the* commanding figure in the current literatures of the world." But much of the summer of 1894 Clemens necessarily devoted to business in America. On the way there he was able to revise what he had written and, he wrote to Olivia, make "some good corrections & reductions." He evidently decided he was finished, for he soon showed his manuscript to Henry M. Alden, editor of *Harper's Magazine.* Alden, however, argued persuasively, "You have told the story of a success, and have abandoned it at the culminating point of the triumph. It is as if the story of the Saviour stopped with His entry into Jerusalem, amid the hosannas of the children."[35] Resigned to a continuation of his story, the writer was nonetheless determined to obtain income from what he had written so far. He returned to the house of Harper, and after various delays managed to discuss with Harry Harper the possibility of publishing in his magazine what he had written — "the first part of Joan" — and to reach an agreement on price. The author assumed that the book would appear anonymously; his agreement with Harper included a proviso that the price would go up substantially if the identity of the author became known. He had told Olivia and Susy, "I shall never be accepted seriously over my own signature. People always want to laugh over what I write and are disappointed if they don't find a joke in it. This is to be a serious book. It means more to me than anything I have ever undertaken. I shall write it anonymously." The agreement so encouraged him that he returned to France and full-time work on the book.

The scope of the book continued to grow. As he told Henry Rogers — now a regular correspondent — in September, he had thought for a time that he would describe "Joan's childhood and military career alone." He was, he explained a week later to Rogers, trying to write the book "at my level best," with help from Olivia and Susy. Taking satisfaction in his accomplishment, he made frequent reports to Rogers. The writing and the reading on which it was based were going on simultaneously in France throughout the fall of 1894, when the writer elected to tell the whole of Joan's dramatic story. The book became the longest of Mark Twain's novels, almost as long as his huge travel books, 150,000 words. When he reached Joan of Arc's death, he found himself exhausted. He finished on February 8, 1895, in Paris. Already the earlier chapters had been prepared for publication, which began in *Harper's* in March. There the publication was anonymous, as the author wished it to be. Soon, however, he requested that Harper put his name on the book, intending to create publicity for an American lecture tour; then he found his wife vetoing the idea and had to cancel the instructions.[36] When the book was published in May 1896, Mark Twain's name appeared on both the spine and the cover but was missing from the title page, where the narrator, Sieur Louis de Conte, is identified as the author. (His initials are those of Clemens.) This arrangement did not please the real author, who wrote a rather confused letter to Harper in August, complaining that he wanted people to know he deserved credit for the *writing,* whereas readers would presume he was cashing in on another person's work. He told Henry Harper that he wanted the title page to cite him as *author,* not editor; actually, however, it was the English edition that had cited the work as "Edited by Mark Twain."

Joan of Arc is truly not Mark Twain's book in the sense that *Huckleberry Finn* or *A Connecticut Yankee* is. For one thing, it is highly derivative. During the composition of the first two-thirds, the story of Joan's childhood and military leadership, the writer made heavy use of Janet Tuckey's biography and Michelet's *Jeanne d'Arc.* He acknowledged this debt to Rogers in January 1895: "I used for reference only one French history and one English one—and shoveled in as much fancy-work and invention on both sides of the historical road as I pleased." But for the last third, the story of Joan's trial and death, he "constantly used five French sources and five English ones." These are the sources cited at the beginning of the book as "Authorities examined in verification of the truthfulness of this narrative." Because of the author's reliance on his reading, *Joan* is best described as a fictionalized biography. The title page identifies it as *Personal Recollections of Joan of Arc by the Sieur Louis de Conte (Her Page and Secretary) Freely Translated out of the Ancient French into Modern English from the Original Unpublished Manuscript in the National Archives of France by Jean François Alden.* (The translator's name seems to have been derived from that of the editor of *Harper's.*)[37] The book is illustrated "from original drawings by F. V. Du Mond and from reproductions of old paintings and statues." Du Mond had studied art in France, where Clemens had met him.

Mark Twain wanted his reader to think of this work as fact, not fiction. His preface, "A Peculiarity of Joan of Arc's History" by "The Translator," reminds readers that her biography is *"the only story of a human life which comes to us under oath."* He cites the official records of the Great Trial of 1431. Sieur Louis de Conte, an actual historical personage, was selected, apparently, as narrator because he shared Clemens's initials. He writes from a viewpoint so close to Mark Twain's that it required little effort at characterization: an older man (he was eighty-two, Clemens sixty), he is Joan's ardent admirer. Now disillusioned with life, Mark Twain more comfortably than ever employed the narrative technique he had employed successfully in *Roughing It* and "Old Times," emphasizing differences between the youthful person whose experiences are being described and the mature veteran who is telling the story. But this distinction is seldom clear. Instead, Mark Twain presents Conte as having simultaneously two attitudes that the author himself shared: sentimentality and cynicism. In writing about this heroic young woman, he could indulge both attitudes. Cynical about mankind, seeing adulthood as a time of defeat, he nevertheless had something to hold dear, for to him youth continued to be appealing, and as the father of three daughters, he looked at young girls as symbols of purity such as he needed to believe in after the defeats he had recently experienced. Significantly, Mark Twain's Joan grows in beauty yet experiences no sexual development. In his copy of Michelet he wrote, "The higher life absorbed her & suppressed her physical (sexual) development."[38]

It has been plausibly suggested that Mark Twain enjoyed writing about Joan because she did not have the failings he had, the cowardice he showed in his "Private History of a Campaign That Failed" and the bad conscience he showed, comically, in "The Carnival of Crime in Connecticut."[39] Like the Yankee, Joan was a personage with power, but unlike that imagined character Joan influenced actual human history, as the writer's narrator repeatedly observes. On the other hand, Joan's martyrdom reflects the author's growing pessimism, as does the presence of many weaklings in the book. The one aspect of Joan's career that, predictably, gave the writer difficulty was her religious devotion and specifically her belief that she was guided by supernatural voices. As his *Connecticut Yankee* shows, the writer had concluded that the Catholic Church was the greatest enemy to human freedom and progress. Even while reading for *Joan,* he expressed contempt for her religion. In the margin of the countess de Charbannes's *La Vierge Lorraine: Jeanne d'Arc,* for instance, he commented that only her "base superstition could lift her to that fearless height."[40] In his own book, he limited this skepticism severely. His interpretation of Joan is very close to that of his Catholic sources. Even a passage in which the narrator suggests reservations about Joan's voices was omitted from the manuscript:

Privately, I myself never had a high opinion of Joan's Voices — I mean in some respects — but that they were devils I do not believe. I think they were saints, holy & pure & well meaning, but with the saint's natural incapacity for business. Whatever a saint is, he is not clever. There are acres of history to prove it. . . . The voices meant Joan nothing but good,

& I am sure they did the very best they could with their equipment; but I also feel sure that if they had let her alone her matters would sometimes have gone much better. Remember, these things I have been saying are privacies — let them go no further; for I have no more desire to be damned than another.[41]

The last sentiments exactly mimic the cautious Mark Twain, anxious lest his reputation be damaged by a full revelation of his deterministic philosophy.

Joan of Arc was an unsuitable subject for Twain's talents; few of the qualities that one looks for in his best work are here. What one misses most is his ruggedly realistic point of view. In particular, Conte's unqualified admiration, even worship, of his heroine's perfection contrasts sharply with Huck's skepticism. Nonetheless, there is much evidence of Mark Twain's style, techniques, and interests. Sometimes a digression is required for the writer to indulge himself, as in Uncle Laxart's bull-ride story in chapter 36 of book 2, originally intended for *The Prince and the Pauper*. This story is rendered as repeated by Conte, deadpan, for he does not understand why Joan found it hilarious. Scenes and characters just off center stage, the fancywork that Mark Twain shoveled in, are drawn from the author's western experiences. Of these the most important are the boastful but heroic Paladin, whom the writer invented, and Joan's favorite general, La Hire. The Paladin's ability as a storyteller (he exaggerates more each time he repeats a story) represents Mark Twain's continuing commitment to the art of oral narrative. The figure who dominates the scene, the modest but confident Joan, is portrayed with more effectiveness than critics have usually been willing to grant, once the reader has passed some early mawkish sentimentality, especially that concerning the "fairy tree" of Joan's village. The trial scenes are potent melodrama, with Joan's goodness struggling against the archvillain Cauchon's deceitful malice. Joan talks too much in these scenes — apparently because the trial records that the writer consulted were very full.

Besides her innocence and purity, Joan's role as liberator of France appealed strongly to Mark Twain because he was devoted to freedom, whether that of Huck on a raft or of the prisoners released by the Yankee. So ignorant of the Middle Ages that he was unable to maintain even a pretense of a medieval point of view, he was nonetheless deeply engaged by Joan's personality. Moreover, he was delighted to have as his protagonist a person whose innocence is not destroyed and whose dedication to liberty is powerfully sanctioned. Eventually Joan loses her freedom and her life, but she never yields her determination. Her story as Mark Twain tells it is not one of defeat but of qualified success. He judged that "Joan of Arc was not made as others are. Fidelity to principle, fidelity to truth, fidelity to her word, all these were in her bone and in her flesh — they were parts of her. She could not change, she could not cast them out. . . . Where she had taken her stand and planted her foot, there she would abide; hell itself could not move her from that place" (book 3, chap. 14).

In time Clemens looked back at *Joan* as his favorite book and his best, perhaps because he identified it with Susy, who liked it especially. Also, it happened to be published in book form the year of her death. He later wrote that Susy had taken "as deep & earnest an interest in the book as if it were her own. The nightly readings and editings covered many months." Moreover, he wrote that Susy had provided a model for Joan:

Susy at 17 — Joan of Arc at 17. Secretly, I drew Joan's physical portrait from the Susy of that age, when I came to write that book. Apart from that, I had no formally-appointed model for Joan but her own historical self. [Yet there were several points of resemblance between the girls: such as vivacity, enthusiasm, precocious wisdom, wit, eloquence, penetration, nobility of character. In Joan the five latter qualities were of a measure that has not been paralleled in any other person of like age in history; but I comprehended them in her all the better from comprehending them in their lesser measure in Susy.][42] (The bracketed passage is deleted in the manuscript.)

Joan of Arc was the last book that the Clemens family heard the author read for their editing.

Surprisingly, *Joan* was well received in England. Andrew Lang described the book as "honest, spirited, and stirring." Sir Walter Besant found Mark Twain's Joan "more noble, more spiritual, of a loftier type than we could have conceived possible in the author of 'Huckleberry Finn.'" The *London Daily Chronicle* now declared that Mark Twain was "far more than a mere man of letters . . . he is a great writer." The *Glasgow Herald* "doubted whether the Church's decree of beatification [of Joan] was as significant a compliment as is this tribute from the pen of Mark Twain."[43] Richard Le Gallienne reported in the *Idler* that in *Joan* Twain revealed "a great imagination" and "a great heart."[44] The reviewer for the *Outlook*, writing in the August 22, 1896, issue, declared that "Mark Twain's book is a historical novel, executed with fidelity to the original documents and records." A reviewer in the July 23, 1896, issue of the *Independent* called the book a "brilliant picture of the life and times of Joan of Arc." The *Bookman* for July 1896 found *Joan* "much finer in texture than, we confess, we had expected from this writer."[45] American reviewers, by contrast, were divided. The author's friend Laurence Hutton, writing in *Harper's Magazine,* found that "for the first time, to one reader at least, does she appear to be an actual person, absolutely alive, with the bloom of youth on her cheeks, and with quite as much of the woman as the saint in her composition."[46] Dissenting from this view, William P. Trent in the *Bookman* asserted that Mark Twain had made his contribution elsewhere.[47] In the *Dial,* historian James Westfall Thompson called *Joan* "a gorgeous failure."[48] Another reviewer called it "the best book he [Mark Twain] has ever written."[49]

William Dean Howells, whose reviews usually praised his friend's work, was troubled by his friend's efforts at "the supposed medieval thing." Howells warned that it was "impossible for any one who was not a prig to keep to the archaic attitude and parlance which the author attempts here and there." He aptly noted, "I wish he had frankly refused to attempt it at all. I wish his personal recollections of Joan could have been written by some Southwestern American, translated to Domremy by some such mighty magic of imagination as launched the Connecticut Yankee into the streets of many-towered Camelot; but I make the most of the moments when Sieur Louis de Conte forgets himself into the sort of witness I could wish him to be."[50] In 1924, when George Bernard Shaw offered to the world his own *Saint Joan,* he lamented in his preface that Mark Twain's theory of progress had obstructed an understanding of why Joan was burned and that his lack of appreciation of medieval churches and chivalry made him unqualified to deal with her epoch.[51]

Joan of Arc has recently received renewed attention from feminist critics. Rolande Ballorain writes appreciatively of the book as a vehicle for Twain's ideas and as a "well written," even "elegant" book. Other modern-day critics, though less favorably disposed, are at least starting to attend to this long-neglected book.[52]

Just before Mark Twain finished *Joan of Arc,* he completed another work, a short novel or long story. During a business trip to America in November 1893, he began what he told Olivia he was calling "Tom Sawyer's Mystery." The trouble was, he had not yet located a mystery for Tom to solve. Nevertheless, he wrote several chapters the following spring, determined to take advantage of the interest in detective stories and the possibilities of an exciting courtroom scene. During his career he wrote, or attempted to write, a number of stories that involve crime detection or else make fun of its methods: "The Stolen White Elephant," *Simon Wheeler, Detective,* "A Double-Barrelled Detective Story," *Pudd'nhead Wilson,* and "The Chronicle of Young Satan." Courtroom dramas are features of several of these works, as well as of *The Gilded Age* and *Joan of Arc.* An early idea for the plot of *Huckleberry Finn* may also have included this element.

While he was still looking for a plot, Twain wrote some pages having to do with stolen diamonds; eventually he was able to incorporate these passages into Tom Sawyer's startling revelation in the courtroom. Only afterward did he find his plot. Late in 1894, he attended a social gathering in Paris, where he met Lady Hegermann-Lindercrone, a Dane, who told him about an unusual murder trial that had taken place in her country in the sixteenth century. The story had become so well known that it had served as the basis of a novel, *The Minister of Veilby* (1824; English title), by Steen Steensen Blicher. Seizing on this story, Mark Twain wrote Henry Rogers a few days later on January 2, "I've got a first-rate subject for a book," and then decided instead to integrate it with the plot for the Tom Sawyer story he had already begun. He acknowledged his debt, somewhat inaccurately, with a footnote: "Strange as the incidents of this story are, they are not inventions, but facts—even to the public confession of the accused. I take them from an old-time Swedish criminal trial, change the actors, and transfer the scene to America. I have added some details, but only a couple of them are important ones." Because he did not know Blicher's novel (not then available in English) and because the British edition of Twain's story lacked this note, Danish writers have suggested that he was guilty of plagiarism.[53]

Once the writer had located his plot, he wound up his 28,000-word story with haste. He finished on January 23 and promptly sold it to Harper and Brothers. First published in *Harper's* in August and September 1896, it was included in the same year in a Harper collection, *Tom Sawyer Abroad, Tom Sawyer, Detective, and Other Stories.* He was paid two thousand dollars for the serial rights, plus royalties on the book. From the beginning, the story had been conceived of strictly as a moneymaker. It is the poorest of the stories of Huck and Tom. Jim is absent, and Huck serves simply as Tom's companion. Huck as narrator displays unlimited respect for, almost adoration of, Tom. At one point, though, Huck seems to echo his creator's determinism in justifying one difference in their outlook: "It was always nuts for Tom Sawyer—a mystery was. If you'd lay out a mystery and a pie before me and him, you wouldn't have to say take your choice; it was a thing that would regulate itself. Because in my nature I have always run to pies, whilst in his nature he has always run to mystery. People are made different. And it is the best way" (chap. 2).

Few pleasures are in store for the reader from Huck's telling of this story, except for his reference to the lawyer whose case Tom finally destroys as "the lawyer for the prostitution." (Olivia Clemens presumably let that one through.) In a letter of 1888 to the Baroness Alexandra Gripenberg, Mark Twain had expressed a belief that seemed to condone plot borrowing: "There is no merit in 99 stories out of a hundred except the merit put into them by the teller's *art;* as a rule, nothing about a story is 'original,' and entitled to be regarded as private property and valuable, except the art which the teller puts into the telling of it. . . . One should always begin a story by saying he got it from somebody else." But there is too little of the storyteller's art in *Tom Sawyer, Detective.* Painfully plot-ridden, the story adds far more complications than Mark Twain's source offered. The chief insertion is Jake Dunlap, who returns home after a seven-year absence. The discovery of his dead body before he is known to have arrived leads the community to believe that his identical twin, Jubiter, has been murdered by his employer, Tom's uncle, Silas Phelps, who had appeared in *Huckleberry Finn.* Tom Sawyer establishes Silas's innocence at a sensational trial. In the source, the innocence of the minister had been established twenty-one years after he was found guilty and executed by beheading, after the supposed victim returned and told how he had been forced to leave town. In both narratives, the villain disguises himself by wearing the minister's green gown; in both, the minister mistakenly admits his guilt. The story has a few Mark Twain touches, such as Jubiter disguising himself as a deaf-mute, like the Duke in *Huckleberry Finn,* and the confusion resulting from the introduction of identical twins.

The first four years of Clemens's long European exile saw him experiencing illness and bankruptcy, making half a dozen trips back to the United States on business, and residing in houses, villas, hotels, and apartments in Switzerland, Germany, Italy, and France. According to his daughter Clara, "He never felt at home in Europe, and in any case, as his serious business affairs required his presence in America, Mother was left abroad alone with her children during the major part of four years, except for brief visits from Father."[54] During this time the writer managed to produce a great deal, nearly all of it disappointing (*Pudd'nhead Wilson* and *Tom Sawyer Abroad* being the most striking instances). Much of the material seems too remote from the native novelist's best abilities — *Joan of Arc* is the obvious case. Mark Twain's career had been marked by similarly infertile periods in both the 1870s and 1880s; he had always written both badly and well, switching from the quality of *Huckleberry Finn* to "The 1002^d Arabian Night" by turns. Whether he could recover, at age sixty, his former brilliance must have seemed to any sympathetic observer entirely possible. One threat, presumably, was his developing pessimism. But as *Joan* had shown, he could still see the bright as well as the dark sides, and even beneath the laughter of *Huckleberry Finn* there had already lurked a dark strain in Mark Twain's imagination. The real question now concerned the resilience of his creative imagination. Had all the strains he had experienced been too much for his inventive faculty?

CHAPTER NINE

The House Burns Down

espite the most obvious evidence to the contrary, all through 1894 Clemens managed to persuade himself that he would somehow cash in on his Paige typesetting investments so that he and his family could return to America and live there prosperously ever after. Only just before Christmas did his financial adviser, Henry H. Rogers, manage to break through his defenses and force him to face the truth: the Paige typesetter, which had failed a test in Chicago, was not a reliable machine. His reply to Rogers tells what had happened.

> I *seemed* to be entirely expecting your letter, and also prepared and re-signed; but Lord, it shows how little we know ourselves and how easily we can deceive ourselves. It hit me like a thunderclap. It knocked every rag of sense out of my head, and I went flying here and there and yonder, not knowing what I was doing, and only one clearly-defined thought standing up visible out of the crazy storm-drift — that my dream of ten years was in desperate peril.

From this dream Clemens slowly awoke. The trauma heavily stamped itself on him, and from the experience, augmented by further disasters, he would repeatedly write, or attempt to write, stories of a man whose happy life was completely destroyed.

He was able to finish both *Tom Sawyer, Detective* and *Joan* before he thought of a way to make a dramatic change in his life. In early February, he told Rogers that he was planning "to go around the world on a lecture trip. . . . not for money but to get Mrs. Clemens and myself away from the phantoms and out of the nervous strain for a few months." A year before in New York, he had done three readings with James Whitcomb Riley and Douglass Sherley at $250 a night with some success. After his recent financial defeats, he now needed some more successes. The tour was soon designed to produce the maximum income as well, for Clemens began to realize that *Pudd'nhead Wilson* would not provide him with the funds he had expected. He then wrote to Rogers, "Apparently I've *got* to mount the platform or starve; therefore I am examining into this thing seriously." Just two weeks later he made a quick trip to New York to arrange the tour. James Pond, who had directed his tour with Cable, was to be in charge of the American schedule; R. S. Smythe, an Australian agent, contracted engagements in Hawaii, Australia, New Zealand, Ceylon, India, South Africa, and England. Several of these, however, were never to be.

Smythe saw to it that Australia was prepared for its visitor, and soon after he announced the trip, the *Sydney Daily Telegraph* pointed out on May 1 that Mark Twain was considered by many as one "who has rendered better service to the world than any imaginative writer of our period, not only by making it smile at clean inimitable humor, but in prompting deep and serious thought on many important questions of our time."[1]

Besides the trip around the world, Clemens had become deeply interested in the possibility of having his books issued in a uniform edition. This would be difficult, inasmuch as several different companies had published his books. Fortunately, Henry Rogers was up to the formidable task. On May 23, 1895, Harper and Brothers agreed to publish a uniform edition; all rights to the books Charles L. Webster and Company had published were to be turned over to Harper. More complicated was the American Publishing Company's claims on books published by that Hartford company. Results would not be forthcoming for a considerable time.

In May 1895, the Clemens family returned to Quarry Farm for their first extended visit there since 1889. They seem to have viewed the upcoming tour as a symbolic act, a kind of campaign, not unlike Joan's. (Ulysses S. Grant had made a round-the-world tour in the 1870s.) Clemens prepared himself carefully for his presentations, as his notebooks indicate. He did not plan to lecture or to read. Instead, he would present himself as Mark Twain and call his performances "At Homes"; ostensibly he was a moralist with a scheme for regenerating mankind. In fact, he would speak, from memory, rendering reminiscences, stories, sketches, essays — pieces such as "The Jumping Frog," "The Awful German Language," "The Decay of the Art of Lying," and "The Genuine Mexican Plug." His programs were to last about two hours, with a fifteen-minute intermission. He would present himself again as the old and original Mark Twain.

Clara Clemens accompanied her parents on the tour but Jean and Susy stayed behind in America. Hoping to become a singer, Susy had been advised that she needed to strengthen her chest in order to give her voice more volume. For that purpose she wanted to stay in Elmira, at Quarry Farm, and it was arranged for Jean to attend school in Elmira. The Clemenses' faithful family maid, Katy Leary, took care of the two. Susy, who had been close to her father as a child and had even written a biography of him, was now very unhappy and felt deeply estranged from her father. Eventually Clemens was to bemoan the separation and become torn with guilt. He blamed himself for the financial failure that had resulted in his long separation from two of his daughters, especially Susy.[2] He always found it easier to deal with young girls than with young women, as is suggested by his dedication at the end of his life to the angelfish of his invented Aquarium and his unhappy relationship at that time with Jean.

The yearlong trip began on July 14; the party traveled slowly across the North American continent, stopping for twenty-six presentations from Mark Twain along the way. In Cleveland he attracted more than four thousand people. Other stops were in Michigan, Minnesota, Manitoba, Montana, Oregon, and Washington. His manager, James B. Pond, noted that Clemens "smokes constantly, and I fear it is too much, still he may stand it. Physicians say it will eventually kill him." And Pond noted that he took with him on his trip four pounds of Durham smoking tobacco and "3,000 manilla cheroots."[3] The heart ailments that would eventually destroy the man were thus foreseen fifteen years before he succumbed.

In Seattle, Clemens publicly announced the purpose of the trip: to pay off his debts, even though the law did not require him to do so. "I am not a business man, and Honor is a harder master than the law."[4] The final North American stop was at Vancouver, British Columbia. By late August, the travelers were crossing the Pacific.

Unable to land in Hawaii, to his great disappointment, because of a cholera epidemic, he began his readings in Australia during five weeks in September and October, then moved on for five weeks in New Zealand, despite persistent troubles with a carbuncle. Newspapers noted that he managed to present himself agreeably, even charmingly during his many public appearances, interviews, and official welcomes, despite the fact that he was unwell and increasingly fatigued. Once during a period of fourteen days he lectured eleven times in six different towns, was interviewed three times, and was publicly welcomed at least five times. During the latter part of the tour, R. S. Smythe's son and partner, Carlyle Smith, served as Clemens's agent and guide.[5]

However fatiguing, the trip was also stimulating to the lecturer. At times in interviews he was able to make statements that provide important evidence of his mature attitude toward humor, like this one, found in the *Sydney Morning Herald* of September 17: "Probably there is an imperceptible touch of something permanent that one feels instinctively to adhere to true humour, whereas wit may be the mere conversational shooting up of 'smartness'—a bright feather, to be blown into space the second after it is launched . . . by general, if tacit, consent Wit seems to be counted a very poor relation to Humour."[6]

Although he was later to assert that his experiences in the Pacific made him an anti-imperialist, while there he recorded in his notebook, "How glad I am that all these native races are dead & gone, or nearly so. The work was mercifully swift & horrible in portions of Australia."[7]

In at least one of his readings in Australia, he supplemented the account in *Huckleberry Finn* of Huck's struggles with his conscience. Part of the addition was recorded in a notebook. There Huck tells his conscience, "I wouldn't be as ignorant as you for wages. You don't know right from wrong, you ain't got judgment." Huck continued this attack, suggesting that it was not easy for him to go against what his conscience dictated.[8]

After additional readings in Australia, he sailed again in January 1896. Two months were given over to India. He landed first at Colombo, on the island of Ceylon; there, he reported, "I spent the most enchanting day of my life."[9] Next there were presentations in Bombay, Poona (where they met an Indian prince), and Baroda (where the maharaja heard Mark Twain "At Home in the Great Hall of the Palace"). The *Times of India* described him as "a rugged and even something of a romantic figure . . . with his masses of curly hair, now nearly white, with his keen, kindly eyes looking out from great shaggy brows, and his strangely magnetic smile."[10] Then the party crossed the continent to Calcutta, with stops for performances along the way. From there they made a special side trip to Darjeeling, to see the Himalayas—and to give another presentation. Next they went to the northwestern part of India, as far as Rawalpindi (now part of Pakistan). Illnesses often delayed the trip, once for two weeks. In all there were some twenty "At Homes" on the Indian subcontinent. As a consequence of the Mutiny of 1857, when Indians went to war against British colonial forces, many members of the Indian elite did not wish to attend Mark Twain's programs, which were usually hosted by British officers.[11]

A long trip southward followed; then for eleven days they rested on the island of Mauritius. May, June, and half of July were devoted to South Africa. He made presentations in Natal, the Transvaal, the Orange Free State, and Cape Colony. In Johannesburg alone, he gave seven performances. Finally, after traveling 53,000 miles, the Clemenses began settling in England by the end of July, at Guildford in Surrey.[12]

The trip was not a great financial success. Clemens cleared only about $30,000, with $5,000 of that coming from the American segment; expenses for the rest of the trip were high. By comparison, his fifteen-week tour with Cable in 1884–85 had netted him $15,000. But further profit was anticipated: he had taken many notes and intended to begin work in England on another travel book. He would forego further lectures in England, since he had presented himself well over a hundred times during the previous twelve months and was worn out. He expected Susy and Jean to join the travelers in England until word reached them that Susy was ill. Olivia and Clara hurriedly returned to the United States — but too late, for Susy died of meningitis on August 18, in the Clemenses' Hartford house — while Olivia was still in mid-ocean. The Clemenses, who had been devoted to Susy (although she and her father had not been as close in recent years), were deeply bereaved, and the writer's pessimism was increased exponentially. In a letter to Andrew Chatto, he called Susy "the prodigy of our flock, in intellectuality, in the gift of speech, & in music." With his letter he sent a brief obituary, which he asked Chatto to give out to newspapers to inform his "many personal friends in England." Although Clemens had previously rejected the concept that God worked through "special providences," he now saw Susy's death, as he explained to Howells in September, to be a deliberate act of God, "exactly and precisely . . . planned; . . . remorselessly . . . carried out."

Even before the devastating news had arrived, the writer had begun an account of "Man's Place in the Animal World"; he completed it two months later. There he argued that man *descended* from the animals, not *ascended* from them. To man alone he ascribed revenge, indecency, vulgarity, obscenity, cruelty, slavery, patriotism, religion, and the useless Moral Sense. "Since the Moral Sense had but the one office, the one capacity — to enable man to do wrong — it is plainly without value to him. In fact it manifestly is a disease." The curse of this Moral Sense — an ability to distinguish right from wrong — would be a theme of some of the author's best late fiction. Perhaps because of his recent illnesses, another topic of the essay was man's physical infirmities: "The mere names of the agents appointed to keep this shackly machine out of repair would hide him from sight if printed on his body in the smallest type of the founder's art." Only in his intelligence, then, is man in any way superior to animals.[13]

During the trip Henry Rogers had been successfully arranging for the publication of a uniform edition of Mark Twain's books. Harper announced such an edition, and in 1896 the first five volumes appeared. Clemens was much pleased at this development scheme because of both the prestige and the income it would provide. The American Publishing Company, which owned the rights to copyright renewals of the books it had published, was planning a rival edition of the author's works. An agreement was reached at the end of 1896 for the American Publishing Company to offer, as subscription volumes, a uniform edition "in handsome library style" of Mark Twain's complete works, including those published by Osgood, Webster, and Harper.[14] In fact, there were several editions: the Autograph Edition, the DeLuxe Edition (one hundred sets), and the Royal Edition (1,250 sets), all sold by subscription. Twenty-two volumes appeared in 1898 and 1899, and six more volumes between 1899 and 1907. Also in 1899 Harper and Brothers began the publication, for regular retail sale, of the Uniform Edition, which by the year 1910 would consist of twenty-five volumes. For Great Britain, Chatto and Windus obtained from the American Publishing Company 612 sets of what was called the Author's Edition, but less expensive sets were also available to the British public; these were called the Uniform Library Edition.[15] None of these editions is now in print; however, Oxford University Press recently published a set of Mark Twain's works in facsimiles of American first editions.

Finally, in 1903, Rogers would negotiate an arrangement by which all of Mark Twain's copyrights (mostly held by Mrs. Clemens) were transferred to Harper, and Harper became the exclusive publisher of his writings, an arrangement that was to continue until 1967.[16] The author was delighted: "They *guarantee* me $25,000 a year for 5 years," he wrote in his notebook, "but they will yield twice as much [as] that for many a year, if intelligently handled."[17] That prophecy, for once, was entirely correct.

Perhaps because he had aired his grievances so fully in his "Animal World" essay, which he did not publish, the writer was able to restrain himself while working on what he called for a time "Around the World," an account of his trip. The programmatic writing, merely following the itinerary of his trip, was undertaken in the house the Clemenses rented on Tedworth Square in the Chelsea district of London and proved therapeutic, as the writer himself recognized. Reporters mercifully left him alone, at least for a time. He wrote to Twichell, "I work all the days, and trouble vanishes away when I use that magic." In the midst of these labors — begun on October 24, 1896 — he wrote to Howells in February that he had become indifferent — "Indifferent to nearly everything but work. I like that; I enjoy it, & stick to it." Just as when he had to compose *Life on the Mississippi* in 1882, he made heavy use of published authorities in his account of this trip, about fifty in all. (Some borrowings were later trimmed from both versions of the book.) Although many of these citations seem like padding, Mark Twain could justify them on the grounds that he was dealing with remote areas concerning which he was no expert. He intended to balance his subjective observations with other writers' more nearly objective comments.

As usual, he changed his plans several times. The first five chapters describing the American phase of the tour he later dropped, although he salvaged a few pieces, such as "A Delicately Improper Tale." At one point he planned to write about only the first half of the tour, leaving India and Africa for a sequel. Then in March he decided, as he told Frank Bliss, who would publish the book, he would "end with India — there will be room for nothing more. At a later date I can make a book about South Africa if there is material enough in that rather uninteresting country to make the job worthwhile."

He finished a rough version by March 1 and almost immediately set about revising it. He explained to Bliss: "I must do all this extraordinary revising because this book has to come into comparison with the Innocents, and so I must do my level best to bring it chock up to the mark." Mrs. Clemens was then giving the manuscript a second reading, and by April 13 he felt that the work was finished. Then he announced to his friend Mac-Alister, "I have changed my plans & am extending the book to take in South Africa — a big addition to the job, I can tell you, after I supposed I was done." He finally finished, for the second time, on May 18. As he told Rogers in January 1897, he had felt obliged to write "7 days in the week, 31 in the month," and he noted in a letter to Wayne MacVeagh that this book was the only one "I have ever confined myself to from title page to Finis without relief of shifting to another work meantime." But he was finally delighted with the work. He wrote to Bliss, "I wouldn't trade it for any book I have ever written — & I am not an easy person to please." Chapters of the book appeared in November 1897 in *McClure's* magazine, the publication having been arranged by the American Publishing Company but without his permission.

The title of the new book gave him some difficulty. The author considered "Imitating the Equator," "Another Innocent Abroad," "The Latest Innocent Abroad," and "The Surviving Innocent Abroad," suggesting that the book was a belated sequel to his first. Eventually the book had two titles. In England it was *More Tramps Abroad,* in America *Following the Equator: A Journey Around the World.* As with *Tom Sawyer Abroad,* the English text is superior, even although Mark Twain intended the book as an American subscription book. He wrote to Rogers to ask for the number of words in *Roughing It,* since he wished to make the new book of the same length. (Actually it is longer, despite the publisher's trimming.) In arguing with Rogers for publication through subscription sales, Clemens noted in November that whereas the market of educated readers had been saturated with travel books, he would be able to appeal to factory hands and farmers who never visit a bookstore.

The author consciously revised his text with an eye to the image of himself—humble but clever and physically vigorous (although in fact he had not been well during much of the trip). On occasion, he deleted sardonic remarks, as when he wrote about an irritating woman he had met on a ship in New Zealand. Eventually he softened his feelings toward her, he explained, "softened them infinitely; & so, when by & by she started ashore & slipped & fell in the water, I saw her fished out without regret."[18] He canceled comments on his health problems and removed remarks that amounted to bragging or self-pity. Two long sections written for the book were cut at an early point: a short story, "Newhouse's Jew Story," published in 1972 in *Fables of Man,* and "The Enchanted Sea-Wilderness," an incomplete narrative published in 1966 in the collection *Which Was the Dream?* In April 1899, he looked back at these experiences, both the lecture tour and the authorship, in a letter to Howells: "I wrote my last travel book in hell; but I let on, the best I could, that it was an excursion through heaven. Some day I will read it, & if its lying cheerfulness fools me, then I shall believe it fooled the reader. How I did loathe that journey round the world! — except the sea-part and India."

In May 1897, after the author had finished his editing, his wife took her turn. A full record of Olivia Clemens's responses survives. She acted mostly as a proofreader who wanted her husband to get his facts straight (after all, she had been with him much of the time), but she also tried to restrain her husband's irreverence.[19] (That tendency is rather prominent, nonetheless, in the selections from "Pudd'nhead Wilson's New Calendar" that introduce the chapters. He asserted there, for example, "There are those who scoff at the school-boy, calling him frivolous and shallow. Yet it was the school-boy who said, 'Faith is believing what you know ain't so.'") Van Wyck Brooks made much of Olivia's criticisms, some of which Paine had quoted in his biography, but the author was by no means ready to accept her suggestions uncritically when it was his turn again to review the manuscript. Next the work went to the two publishers. What Bliss did was far more destructive than any cuts Olivia Clemens made; moreover, many of his changes were made at proof stage, without the author's approval. An unenthusiastic reader, he marred the book by deletions that create incoherence. He cut off the ends of chapters, trimmed anti-British remarks, and excised much that he found boring. He partly made up for his reductions by providing the book with a splendid appearance. *Following the Equator* is the most elegant of Mark Twain's books, with an elephant in color on the cover and over two hundred illustrations, many of them photographs, printed on thick, glossy "plate" paper. In appearance, *More Tramps Abroad* is much more ordinary, but at least Chatto and Windus made fewer cuts; moreover, it was the British edition that the author read in proof. Fortunately, the manuscript survives in the Berg Collection of the New York Public Library, and one can see what kinds of editing the book was given — by the author, his wife, and the two publishers.[20] Of all Mark Twain's books, this one most deserves a new edition with passages restored that the author had no intention of deleting.

Compared with his earlier travel accounts, this last one is less uneven, though it contains no such glories as "Jim Baker's Blue Jay Yarn" of *A Tramp Abroad*. One passage does, however, echo Baker's comments on the jay's intelligence. Of the Indian crow, which he labeled an "Indian sham Quaker," Mark Twain remarked that he is

> just a rowdy, and is always noisy when awake — always chaffing, scold-ing, scoffing, laughing, ripping, and cursing, and carrying on about something or other. I never saw such a bird for delivering opinions. Nothing escapes him; he notices everything that happens, and brings out his opinion about it, particularly if it is a matter that is none of his business. And it is never a mild opinion but always violent — violent and profane — the presence of ladies does not affect him." (chap. 38)

Mark Twain very likely saw in this bird an exaggerated version of his earlier, authentic self. Introducing very little of the forced humor and burlesque that mars the account of his European adventures, *Following the Equator* has some exquisite purple prose, such as the famous account of a New England ice storm. The weakest pages are those written last. There the author leaned heavily on his notes, even going so far as to place pages from his notebook directly into the manuscript.

Joan was written to meet the author's need, and so, in a way, was this book. He needed to believe he could live again after the loss of both his daughter Susy and his fantasies of wealth. As he wrote, memories of the teeming life and color of India did much to comfort him: it was "the one sole country under the sun that is endowed with an imperishable interest for alien prince and alien peasant, for lettered and ignorant, wise and fool, rich and poor, bond and free, the one land that *all* men desire to see, and having seen once, by even a glimpse, would not give that glimpse for the shows of all the rest of the globe combined" (chap. 38). His recollections of India brightened his last years.

Later he was to identify himself as anti-imperialist and testify that his travels in 1895–96 had dramatically changed him. In *Following the Equator* he frequently relates how colonial powers had brutally destroyed indigenous populations, for example in Australia. But his attitude was inconsistent, as is suggested by the fact that his usual term for aborigines, Pacific Islanders, Maori, and native South Africans is *savage*. As early as the third chapter he comments, "Savages are eager to learn from the white man any new way to kill each other, but it is not their habit to seize with avidity and apply with energy the white man's ideas." Moreover, he frequently expressed admiration for British colonial rule.[21]

Financially, Clemens realized far more from the book than from his lectures. His American royalties were 12.5 percent, and he was given a $10,000 advance. Published in November 1897, the book, along with the tour and other income, permitted Rogers to pay off *all* Clemens's debts by the end of January 1898. (Clemens had formerly been ready to accept Rogers's proposal for an easier settlement, but Olivia had insisted on complete restitution.) The final payments were given wide publicity, and Mark Twain was acclaimed as a hero for his strenuous efforts. In both America and Great Britain, the book sold well, with 28,500 copies sold in the first five months in the United States. Most American reviews were favorable; readers praised the author's poetic feelings as well as his humor. His friend Laurence Hutton reminded his readers in the January 1898 *Harper's Magazine* that the book "was undertaken to raise the burden of a business debt which he [Clemens] considers a personal obligation." A few English reviews found the book padded, labored, and disappointing; others called it "a first-class book of travel," marked by "humor, good sense, good nature, shrewd observation." Perhaps the frankest appraisal was that in the May 21, 1898, *Spectator:* "Although the book is not likely to add to the author's reputation, it is readable and sometimes entertaining."[22]

If Mark Twain had managed with some success to make the account of his round-the-world tour a sunny book, still the disasters he had experienced were beginning to have a powerful effect on his imagination. From now on, most of what he wrote was to be distinctly different from his earlier works, both travel books and fiction. To set forth his new sense of his situation, he tried a variety of experimental fictional forms. The narrative fragment he had written for the book toward the end of 1896, "The En-chanted Sea-Wilderness," for example, charts his mental state. It tells of a ship becoming trapped in a region called the Devil's Race Track, in the southern Indian Ocean, and eventually being confined at its center, the Everlasting Sunday. The plight of the voyagers seems to reflect the author's perception of his own situation. He had written of Susy's death to his old family friend, Joseph Twichell: "You have seen our whole voyage. You have seen us go to sea, a cloud of sail, and the flag at the peak, and you see us now, chartless, adrift—derelicts; battered, water-logged, our sails a ruck of rags, our pride gone. For it is gone. And there is nothing in its place. The vanity of life was all we had, and there is no vanity left in us." The summary matches the hopelessness in the story, with the voyagers seeing only death around them. In an early part of the "Sea-Wilderness" fragment, an un-usually smart dog, "just a darling," saves the crew of a ship by rousing the sleeping captain when the ship catches fire. The sailors flee the ship, with the captain insisting that the dog be left behind to die rather than being permitted to escape in the lifeboat. This piece first appeared in *Fables of Man*. The writer seems to have been hinting at his own sense of guilt in leaving Susy behind as he circled the globe; she had died, feverishly, in the Clemenses' Hartford home. The fragment was only one of a series of disas-ter stories that Mark Twain was to write over the next several years; he finished none.

But even before he had completed the book about his trip, he was plan-ning other stories and books, not sequels to earlier successful books, but new forms registering new themes. He wrote to Rogers in January 1897, "I've got a new book in my head—3 or 4 of them, for that matter. . . . I shall write *All* of them, a whole dam library." The first of these he had meant to begin after finishing *Joan* in 1895, but illness and tour plans intervened. The plot idea was based on one of Clemens's own experiences: a dream that made him question the reality of his own life. He had written to Susan Crane in 1893, "I dreamed I was born & grew up & was a pilot on the Mississippi, & a miner & journalist in Nevada, & a pilgrim in the Quaker City, & had a wife & children & went to live in a Villa out of Florence—& this dream goes on and *on*, & sometimes seems so real that I almost believe it *is* real. I wonder if it is? But there is no way to tell; for if one applies tests, *they* would be part of the dream, too, & so would simply aid the deceit. I wish I knew whether it is a dream or real." When the Paige machine had finally proved to be valueless, Clemens had described himself as shocked at finding that his "ten-year dream" had dissolved, and when he visited his Hartford house in March 1895, he had written to his wife that it "seemed as if I had burst awake out of a hellish dream, & had never been away." The death of Susy had intensified the feeling that his happy life in Hartford had actually been only a passing dream. Afterward, the Clemenses felt that they could never go back to their Hartford house, the location of Susy's final days and nights. In his autobiography, Mark Twain compared the death of Susy to the burning down of a man's house.

> The smoking wreckage represents only a ruined home that was dear through the years of use and pleasant associations. By and by, as the years go on, first he misses this, then that, then the other thing. And when he casts about he finds that it was in that house. And always it is an *essential* — there was but one of its kind. It cannot be replaced. It was in that house. It is irrevocably lost. He did not realize that it was an essential when he had it; he only discovers it now when he finds himself balked, hampered, by its absence. It will be years before the tale of lost essentials is complete, and not till then can he truly know the magnitude of his disaster.[23]

These dream images remained vivid in his consciousness.

On May 23, 1897, just five days after his story of the round-the-world trip was finished, Mark Twain began "Which Was the Dream?" Although inspired by his own disaster, the author also drew on the experiences of his hero General Ulysses Grant, as sketched in some pages he had written in 1885. The protagonist and narrator of the story, Major General X, is a successful politician who first undergoes the loss of his house to fire, then bankruptcy when his wife's cousin swindles him. In the stress of the situation, the general loses consciousness, awakening eighteen months later in California, in poverty. The general's daughter Bessie in this fragment is modeled after Susy Clemens. In his autobiography, Mark Twain tells how when Susy was told as a child not to cry over little things, she asked, "Mama, what is 'little things'?"[24] Bessie raises the same question. Other parallels abound. But Bessie, unlike Susy, survives the disaster: fiction could restore what had been irreparably lost.

Notes for the continuation of the story show that it would involve the family's traveling toward Australia, into the Devil's Race Track of "The Enchanted Sea-Wilderness."[25] They also suggest that the story was to be long and complicated. What may not be clear from the surviving text is that after describing his own life and, too lengthily, the charming ways of young Bessie, the general, falling asleep, *dreams* his disasters. Mark Twain tried to suggest that the narrator was dreaming by adding a prefatory entry from the diary of the general's wife, in which she sees him drowse while trying to write his narrative. This part, the beginning of the story, was added during the summer. The abandoned manuscript is engrossing, but the section on Bessie mars the focus badly.

Still mourning, Mark Twain agreed before he left England to write a report of Queen Victoria's jubilee for American newspapers. The date of June 22, 1897, was chosen to celebrate her sixty-year reign. The account Mark Twain produced is a pleasant piece of journalism with a few humorous touches. Albert Bigelow Paine later put it into the volume he called *Europe and Elsewhere* (1923). In July, the Clemenses moved back to the Continent, to Weggis in Switzerland, for the summer. There, returning to an old pattern, the writer devoted the summer to composition. On the anniversary of Susy's death, he wrote a poem, "In Memoriam Olivia Susan Clemens," published in November 1897 in *Harper's Magazine*. He also wrote "In My Bitterness," a statement which he himself called "blaspheming," unpublished until 1973. This piece attacks the God who "gives you a wife and children whom you adore, only that through the spectacle of the wanton shame and miseries which He will inflict upon them He may tear the palpitating heart out of your breast and slap you in the face with it."[26]

After this outburst, Mark Twain was able to return to his earlier humorous manner, if only briefly. In Switzerland he fictionalized slightly, without reference to Susy, his own recent experiences in England and on his way to Switzerland as "Letters to Satan." (One letter was published by Paine in 1923.) This piece demonstrates that under the proper conditions he could penetrate the fog of his despair and produce literature that rewards readers. Another indication is a nearly complete novelette of approaching thirty thousand words, "Tom Sawyer's Conspiracy." Notebook entries of 1896 and 1897 suggest plot ideas for a "New Huck Finn," one of which was adopted: "Tom is disguised as a negro and sold in Ark[ansas] for $10, then he & Huck help hunt for him after the disguise is removed."[27] Mark Twain wrote four chapters in Switzerland, then ran out of ideas. In these chapters, Tom plans the adventure, and he and Huck undertake the elaborate scheme. The vividly realized setting once again is the author's hometown, Hannibal/St. Petersburg, Missouri. An incident from the author's childhood is introduced when Tom chooses to catch the measles by getting into bed with Joe Harper, although the disease turns out to be scarlet fever. Later the author found a way to go on with the story, and over the next several years he returned to it several times, as he had with *Huckleberry Finn*. Instead of Tom's invented "conspiracy," the boys ultimately contend with a murder, and Jim is the suspect. This development permits Twain to provide another dramatic courtroom scene, with Tom in a very difficult situation as his plans backfire and Jim seems likely to be found guilty. The Duke and the King appear briefly, too, but within a few pages of the apparent ending, the writer broke off, and by 1902 he was referring to "the discarded Conspiracy."[28]

Unfortunately, admirers of *Huckleberry Finn* will discover that Mark Twain had forgotten the essential virtues of his masterpiece in trying to write this sequel. The issue of race, for example, is made frivolous here. This time the narrator is telling his story after the Civil War, and it too is made to seem inconsequential. Huck tells how Tom himself had invented plans for a civil war, "and it is one of the brightest things to his credit. And he could a had it easy enough if he had sejested it, anybody can see it now. And it don't seem right and fair that Harriet Beacher Stow and all of them other second-handers gets all the credit of starting that war and you never hear Tom Sawyer mentioned in the histories ransack them how you will, and yet he was the first that thought of it. Yes, and years and years before ever they had the idea."

The story is almost as badly plotted as *Tom Sawyer, Detective*. Again the writer introduces detectives; again he simultaneously both glamorizes and satirizes detective methodology. He may have become more sympathetic from his recent reading of Arthur Conan Doyle's stories of Sherlock Holmes, from which he derived some ideas. But chiefly he was trying once more to exploit the enduring popularity of Huck, Jim, and Tom. Perhaps the diminishment of Jim here showed that Mark Twain had become more aware of the lasting psychological effects of slavery on turn-of-the-century African Americans. The unfinished "Tom Sawyer's Conspiracy" was first published in 1969 in *Hannibal, Huck, and Tom*.

A partially redeeming feature, in stretches, is that occasionally Huck Finn's narrative style is almost up to that of the book that made him famous. The story begins with summer just coming on and Huck explaining, "Winter is plenty lovely enough if it *is* winter and the river is froze over and there's hail and sleet and bitter cold and booming storms and all that, but spring is no good — just rainy and slushy and sloppy and dismal and ornery and uncomfortable, and ought to be stopped. Tom Sawyer he says the same."[29]

In a series of profiles written in Switzerland about the same time, "Villagers of 1840–3," Mark Twain recalls his fellow Hannibal townsfolk of his youth with what is mostly a cynical attitude. The sordid and seamy side of life in the village is emphasized in this remarkable catalog, a caustic commentary on 168 people. The manuscript amounts to a biographical document, not literature, and was to have been utilized, for instance, in such stories as "Hellfire Hotchkiss," which explores sexual identity.[30]

This latter fragment, featuring Orion, here called Oscar and ironically nicknamed "Thug" for his gentleness, begins by making much of Orion's short-lived religious enthusiasms, a trait of Orion's that Mark Twain returned to often. Employing Dawson's Landing as a setting, with Pudd'nhead Wilson serving as a minor chorus character, the author found his attention drawn more and more to another, to whom he assigned Susy-like qualities. Her name was given to the story: "Hellfire" (properly Rachel) Hotchkiss, a tomboy. She and Thug have one thing in common: both are hampered by their "misplaced sexes." "Pudd'nhead Wilson says Hellfire Hotchkiss is the only genuwyne male man in town and Thug Carpenter's the only genuwyne female girl, if you leave out sex and just consider the business facts."[31] But neither this idea, which recalls the plot of "The 1002^d Arabian Night," nor any other remains in focus. Oscar's mother, who is introduced at the beginning of the story in a long dialogue with his father, becomes a dominant figure before the story breaks off; she is obviously based on Jane Lampton Clemens, the author's mother. But like "Which Was the Dream?," "Hellfire Hotchkiss" is marred by the writer's obsessive memories of his family. The fragment was finally published in *Satires and Burlesques* (1967).

A thematically related piece begun during that same summer of 1897 in Weggis is "Wapping Alice." Based on an incident of the Clemens household of 1877, when the author forced the lover of one of his housemaids to marry her, the story had a new setting in London. Revising it in the autumn, Twain changed the name of the narrator from Clemens to Jackson and tried to pass the narrative off as fiction. He made another crucial change, a twist that had never happened in Hartford. After the wedding, "Alice" is discovered to be a man who had invented the entire romance as a lark. The story is interesting chiefly because of its treatment, yet again, of sexual identity.[32] The author's attitude toward this piece is both curious and amusing. After it had failed to find acceptance, in August 1899, he wrote to Rogers, "I perceive that a part of Alice needs re-writing—so *she* isn't publishable as she stands. She'll never get that re-writing. She should have applied when I was interested in her—and she didn't. I wash *my* hands of the business." And so "Alice" remained unpublished until 1981.

Another piece attempted in this busy summer was a historical novel based on the life of Wilhelmina, Margravine of Bayreuth. Mark Twain drafted a chapter and pages of notes, then gave it up.[33] Thus the summer of 1897 was in retrospect an unsuccessful one—a fact the author admitted to Howells in August 1898. "I started 16 things wrong—3 books and 13 mag. articles—& could make only 2 little wee things, 1500 words altogether, succeed; — only that out of piles & stacks of diligently-wrought MS., the labor of 6 weeks' unremitting effort." He dismissed all of them as unimportant except one, "Which Was the Dream?" (One of the completed pieces appears to be merely an obituary for a Hartford friend, J. Hammond Trumbull, who had provided learned chapter headings for *The Gilded Age*.) Back in New York, Harper published a collection of Mark Twain's nonfiction, *How to Tell a Story and Other Essays*.

The period from 1894 through the summer of 1897, then, was a low point in Clemens's life; within this short period he experienced both bankruptcy and the death of his oldest daughter. Although he was able to meet his financial obligations, and in time return to prosperity, the loss of Susy confirmed a pessimistic attitude he had been developing for some fifteen years. He could no longer think of his Hartford years with his growing family as a halcyon period; instead, in his bereavement the memories had become for him a dream from which he had been roughly awakened.

CHAPTER TEN

Second Harvest

A fter the defeats of the summer of 1897 and despite his penchant for taking on projects for which he had no talent and his inability to resist trying his hand at business, Mark Twain nonetheless underwent a remarkable recovery. In September, the Clemenses moved to Vienna, and for twenty months they made their home in that cultural capital and in the nearby summer resort community of Kaltenleutgeben, in the southern sector of the Vienna Woods. During this period, the writer enjoyed extensive public attention and gained a new sense of his possibilities as a writer.[1] For example, soon after he arrived, he was invited to address the Concordia, Vienna's celebrated press club. (He could not have known that the club was shunned by anti-Semitic newspapermen.) Then in March 1899 he traveled to Budapest to speak to the Hungarian Journalists' Association. Before he ended his Vienna sojourn, he had a private audience with Emperor Franz Josef. No wonder he could write in his notebook, "During 8 years I have now filled the post — with some credit, I trust — of self-appointed Ambassador at Large of the U.S. of America — without salary."[2] He found the political and cultural life of Vienna very engaging and was also stimulated by the Dreyfus case in France, which he watched closely. (He was so moved by Emile Zola's defense of Dreyfus that he composed, but apparently did not send, a brief note of appreciation to Zola.)

A step toward the author's recovery occurred in early 1898, when, as his letters to Henry H. Rogers show, he was able to pay his creditors fully, to his great relief. Newspapers compared him to an earlier writer who had courageously redeemed himself from bankruptcy, Sir Walter Scott. Besides regaining self-confidence, he was now able to collect generous remuneration from his writing, although he still squandered much time on fruitless efforts, especially in writing for the stage.

The reason for the visit to Vienna, although the writer was not to admit it to the Viennese, was to accommodate his daughter Clara's wish to study the piano with a famous professor, Theodor Leschetizky, and voice with a noted Wagnerian contralto, Marianne Brandt. Leschetizky's students included Ignace Jan Paderewski, Alexander Brailowsky, Paul Wittgenstein, Arthur Schnabel, and the man who was to become Clara's husband, Ossip Gabrilowitsch. Clara's parents were eager to cater to their daughter and keep her near them, for they still felt acutely the death of Susy. As Clemens wrote to Rogers on March 7, "Clara has to stay here a year yet, to study music, and the rest of us must stay, too, for Mrs. Clemens will not hear of the family ever being divided again."

Ossip Gabrilowitsch, a Russian Jew, had come to Vienna to study with Leschetizky at age sixteen. Four years younger than Clara, Gabrilowitsch had already made his debut in Berlin before they met. Eventually, in 1909, they would marry. Much later, in 1930, Gabrilowitsch was to recall, "The Clemens drawing-room in Vienna was a rendez-vous for distinguished men and women of all types and nationalities. Clara enjoyed great popularity in musical circles; and I was by no means the only young man whose head was turned and whose heart needed mending."[3]

During their first year in Vienna, the Clemenses resided at the fashionable Hotel Metropole, not far from the center of the city. During the second year, from October 1898 till May 1899, they lived at the new and handsomely furnished Hotel Krantz, in an even choicer location. (Today that hotel, partly rebuilt after World War II, is called the Ambassador.) Finding the complicated and volatile politics of the Austro-Hungarian Empire intriguing, the writer made several visits to the parliament soon after his arrival. There, in late November 1897, he witnessed the eviction of ten members of parliament by armed police and was so deeply moved by the frightening experience that he wrote a long essay on the politics of the day, "Stirring Times in Austria," published in *Harper's* in August 1898. He judged that he had seen one of "the world's unforgettable things." In September 1898, an event occurred foreshadowing the events that were later to begin World War I, and he wrote about it. "The Memorable Assassination" reports on the assassination of Empress Elisabeth and the funeral that followed. He labeled "the murder of an empress" the "largest of large events." From the balcony of a room in the Krantz Hotel he observed the funeral procession heading for the Capuchin church just across the square. The essay, essentially journalism, was rejected by three magazines, including *Harper's*. Paine included it in his 1917 collection *What Is Man?* Its chief importance is its acknowledgment of Mark Twain's misanthropy. "Without our clothes and our pedestals we are poor things and much of a size; our dignities are not real, our pomps are shams."

In the spring and summer of 1898, Mark Twain drafted another essay, "Concerning the Jews." According to it, a remark he made in "Stirring Times" had prompted several American Jews to write to the author, one asking for his explanation of anti-Semitism. Ostensibly his next essay was a response to the letter-writers. But he had better reasons for writing on the subject: his Vienna experiences and his keen interest in the Dreyfus affair in France. The Jews he had come to know personally were highly successful and had been largely assimilated in Vienna. Jewish musicians, writers, and intellectuals were in fact largely responsible for Vienna's status as a great center of culture. In the years just before the Clemenses settled there, Jews of a different kind had flooded into Vienna. Poverty-stricken immigrants, many of them orthodox, from Bukovina and Galicia, created a readily identifiable Jewish proletariat. Like the Irish who flooded Massachusetts in the late nineteenth century, they were considered unwelcome. Soon there was a strong anti-Semitic movement at work.

Clemens found himself entangled in the conflict because the leading newspapers of Vienna were mostly liberal, owned and edited by Jews, yet others were harshly anti-Semitic. That the newcomer had been courted by the liberal press and had granted interviews to Jewish journalists was not lost on the anti-Semitic newspapermen. Moreover, the name Samuel was considered a Jewish (Old Testament) name, not a suitable Christian name by local standards: the Catholic requirement was to adopt the name of a saint. As a result Clemens himself was identified in the anti-Semitic press as a Jew, even ridiculed in newspaper cartoons, and vigorously attacked. He was referred to as "der jüdische amerikanische Humorist."[4]

Thus Mark Twain had very good reason to think seriously about anti-Semitism. Whereas the earlier piece had been a competent piece of topical journalism, in "Concerning the Jews" he was much more engaged by his topic, although he made no reference to his Vienna experiences. He presents himself as a philo-Semite and identifies Jews as good citizens, law-abiding, benevolent, devoted to family, "not a burden upon public charities." Why then are they subject to such abuse? Anti-Semitism is based, according to Mark Twain, simply on the Jew's superior ability as "a money-getter." "The cost to him has been heavy; his success has made the whole human race his enemy."

How might Jews seek to eliminate the "maltreatment, injustice, and oppression" they suffer? They should seek election to legislatures in "all parliamentary countries" and organize themselves to achieve political power. But Mark Twain expresses opposition to the creation of a Jewish state in Palestine because such a concentration of "the cunningest brains in the world" would have the unfortunate effect of letting "that race find out its strength," a remark that can be interpreted as implicitly anti-Semitic, although he asserted, "I *am* without prejudice." He judged that despite splendid contributions to civilization, the Jew would always suffer because "By his make and ways he is substantially a foreigner wherever he may be, and even the angels dislike a foreigner." Thus the only way for Jews to escape anti-Semitism was for them to change their identity, their "make and ways." Most readers will find the essay unsatisfactory, although one's reading is inevitably colored by what has taken place since the essay was written. At any rate, the author was very proud of it and told Rogers in July 1898 that it was a "gem," and that if Jews and Christians did not admire it, "people who are neither Jews *nor* Christians will." *Harper's* accepted "Concerning the Jews" and published it in September 1899.

One aspect of Vienna's rich cultural life that especially nourished and delighted Clemens was its vibrant theater. Vienna was the preeminent headquarters of the theater on the European continent, and one of the most magnificent buildings of the city was the Burgtheater, where he saw many performances. One play interested him so much that he attended several performances: Adolf von Wilbrandt's *Der Meister von Palmyra*. The theme of the play is that only death makes life meaningful, an argument that appealed to the increasingly pessimistic author. In late May and early June 1898, he wrote a highly appreciative essay on von Wilbrandt's work in an essay he called "About Play Acting," published in *Forum* magazine in October 1898. Such serious drama greatly attracted the aging author because he was becoming more and more interested in philosophical literature, both as reader and as writer. He praised it as "just one long, soulful, sardonic laugh at human life." Soon the impact of the play on the author was to reveal itself in his masterwork, "The Chronicle of Young Satan."

A few months earlier, in February 1898, Clemens had told Rogers that he had "resolved to stop book-writing and go at something else." Not surprisingly, his interest turned again to the writing of plays. He explained that he was "learning the trade pretty fast" and would "stick to the business" until he found out whether or not he could succeed at it. He was less optimistic with Howells, to whom he had written a few days earlier: "I have made a change lately — into dramatic work — & I find it absorbingly entertaining. I don't know that I can write a play that will play; but no matter, I'll write half a dozen that won't anyway."

That prediction was not much off the mark. None of the several play-writing projects — to which he devoted a number of months — was of any consequence. First, he wrote "Is He Dead?" — a dramatization of a story he had written in 1894, "Is He Living or Is He Dead?" Bram Stoker, acting as his agent in London, was unable to muster any interest in it. The un-published "Is He Dead?" does survive, despite what Clemens wrote to Rogers in August: "*Put 'Is He Dead' in the fire.* God will bless you. I too. I started in to convince myself that I could write a play or couldn't. I'm convinced. Nothing can disturb that conviction."

But this resolution was to be short-lived. Next he took on what he told Rogers was "a joint production": "An Austrian playwright is plotting it out, and we are going to write it together." It was to be called *Der Gegenkandidat, oder die Frauen Politiker* (The Opposing Candidate, or the Women Politicians), and it was an attempt to write a topical play, there being interest at the time in women's suffrage in Austria, Britain, and the United States. The arrangements for the collaboration were complicated. Siegmund Schlesinger, an established dramatist whom he had met early in his visit, sketched out the plot; Mark Twain then wrote the play in English, and Schlesinger translated it into German. What happened to the result is not clear; perhaps the American writer realized that the result was worthless. A second attempt at collaboration, *Die Goldgräberin* (The Lady Goldminer), appears never to have been completed.[5]

Earlier, when he was preparing "Is He Dead?" Clemens obtained — as he wrote to Rogers — "American and English rights in a new and powerful and successful Austrian drama." This was Philip Langmann's naturalistic play *Bartel Turaser,* concerning the corrupting power of money. Next, he translated Ernest Gettke and Alexander Engel's farce *Im Fegefeuer* (In Purgatory). His efforts to have each of these plays accepted by New York producers were unsuccessful. The translations have not survived. Once again, the writer had wasted his talents.[6]

On May 20, 1898, the Clemenses began residing at Villa Paulhof in Kaltenleutgeben, some fifteen miles from central Vienna. There, in part because of cool, wet weather, Mark Twain had an unusually productive five-month period of writing. Probably the first piece he wrote there is "At the Appetite Cure," based on an imagined visit to a health resort where he is abused by being alternately starved and fed disgusting food.

Other works written in whole or in part at the summer retreat were among his most important works of the 1890s. In 1897, he had drafted a discussion of "The Moral Sense." Now, between April and July, he gave serious attention to what he later called his "gospel": a dialogue between a young man and an old man on moral and ethical issues. Originally he called it "Selfishness" or "What Is the Real Character of Conscience?" Elaborated, edited, and reorganized over the next seven years, *What Is Man?* was privately printed in 250 copies for the author in 1906, after his wife's death, with no indication of the author's identity. Some copies were distributed, but not until April 23, 1910, two days after Clemens's death, was the work given any public attention. Then the *New York Tribune* published excerpts in a feature article, and other periodicals, English and American, gave the piece further publicity. The first American trade edition was published in 1917 in *What Is Man? and Other Essays*. Thereafter, it was routinely included in some editions of Mark Twain's works.[7]

Clearly Mark Twain was beginning to think of himself as a philosopher. In 1902 he received a letter from a European reader who thought he had been able to read Mark Twain's views between the lines of his most recent pieces. He wanted to know if the writer didn't believe that American civilization was better than the dreadful European civilization. In response Mark Twain described his work as the result of using a "microscope."

> I believe that many a person has examined man with a microscope in every age of the world; has found that he did not even resemble the creature he was pretending to be; has perceived that a civilization not proper matter for derision has always been and must always remain impossible to him — and has put away his microscope. . . . Perhaps because the microscopist (besides having an influential wife) was built like the rest of the human race — 99 parts of him being moral cowardice. I am such a person myself. I used my microscope during fifteen years, and then put the result on paper five years ago. Whenever I wish to account for any new outbreak of hypocrisy, stupidity or crime on the part of the race I get out that manuscript and read it, and am consoled, perceiving that the outbreak was in obedience to the law of man's make, and was not preventable. My wife does not allow this manuscript to be published, and as 99 parts of me forbid me to make myself comprehensively and uncompromisingly odious, it has not been difficult to persuade me to restrict the reading of it to myself.[8]

In the 1906 edition, the roughly thirty thousand words are divided into six chapters. These discuss determinism, personal merit, human motivation, training, instinct, thought, and free will. Other sections, including a long disquisition on God, were not included in the 1906 version but were finally published in 1973.

The dialogue argues that man is a machine whose performance is determined by training. Man is "moved, directed, COMMANDED, by *exterior* influences — *solely.*" Everything he does is done in order to secure his own approval and that of his neighbors and the public. Many examples are cited. The effect of outside influences in training is explored, with the old man offering, with much ado, a plan for man's betterment. "Diligently train your ideals *upward* and *still upward* toward a summit where you will find your chiefest pleasure in conduct which, while contenting you, will be sure to confer benefits upon your neighbor and the community" (chap. 4). Yet there is no free will, and man has absolutely no reason to be proud. (The early versions of the dialogue stress this last argument.) Man can be happy only *if* he is born with a happy temperament. Nonetheless, the work itself is not entirely gloomy, and some of the examples cited are engrossing.[9]

The deterministic side of the would-be philosopher found in *What Is Man?* has often been ascribed to Clemens's need not to be relieved of responsibility for his failures. But his reading over many years seems a far more important source, especially his favorite, Lecky's *History of European Morals,* Darwin (whom he cites in the dialogue), and other contemporary scientists such as Huxley and William James. He had been heading toward determinism since the early 1880s; in 1883, for instance, he discussed some of his ideas in a talk on "What Is Happiness?" before the Monday Evening Club of Hartford. Some of what he read while he was in Austria also contributed to his philosophy. These works include Schopenhauer's *World as Will and Idea.*[10] Although it has been treated as literature, *What Is Man?* is chiefly of interest to those concerned with the writer: it provides a careful statement of one dimension of his philosophy during his later years. Although most readers find the work prosaic and unsophisticated, Sherwood Cummings has recently looked at it appreciatively. He writes:

> Without connecting with the movement of naturalism [identified with such contemporary American novelists as Stephen Crane and Theodore Dreiser], Mark Twain expressed naturalistic ideas and emphases. Without studying two centuries of behavioralistic science, he apprehended its ideas in historical order. He did all that in spite of his friends' and family's disapproval of his notions. In the matter of *What Is Man?* he was a stubborn literary circle of one, depending on a few seminal books read years before, on private thoughts, and on an exquisite sensitiveness to ideas in the air.[11]

Much more personal than *What Is Man?* is the long poem, some fifty quatrains, that Mark Twain wrote in the same year, 1898; it is entitled

"Omar's Old Age," and it echoes a work that the author had read as early as 1876 and that had become a favorite with him, the *Rubáiyát* of Omar Khayyám. Its forty-five stanzas were published in 1983. The poem deals with the enfeeblements of old age and complains of the efficacy of newly discovered germs and the failure of bodily functions and sexual ability. Midway through the collection can be found this bittersweet stanza.

> Some happy Day my Voice will Silent fall,
> And answer not when some that love it call:
> > Be glad for Me when this you note — and think
> I've found the Voices lost, beyond the Pall.

One line jokes, "Behold! The Penis mightier than the Sword." The "poet" went so far as to urge his English publisher to make a book of the verses, a limited edition, with the aim of making money. Not surprisingly, Andrew Chatto opposed the idea.[12] In all, Mark Twain wrote over 120 poems. Of those identified, 95 are comic and 31 are serious. In addition to the ones inspired by Omar Khayyám, a thin volume of the more appealing ones was published as *On the Poetry of Mark Twain*.

Similar in theme, but different in genre from his philosophical dialogue was the writer's completion at Kaltenleutgeben of a piece of serious fiction, "The Man That Corrupted Hadleyburg," which may reflect the author's recent experiences with pandemonium in the Austrian parliament. His most elaborately plotted story, highly economical and suspenseful, it is rich in implications. What strikes most readers is the pessimism of its biting satire: all nineteen of the town's leading citizens are quickly corrupted by greed as the result of a cunning hoax. Part of the reason for their failing is that "through the formative years temptations were kept out of the way of young people." Consequently, at the end of the story the inhabitants of Hadleyburg adopt a new town motto by dropping the word *not:* "Lead us into temptation." The story focuses, almost clinically, on the mental processes of two main characters, Mary and Edward Richards, who rationalize themselves into dishonesty. Richards declares that their action "was ordered. *All* things are ordered." Their moral degeneration leads them first to a fear of humiliating exposure, then to delirium; even their eventual confession and misdirected self-recrimination destroy rather than redeem them. While not villains in a conventional sense, they are thoroughly reprehensible. Unlike *What Is Man?* "Hadleyburg" essentially implies man's responsibility for his actions. Published in *Harper's* in December 1899, the tale proved profitable. Mark Twain made two thousand dollars.

For several years the writer had longed to write an autobiography. Inspired by the example of Grant's dictating his memoirs in 1885, Mark Twain dictated an account of his dealings with Grant during the same year, and in 1890 he wrote (rather than dictated) a brief account of his dealings with James W. Paige, the inventor of the typesetter. While he was in Vienna, he wrote seven autobiographical pieces, including an absolute masterpiece, "Early Days." Perhaps because of his recent failures and disappointments, the writer here sees his own youthful past with a good deal of nostalgia, but he is never sentimental and he never lingers over incidents or persons. Among the high spots are the sketch of James Lampton, the original of Colonel Sellers, and the affectionate description of the Quarles farm, where he spent his boyhood summers. His memories bring image after image into sharp focus.

> I know the taste of the watermelon which has been honestly come by, and I know the taste of the watermelon that has been acquired by art. Both taste good, but the experienced know which tastes best. I know the look of green apples and peaches and pears on the trees, and I know how entertaining they are when they are inside of a person. I know how ripe ones look when they are piled in pyramids under the trees, and how pretty they are and how vivid their colors. I know how a frozen apple looks, in a barrel down cellar in the wintertime, and how hard it is to bite, and how the frost makes the teeth ache, and yet how good it is, notwithstanding. I know the disposition of elderly people to select the specked apples for the children, and I once knew ways to beat the game.[13]

Later, when he began to dictate his autobiography on a regular basis, he indulged himself by taking up whatever subject suited his fancy. In "Early Days," however, there are only brief digressions. It is the highlight of the autobiography, much the finest of the pieces written in Austria. Yet despite its virtues, the author declared to Rogers in November that he would "never write the Autobiography" till he was "in a hole." Fiction still seemed to him the worthiest challenge.

About the same time that he wrote the pages on his boyhood, he began a story set in the fictional Austrian village of Eseldorf in 1702. He called his new work "The Chronicle of Young Satan." This fragment forms the basis of the much-admired book that Albert Bigelow Paine and Frederick A. Duneka of Harper and Brothers edited and published in 1916 as *The Mysterious Stranger*. Since the composition took place over a period of years, the work is discussed later in this chapter.

Despite his lack of success with the Paige typesetting machine and other investments, Clemens was still pulled toward "business." In March 1898, he had met Jan Szczepanik, an inventor who had developed a device for copying images onto woven fabric. Immediately he thought of his own financial advantage and sought an option on American rights to the device. He befriended the inventor, and for more than two months his correspondence with Rogers is full of his preoccupation with the invention. Nothing was to come of his efforts, but he was able to write as a result of his enthusiasm two pieces good enough to be published in the *Century* magazine in 1898. Both "The Austrian Edison Keeping School Again" and "From the 'London Times' of 1904" merely show that the author retained an ability to produce what he could sell. The former is derived from his experiences with the inventor. The latter, which is science fiction, also involves "the Austrian Edison." A little of the author's outlook is suggested by the surprising, and unconvincing, ending of the "London Times" piece, which is bitter: an innocent man is executed. (The reader is told to find an analogue in the Dreyfus affair.)

Another highly personal statement is "My Platonic Sweetheart," written in late July 1898 and rejected by three periodicals. Originally entitled "My Lost Sweetheart," this autobiographical piece tells of the author's recurring dream of his unnamed childhood sweetheart (actually Laura M. Wright). He dreamed of being with her in a Missouri village, then in a magnolia forest in Natchez, in a Hawaiian valley, in Athens, and in India. Always he is seventeen, she fifteen. The experiences are so powerful that they persuade the writer that dreams are true and the dreamers immortal. Here the writer reveals his continuing interest in "the duality idea," which he had taken up more comically many years before in "The Facts Concerning the Recent Carnival of Crime in Connecticut." He tells how from a conversation with his conscience he had learned "he was not *me*, nor a part of me, but merely resided in me." Then the author was further enlightened, first by Robert Louis Stevenson's *Dr. Jekyll and Mr. Hyde*, then by French experiments with hypnosis and the work of William James. He concluded that he consists of a "waking self," a "somnambulic self," and a "dream self." This last self especially intrigued the writer. He is a

spiritualized self who nightly or daily, at home or church or wherever the chance offers, takes a holiday for a couple of seconds and goes larking about the world for hours during those seconds, has adventures, sees wonderful things, makes love, falls over precipices, gets lost in mazes, is pursued by shrouded corpses and other horrors and cannot make headway for fright, gets mixed up in quarrels while doing his best to avoid them, enlists for the war and retreats from the field in front of the first volley, gets run away with by scared horses, tries to deliver lectures without any subject, appears in crowded drawing rooms with nothing on but a shirt; in a word, does a thousand rash and foolish things which nothing could ever persuade my workaday "me" to do—then comes back home and remembers it all, re-sees it all, with a memory for form, color and detail compared to which mine is as blank paper to a printed book, and I get up in the morning and innocently tell the family what *I* have been seeing and doing![14]

This idea of the three selves would soon form the basis of a long, uncompleted novel, "No. 44, The Mysterious Stranger."

That "My Platonic Sweetheart" was written so soon after the first draft of *What Is Man?* shows clearly that Mark Twain's deterministic philosophy and his bitter pessimism and misanthropy were to some extent counterbalanced by his delighted fascination with the mysteries of identity and multiple personality and even by a readiness to believe in an immortal self. The cheerfulness of "My Platonic Sweetheart" even includes a joke the author calls "much the best I ever made in a dream." He found himself in his dream to be the seven-year-old son of a fashionably dressed couple in Paris—Adam and Eve. He was an impertinent child, calling his father "Ad." "Eve was shocked at my abbreviating my father's name in that irreverent way, and told me to say it again and put on the rest of it. I refused, and said 'Ad' again. She told me to get under the table and stay there until I was willing to obey that order. I was under the table a while, then I had an idea, and crawled out and stood by her knee and said—'Dam!'"[15] Despite its appeal, "My Platonic Sweetheart" was rejected by three magazines, and only after the author's death did an abridged version, published by *Harper's,* appear in 1912.

Another attempt at fiction written at the summer resort is wholly serious, even somber: "An Adventure in Remote Seas." A surviving fragment of just two chapters again deals with the area toward the South Pole that had attracted his imagination since his trip to Australia. The argument of the story—that nothing has value apart from use—is demonstated when a group of sailors discover, first, sixty million dollars' worth of gold coins, and second, that they have been left stranded with no way to escape. The author too found himself with nowhere to go and abandoned the story.

In August 1898, Mark Twain recorded in his notebook: "Last night dreamed of a whaling cruise in a drop of water. Not by microscope, but actually. This would mean a reduction of the participants to a minuteness which would make them nearly invisible to God, and he wouldn't be interested in them any longer."[16] The dream led him to try another version of his dream-disaster story. This time he decided to make the first half or two-thirds comedy. He now wrote to Howells, "I think I can carry the reader a long way before he suspects I am laying a tragedy-trap." DeVoto, who edited it for publication, called the new story "The Great Dark." In it the narrator, Mr. Edwards, and his family have been examining a drop of polluted water under a microscope, when Edwards takes a nap. Before he falls asleep, he mentions to the "Superintendent of Dreams" his wish to explore the world of a drop of water in a comfortable ship with his family. Soon his wish is realized: he finds himself on a frightening, nightmarish voyage, sailing in perpetual night. There are some light touches, but the mood is by no means comic. The superintendent is along, and when he and Edwards have a small falling-out, Edwards tells him he can end the dream if he wants — to which the superintendent replies: "The dream? *Are you quite sure it is a dream?*" He continues, "You have spent your whole life in this ship. And this is *real* life. Your other life was the dream!"[17] Soon Edwards realizes that his wife and children know no other life than the one on shipboard and have no memories to correspond with his, except memories of dreams. "And now another past began to rise, dim and spiritual before me and stretch down and down and down into dreaming remoteness of bygone years — a past spent in a ship!"[18] The dream manages to suggest the horror that lurks within the human psyche, below consciousness. The discussion of the difference between dreams and reality is decidedly engaging. (In a related fragment, the writer records that in one of the countries of "Dreamland" there are "no exact equivalents for our words *modesty, immodesty, decency, indecency, right, wrong, sin.*")[19]

Soon the narrator and the reader are plunged deeper into nightmare as the ship and its crew are attacked by a giant squid. Though blinded, the creature remains threateningly nearby. Mutiny adds to the terror, even after Captain Davis, a figure based on Mark Twain's old hero Ned Wakeman, is able to put it down. (For some of these events, the author obviously drew on materials from an article he was writing at the time, "My Début as a Literary Person," about the *Hornet* disaster at sea.) At this point, unfortunately, the writer interrupted the story. Notes suggest how he might have continued, with horror piled on horror: the crew going crazy, the narrator's son and the captain's daughter being taken to another ship, the seas drying up. Finally the narrator "Looks up — is at home — his wife & the children coming to say goodnight. His hair is white."[20] Despite some burlesque elements and a story about a seaman who takes the temperance pledge, the dominant mood of this 35,000-word fragment is incredibly black; it is the best of the author's several attempts to write dream-disaster stories.

The year 1898 was truly a strange one in Mark Twain's writing career. A play, translations, serious and commercial fiction, philosophy, and auto-biography are among the forms that his writing took. He wrote one other work before he returned to the United States, a piece that seems at first a most unlikely one. He began the piece after completing "Hadleyburg" and continued to work on it until the following spring. When published in *Cosmopolitan* in October 1899, the piece was entitled "Christian Science and the Book of Mrs. Eddy."

Christian Science at this time was a highly controversial, much discussed topic of journalistic investigation. Moreover, Clemens himself had long been fascinated by mental healing. That his daughter Susy had been a devotee was a factor; he had written to her during his world tour, "I am perfectly certain that the exasperating colds and the carbuncles came from a diseased mind, and that your mental science could drive them away." But belief in the principle, which he called "Humanity's boon," was not the same, he told a correspondent, as reverence for the founder of Christian Science, Mary Baker Eddy, whom he scoffed at in 1903 as "the monumental sarcasm of the Ages." He continued, "It seems to me that when we contemplate her & what she has achieved, it is blasphemy to longer deny the Supreme Being the possession of a sense of humor." In a March 1903 letter, Mark Twain called her "the queen of frauds and hypocrites." His interest in both Mrs. Eddy and Christian Science was enduring; the first essay he wrote became, somewhat revised, chapters 1–4 of book 1 of Mark Twain's book *Christian Science* (1907).

In "Christian Science and the Book of Mrs. Eddy," Mark Twain imagines that he meets an American practitioner of Christian Science, a Mrs. Fuller, in Austria when he has a bad fall. In the sketch Mark Twain returns to one of his most dependable roles, that of victim, as he tries to contend first with the resolute woman who lectures him on metaphysics, then with a horse doctor whom he calls in when he finds his recovery slow. In his conversation with Mrs. Fuller, the writer is eager to submit and be rid of his pains, which he has been informed are unreal.

> "I am full of imaginary tortures," I said, "but I do not think I could be any more uncomfortable if they were real ones. What must I do to get rid of them?"
>
> "There is no occasion to get rid of them, since they do not exist. They are illusions propagated by matter, and matter has no existence; there is no such thing as matter."
>
> "It sounds right and clear, but yet it seems in a degree elusive; it seems to slip through, just when you think you are getting a grip on it." (chap. 2)

Mrs. Fuller leaves behind a copy of Mrs. Eddy's *Science and Health,* a book that Mark Twain finds even more amusing than Fenimore Cooper's *Deerslayer.* "When you read it you seem to be listening to a lively and aggressive and oracular speech delivered in an unknown tongue, a speech whose spirit you get but not the particulars; or, to change the figure, you seem to be listening to a vigorous instrument which is making a noise which it thinks is a tune, but which, to persons not members of the band, is only the martial tooting of a trombone, and merely stirs the soul through the noise, but does not convey a meaning" (chap. 3).

This polemical but richly varied essay was well received. Twichell wrote to his friend, "Some judge it the best you ever did."[21] The editor of *Cosmopolitan* was so pleased with the attention the essay received that he increased his payment by two hundred dollars, to one thousand dollars. Much less good are some pages on Christian Science also written in 1899 but not published in America for several years. They did appear, however, in England and Germany in 1900 in *The Man That Corrupted Hadleyburg and Other Stories and Sketches.*

While he was living in Vienna, in November 1898, the writer recorded a long note for a story. It begins: "Story of little Satan, jr., who came to Petersburg (Hannibal) went to school, was popular and greatly liked by (Huck and Tom) who knew his secret. The others were jealous, and the girls didn't like him because he smelt of brimstone."[22] The resulting story fragment of sixteen thousand words entitled "Schoolhouse Hill" combines the world of Huck and Tom with another portrait of Orion Clemens, here Oliver Hotchkiss, along with a charming portrait of the miracle-working, amoral Number Forty-four, the son of Satan. Because his father erroneously tempted Adam and Eve and thereby "*poisoned* the men of this planet—poisoned them in mind and body,"[23] Number Forty-four aims to improve man's lot. The author intended to subvert this plan, ironically, by converting him to Christianity. According to the very full notes, he was to fall in love with Hotchkiss's niece, Annie Fleming, who is a version of Hellfire Hotchkiss, heroine of an earlier fragment.[24] Despite its diffuseness, "Schoolhouse Hill" is a fascinating return to the evocative St. Petersburg, Mark Twain's last.

The writer's interest in Satan was long-standing. His own mother, he recounts, prayed for Satan, who she felt was especially in need of such help.[25] According to his 1909 publication *Is Shakespeare Dead?* (which the author identified as "From My Autobiography") Clemens's interest originated during his school days, when he wrote Satan's biography. In "Concerning the Jews," written in the summer of 1898, the author had asserted, "Of course Satan has some kind of case, it goes without saying. . . . As soon as I can get at the facts I will undertake his rehabilitation myself, if I can find an unpolitic publisher." One source of this interest and sympathy was Clemens's conception of Satan as both an underdog and a rebel against the God that Clemens was more and more considering his personal antagonist. And he had at least begun "Letters to Satan" by 1897.

In late May 1899, the Clemenses left Austria. Just as the reason for their visit was a daughter, their reason for leaving was a daughter, this time Jean. She had been suffering frequent attacks of epilepsy. An osteopath in London had been recommended, and it was there that they went. By this time Clara had given up the piano and had moved on to singing. She now wanted to continue voice lessons with Blanche Marchesi, a famous coach, in London.

In May 1899, on the eve of his departure, Mark Twain returned to "The Chronicle of Young Satan." He had abandoned it in early 1898 because he thought he had not started it right. But now believing that he had found the way to do what he intended, he was so relieved that he called his writing "an intellectual drunk." What he was up to, he confided to Howells in May 1899, he considered crucial to his career.

> For several years I have been intending to stop writing for print as soon as I could afford it. At last I can afford it, & have put the pot-boiler pen away. What I have been wanting was a chance to write a book without reserves — a book which should take account of no one's feelings, no one's prejudices, opinions, beliefs, hopes, illusions, delusions; a book which should say my say, right out of my heart, in the plainest language & without limitations of any sort. I judged that that would be an unimaginable luxury, heaven on earth. There was no condition but one under which the writing of such a book could be possible; only one — the consciousness that it would not see print.

Now engaged in writing such an unbridled statement, he told Howells:

> It is in tale-form. I believe I can make it tell what I think of Man, & how he is constructed, & what a shabby poor ridiculous thing he is, & how mistaken he is in his estimate of his character & powers & qualities & his place among the animals.

Mrs. Clemens, he reported to Howells, found the tale "perfectly horrible — and perfectly beautiful."[26]

Returning to his manuscript of the previous year, he discovered that in "The Chronicle of Young Satan" he had telescoped the story by coming too soon to the trial scene that serves as a climax. He therefore began to insert

1902: *Mark Twain at age sixty-six, in York Harbor, Maine. The Clemenses had returned to the United States in the fall of 1900. In 1902, they summered in York Harbor, where in August Olivia suffered a severe heart attack from which she never fully recovered. She had been an invalid for two years in her teens, never strong, and since 1870 she had regularly breathed her husband's tobacco smoke without his realizing that he was damaging her health. (Courtesy of the Mark Twain Papers, University of California, Berkeley)*

1903: *Sam at age sixty-seven and Olivia at age fifty-seven, at Quarry Farm, not long before they sailed for Italy to avoid the winter cold for Livy's sake. In Florence she was soon confined to bed, suffered two more heart attacks, and died of heart failure on June 5, 1904. (Courtesy of the Mark Twain House, Hartford)*

(Opposite) 1903: *Mark Twain at age sixty-seven at Quarry Farm, above Elmira, where the Clemenses resided again during the summer. Always apprecia-tive of cats, Mark Twain in* Pudd'nhead Wilson *asserted, "A home without a cat — and a well-fed, well-petted and properly revered cat — may be a perfect home, but how can it prove it?" This cat, however, is porcelain. (Courtesy of the Mark Twain House, Hartford).*

1906: *Mark Twain at age seventy. His secretary, Isabel Lyon, recorded on October 8, 1906, that he was "filled with the idea of defying conventionalities and wearing his suitable white clothes all winter." He then ordered five white suits and later fourteen, one for each day of the week and seven at the dry cleaner's; he even had one with tails for evening wear. (Courtesy of the Mark Twain Papers, University of California, Berkeley; location of original not known)*

(Opposite) 1907: *Mark Twain at age seventy, in his Oxford gown. Being awarded the degree of doctor of laws by Oxford University on June 26 was surely the high point of the writer's life. On October 6, 1909, he wore this gown over a white suit at the wedding of his daughter Clara to Ossip Gabrilowitsch at Stormfield. (Courtesy of Nick Karanovitch, Fort Wayne, Indiana, from his private collection)*

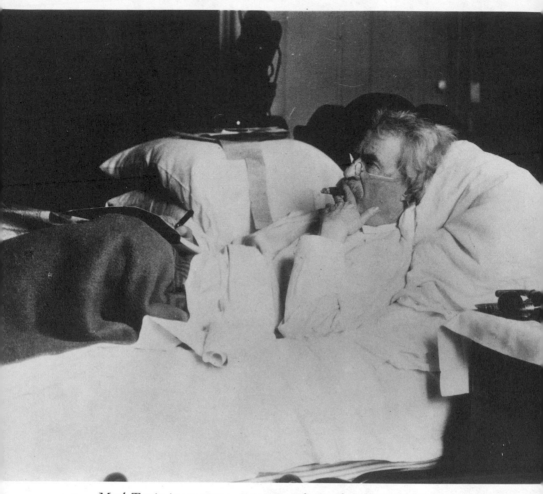

Mark Twain in 1906, at age seventy, at his residence on Fifth Avenue, New York. His favorite place to smoke was in bed. When he hit a snag in what he was writing, he sought inspiration from staying in bed and smoking there. (Courtesy of the Mark Twain Papers, Bancroft Library, University of California, Berkeley)

Mark Twain at age seventy-three with William Dean Howells. Howells read many of his friend's works in manuscript, regularly reviewed his books, and, following Clemens's death, published My Mark Twain *(1910). (Courtesy of the Mark Twain Papers, University of California, Berkeley; location of original not known)*

1910: *Mark Twain at age seventy-four, returning from Bermuda on April 14. He had begun to smoke as a child and for years had been a chain cigar-smoker. At first the result was simply a smoker's cough; later he experienced shortness of breath. From June 1909 onward he suffered from angina pectoris and admitted to reporters that smoking gave him a sharp pain in the heart. He died at Stormfield on April 21, 1910. (Courtesy of the Mark Twain Papers, University of California, Berkeley).*

new philosophic materials between two blocks that he had already written: what are now chapters 1, 2, and the beginning of 3, and the trial scene that would become part of chapter 10. These he wrote mostly in London, where the Clemenses moved in May, and in Sanna, Sweden, where Jean Clemens was treated for epilepsy during the summer. At that time he wrote the rest of chapter 3, then 4, 5, and the early part of chapter 6. All the rest that he finished — chapters 6, 7, 8, 9, part of 10, and what was written of chapter 11, were composed between June and August of 1900, just outside London at Dollis Hill.

One germ of this story is a notebook entry made at the end of June 1897: "Satan's boyhood — going around with other boys & surprising them with devilish miracles."[27] As he developed the story, the author suggested that this young Satan is a dream such as those he had described in "My Platonic Sweetheart": Satan gives himself the name of Philip Traum (dream). Clemens's reading of a book on psychic phenomena, *Phantasms of the Living* (1886), may have contributed to the story; the book deals with materialization, dematerialization, and dream experiences.[28] Almost like a wish fulfillment, Satan is introduced into Mark Twain's story the day after the boys to whom he appears have heard an old man's tale of "actual angels out of heaven" who "had no wings, and wore clothes, and talked and looked and acted like any natural person." The boys have "stretched out on the grass in the shade to rest . . . and talk over strange things" when an unfamiliar boy appears, to their great pleasure, in chapter 2.

Even as a fragment, "The Chronicle of Young Satan" is a masterpiece, horrible *and* beautiful, as Olivia Clemens said. In fifty-four thousand words, Mark Twain creates a world of both fantasy and reality, with a transcendent hero, Young Satan, nephew of the famous one. He resembles the boy Jesus of the apocryphal gospels, with which the writer had long been familiar. In 1867 he had quoted a description: "Jesus and other boys play together and make clay figures of animals. Jesus causes them to walk; also makes clay birds which he causes to fly, and eat and drink. The children's parents are alarmed and take Jesus for a sorcerer."[29] Mark Twain's narrator, Theodor Fischer, looks back at his youth from the vantage point of maturity, the same technique that the author had employed with effect in the 1870s but less aptly in *Joan of Arc*. One sign here of the narrator's double point of view is that he remembers his own identification with his community, Eseldorf (i.e., Jackassville), which was and has presumably remained naive and deluded. The story begins with this emphasis: "It was 1702 — May. Austria was far away from the world, and asleep; it was still the Middle Ages in Austria, and promised to remain so forever. Some even set it away back centuries upon centuries and said that by the mental and spiritual clock it was still the Age of Faith in Austria."[30] Theodor remembers his boyhood identification with an ignorant brand of Catholicism. He and his friends "were trained to be good Catholics; to revere the Virgin, the Church and the saints above everything. . . . Beyond these matters we were not required to know much; and in fact not allowed to. The priests said that knowledge was not good for the common people" (p. 36). The "Chronicle," then, is a *Bildungsroman,* a story of Theodor's initiation and education. An unobtrusive plot structure enables Satan to teach important lessons about what life offers. Satan educates Theodor by sharing with him the truth about the Moral Sense, man's lack of freedom, and the impossibility of human happiness. He teaches skillfully — far better than the Old Man of *What Is Man?* — for nearly always he finds examples, or creates them, from the boys' very lives. Satan, like the apocryphal Jesus, makes miniature living creatures, then casually destroys them. The incidents that occur in Theodor's village, such as Nikolaus's death, are effectively told. The reader is frequently reminded of Theodor's double perspective, as when he finds fault with Satan for depriving Father Peter of his reason: Satan "didn't seem to know any way to do a person a favor except by killing him or making a lunatic out of him." (p. 164).

Mark Twain's exuberant joy in depicting spectacle and showmanship (demonstrated by Tom Sawyer, the Yankee, and Pudd'nhead Wilson) reaches its most effective use in the "Chronicle." Like the bored boys of Hannibal who are roused by the arrival of a steamboat, the youth of Eseldorf are charmed by Satan's miracles. No dull lessons here. Ironically, Satan's most startling news is that the seemingly youthful innocence of the boys is not what it appears to be, and that it is Satan, despite his name, who is unfallen, and not the boys, for they are the victims of the Moral Sense. Satan explains:

> No brute ever does a cruel thing — that is the monopoly of the snob with the Moral Sense. When a brute inflicts pain he does it innocently; it is not wrong; for him there is no such thing as wrong. And he does not inflict pain for the pleasure of inflicting it — only man does that. Inspired by that mongrel Moral Sense of his! A Sense whose function is to distinguish between right and wrong, with liberty to choose which of them he will do. Now what advantage can he get out of that? He is always choosing, and in nine cases out of ten he prefers the wrong. There shouldn't *be* any wrong; and without the Moral Sense there *couldn't* be any. (pp. 72–73)

Satan's own lack of grief and guilt — since he is not burdened with a moral sense — emphasizes the pathetic absurdity of man.

The creator of "The Chronicle of Young Satan" had written to Howells in April 1899 that "man is not to me the respect-worthy person he was before" and therefore he could not "write gaily nor praisefully about him any more." To this he added, "And I don't intend to try." All the same, "Young Satan" is marked by much humor and vitality as well as pessimism and misanthropy. Above all, the story is almost magically imagined. Indeed, Satan speaks in praise of the power the author has given him:

> I *think* a poem — music — the record of a game of chess — anything — and it is there. This is the immortal mind — nothing is beyond its reach. Nothing can obstruct my vision — the rocks are transparent to me, and darkness is daylight. I do not need to open a book; I take the whole of its contents into my mind at a single glance, through its cover; and in a million years I could not forget a single word of it, or its place in the volume. Nothing goes on in the skull of any man, bird, fish, insect or other creature which can be hidden from me. I pierce the learned man's brain with a single glance, and the treasures which cost him three-score years to accumulate are mine; he can forget, and he does forget, but I retain. (p. 114)

Perhaps the most memorable passage is Mark Twain's encomium to humor. He argues, through Satan, that mankind "has unquestionably one really effective weapon — laughter. Power, Money, Persuasion, Supplication, Persecution — these can lift at a colossal humbug, — push it a little — crowd it a little, century by century: but only Laughter can blow it to rags and atoms at a blast. Against the assault of laughter nothing can stand" (pp. 165–66). The last episode that Twain wrote (he stopped in the middle of it) takes Theodor to India and Ceylon, where he had recently visited. As he abandoned Theodor's village to display Satan's mastery over time and distance, he developed a "centrifugal tendency" that led everywhere and nowhere; the travels through geography and history vitiate the story.

Before he stopped writing "The Chronicle of Young Satan," Mark Twain started — and dropped — another novel. This one he seems to have conceived of as written for publication. "Indiantown" occupied him for only a short time, perhaps two weeks, during the summer of 1899. While only three chapters (less than ten thousand words) were written, the setting sketched in these pages would reappear in a longer fragment, "Which Was It?" A Mississippi River town well south of St. Louis in cotton-growing country, Indiantown is viewed from an adult's perspective. The narrator is genial, kindly, leisurely. He introduces characters based on Orion Clemens, his sister Pamela (the widow Wilkinson), and Joseph Twichell. David Gridley is a self-portrait of the author, and his wife Susan is recognizably based on Olivia Clemens. Described as flawless, Susan devotes herself to the manufacture of an "elaborate sham" to replace the man she had married: "as far as his outside was concerned she made a master-work of it that would have deceived the elect."[31] She went so far as to try to cure David of swearing by quoting him; this incident is parallel to one that Mark Twain describes in his autobiography.[32] Both Susan Gridley and Olivia Clemens had made a practice of "dusting off" their husbands, to their children's great satisfaction, and both allowed their husbands to blow off steam at home. "Otherwise there would have been explosions in public."[33] A long passage makes clear the duplicity of David Gridley, and one is tempted to see in it the origins of the writer's obsession with identity and multiple personalities as well as a suggestion that the original Sam Clemens of Hannibal, the river, and Washoe had somehow survived despite his wife's efforts, and Clemens's own, to make him genteel. How thoroughly did Clemens create in Gridley a version of himself? Gridley remained in his own eyes "just a piece of honest kitchen furniture transferred to the drawing-room and glorified and masked from view in gorgeous cloth of gold."[34]

Joseph Twichell would have understood what his longtime friend was saying. He once told Isabel Lyon, who later became Clemens's secretary, "how much Mrs Clemens had done toward remodelling Mr Clemens. The Hooker girls of Hartford had been quite shocked when Mrs Clemens became engaged to him. But Mrs Clemens knew what she was about. . . . Of course there couldn't ever be anybody who could train him so that he wouldn't drop away a little back to his wildnesses, & his strengths. But Mrs Clemens did more than anyone else in the world could have done."[35] Why did the writer produce this self-portrait in David Gridley? One can only guess that it relieved by a kind of confession his guilt at being a hypocrite, what in "Indiantown" he called "a comprehensive, complete and symmetrical humbug."[36]

In Sweden, Mark Twain wrote "My Boyhood Dreams," which joshingly discusses the author's youthful ambitions as well as those of his friends Thomas Bailey Aldrich and John Hay. In London, to which the Clemenses returned in October, he wrote some slight but publishable pieces showing that his disdain for writing for money was not complete. "Two Little Tales," "The Death Disk," and "My First Lie and How I Got Out of It" represented a step backward. Some time was given over to preparing *The Man That Corrupted Hadleyburg and Other Stories and Essays,* published by Harper in

1900; some days were wasted on notes for an edition of the trial records of Joan of Arc and some others on "Proposition for a Postal Check," a dialogue that went unpublished. But until he returned to "The Chronicle of Young Satan" in the summer (he continued out of habit to think of summer as a time for writing), the remainder of his European decade was not fruitful. He expected to return at last to America, perhaps even to a position as magazine editor, an idea he soon abandoned. He indicated a developing interest in international affairs by writing "The Missionary in World Politics," which attacked Christian missionaries in China. He intended to publish this piece anonymously in the London *Times,* fearful of hurting the selling power of his name, then decided not to send it off. The year was 1900, and Clemens, who had reached the end of a decade without a home, told Laurence Hutton that he was "getting heartbreakingly anxious to get home — to get home and never budge again." He did not ask himself, apparently, where his *home* now was.

Perhaps one reason for the writer's homesickness was that he had been reminiscing again for his autobiography. "Playing 'Bear' — Herrings — Jim Wolf and the Cats" was published in the *Autobiography* in 1924, when Paine dated it "about 1898." But the holograph manuscript, in the Mark Twain Papers, is marked with both Paine's dating and a later correction to "1900." These vivid reminiscences both focus on youthful embarrassment. "Jim Wolf and the Cats" retells and improves the story that Mark Twain had published in 1867 and goes on to describe how later writers appropriated it and published it as their own. The other sketch is one of the best parts of the autobiography, almost on a par with "Early Days." It begins by telling of the author's acute distress at age twelve on discovering that while donning a bear costume for an entertainment he had unknowingly undressed in front of two young women in hiding. They revealed their presence when the black boy accompanying young Sam asked:

> "Mars Sam, has you ever seed a dried herring?"
> "No. What is that?"
> "It's a fish."
> "Well, what of it? Anything peculiar about it?"
> "Yes, suh, you bet dey is. *Dey* eats 'em innards and all!"[37]

[The manuscript originally read "guts and all."] After telling of meeting in Calcutta one of the young women whose "burst of feminine snickers" he had heard from behind the screen (only in India did she identify herself, by means of the slave boy's description of how herrings are eaten), the writer then summarizes, in seven paragraphs, his experiences with violence during his boyhood. The power of these pages suggests the strength of feeling behind the author's boy books. "There was the slave man who was struck down with a chunk of slag for some small offense; I saw him die. And the young Californian emigrant who was stabbed with a bowie knife by a drunken comrade; I saw the red life gush from his breast."[38]

For the writer, the second half of the 1890s had been far more productive than the first. *Joan of Arc* proved that the writer, even in his fifties, could do something entirely out of his line. Purely by an act of iron will, he had finished an account of his world tour. It proved, if nothing more, that he could give fans of his earlier travel books what they still seemed to want. After his daughter's death, he longed to find adequate expression of his unflinching view of the human condition and his own. Perhaps most important, he had discovered that he could return to his youth through autobiography. Much of what he wrote was never finished, but he proved that he could abandon the strictly commercial spirit he had shown in writing *Tom Sawyer, Detective* and adopt a truly experimental approach to the writing of fiction, most notably in "The Great Dark" and "The Chronicle of Young Satan." But while there was an occasional solid achievement, especially "The Man That Corrupted Hadleyburg," the writer's increasing indifference to publication meant that while he was writing a great deal, his contemporary readers were often getting mere journalism — and only a few samples of that.

The Clemenses remained near London at Dollis Hill House from July till early October 1900, with Jean continuing to receive treatments for epilepsy. There Clemens was relatively happy. Paine quotes him as writing, "Dollis Hill comes nearer to being a paradise than any other home I ever occupied." The trip to London's Baker Street took seventeen minutes or less, he told Twichell. Incredibly, he could not resist making another speculative investment, this one in a health food supplement called Plasmon; he became director of the English Plasmon syndicate. (Eventually he lost some $50,000 from this unfortunate venture.)[39] When he found that osteopathic treatments similar to the kind Jean was having in London were available in the United States, he judged it was time to return home. The Clemenses sailed on October 6, 1900.

CHAPTER ELEVEN

The Humorist as Philosopher

On October 15, 1900, Mark Twain came home. Having finally succeeded in paying his debts, he had also created a new image of himself. Now he was heralded as "one who has borne great burdens with manliness and courage."[1] Moreover, as the result of such recent writing as "The Man That Corrupted Hadleyburg," he was hailed as a "critic and censor" who had become "more philosophical" and more dedicated to "justice, absolute democracy, and humanity."[2] He had indeed developed a strong interest in justice, democracy, and humanity — all over the world. He had become especially concerned about imperialist conflicts. Western nations, including the United States, were involved in wars outside their natural sphere of influence: the Boer War, the Boxer Rebellion, the war between the United States and Spain over possessions in the Pacific and the Caribbean. In "The Chronicle of Young Satan," his Satan prophesies with disgust in chapter 8: "The Christian missionary will exasperate the Chinese; they will kill him in a riot. They will have to pay for him, in territory, cash, and churches, sixty-two million times his value. They will exasperate the Chinese still more, and they will injudiciously rise in revolt against the insults and oppressions of the intruder. This will be Europe's chance to interfere and swallow China, and her band of royal Christian pirates will not waste it." To his friend Twichell, Clemens had written that he hoped the Chinese "will drive all foreigners out and keep them out for good." Such an occurrence, the British exodus from Hong Kong, was not to happen for more than one hundred years.

Because his return to America was a front-page story, Mark Twain talked to many reporters. He told one interviewer that he had become an anti-imperialist as a result of his travels: "I left these shores, at Vancouver [in 1895], a red-hot imperialist. I wanted the American eagle to go screaming into the Pacific." But since then his eyes had been opened. "I have read carefully the treaty of Paris, and I have seen that we do not intend to free, but to subjugate the people of the Philippines. We have gone there to conquer, not to redeem. . . . And so I am an anti-imperialist. I am opposed to having the eagle put his talons on any other land."[3] He was referring to the so-called Philippine Insurrection, actually a war to crush a movement for Philippine independence, which followed the Spanish-American War. The United States had purchased the islands from Spain, but was soon involved in a costly war to subjugate them, lasting from February 1899 to July 1902.

In the interview quoted above, Clemens said, "In the spring I shall return to Hartford, Conn., where Mrs. Clemens, my daughters and myself will settle down for some home life, after nine years of wandering up and down the earth." But just five days after his arrival, he traveled to Hartford to attend the funeral of his onetime coauthor, Charles Dudley Warner. The emotional visit persuaded him that the Clemenses could never live in Hartford again. As Clara Clemens was later to note, "None of us felt able to face the Hartford home without Susy."[4] Moreover, after living in Vienna, Paris, and London, the writer felt a craving to be close to the center of American cultural and political life. Although he criticized American (and British) imperialism, he proudly called New York "our city" and "the envy of the cities of the world."[5] The Clemenses soon settled down in New York City, their first location being 14 West Tenth Street. They would make the city and its suburbs their home for three years, with summers, as usual, in the country.

Between his arrival in mid-October and the end of the year 1900, Mark Twain was in great demand as a speaker. The standard collection of his speeches provides the texts of ten talks delivered during this time, including several made for the New York Press Club and the Woman's Press Club. He and his family were honored by the Society of American Authors, and he addressed the Lotos Club, the Nineteenth Century Club, the Public Education Association, and the Saint Nicholas Society. At the end of the year, he wrote for newspaper publication "A salutation speech from the Nineteenth Century to the Twentieth, taken down in shorthand by Mark Twain." It is short but sardonic: "I bring you the stately matron named Christendom, returning bedraggled, besmirched and dishonored from pirate-raids in

Kiao-Chou, Manchuria, South Africa & the Philippines, with her soul full of meanness, her pocket full of boodle, and her mouth full of pious hypocrisies. Give her soap and a towel, but hide the looking glass."[6] Here spoke a citizen of the world.

In January 1901, he became a vice president of the Anti-Imperialist League of New York. He told a correspondent that his position would be "a useless because non-laboring one, but prodigally endowed with sympathy for the cause." In reality he accepted an active role, although he fretted to Twichell that he expected the result would be "a diminution of my bread and butter." One of his finest polemical pieces, "To the Person Sitting in Darkness," appeared in the February 1901 *North American Review*. The title is an ironic reference to Matthew 4:16 — "The people who sat in darkness have seen a great light." Pretending to defend the actions of Western nations in South Africa, China, and particularly the Philippines, he writes, "Extending the Blessings of Civilization to our Brother who sits in Darkness has been a good trade and has paid well, on the whole; and there is money in it yet, if carefully worked." The commentator's special target is the Rev. William Ament of the American Board of Commissioners for Foreign Missions, who required the Chinese to pay inordinate fines for damages suffered by his converts during the Boxer Rebellion.

After its magazine publication, the Anti-Imperialist League of New York published the essay as a pamphlet and seems to have distributed as many as 125,000 copies; despite the author's fears, the essay was mostly well received.[7] He was encouraged to continue writing political commentary. Even before the verdict was in, he had begun another piece, "The Stupendous Procession." Here he imagines the funeral procession for Queen Victoria, who had died on January 22, 1901. Among the marching mourners are "THE TWENTIETH CENTURY, a fair young creature, drunk and disorderly, borne in the arms of Satan," and "Christendom, in flowing robes drenched in blood." England, Spain, Russia, France, Germany, and America, all are guilty of blood crimes. He sees one of America's supporters as a "*Mutilated Figure in Chains,* labelled 'Philipino Independence,' and an allegorical Figure of the Administration caressing it with one hand, and stabbing it in the back with the other." Here the author's anger is less controlled, and perhaps as a result the piece remained unpublished until 1972.[8]

Probably in February 1901, Mark Twain wrote a brief, modest essay, "Corn-Pone Opinions," which was not published in his lifetime. Based on a text the author says he heard in his youth from a slave ("You tell me where a man gets his corn-pone, en I'll tell you what his 'pinions are"), the essay takes up the philosopher's now-favorite subject, the effect of outside influences and the human need for self-approval. This reflects his concept of his own situation: he was writing social and political opinion because he had been encouraged to think he was a writer whose opinions were widely respected. He liked the attention he was getting and wrote to a correspondent that he was in "hot water with the clergy and other goody-goody people, but I am enjoying it more than I have ever enjoyed hot water before." Instead of dropping the subject when he was attacked by clergymen, he penned "To My Missionary Critics," which offered no apologies, although it ended by acknowledging that missionaries no doubt mean well. The essay, originally entitled "The Case of Rev. Dr. Ament, Missionary," was published in the *North American Review* in April 1901. It relies on specific details from newspaper stories rather than literary argument.

Mark Twain was now a highly visible person. When Lincoln's birthday was celebrated at Carnegie Hall, he presided over the affair. Howells was living in New York and wrote to his sister, "I see a great deal of Mark Twain nowadays, and we have high good old times denouncing everything. We agree perfectly about the Boer war and the Filipino war, and war generally. Then, we are old fellows [they were in their mid-sixties], and it is pleasant to find the world so much worse than it was when we were young."⁹

In early February 1901, Mark Twain recorded in his notebook: "Write Introduction to 100-Year Book." Three days later he recorded, "Introduction 100-year. Gov't in hands of Xn Sci, or R. Catholic? *Whole* suffrage introduced to save Protestantism in 1950, but too late; RC and XCᶜ ahead —got the field."¹⁰ These notes about the future dominance of Christian Scientists and Roman Catholics suggest the revival of an idea he had jotted down in 1883 or 1884: "For a play: America in 1985. The Pope here & an Inquisition. The age of darkness back again. Pope is temporal despot, *too*."¹¹ He was now zeroing in on Mary Baker Eddy and planned a work in which Christian Science dominated America, "The Secret History of Eddypus, the World Empire." He wrote twenty thousand words before he stopped, probably in March, then began again in February 1902 after reading Andrew D. White's *History of the Warfare of Science with Theology*. Finally he added five thousand words before giving up the notion. While his interest was still hot, in February, he described the work to Frederick Duneka of Harper as "a mine of learning . . . a little distorted, a trifle out of focus, recognizably drunk. But interesting, & don't you forget it!"

In the "Secret History" (published in 1972 in *Fables of Man*), Mark Twain looks at an imagined future as well as the past he himself has experienced. The future is the year 2901, here dated A.M. 1001 — the "Year of Our Mother," for Mary Baker Eddy has replaced Christ, just as Eddy-mania has replaced Christianity. In the preface to book 1, she is described as "Fourth Person of the Godhead and Second Person in Rank." The ruler of the church-state that she founded uses her name as a title, even though, since the consolidation of the Christian Science Church and the Roman Catholic Church, all popes have been men. As usual, Mark Twain delights in gender confusion; here he explains how, following the death of M. B. G. Eddy XXIV, the last Catholic pope "relinquished his title, abolished his Papacy and his Church, put on the late [Christian Science] Pope's clothes, and became Mistress of the World and of Christian Sciencedom, under the name and style of Her Divine Grace Mary Baker G. Eddy XXV, and went to demonstrating over things like an Old Hand. She (that is, he) was English, and in his boyhood her name was Thomas Atkins. She (that is, he) reigned sixteen years; and when she died she left the cards most competently stacked, and secure in the hands of such as knew the Game."[12] Early in the new era, even before the consolidation, all libraries were destroyed, and "intellectual Night followed" (p. 325). Consequently, history becomes a jumble. It is known, however, that "Louis XIV, King of England, . . . was beheaded by his own subjects for marrying the Lady Mary Ann Bullion when he already had wives sufficient. He was succeeded by his son, William the Conqueror, called the Young Pretender, who became embroiled in the War of the Roses, and fell gallantly fighting for his crown at Bunker Hill" (p. 326).

The chief authority for book 2 of the "History" is "his Grace Mark Twain, Bishop of New Jersey in the noonday glory of the Great Civilization." The bishop's chief work is "Old Comrades," which seems to be a kind of autobiography. In the "Author's Introduction" to that work, reproduced in the "History," he speaks from the grave and tells of his dear friends Thomas Bailey Aldrich and Howells. His greatest gift was philosophizing; his weakness was his lack of a sense of humor. Another of his works, "The Gospel of Self," was for a time influential, but nevertheless it led to the bishop's death by hanging. He seems to have had many offspring, two of them being Huck Finn and Tom Sawyer. One of his interests was books, his favorites being several ones of unknown authorship, among them "Innocents Abroad; Roughing It; Tramp Abroad; Pudd'nhead Wilson; Joan of Arc; Prince and Pauper."

In chapter 3, drawing presumably on the great bishop's writings, the unidentified author describes the primitive ways of life in the early nineteenth century (A.D.), recognizably in America. But then the *"creators of the Great Civilization"* began their work, the burden of chapters 4 and 5. One such hero is Sir Izaac Walton, who "discovered the law of the Attraction of

Gravitation, or the Gravitation of Attraction, which is the same thing," and another is John Calvin Galileo. The work of astronomers had an especially great impact. With their discoveries, "the lid had been taken off the universe, so to speak, there was vastness, emptiness, vacancy all around everywhere, the snug cosiness was gone, the world was a homeless little vagrant, a bewildered little orphan left out in the cold, a long way from any place and nowhere to go." The painfully distorted history may indicate the author's belief that historical records are another joke played on man, or perhaps he was simply letting his imagination have free play. However self-indulgent, "Eddypus" deserves the attention of readers, who will, however, discover that just as Mark Twain's appetite for the work dulled, so does theirs.

In June, the Clemenses began a summer at a remote log cabin on Saranac Lake in the Adirondacks of New York State, where the author received from someone at the *Century* magazine a batch of newspaper clippings about lynchings that had recently occurred. As a result, he envisioned "a large subscription book to be called 'History of Lynching' or 'Rise and Progress of Lynching' or some such title," as he told Frank Bliss of the American Publishing Company. But then, overtaken by concerns about money rather than social reform, he developed second thoughts. He deduced that his identification with a book on lynching would likely hurt his southern sales. Only a few days after sending his proposal to Hartford, he wrote again: "I shouldn't have even half a dozen friends left, after it issued from the press." He had already written an essay, perhaps to serve as an introduction, for he told Bliss, "I shan't destroy the article I have written, but I see it won't do to print it."

"The United States of Lyncherdom" did not appear in his lifetime; it was first published in Paine's collection *Europe and Elsewhere* in 1923. Using the occasion of a lynching in his home state of Missouri, Mark Twain examines mob violence within the context of public opinion. He sees lynching as a fashion that spreads like a disease. As early as 1883, when he composed the account of an effort to lynch Colonel Sherburn in *Huckleberry Finn,* he had argued this same position. Despite its striking title, itself a powerful indictment, "The United States of Lyncherdom" is not the statement one might expect from a man ready to prepare a history of lynching in America. Although the lynchings that are his subject all involved blacks, the author did not confront the inescapable fact that a major purpose of this form of violence was to keep blacks in a place of subservience. Indeed, not only is the racial basis disregarded but the polemicist even accepts the notion that mob violence results from legitimate provocations. His suggestion that American missionaries be brought home from China to stop the "bloody insanities" indicates that the writer was still glorying in his earlier essays, of whose authorship Mark Twain reminds his readers none too subtly.

Another undertaking of the summer of 1901, "A Double-Barrelled Detective Story," is probably the worst story that he ever wrote, yet he published it in two installments in *Harper's Magazine* in early 1902. The first chapters appear to be painfully serious, with cruelty, even sadism, as a theme. With chapter 4 (the second barrel), the story seems to start again, beginning with a long description of an October morning, obviously a parody of someone's purple prose, and now the story becomes a farcical burlesque, featuring Sherlock Holmes as an incompetent detective, with no explanation provided. Mark Twain was apparently inspired by the first installment of A. Conan Doyle's *Hound of the Baskervilles* (published in August) to attempt a burlesque, targeting both Doyle's new novel and his earlier *Study in Scarlet* (1887). The latter work had a similar break in the narrative, followed by a long descriptive passage. But the fact that the whole story is meant to be a burlesque of the Sherlock Holmes stories is not clear unless one has just read the objects of the attack; otherwise, it is merely confusing. In a letter to Twichell, who had loaned him *A Study in Scarlet,* Clemens describes his story as a "condensed novel" satirizing Doyle's "pompous sentimental 'extraordinary man' with his cheap & ineffectual ingenuities." Perhaps because even the author recognized in time that the satirical purpose is not clear enough, he inserted—when the story was included in a book—a lengthy footnote at the beginning of chapter 4 that includes letters he had received in response to the story, and refers to it as "the most elaborate of burlesques of detective fiction."

Following their summer at Saranac and a week in Elmira, the Clemenses began a two-year stay in a house in Riverdale, just inside the northern limits of New York City. (Now called Wave Hill House and surrounded by twenty-eight acres of garden and greenhouses, it dates from 1843; its other notable occupants have included Theodore Roosevelt and Arturo Toscanini.) There the Clemenses returned to their extensive socializing; Paine reports that because of easy access from New York, they entertained guests at as many as seventeen meals in a single week.

Although he seldom stayed with any substantial work long enough to finish it, Mark Twain was now writing a great deal. His literary output had always been uneven, good works following inferior ones; now most of what he wrote was either inferior or seriously flawed, if not altogether botched. Perhaps the prize specimen of his unevenness in the early years of the twentieth century was the longest of his novel fragments, *Which Was It?* Begun in the summer of 1899, this story—another version of "Which Was the Dream?" — occupied the writer at Saranac Lake in the summer and later at Riverdale. Discounting a few exceptions, the pages are tedious, especially the early ones. In the following summer, when the Clemenses were at York Harbor, Maine, the author added to it and brought it close to an ending. He thought he could publish it, first "serialized in a *weekly* only."[13] Still it was never finished, and it remains a long — 100,000-word — fragment. In the summer of 1906, he looked back at it in an autobiographical dictation. He remained sure he could finish the book, "but I shan't do it. The pen is irksome to me. I was born lazy, and dictating [the autobiography] has spoiled me." And so, despite all his effort, he decided that "that book will remain unfinished."[14]

This novel is the story of George Harrison, who like General X in "Which Was the Dream?" falls asleep and dreams catastrophes for "fifteen bleak years." Before the narrative begins, his house burns, killing his wife and daughters. This time, however, the story is not about disasters but about the protagonist's failings, or apparent failings, and their effect on his conscience. Harrison begins his story by explaining that he cannot tell it as *his* story: "I could not say, 'I did such things,' it would revolt me, and the pen would refuse." So he writes his story in the third person. Harrison is, or appears to be, a hypocrite. Tempted like the Richardses of Hadleyburg, he becomes a robber and a murderer, then finds that he must live with his guilt, for he is too cowardly to confess it. In the manuscript, Mark Twain sketched a tree, labeled "disaster," with its base in false pride and its fruits depicted as seven distinct crimes. Since Harrison corresponds to General X and to David Gridley of "Indiantown," earlier efforts to tell the dream-disaster story, he assuredly represents in some sense the author. Was the story Mark Twain's way of examining his own sense of guilt, originating either in the hypocrisy he emphasized so fiercely in "Indiantown" or in his sense of responsibility for his bankruptcy and the death of Susy? It is perhaps signifi-cant that Harrison loses his mask at the time of the robbery and murder and that it is later used to blackmail him. Throughout the story, Harrison's guilt is associated with a counterfeit theme — counterfeit money, Mrs. Gunning's mail-investment swindle, forged letters.

By far the most gripping feature of the narrative, which is alternately either too leisurely told or too condensed, is the role taken by Jasper, the mulatto extortionist, who forces Harrison to become his servant. Victim-ized again and again by whites, forced to purchase his freedom three times, and beaten for being out at night without a pass, he takes all his grievances out on Harrison and shows no compassion. The episode has been read as a turning point in Mark Twain's response to blacks and the South, with

Huck's genial friend Jim now being replaced by a vengeful mulatto and the onetime humorist advocating the punishment of white sins. Writing in the era of Jim Crow laws, Mark Twain saw the whites who had earlier enslaved blacks now extending their domination by means of strict segregation.[15] (In the 1880s, he had imagined a scenario in 1985 in which blacks would be on the verge of supremacy in America. And he was plotting a story he called "The Man with the Negro Blood.")[16] Here it is Harrison who is being tyrannized. It would appear that he needs some form of punishment to help atone for his crimes; his fate seems intertwined with the collective guilt of whites. The story breaks off before anything can be made of the matter, although the original idea was for Harrison to have dreamed both his disaster and his crimes. A related fragment informs readers that Harrison's guilt is misplaced, since his father was the real criminal. Both these pieces of evidence imply that Harrison's suffering from his guilt was unwarranted — that he was in fact not guilty. But such subtleties as misplaced masochism were beyond the skills (or the nerve) of the author.

In the fall of 1901, Clemens, along with his longtime friend William Dean Howells, was awarded an honorary doctorate from Yale. The degree if anything increased his sense of responsibility to the public. His chief concerns for a time involved politics and his opponent, Richard Croker, and the latter's Tammany Hall gang. For this once he became thoroughly engaged in politics. He gave speeches and marched in a political parade. When Tammany lost, one newspaper identified Mark Twain as the responsible force.

> Who killed Croker?
> I, said Mark Twain,
> I killed Croker,
> I, the Jolly Joker![17]

At least privately, he did claim credit.[18] Whatever the status of his literary career, Samuel Clemens was feeling good about himself as an icon of common sense and public virtue. At the end of 1901, he wrote to his friend Aldrich: "I am having a noble good time — the best I have ever had. All my days are my own — all of them: & I spend them in my study. It comes of wisdom; of establishing a rational rule & then sticking to it: to take no engagement outside the city, & not more than 2 per month. They can't improve on this happiness in heaven."

In early 1902, Mark Twain expanded his role as social philosopher with two additional opinion pieces. To the question "Does the race of man love a lord?" he volunteered an emphatic *yes* in an essay in the April *North Ameri-*

can Review. The next month, a more timely piece appeared in the same journal, an ironic "Defence of General Funston," in which he castigated the American military leader who had captured, through trickery, the Philippine patriotic leader Aguinaldo.[19] Here the writing is under control, although one may wonder whether the author's displacement of blame from the man to his disposition—which manifested "a native predilection for unsavory conduct"[20]—is plausible. The expression of determinism in this essay suggests the author's new willingness to share his thoughts and feelings with the world more fully than previously. But there were limitations to his political writings. When an American army captain was charged with responsibility for the fatal torture of a Philippine priest, Howells urged him to write about the incident, but he begged off, unable to achieve control of his strong feelings.

A little sketch published in the summer of 1902 expresses strong pessimism. The piece names "the five boons of life": fame, love, riches, pleasure, and death. They are, from time to time, offered to a man who eagerly selects first one, then another, always to be disappointed. Finally he would gratefully take the one boon he had thus far avoided, but death is now no longer available to him. Having waited too long, he now must experience "the wanton insult of Old Age." The theme resembles that of *The Master of Palmyra,* the drama Twain had liked so much in Vienna. "The Five Boons of Life," which Paine calls a "beautiful fairy tale,"[21] should be put beside the recently published sketch that Paine identified as being written the same year, "The Victims." Among the philosophical, religious, and historical fantasies published in 1972, this one stands out because of its imaginative treatment of man's vulnerability to disease and the native disposition of animals to behave according to their kind. "The Victims," a skeletal fable for children, tells of a picnic attended by "all the nicest creatures." Yet the adult mothers of the baby animals promptly set about catching and devouring their offspring's playmates of different species.[22]

Perhaps this grim little fable was inspired by one of the major events of 1902 for Clemens, his last return to his boyhood home. In May he traveled to Missouri to receive an honorary degree from the University of Missouri, after which he made a five-day visit to Hannibal and took a trip on the Mississippi with Horace Bixby, who had taught him to be a steamboat pilot. He found his mind swarming with images of his youth. He took up, apparently as a result of the trip, an idea he had recorded in his notebook in 1891: the reunion of Huck and Tom at the age of sixty, by which time their experiences have proved to be as bitter as those of the youth of "The Five Boons": "Life has been a failure, all that was lovable, all that was beautiful is under the mound. They die together."[23] Now, in 1902, he made more notes on what he called "the final Huck Finn book," to which he gave the working title "50 Years Later."[24] Many notebook entries offer tantalizing clues concerning what might have been. "Huck a doubter — or believer? (for he is superstitious) — Tom tells him the facts. Aunt Polly believes. Take Aunt Polly & Betsy to prayer-meeting — nigger show — old jokes." One entry suggests that the story was to have two parts, the first ending in a "moonlight parting on the hill — the entire gang. 'Say, let's all come back in 50 years and talk over old times.'" The story was begun during the summer, when the Clemenses were vacationing in Maine, and by October the first part had been completed and sent to Howells, who was residing nearby. Then, apparently, Clemens gave the idea up. In 1906 he said, "I carried it as far as thirty-eight thousand words four years ago, then destroyed it for fear I might someday finish it."[25] Unlike other manuscripts he said he discarded, this one does seem not to have survived.

During the same summer of 1902, while the Clemenses were at York Harbor, Maine, the author did manage to finish two short stories, soon published. "The Belated Russian Passport" is an O. Henry kind of story, seemingly pathetic; the comic twist at the end put Mark Twain's talents to no good purpose. Better but painfully sentimental is "Was It Heaven? or Hell?" Based on a true story that Howells had told him earlier in the summer, it tells of the efforts of two elderly women to protect their dying niece from knowledge of her daughter's illness and subsequent death.

Soon the author found himself in an excruciatingly similar situation. On August 12, Olivia Clemens had a severe heart attack; she could not breathe and had strong heart palpitations. She believed she was dying as did her husband. She was left an invalid. In October, Olivia was moved with difficulty back to Riverdale. Hereafter Clemens was often permitted only brief visits with his wife; sometimes these were restricted to two minutes a day. When Jean became seriously ill from pneumonia in December, the family felt that they had to protect Mrs. Clemens from worrying about her, exactly as in "Was It Heaven? or Hell?"

At this time an important member was added to the Clemens household, Isabel Lyon. The Clemenses had known her during their Hartford days; she had served as governess for the Whitmores of Nook Farm. Because of Olivia's illness, she needed household help. Mrs. Whitmore recommended Lyon. (Whitmore was Clemens's business manager). She served as Olivia's secretary but soon became manager of the household and took on some of Olivia's roles. How she fitted in is explained by Clara, who wrote to Mrs. Whitmore, "I want to tell you how thankful we are that you told us about

Miss Lyon for she is really a treasure and enormous comfort. She not only is sweet and attractive entirely lacking any disagreeable qualities but she has a cheerful manner and way which are welcome in a house at time of illness & depression."[26] She played an increasingly important role in the Clemens family, becoming in time Clemens's own assistant.

Clemens recorded in an autobiographical dictation of February 15, 1906, "All through her life Mrs. Clemens was physically feeble, but her spirit was never weak. She lived upon it all her life, and it was as effective as bodily strength could have been."[27] It was inevitable, however, that she would be affected by her husband's behavior. His irascibility and mood swings took their toll on her nerves. For years, too, she had been breathing her husband's cigar and pipe smoke, even at night in their bedroom, where, by the practice of the day, the windows were usually closed. In fact, his favorite place to smoke was while he was in bed. The Clemenses' longtime maid, Katy Leary, quotes Clemens as saying, "My wife thinks there's no place in this house too good for me to smoke in, and so I smoke everywhere — in the bedroom or in the parlor — any place I like."[28]

At the celebration of his seventieth birthday — after the death of his wife — Clemens reported on what he called his permanent habits: "I smoke in bed until I have to go to sleep. I wake up in the night, sometimes once, sometimes twice, sometimes three times, and I never waste any of these opportunities to smoke. The habit is so old and dear and precious to me that . . . I am making no changes."[29]

In his appreciative book *My Mark Twain* (1910), William Dean Howells had this to say:

Whenever he had been a few days with us, the whole house had to be aired, for he smoked all over it from breakfast to bedtime. He always went to bed with a cigar in his mouth, and sometimes, mindful of my fire insurance, I went up and took it away, still burning, after he had fallen asleep. I do not know how much a man may smoke and live, but apparently he smoked as much as a man could, for he smoked incessantly.[30]

Although the dangers of tobacco smoke were not fully recognized at this time, Clemens had been told frequently that his excessive smoking was dangerous to his health. It is not difficult, with hindsight, to recognize that it was not simply a matter of the smoker's health but that of his wife and his children, too.

Sometime in the summer or fall of 1902, Mark Twain returned to his 1899 Christian Science writings and revised them for publication in the *North American Review,* where they appeared in December and January.

Soon after, he added a new essay, on the growth of the religion, published in February, and another, "Mrs. Eddy in Error," a rejoinder to Mrs. Eddy's comments on the writer's criticism, appeared in April, again in the *North American Review*. This latter piece is a discussion of the title "Mother" used as a form for addressing Mrs. Eddy. In the meantime, the humorist–novelist–social critic had decided to put together an entire book on the subject, and Harper agreed to such a publication — a testimony to the newsworthiness of what many contemporaries still considered to be a dangerous cult. The author was pressured to finish his book as early as possible. In mid-February, Frederick Duneka of Harper and Brothers wrote: "There should be an interval of six weeks between the receipt of a manuscript and the publication of the book. This can be cut down, of course, but not very much. It is our wish to issue the Christian Science volume not later than the last of April. Will this impose too great a burden on you."[31] (The question mark was omitted.) Under such prodding, the author finished the manuscript, the book was set in type, and publication was announced as forthcoming. Then, presumably fearful of stirring up too much controversy about Christian Scientists, the Harper editors changed their minds, and publication was indefinitely postponed. After waiting three years, Mark Twain tried unsuccessfully to retrieve the manuscript. Finally, in February 1907, Harper published the work as *Christian Science* (a better title might have been *Mary Baker Eddy*) when the new religion was once again being attacked in the newspapers.

Mark Twain wrote the bulk of his post-1899 material under difficult circumstances. He was staying close to his ailing wife and working quickly. Perhaps as a result, he took the easiest way he could find to produce this book. The new parts are chiefly an examination of various Christian Science publications. Throughout the work, his target is Mrs. Eddy's dictatorial rule, which he refers to as "The New Infallibility." Little is said about the practice of Christian Science, and much of that little is implicitly favorable. But unlike the early chapters, the last two-thirds of the book is unequivocally dull. The reader must wade through Mark Twain's excessively thorough analysis of the organizational structure of the church, with extended quotations from documents, followed by appendixes — padding, really — of quoted documents. The good-humored tone of the early chapters is entirely different from that of book 2, which was written, doggedly, to supplement sufficiently the pieces written four years earlier to make a book. While no reader could wish it longer, it is far shorter than the writer's earlier books. Since the author was of two minds about Christian Science, the book lacks coherence.

At an elaborate sixty-seventh birthday party given him by Colonel George Harvey, Mark Twain spoke at length. He made a particular point to express gratitude to his wife.

> A part of me is present; the larger part, the better part, is yonder at home; that is my wife, and she has a good many personal friends here, . . . and I think it is quite appropriate that I should speak of her. I knew her for the first time just in the same year that I first knew John Hay [diplomat and writer] and [former congressman and Speaker of the House] Tom Reed and Mr. Twichell — thirty-six years ago — and she has been the best friend I have ever had, and that is saying a good deal; she has reared me — she and Twichell together — and what I am I owe to them.[32]

Those who insist that Olivia's influence on her husband has been overstated will find that Clemens himself repeatedly and publicly announced what she had done for him; it is doubtful that he was fully aware of what he had done to her.

In *Harper's Weekly* for May 2, 1903, Mark Twain published a short essay that he never saw fit to include in any collection, nor did Paine include it. The title is "Why Not Abolish It?" — and the "it" is the age of consent to sexual intercourse. Mark Twain calls seduction "this crime of crimes."

> There is *no* age at which the good name of a member of a family ceases to be a part of the *property* of that family — an asset, and worth more than all its bonds and moneys. There is no age at which a member of the family may by consent, and under authority of the law, help a criminal to destroy the family's money and bonds. Then why should there be an age at which a member, by consent, and under connivance of the law, may help a criminal to destroy that far more valuable asset, the family's honor?[33]

The ostensible occasion of the composition of this piece was a story in the *New York Herald* of May 2 about an unwed girl who was "convicted of murder in the second degree . . . for drowning her baby," after failing to get any help from the baby's father. Mark Twain was ready to sign a petition protesting her sentence. Just possibly he was thinking about the honor of his own family, for daughter Clara was in Paris, where she saw much of Ossip Gabrilowitsch.

Even a summer at Quarry Farm, where Mark Twain might have been inspired by memories of his best periods of productivity, was not fruitful in 1903. He was preoccupied with business and his plans to move to Italy, to Florence, in the autumn, for the sake of Olivia Clemens's health. At Quarry

Farm Olivia seemed temporarily revived. She practically lived in the fresh air on the front porch with its sweeping view of the Chemung River.

The author did manage to complete one short story, "A Dog's Tale," soon published in *Harper's Magazine.* Intended for Jean Clemens, who was strongly opposed to vivisection, the little story is told by a heroic dog who saves a baby from a fire but dies of a broken heart after her own offspring is destroyed by curious but cruel scientists, led by the baby's father. The onetime archfoe of sentimentalism had drifted over to the enemy's camp with such stories as "The Californian's Tale" and "Was It Heaven? or Hell?" This most determinedly softhearted — and contrived — tale showed that Mark Twain had all but given up his aim of authenticity.

In October 1903, the Clemenses left for Florence; Howells wrote his sister: "Clemens, I suppose, will always live at Florence, hereafter. He goes for his wife's health, and then because he can't stand the nervous storm and stress here. He takes things intensely hard, and America is too much for him."[34] Isabel Lyon organized the writer's manuscripts and correspondence for the trip; increasingly, she was winning a place in the writer's life.

In Italy, Clemens did settle down to business early, and despite Olivia's illness and his own illnesses, the stay was for him remarkably productive. Their residence was the Villa Quarto, beautiful but gloomy, and the weather proved cold and wet. Nevertheless, the writer supposed that he and his wife would be permanent residents of Florence; he was hunting for a suitable villa. Therefore he was eager to make money. He hoped he would soon have ten thousand dollars from what he could publish to invest in the stock market, and he was able to achieve his goal in just a month of writing. The first of his pieces, "Italian Without a Master," begins: "It is almost a fortnight now that I am domiciled in a medieval villa in the country, a mile or two from Florence." In this pleasant return to his earlier manner, Mark Twain reveals an amusing ignorance of Italian as he confidently attempts to cope with Italian newspapers. Even better is "Italian with Grammar," in which he tells of his efforts to master the fifty-seven forms of the Italian verb system. It is a highly imaginative, good-humored sketch. But the original was too long; only the first half was published.

A third piece was a story, "The $30,000 Bequest." Like "Hadleyburg," it analyzes the destructive consequences of greed, a subject on which the author might well have considered himself an authority; he took up this theme repeatedly. As the story opens, an unusually honorable couple, Saladin and Electra Foster, have established a rewarding life by dint of hard work and economy. They are, however, soon victimized by their romantic dreams of "comrading with kings and princes and stately lords and ladies"

when they hear that Foster's uncle is intending to bequeath them $30,000 —
"Not for love," he explains, "but because money had given him most of his
troubles and exasperations," and he wishes to place his wealth "where there
was hope that it would continue its malignant work." The money never
comes, but the very expectation itself proves malignant and destructive.
Like "Indiantown," the story is partly autobiographical. Mr. Foster's bad
temper, rashness, and eventual dishonesty may be understood as the author's admission of responsibility for the disaster that had resulted from his
preoccupation with wealth during the late 1880s. If so, it may also suggest
that he was provoked by circumstances and encouraged by his wife.

Mark Twain's financial needs presumably explain the preoccupation with
money in these three stories. Early in 1904, in a letter to Twichell, he
described his "sort of half promise to Harpers magazines to supply 30,000
words each year" to augment what he would receive from the collected
edition Harper was issuing. To his surprise and pleasure, in "25 working
days" he was not only able to produce 37,000 words of "magazining," but
found that both he and his wife judged them publishable. These already
produced, he could now declare with satisfaction, in a letter to Twichell,
"No more magazine-work hanging over my head."

Even though he was away from the United States, Mark Twain was still
much interested in the fate of the Philippines. He had read of Leonard
Wood's appointment as governor of Moro Province and his subsequent
promotion. In December 1903, according to a letter he wrote to Frederick
Duneka at Harper, he had written "a pretty pison article about 'Major
General Wood, M.D.,' and took great pains with it, and worked at it several
days and got it to suit me exactly — then pigeonholed it with a sigh." Why
did he drop it? Because of his contract with Harper: "I'm not as free to
make enemies as I was before the contract was signed." The short piece was
first published in 1992, in *Mark Twain's Weapons of Satire*.

Thereafter in Florence, Mark Twain devoted himself to two other works
that remained unpublished until after his death — indeed, portions are yet
to appear. One was the autobiography, his off-and-on project over the
years. Now he was so pleased with a new method that he thought he might
destroy his earlier efforts. (He did not.) In January 1904, three weeks
before writing his letter to Twichell, he wrote to Howells:

> I've struck it! And I will give it away — to you. You will never know how
> much enjoyment you have lost until you get to dictating your auto-
> biography; then you will realize, with a pang, that you might have been
> doing it all your life if you had only the luck to think of it. And you will
> be astonished (& charmed) to see how like *talk* it is, & how real it

sounds, & how well & compactly & sequentially it constructs itself, & what a dewy & breezy & woodsy freshness it has, & what a darling & worshipful absence of the signs of starch, & flatiron, & labor & fuss & the other artificialities!

His purpose at this time, he told Howells, was to provide "notes" to the books he had already written, in order to add to their copyright life. He dictated to Isabel Lyon two hours or so a day, about fifteen hundred words each time, but was soon interrupted by illness and did not start up again for two months. Only about eighteen thousand words of these vernacular dictations, supplemented by some written portions, have been published— rather flat despite the author's enthusiasm: pages about the Clemenses' Florence residences of 1892–93 and 1903–4, a few pages on John Hay and some on Henry Rogers, some entertaining ones on the writing of *The Innocents Abroad*. Unpublished portions at the Mark Twain Papers describe the writer's study at the time he was dictating and recount his difficulties with the character who owned the house he occupied. What he had written in earlier years was far superior.

The most remarkable portion of the autobiography composed at Florence is the "Preface. As from the Grave." It reads, in part: "In this Autobiography I shall keep in mind the fact that I am speaking from the grave. I am literally speaking from the grave, because I shall be dead when the book issues from the press." A similar preface, it may be recalled, was attached to the work of the Father of History, "Old Comrades," on which "Eddypus" was purportedly based. But here the writer went on, rather cautiously: "It has seemed to me that I could be as frank and free and unembarrassed as a love letter if I knew that what I was writing would be exposed to no eye until I was dead, and unawares, and indifferent."[35] He hoped to ignore all previous inhibitions: his wife's censorship or Howells's, his concern with his reputation and its effect on the sale of his books. He wanted to be frank and free, as did Gridley of "Indiantown." But it was never to be, in Florence or elsewhere. In time he would recognize that he would always feel contained. Although he aimed at frankness, even the presence of a stenographer, "that petrified audience-person" who "is always there," was enough, he informed Howells in April 1909, "to block that game."

On January 5, 1904, he wrote to Duneka to report that having trimmed "Italian with Grammar" and written, revised, and rerevised "Sold to Satan," he had supplied Harper with all that was expected and could therefore "dig out one of my unfinished novels—a couple of them. Not for issue as single books, & not serially, but only to be added to the Complete Subscription Set."

The novel he turned to now was the one he would later allude to as "the book I wrote in Florence"; he called this story "No. 44, The Mysterious Stranger." That version supplied the attractive title for what Paine and Duneka published in 1916, although their heavily edited *Mysterious Stranger* included only the last chapter of the "Florence" book. "No. 44" belongs to no one period of the author's last years. The first chapter is a revision of "The Chronicle of Young Satan" of 1897–98. Chapters 2–7 (and perhaps 8) were written sometime between April 1902 and October 1903. Begun at Quarry Farm, they were mostly written in Florence; also while there, he wrote chapters 8–25 before June 1904. After he had returned to America, he wrote the six pages of what he called the "Conclusion of the book" (eventually published as chapter 34 when the whole surviving manuscript was published in 1969). Like "Which Was the Dream?" it reflects the author's fantasy that the calamities of his life might be dreams, not realities. In some ways it echoes Prospero's speech in Shakespeare's *Tempest,* beginning "Our revels now are ended." In 1905, after destroying at least 125 manuscript pages written in Florence, he wrote chapters 26–32. Then in order to ready something else for publication — or because Frederick Duneka did not like the way the priest in the story was presented — he laid it aside. In the following summer, he recorded in his autobiography that he would "dearly like" to finish the story but was "tired of the pen."[36] Nonetheless, at the end of the summer of 1908, he wrote one additional chapter, published in 1969 as chapter 33. Both it and chapter 34 serve as conclusions, although they have quite different implications. The whole of the story does not quite fit together; more than a fragment, it amounts to less than a finished whole.[37]

The last of the long fictions composed after Susy's death, "No. 44" was not clearly identified until the publication in 1963 of John Tuckey's *Mark Twain and Little Satan,* because before that date attention had been given exclusively to the 1916 publication, *The Mysterious Stranger.* In 1942 Bernard DeVoto, who had succeeded Paine as custodian of the Mark Twain Papers, observed about it only that "this story includes a print-shop such as young Sam Clemens worked in." He added, "I will say nothing except that it led directly to the one that came through to triumph at last, the book which, after it had been painfully written over and changed and adjusted and transformed, was to achieve the completion denied its many predecessors, the book we know as *The Mysterious Stranger.*"[38] Regrettably, DeVoto was mistaken on several counts. "No. 44," the print-shop story, was begun four years *after* Mark Twain had last worked on "The Chronicle of Young Satan," which DeVoto identifies as the work that came "to triumph at last." The latter, which Paine and DeVoto call *The Mysterious Stranger,* is misnamed, for the "Satan" figure is mysterious about his identity only in the print-shop story. Finally, too, it is the print-shop story that is more nearly complete than "Young Satan."

While "No. 44" lacks the blend of fairy-tale whimsy and pessimistic determinism of "The Chronicle of Young Satan," it has its own merits. It is highly, even wildly, imaginative, at the same time that its basic setting, the print shop, is based solidly on the author's memories of his first occupation. More fully than any other of Mark Twain's stories, it takes up what the author liked, even relished: food (especially that described in chapter 22: hot corn pone, fried spring chicken, "cream-smothered strawberries, with the prairie dew still on them," "coffee from Vienna, fluffed cream"), cats (including the charming Mary Florence Fortescue Baker G. Nightingale), and a minstrel show, complete with the singing of "Buffalo Gals, Can't You Come Out Tonight?" These elements enrich the central fantasy of the story and make it seem authentic despite its shapelessness. Thoroughly liberated from the demands of commercial book publication, Mark Twain is even able to provide for the first time a credible portrayal of romantic, even passionate, love.

In "No. 44," the old author returns to the motif that made *Huckleberry Finn* so memorable: the celebration of freedom. What he had played with in the unpublished part of "My Platonic Sweetheart" becomes the focus of this story, taken up with great imaginative zest. Like young Satan of "The Chronicle," No. 44 serves as the *raisonneur* of the novel; he opens the eyes of August Feldner, the narrator, to the author's more than half-serious ideas. A central idea is that

> each human being contains not merely two independent entities, but three — the Waking-Self, the Dream-Self, and the Soul. This last is immortal, the others are functioned by the brain and the nerves, and are physical and mortal. . . . When [Feldner explains] I was invisible the whole of my physical make-up was gone, nothing connected with it or depending upon it was left. My soul — my immortal soul — alone remained. Freed from the encumbering flesh, it was able to exhibit forces, passions and emotions of a quite tremendously effective character.[39]

Here Mark Twain posits a higher, bodiless form of freedom. But the story consists of fun as well as philosophy. No. 44 puts flesh on August's dream-self, who is devoted to "romance and excursions and adventure" (chap. 18). This "fleshing" of the dream-self is both mysterious and comic in an imaginative episode in which the various selves of August and Marget, whom he loves, interact. It is highly serious when August's dream-self, Emil Schwarz, tells of his desire for the fleshed version of Marget. The dream-selves of this story are Twain's final and most fascinating treatment of the double concept that had interested him so long. What seems to be implied is that No. 44's purpose is to help August Feldner, an ordinary mortal, discover powers that mankind has neglected. The continuing process of educating August, not fully described since the story is incomplete, was to lead to a conclusion, chapter 34, in which No. 44 disappears after announcing to August that he has "revealed you to yourself and set you free."

Mark Twain's productive Florence sojourn ended when, on June 5, 1904, Olivia Clemens died, not yet sixty years old. Her death was much less of a shock than that of Susy, for she had been very ill for almost two years, but her death deepened, at least for a time, the author's pessimism. The ending to "No. 44," which he wrote in 1904 (although he was still far from bringing his story to an ending), seems to have been written under the influence of his loss, and it suggests a further step beyond the "dream-disaster" ideas he had been fictionalizing. The lessons that 44 teaches to August are similar to those Clemens set forth in a letter to Joseph Twichell in July 1904. But in the letter about how life and the world had appeared to him for "the past seven years," since the death of his daughter, he qualified his statement: his dreadful vision was seen only a "part of each day—or night." In the story, on the other hand, the ideas are presented without any such qualification.

> *"Life itself is only a vision, a dream.* . . . *Nothing exists save empty space — and you!* . . . you will remain a *Thought,* the only existent Thought, and by your nature inextinguishable, indestructible. . . . Strange, indeed, that you should not have suspected that your universe and its contents were only dreams, visions, fictions! Strange, because they are so frankly and hysterically insane — like all dreams: a God who could make good children as easily as bad, yet preferred to make bad ones; who could have made every one of them happy, yet never made a single happy one; who made them prize their bitter life, yet stingily cut it short." (chap. 33)

No. 44's long speech is not fully prepared for. The ending was not attached to the chapters that go before it, and it conflicts with the author's belief that each person has an immortal soul. Still, this conclusion is deeply moving.

In his last years, Mark Twain made more than ten attempts to write another novel: three stories about Satan figures, two on Huck and Tom, at least five on the dream-disaster theme, and the "Eddypus" history, if that can be called a novel. These were all left unfinished and not published in the author's lifetime. He was still interested in marketing his writings, as shown by his eagerness to publish even the inferior *Christian Science.* That, sadly, was Mark Twain's last completed book — as distinguished from collections of shorter pieces, booklets, pamphlets — and his only volume to appear after his book about his world tour.[40]

Huckleberry Finn, The Prince and the Pauper, and *A Connecticut Yankee* all were written over a period of several years and completed only after several interruptions. Had Mark Twain not "tired of the pen," as he put it, some of these later novels might well have been finished, even if not given satisfactory endings. Some of the unpublished fictional fragments are tantalizing, and one bizarrely attractive fragment has found its way into print: "How Nancy Jackson Married Kate Wilson," the story of a girl who is obliged to present herself as a man to avoid being lynched.[41]

At the age of sixty-nine, Clemens had established ways, although eccentric in certain respects. He experienced immense loneliness following the death of Olivia, but the principal observable difference the loss made in his literary career is that he now dared to publish a few things that his wife had disapproved of. While his daughter Clara acted for a time as his censor, he finally felt free to publish an extract from the never-finished "Captain Stormfield's Visit to Heaven" in 1907–8. *Stormfield* had been held back so long that the author was surprised when it went over as inoffensive. But he was rapidly losing his inclination to write at all, especially as he found out how much more pleasurable it was to dictate segments of his autobiography.

CHAPTER TWELVE

Still Writing Till the End

hen Clemens returned from abroad after the death of his wife in 1904, he was utterly repelled by politics. His frame of mind was distinctly different from his attitude when he had returned in 1900. He advised Joseph Twichell, "Oh, dear! get out of that sewer — party politics." He added, echoing the language of his gospel, "I wish I could learn to pity the human race instead of censuring it and laughing at it; and I could, if the outside influences of old habits were not so strong upon my machine." After a quiet summer on the estate of his friend Richard Watson Gilder in the Berkshires of western Massachusetts, a brief trip to Elmira, and some days at a New Jersey beach, where he visited with Henry James, Clemens — along with Isabel Lyon and the remaining members of his family — settled again in December in New York City, this time at 21 Fifth Avenue, at Ninth Street; he signed a three-year lease. The house had been designed by James A. Renwick, the owner, who had been the architect of Grace Church, built in gothic style. Furnishings were brought from the Hartford house; they had not been seen for thirteen years. In time Clemens would dislike the house and feel lonely there, although his life was brightened when the wife of his friend Henry Rogers gave him a billiard table in October 1907.

Following a siege of bronchitis, the old habits, aroused by contemporary events, stirred Mark Twain into writing. On January 22, 1905, the Russian czar's guards in St. Petersburg fired on strikers, and within a few days Twain composed "The Czar's Soliloquy," published in the *North American Review* in March. In twenty-five hundred words, he takes up once again a theme looked at in an 1899 piece, "Diplomatic Pay and Clothes," in which he argued that clothes make the diplomat. Standing naked before a mirror (as a newspaper story reported that the czar regularly did), the czar proclaims, "There is no power without clothes." In his nakedness the czar candidly accepts responsibility for his actions, some of which are described from his collection of newspaper clippings. The czar fears the growth of genuine patriotism; *"loyalty to the Nation* ALL *the time, loyalty to the government when it deserves it."*[1] This time Mark Twain's personal philosophy is not permitted to intrude: nothing is introduced about the czar's training or his disposition in this forceful attack.

The brief gibe at the end of the "Soliloquy" ("Is the human race a joke?") is developed in a continuation, "Flies and Russians," which extended the czar's remarks. Here his ruminations lead him to conclude that Nature made a mistake in creating *both* flies and Russians and that "the grotesque nature of the result was not clearly foreseen."[2] It is amusing in places, but the illusion that the czar is speaking is not maintained. Perhaps for that reason the piece remained unpublished until 1972, when it appeared in *Fables of Man.*

The real sequel to "The Czar's Soliloquy" was *King Leopold's Soliloquy: A Defense of His Congo Rule,* begun in February 1905. The history of this piece is complex. In October 1904, the founder of the English Congo Reform Association, E. D. Morel, sought Clemens out and asked him to work for his cause. King Leopold was squeezing immense profits out of the Congo and committing unthinkable atrocities in the process. Morel won from Clemens a promise that the Congo would receive his attention. The piece that resulted was turned down by the *North American Review* and then was issued as a pamphlet in September 1905 by the Congo Reform Association, with proceeds going to the association. Published in England as well, *King Leopold's Soliloquy* was so incisive that *An Answer to Mark Twain* was published for distribution in England.

King Leopold's Soliloquy is four times as long as its predecessor and more ambitious. The characterization of the speaker is much fuller, and the gradual shift from a pose of wounded innocence to outright cynicism is skillful. The piece presents a detailed case against the Belgian king, based on quotations from newspaper accounts and reports from missionaries about the crimes committed by greedy imperialists. Unfortunately, in this essay Mark Twain made the error of assuming that the U.S. government had endorsed Leopold's rule in the Congo. The soliloquy labors under other difficulties as well. Although missionaries were among the supporters of the Congo Reform Movement, the piece has a strenuously antireligious bias. Moreover, the pamphlet adopts a discouragingly pessimistic attitude toward the possibility of reform.

In November 1905, despite these shortcomings, Clemens became vice president of the American Congo Reform Association and took up his pen again for the cause, but neither of the pieces he wrote, "A Thanksgiving Sentiment" and another without a title, was published. In his capacity as reform leader, Clemens made three visits to Washington, D.C., to confer with the president and State Department authorities before he grasped what the policy of the United States toward the Congo really was. Vexed and discomforted, he thought that he should withdraw his soliloquy; even though he did not, he became disillusioned about reformist activities and resigned his office. Ironically, the *Soliloquy* proved to be a genuinely significant contribution to the effort to stop abuses in the Congo. Improvements in conditions there were rapidly effected. Although Clemens never completely understood what he had done, this last commitment to reform was Mark Twain's most successful.[3]

A third and quite different kind of soliloquy, although apparently generated by his growing awareness of the potentialities of the genre, is "Adam's Soliloquy."[4] The piece itself is negligible, but it revived Mark Twain's interest in Adam and Eve, for whom he thereupon wrote diaries and an autobiography. But for the moment he continued his social and political criticism with what is usually considered his most eloquent piece of this kind, "The War Prayer," written in February or March 1905. Basing his sketch on a story he had heard in 1862 and recorded in *Life on the Mississippi* (chap. 57), he describes a timeless wartime scene — any war will do. Patriotism at the time is rampant, and opposition is a very risky business. At a church service, God is grandly invoked to "watch over our noble young soldiers, and aid, comfort, and encourage them in their patriotic work; bless them, shield them in the day of battle and the hour of peril, bear them in His mighty hand, make them strong and confident, invincible in the bloody onset; help them to crush the foe, grant to them and to their flag and country imperishable honor and glory."

A chronic disbeliever in special providences, Mark Twain might be expected to question such a plea. In this case, he introduces an "aged stranger" who announces that God has interpreted their prayer in literal terms:

O Lord our God, help us to tear their soldiers to bloody shreds with our shells; help us to cover their smiling fields with the pale forms of their patriot dead; help us to drown the thunder of the guns with the shrieks of their wounded, writhing in pain; help us to lay waste their humble homes with a hurricane of fire; help us to wring the hearts of their unoffending widows with unavailing grief; help us to turn them out roofless with their little children to wander unfriended the wastes of their desolated lands in rags and hunger and thirst . . . for our sakes who adore Thee, Lord, blast their hopes, blight their lives, protract their bitter pilgrimage, make heavy their steps, water their way with their tears, stain the white snow with the blood of their wounded feet! We ask it, in the spirit of love, of Him Who is the Source of Love, and who is the ever-faithful refuge and friend of all that are sore beset and seek His aid with humble and contrite hearts. Amen.

But the angelic visitor receives an ironic dismissal: "It was believed afterwards, that the man was a lunatic, because there was no sense in what he said." After the sketch was rejected by *Harper's Bazar* as "not quite suited to a woman's magazine,"[5] "The War Prayer" was filed away until posthumous publication in *Europe and Elsewhere* in 1923.

Throughout 1905 and into 1906, Mark Twain regularly contributed short pieces, many in the form of letters, to several periodicals, especially *Harper's Weekly* — ten in all, and all slight. They show that the author was a man of rapidly changing moods, sometimes playing the part of philosophical observer. He had not altogether lost his sense of humor and his enjoyment, even delight, in life's daily offerings, as his letters to Henry Rogers's daughter-in-law show. Blending humor and tragedy to reflect the comprehensive human condition was, however, usually beyond his ability. Even his shorter, less ambitious efforts gave him trouble, chiefly in their structural demands. He never recognized the new possibilities in fictional structure being created by his contemporaries. Indeed, he had described himself in the prefatory note to "Those Extraordinary Twins" as a man "not born with the novel-writing gift."

He began the first of his two remaining efforts at extended fiction at the end of the winter of 1904–5, nine months after his wife's death. "The Refuge of the Derelicts" (also called the "Adam Monument") reveals how the writer's literary imagination was working late in his life. He created a dubious fictional vehicle for his philosophy, resurrecting the idea of a monument to Adam. He then attempted to introduce figures that haunted his memory and imagination.

Much information about Clemens's last years is provided by Isabel Lyon, for she was the person closest to him for several years: at one time he intended for Lyon to prepare his letters for publication. On March 17, 1905, she recorded in her diary that the author had read to her the beginning of a new story of a "poet who had a marvellous idea of erecting a statue to

Adam, & he tells a friend of the project. He had no money & so would have to interest other people in the idea. The first person he goes to is an old Admiral."[6] The focus of the fragmentary novel then becomes reports in the poet's diary (with little revealed about the personality of the diarist) dealing with Admiral Stormfield, based again on Captain Ned Wakeman, as well as Clemens's old friend and adviser Henry H. Rogers, along with Stormfield's collection of failed and defeated derelicts. (Mark Twain told Paine that there is "no such figure for the storm-beaten human drift as the derelict.")[7] The structure of the fragment is loose; the slight plot supplied by the poet's efforts to induce the admiral to contribute to the monument fund serves as a peg on which the author strains to hang philosophy, anecdotes, and portraits.[8]

At the end of March 1905, Mark Twain read to his household a newly composed essay on William Dean Howells. It was published in *Harper's Magazine,* but not until July 1906. Deeply in Howells's debt because of his friend's support and helpful criticism, private and public, Mark Twain here celebrates literary standards that he and Howells shared: choice of the right word, graceful and unbroken meters, compactness, and unobtrusive stage directions, "those artifices which authors employ to throw a kind of human naturalness around a scene and a conversation." These were in fact the writer's stylistic views, although the virtue of compactness is found more commonly in his sentences than in his larger units.

On May 18, 1905, Clemens and his household, including Isabel Lyon and Jean, began the first of two long summers at Dublin, New Hampshire, near Mount Monadnock, where he found himself surrounded by people he had known for many years. Almost as soon as he arrived, he began his last effort at a novel, "Three Thousand Years Among the Microbes." He was soon delighted both with his productivity and with the story itself, which he said yielded more enjoyment than any book he had undertaken in twenty years. Although he hoped he could work on it all summer, his inspiration lagged after a little over a month. Moreover, he was bothered by gout, dyspepsia, and bronchitis, the latter not altogether surprising in view of his status as an "excessive smoker."

"Microbes" differs from the other late fragments in being chiefly a satire. It is based on an idea he had recorded in his notebook in 1883 and later dreamed: that "we are only the microscopic trichina concealed in the blood of some vast creature's veins, & that it is that vast creature whom God concerns himself about, & not us."[9] Paine published selections from this work in his 1912 biography; a complete edition appears in *Which Was the Dream?* (1968). The fragment is about fifty thousand words long.

Unlike "The Refuge of the Derelicts," this last long story is original in conception and, up to a point, provocative. It tells the story of a scientist who has been magically transformed into a cholera germ in the body of an aged and malicious tramp named Blitzowski. There he finds that a whole world exists, a world of microbes analogous to man's world, although more densely populated. Measurements naturally have a different scale, with three thousand years amounting to three human weeks. The scientist-narrator is named Bkshp, but he is familiarly known as "Huck," an abbreviation for his American middle name, Huxley. (Bkshp appears to be an abbreviation for the name of Huckleberry Finn's real-life model, Tom Blankenship.) Because of his previous human experience, Huck is able to tell his adventures from a double point of view. Happy in the germ world, he is, according to chapter 1, "the germiest of the germs," and so he can observe the germs from their point of view as well as from his human memories. Although wildly inventive, the story is for a time kept under control through the author's satiric purpose. The United States is satirized as GRQ — Getrichquick — and Christian Science becomes another object of satire. In a preface, the "translator" describes the style of the original microbic as that of a stevedore in short sleeves and overalls, but he is by no means a grown-up Huck Finn. Here and there one finds touches of the early exuberance of Mark Twain, for the first half is told with considerable zest, but eventually the ingenuity dominates the narrative, and the work falters, much as in "Eddypus."

The author explained to Clara in June that he was dropping "Microbes" in order to finish "No. 44," and as already noted he did work on this project in June and July. In June he also wrote "As Concerns Interpreting the Deity," not published until 1917, when Paine included it in *What Is Man? and Other Essays* — minus its last 750 words. A complete version appears in *What Is Man? and Other Philosophical Writings* (1973). This delightful and quite successful hoax begins with what appears to be a learned discussion of Egyptian and Dighton Rock inscriptions, but the real purpose was to mock the pastor of the Plymouth Church of Brooklyn, who had construed the Russo-Japanese War of 1904–5 as God's work.

On July 12, Mark Twain felt obliged to meet requests from Duneka for contributions to *Harper's Magazine* and turned from "No. 44" to "Eve's Diary." His technique, he explained in a letter to Duneka, was for Eve to use "Extracts from Adam's Diary," written some dozen years before, as "her (unwitting and un[con]scious) text." As a tribute of sorts to Olivia Clemens, the diary emphasizes what the author believed to be distinctively female characteristics: love of beauty and nature, affection, reliance on intuition, curiosity. Eve is a young girl, full of wonder at the creation and at herself. She considers herself an experiment, and when she sees Adam, she calls him the "other Experiment." Since she is quickly attracted to him, her efforts to win his love apparently lead to the Fall. "I tried to get him some of those apples, but I cannot learn to throw straight. I failed, but I think the good intentions pleased him. They are forbidden, and he says I shall come to harm; but so I come to harm through pleasing him, why shall I care for that harm?" She does not report the event of the Fall, but afterward she records, "The Garden is lost, but I have found *him,* and am content." A long examination of *why* she loves him concludes, "*Merely because he is masculine,* I think." "Eve's Diary" ends with an epitaph for Eve—and Olivia Clemens. Adam touchingly records, "Wherever she was, *there* was Eden." The good-humored diary is so full of Eve's delightful naivete that its sentimentality is never offensive; one welcomes Mark Twain's return to a portrayal of youthful innocence. Of his Eve, Mark Twain wrote to his daughter Clara, she "has no refinements, either of conduct or speech, & I think she is charming." The "Diary" was published in the Christmas issue of *Harper's Magazine* and made into a book in 1906, with many illustrations, but without any part of "Adam's Diary." (Nor was it included with "Eve's Diary" in *Their Husbands' Wives,* edited by William Dean Howells and Henry Mills Alden and published by Harper in 1906). The 1905 addition to "Adam's Diary" first appeared in *Eve's Diary,* published by Harper, also in 1906.

Thereafter Mark Twain revised "Adam's Diary," which for a time he judged "not literature." "I have struck out 700 words," he wrote Duneka, "and inserted 5 MS pages of new matter (650 words) and now Adam's Diary is *dam* good—sixty times as good as it was." He added, "I hate to have the old Adam go out any more—*don't* put it on the presses again, let's put the new one in place of it." What happened next is quite strange; it suggests either that Duneka had a casual attitude toward his responsibilities as editor or that the writer had a change of heart, for when "Adam's Diary" next appeared, it was the same old Adam that his creator had rejected. Duneka had received the revised manuscript and written to Clemens, "Thank you ever so much for the corrections of 'Adam's Diary,' which I shall have made at once."[10] The five new pages, extant at the Mark Twain Papers,[11] *were* published, but not in "Adam's Diary"—they appear toward the end of Eve's, where they are introduced as "Extract from Adam's Diary," although they hardly belong there. A proper text of "Extracts from Adam's Diary" finally appeared in *The Bible According to Mark Twain* in 1995.

While Eve is a man's view of a woman, Adam is almost a comic character. Paine says, "Mark Twain created Adam in his own image"[12]—he should have said "in the image of the prime Mark Twain." Adam first sees Eve as competition; she is preempting his territory. His comments are full of delicious anachronisms: "The new creature eats too much fruit. We are going to run short, most likely." (In the original version, it was not an apple but a chestnut, a moldy joke, that caused the Fall.) In both Adam's diary and Eve's, the Fall is treated in a wholly human, nonmythic context.

One charming passage written some years earlier for "Adam's Diary" has yet to be published in any collection of Mark Twain's writings. The passage reads:

> *Saturday.* The Voice says he made this property in six consecutive days, and is resting to-day. (Consecutive — a good word; will set it down and use it again.) He says he made me yesterday. Also the creature with the long hair, that follows me about, and calls herself Eve and says she is a Woman — whatever that may be. Seems bent upon living with me — *is* bent upon living with me, in fact. . . . I said it would cause remark. She said there was nobody but the animals to take notice of it. I reminded her that there was herself, and also me, and added that the true basis of right living is principle, not expediency; that an upright life uprightly lived for show would be a sham, and valueless. She tossed her head and sniffed at that, and said "I wouldn't be as goody-goody as you for wages." I reminded her, coldly, that such a speech was hardly proper, from one mere acquaintance to another; that I had no formal introduction to her, knew nothing about her character and antecedents, that she had intruded upon the estate unasked, and that I must be excused if I regarded her ways as somewhat too familiar, in the circumstances. She retorted that I was as much as intimating that she was an adventuress. This being the truth, I was not willing to deny it, therefore an uncomfortable silence supervened. Then she said that if all respectability was lodged in me, some share could hardly be denied her, since out of a rib of my body she had been made.[13]

Read in the context of a knowledge of Mark Twain's literary career, the passage has a great deal to offer. He returns to his amused attitude toward gentility by creating the ultimate snob, the first one. (This Adam and the Adam of the rest of the diary are utterly different.) It is further evidence that the social graces Clemens adopted under his wife's tutelage were mainly a veneer.

The longest of the several pieces on man's earliest ancestors is "Autobiography of Eve." Here Eve looks back at her nine hundred years of life and quotes at length from her diary record of the years before the Fall. She records how she found that all the creatures except herself had mates. Only after a year's strenuous search does she find Adam. This sketch, unlike the other ones, is both humorous and bitter, but mostly humorous. For example, Adam and Eve are both scientists, with dictionary-making as an avocation. Although uneven, the piece has some delightful touches. Here is the way the manuscript of Eve's diary ends with the entry for the year 15: "The children promise well. . . . Cain is the cleverest of all. He is really an expert at making the simpler kind of fossils, and will soon be taking the most of that work off our hands, I think. And he has invented one fossil, all by himself—the planning & arranging of prehistoric deposits."[14]

During the summer of 1905, one more piece came from Mark Twain's pen. In April, Jean Clemens had published in *Harper's Weekly* "A Word for the Horses," on the evils of checkreins and martingales—both punishing harness restraints. Perhaps as a result, in mid-September Mark Twain received a letter from Minnie Maddern Fiske, an animal-rights advocate, encouraging him "to write a story of an old horse that is finally given over to the bull-ring."[15] She was campaigning to put a stop to bullfighting. The obliging author replied that he would try. After a good deal of effort, he finished the story later that month, pleased because he had been able to draw on his memories of Susy in the portrait of Cathy, a little girl who is devoted to Soldier Boy, the horse eventually killed in the bullring. A long story, over seventeen thousand words, "A Horse's Tale" was published in two installments in *Harper's Magazine,* in August and September of 1906, and as an illustrated book in 1907. The story might well have been written as the basis for a Shirley Temple movie. Told in part by the horse himself, in part through letters, interspersed with chapters wholly in dialogue—one between Soldier Boy and a Mexican Plug—the story is readable, but with two objects of sentimental interest, the remarkably assertive girl and her horse (both mortally wounded in the bullring), it is distinctly overdone. Mark Twain may have been trying to comply with what had been requested of him.

Perhaps the most interesting aspect of the story is that Cathy is described as "twins, and . . . one of them is a boy-twin and failed to get segregated." Thus the story belongs to a group that features a masculinized female, others being "A Medieval Romance" (1869–70), "The 1002ᵈ Arabian Night," *Joan of Arc,* "Hellfire Hotchkiss," "Wapping Alice," and "How Nancy Jackson Married Kate Wilson." These stories show Mark Twain taking a further step beyond stories about role-changing, such as *The Prince and the Pauper* and *Pudd'nhead Wilson,* to stories about gender-changing. Despite his social acceptance of the traditional gender roles, in his fiction he repeatedly questioned these roles. But he was not sure of himself: of the five, he published only *Joan of Arc*, and in it he made sure that Joan had many of the conventional feminine characteristics (innocence and compassion) as well as the "masculine" ones of daring and leadership.

After leaving New Hampshire, Clemens returned to New York in October. Now his life was largely devoted to social engagements, the most monumental of which was a seventieth-birthday celebration, with 172 guests who, according to the *New York Times,* "showed by word and manner and act that they looked upon the chief guest as the master" and "the uncrowned king of American letters."[16]

At this point, early in 1906, the writer Albert Bigelow Paine entered Clemens's life. Paine soon arranged to become the author's authorized biographer and was permitted to examine his manuscripts and letters. On January 9, Mark Twain began to prepare materials for Paine, and once more he returned to his autobiography, now with an added motive. The task was to be enormous yet almost easy. On the first day, the writer stated his plans to Paine. The stenographer present for this auspicious occasion recorded:

> The only thing possible for me is to talk about the thing that something suggests at the moment — something in the middle of my life, perhaps, or something that happened only a few months ago. It is my purpose to extend these notes to 600,000 words, and possibly more. But that is going to take a long time — a long time.
>
> My idea is this — that I write an autobiography. When that autobiography is finished — or before it is finished — then you take the manuscript and decide on how much of a biography to make. But this is no holiday excursion — it is a journey.[17]

It was to be a long journey. Thereafter dictations became a regular, often daily event. Although Mark Twain made much of the dangerously frank character of what he dictated, those closest to him soon knew that his comments had distinct boundaries. He told Isabel Lyon that he would tell the truth about himself with one reservation: "There were the Rousseau confessions, but I am going to leave that kind alone, for Rousseau seems to have looked after that end."[18] Howells reports in *My Mark Twain* that one day Clemens told him that "as to veracity it [the autobiographical dictating] was a failure; he had begun to lie, and that if no man ever yet told the truth about himself it was because no man ever could."[19] Paine soon concluded that as source materials the dictations had to be checked, for "these marvelous reminiscences bore only an atmospheric relation to history."[20]

Beginning with twelve dictations in January, Mark Twain continued for three years. Until June in the first year, there were each month from seven to seventeen sessions; then there was a short break. Of this early group, a month was devoted to comments inspired by Susy's biography of her father, which she had begun in 1885 when she was fourteen. Often he proceeded by process of association. Sometimes he worked from obituaries. For five days in June, back in Dublin, New Hampshire, he dictated reflections on religion that he promised Howells "will get my heirs & assigns burnt alive" if they are published "this side of 2006 A.D." By this time he was describing the dictations as "already perfectly outrageous in spots." He liked the results. "I don't care for my other books, now, but I dote on this one." He described "the law of this book: the newest & hottest interest takes precedence of *anything* I may be talking about."

Isabel Lyon played an important role in these dictations. She helped to ready Clemens by visiting him early in the morning. In June 1906, she recorded, "The morning bedroom talks are vastly interesting. I go into Mr. Clemens's room a little before 9, after he has finished his breakfast. I make a good enough audience for him to talk against in order to get himself into his dictating swing."[21]

Clemens took another break in late June and July, when he visited New York to make publishing arrangements. There he frequently spent the night on Henry Rogers's yacht. Throughout 1906, he continued on his autobiography, when 134 dictations were recorded. In 1907, as enthusiasm cooled, there were fewer, seventy in all, with only four during November and December. In 1908 there were just thirty-four, including several in which the author expressed his dislike of Lilian Aldrich, wife of his friend Thomas Bailey Aldrich. The last dictations were made in early 1909, when fourteen were completed, the very last being dated April 16. The dictations averaged about 1,500 words each, making the total (including undated dictations) about 450,000 words, to which should be added some 60,000 words written or dictated before 1906. But what could be done with such a huge and shapeless mass of material?

Although Mark Twain referred to the autobiography as a work intended to be published posthumously, he took a first step toward publication in August 1906, less than nine months after the project was conceived, by arranging with George Harvey, president of Harper and editor of the *North American Review,* to publish selections. These appeared in what was at the time a fortnightly, from September 7, 1906, until December, then in monthly installments from January through October 1907, twenty-five installments in all; they represented only the dictations of winter and spring 1906. For them, the author received thirty thousand dollars, which he eventually used to build a house at Redding, Connecticut.

Harvey himself designated the portions that the *North American Review* published. As the author told Howells, "He has selected five 5,000 word installments, & pieced them together so cleverly that the seams don't show, & each seems to have been written by itself." Recently Michael Kiskis has collected and published the *North American Review* chapters as a book, attaching an extended introduction and annotations. (They also appear in the Oxford Mark Twain.) Kiskis argues convincingly that this collection, rather than others, constitute "the text of Clemens' life story" inasmuch as the author "was involved in the choices for the installments, had final control over the revisions that were made to the texts, and gave his approval for their publication," and because "the twenty-five chapters compressed into a single volume present a unified tale of Clemens's life."[22]

Mark Twain's autobiography has been put to many uses. In 1909, the writer himself used materials from his dictations to compile *Is Shakespeare Dead?* After Clemens's death, Paine published a few pages and many passages in his *Mark Twain: A Biography* (1912). In 1922 Paine published a few more pages in *Harper's Magazine,* and a little more in 1923 in his collection *Mark Twain's Speeches*. Finally in 1924 Paine published a two-volume edition of *Mark Twain's Autobiography,* including much of the pre-1906 material but only selections from the dictations through April 11, 1906. He thus drew on merely 71 of 252. These he published in the order of composition, "in accordance with the author's wishes," according to Paine.[23] He did not include in these volumes all that had been published in the earlier periodical selections. Apparently Paine intended to publish at least another volume from dictations following those of April 1906, but probably because the reviews of the first two volumes were not enthusiastic, he did not proceed. Paine's successor as literary editor, Bernard DeVoto, published another volume of selections, chiefly from dictations later than those Paine had used; he called it *Mark Twain in Eruption: Hitherto Unpublished Pages About Men and Events* (1940). Whereas Paine's selections had emphasized the author's life, DeVoto presented selections on Hannibal and Mark Twain's comments on his own work, plus many discussions of political figures, especially Theodore Roosevelt.

DeVoto includes passages about an important feature of Twain's last years: the fact that he began but did not finish many works of fiction.

> As long as a book would write itself I was a faithful and interested amanuensis and my industry did not flag, but the minute that the book tried to shift to *my* head the labor of contriving its situations, inventing its adventures and conducting its conversations, I put it away and dropped it out of my mind.[24]

Later, as with *Huckleberry Finn,* he could return and finish a few works. But others turned out to be "books that refuse to be written. They stand their ground, year after year, and will not be persuaded. It isn't because the book is not there and worth being written — it is only because the right form for the story does not present itself."[25]

In 1959 Charles Neider made some use of unpublished manuscripts as well as published parts to compile what he called *The Autobiography of Mark Twain.* His arrangement is intended to show Mark Twain telling the story of his life in chronological order, a difficult task since in a single dictation the author often discussed both early events and much later ones. Neider chose to include little of the social and political criticism that DeVoto had published, but he did provide some thirty thousand words of previously unpublished material. Serious readers notice that the selections sometimes do not carry dates, making it hard to locate their source. Neider had hoped to include in his version the reflections on religion that were dictated in June 1906 — even though they were not autobiographical and thus did not fit into his scheme — but Clara Clemens Samossoud denied permission to publish them. They finally appeared in 1963, after her death, in the autumn issue of the *Hudson Review* and then in a collection Neider called *The Outrageous Mark Twain* (1987). Tentative plans to publish a more complete edition of the autobiography were made by Frederick Anderson in his position as literary editor of the Mark Twain estate, but his death in 1979 interrupted the effort.

Pieces of the autobiography continue to appear. The dictations of March 12 and 14, 1906, appeared in *Mark Twain's Weapons of Satire* (1992). They provide a strong condemnation of the "Moro Massacre" — the destruction of a tribe of Filipinos, six hundred men, women, and children — by American troops under General Leonard Wood.

The rationale for Mark Twain's autobiography was best stated in 1907 when he wrote to his friend J. W. Y. MacAllister, "Dictated things are talk, and talk is all the better and all the more natural when it stumbles a little here and there." This principle also animated the talk of the writer's vernacular narrators, such as Simon Wheeler and Captain Stormfield, even Huckleberry Finn. Many of the dictations are natural, easy, comfortable, and informal, but some are also vituperative, unfocused, egotistical, or trivial. Unlike the other long pieces of the author's last years, they are not burdened by expectations of structure or even coherence. But the author was laboring under a mistaken notion in believing that he was at last telling the whole truth. In a letter to Clemens in February 1904, Howells wisely questioned whether anyone could stand to tell the truth about himself:

"The black truth, which we all know of ourselves in our hearts, or only the whity-brown truth of the pericardium, or the nice, whitened truth of the shirtfront?" Even *you* won't tell the black heart's-truth."[26] It is a whity-brown truth that Mark Twain tells, at best. For example, when Clara debuted as a singer at Norfolk, Connecticut, he acknowledged that he had urged her to publicize herself as "Mark Twain's daughter." "This was vinegar for Clara, but saccharine for me." After she sang, he admittedly "made a plunge for the stage . . . to congratulate her and . . . to show off and get my share of the glory."[27] He paraded his egotism: "I like compliments, praises, flatteries, I cordially enjoy all such things, and am grieved and disappointed when what I call a 'barren mail' arrives — a mail that hasn't any compliments in it."[28]

The "Reflections on Religion" are outspoken, but not much more so than others of the author's late comments. He calls God hard names here:

> In His destitution of one and all of the qualities which could grace a God and invite respect for Him and reverence and worship, the real God, the genuine God, the Maker of the mighty universe is just like all the other gods in the list. He proves every day that he takes no interest in man, nor in the other animals, further than to torture them, slay them, and get out of this pastime such entertainment as it may afford — and do what he can not to get weary of the eternal and changeless monotony of it.[29]

Oddly, there are no real revelations in the autobiography. Generally the habits of a lifetime of lecturing and after-dinner speaking enticed the author and he became an entertainer once again. However edited and organized, the autobiography is not a masterful book, if it can be called a book at all. Mark Twain made better use of his memories in *Tom Sawyer, Huckleberry Finn,* and "Old Times on the Mississippi," for there they are shaped, filtered through nostalgia, and refined with art. "Narrative *writing*," he asserted, "is always disappointing. The moment you pick up a pen you begin to lose the spontaneity of the personal relation, which contains the very essence of interest. With shorthand dictation one can talk as if he were at his own dinner-table — always a most inspiring place."[30] No doubt the experience of dictating his memoirs appealed to the speaker, but the reader finds less fulfillment from the process.

Mark Twain ignored large aspects of his literary and personal life because his autobiography became less a record of his life than entertainment — his own chiefly — and a means of profiting from his career as a writer. He relied on it, too, for therapy, to relieve himself of guilt over the deaths of his brother Henry and his son, Langdon. When he had finished his account of another source of guilt, his bankruptcy, he said: "There — Thanks be! A hundred times I have tried to tell this intolerable story with a pen, but I never could do it. It always made me sick before I got half-way to the middle of it. But this time I have held my grip and walked the floor and emptied it all out of my system, and I hope never to hear of it again."[31] Similarly, he wrote to Howells in June 1906 about the relief of getting certain topics "out of my system, where they have been festering for years — & that was the main thing," more important apparently than communicating what he had to say to posterity. "I feel better, now," he added.

Sometimes he simply editorialized on news events, attaching clippings to the dictations. Occasionally he inserted unpublished manuscripts, such as that of "Wapping Alice," part of the dictation of April 9, 1907. A particularly fertile event occurred when he was awarded an honorary doctorate from Oxford University and found himself acclaimed as a national hero in Britain. He reported having received "hundreds of letters from all conditions of people in England — men, women, and children — and there is in them compliment, praise, and above all and better than all, there is in them a note of affection."[32] George Bernard Shaw, with whom he had lunch, called him the greatest American author.[33] After the ceremony, Clemens told the Maharajah of Bikanir, "I like the degree well enough, but I'm crazy about the clothes."[34] On this trip he was accompanied by Ralph Ashcroft as a personal secretary; later, Ashcroft would become a kind of business manager. From this occasion, surely the high point of his life, Mark Twain obtained materials for nineteen days of dictation at Tuxedo Park, New York, where he summered that year. Amusing and valuable remarks are scattered through the unpublished materials, in the midst of opinions he had been volunteering for years. It took him a long time to tire of hearing his own voice.

In the year when he began his autobiographical dictations, 1906, he took up his pen long enough to begin a substantial essay that was also autobiographical. Begun as a commemorative essay on Susy ten years after her death, it was later broadened to include highly amusing descriptions of the people who had influenced Susy and her sisters, such as George Griffin and Patrick McAleer, two longtime Clemens servants, and the "Egyptian volcano," the most productive of Clara's many wet nurses, whose proper name was Maria McLaughlin and whose ability to consume food and drink proved enormous. During the year's shortest month she drank, he reported, 256 pints of beer, although she by no means restricted her liquid intake to that beverage. "A Family Sketch," some twelve thousand words, deserves publication more than any of the still-unpublished autobiographical dictations.[35]

The decision to dictate his autobiography had one definite effect on Mark Twain's career: it all but stopped him from writing anything for some time. His letters of early 1906 are brim full of expressions of satisfaction in the dictations, both process and product, medium and message. The entire exercise encouraged his egotism and his love of showing off. In October he decided that he would defy seasonal conventions by appearing in a white suit. He ordered five and later added others. His explanation was that dark colors help make winters depressing, but the real reason was that he enjoyed receiving attention. Late in 1906, at copyright hearings in Washington, D.C., Clemens made his first winter public appearance in the white suit that was to become habitual. He even ordered white evening clothes.[36] After receiving his honorary degree from Oxford, he found occasions to wear his scarlet Oxford gown over his white suit, for example at Clara's wedding in 1909. In a 1905 notebook entry, he wrote; "White clothes — most conspicuous person on the planet — the only grown-up male, savage or civ who wears clean clothes in cold weather. *None* are clean after 24 hours' wear."[37]

The fact that Paine was preparing notes for a biography and was traveling both to Europe and to the American West to collect materials and that his letters were being assembled for publication must have made the author feel that he had been admitted to the Writers' Pantheon.

During the years 1906–8, Isabel Lyon was in a sense taking the place of Olivia, giving the elderly man constant care. For a time she and Albert Bigelow Paine worked well together. She recorded that the two agreed that "the King can do no wrong," although she pictured Clemens as overcome with rage and anger at a green shade that did not work right and found that when he read letters, he always saw something that so irritated him that he denounced the human race. She devoted herself assiduously to Clemens's welfare, even making use of the telephone to summon billiard players in order to prevent Clemens from feeling lonely. She wrote to Paine on February 1908, and recorded the message in her diary, "I have taken sole care of the King, which meant an hourly attention from 8. am. until 12 midnight."[38] Clemens told Clara and Jean that what Isabel Lyon said to them should be understood as equivalent to what he himself might say; he told his daughters that he knew her "better and more intimately than I have ever known anyone except your mother."[39]

His unceasing commitment to preserving the value of his works and his pen name had important and extended consequences. In 1907, Ashcroft suggested that the author register and protect at the Patent Office products that might be identified by others, for profit, with his name. As a result,

"Mark Twain Whiskey" and "Mark Twain Tobacco" were duly registered. Later the author founded the Mark Twain Company to relieve himself of the task of overseeing his estate and (as the *New York Times* reported) "to keep the earnings of Mr. Clemens's books continually in the family, even after the copyright on the books themselves expires." [40] Upon his death, the three men who were to become executors of his will were the officers of the company, along with Paine and Clemens's attorney. [41] As a result of these arrangements, Clara Clemens, who lived until 1962, was receiving even at the end of her life — according to her biographer — substantial benefits from royalties and from the use of her father's name. In 1964, the value of her estate was determined to be over $925,000. [42] The company survived until 1994, although by the terms of Clara's will the more benevolent Mark Twain Foundation was created after the death of her second husband and (subsequently) of his friend Dr. William E. Seiler, both of whom for a time enjoyed the proceeds of the estate. This foundation still collects the author's royalties. [43]

In his last years, Clemens was frequently lonely. He discovered that Bermuda gave him pleasure and visited there frequently, once for three months, sometimes with Twichell, Ashcroft, Rogers, or Paine. The writer still kept himself in the public eye by entertaining reporters. For example, the *New York Times* for January 10, 1907, headed a story: "More Health Than He Needs: Mark Twain Home from Bermuda Has It to Give Away." Arriving with Isabel Lyon and Joseph Twichell, he is quoted as saying, "I could not stay away any longer. Literature is in a bad way. Mr. Shakespeare is dead, and my old friend, Mr. Milton, has passed away, so I had to come home." He reported that the trip "had given him a chance to create a sensation by wearing the famous white suit in which he appeared in Washington some time ago. He added that the costume suited both his complexion and style of beauty."

In Bermuda Mark Twain made the acquaintance of several young girls between ten and sixteen, whom he called "angelfish." To please them he had Tiffany make enamel angelfish pins; he soon established a considerable correspondence with them. [44]

Writings by Mark Twain besides the autobiography (he revised and corrected the dictation transcripts with pen) continued to appear in print during his last years. As noted, "Eve's Diary" and "A Horse's Tale" were published as books in 1906 and 1907. An "Extract" from Captain Stormfield's story of his visit to heaven appeared in 1909 as a book. But before he let it appear, Twain satisfied himself that it was not offensive. Isabel Lyon recorded that the author "has been so troubled over publishing Captain

Stormfield's Visit to Heaven that he has been collecting opinions. Tonight he read parts of it to the guests, but they have no comment to make save one of approval."[45] What very well might have been found offensive, though some readers would have judged it one of Mark Twain's best short pieces of his last years, is "Little Bessie," which he began on a yachting trip with Rogers in early 1908. It opens with the question that Susy Clemens had asked so plaintively years before: "Mama, why is there so much pain and sorrow and suffering? What is it all for?" In the series of dialogues that follow, little Bessie, almost three, persistently asks her mother probing questions about God's justice, the virgin birth, and the Trinity; she finds it difficult to accept the pious Sunday school answers. Bessie's charming naivete makes these few pages amusing. The skeptical attitude Mark Twain had shown in his western sketches survived for over forty years, indeed becoming deeper dyed. Paine published a selection of "Little Bessie" in his biography; the complete dialogues are in *Fables of Man*.

In June 1908, Clemens moved into a sixteen-room house in Redding, Connecticut, built at a cost of $45,000 with earnings from the autobiography; he appropriately called it Stormfield, after the recently published sketch. The house, designed by Howells's son John, was constructed under the direct supervision of Isabel Lyon, to whom Clemens gave full credit for the residence, which he liked immensely. Originally the house was to be a summer residence, but it pleased Clemens so much that he decided to make Stormfield his sole residence. (He gave Isabel Lyon the task of closing the Fifth Avenue house.) Stormfield, which quite lacked the warmth and charm of the Clemenses' Hartford house, did not survive its owner for long.

Many guests, including several of the angelfish, came for visits. But his pleasure from these visits was counterbalanced by deaths. His close friend Henry Rogers died in May 1909, and Samuel Moffett, his sister's son, drowned in August, while Moffett's young son watched. These deaths shook the author badly and caused depression and illness. Perhaps as a consequence he wrote in September, for inclusion in "No. 44," a chapter in which 44 teaches August Feldner another lesson by providing a gloomy historical pageant of the dead, biblical figures, Caesars, King Arthur, even the Missing Link. This serves as chapter 33 of the published version (1969) and may have been an effort to connect what he had written earlier to the "Conclusion of the Book," in which #44 disappears.

During his later years, Clemens's relationship with his youngest daughter was problematic. Following her mother's death, Jean experienced more epileptic seizures, and in 1906 she entered a sanatorium and did not live with her father again until April 1909. He was unable to deal with her sympathetically; he complained, for example, about the expense of boarding her dog and even told her that the dog should be destroyed.[46] Soon he would have additional reasons for guilty feelings, for she was to die in the same year that she settled in at Stormfield.

For a while Stormfield was too full of guests for its illustrious occupant to undertake any writing. But early in 1909, after receiving proofs of a book elevating the status of Sir Francis Bacon, George Greenwood's *The Shakespeare Problem Restated,* he began the series of dictations that became a little book, *Is Shakespeare Dead?* Here Mark Twain reviews the paucity of biographical information on Shakespeare and suggests that Bacon is the most plausible candidate for authorship of the celebrated plays. Several pages recall the author's piloting days, when he first became familiar with the plays, but when he compares his reputation in Hannibal with Shakespeare's Stratford one, the results are not gratifying. Moreover, he inserted into his work twenty-two pages of Greenwood's work, without permission — which hardly seems like appropriate behavior for an advocate of copyright laws. Whereas Harper had eagerly contracted to publish whatever he wrote, the editors now were becoming eager to shut off a failing old man.

Isabel Lyon had been for some time the person closest to Clemens. On March 18, 1909, she married Ashcroft, Clemens's business manager. Clemens duly attended the wedding. Why these two abruptly married is not clear; on their return to Stormfield, they occupied separate bedrooms. Much later Lyon said that it had been a marriage of convenience, intended "to save the good name of Mr. C."[47] Indeed, she had noted in her diary that a reporter had inquired about reports that linked Clemens's name with hers. She had told the reporter that Clemens would be "as pained as his secretary to hear of such a report."[48] Her explanation to Clemens of her marriage was that she could not "go on alone carrying the dear weight of wonderful Stormfield direction."[49] Meanwhile, Clara Clemens had become deeply resentful of Lyon's expanding role, especially since she curtailed Clara's expenditures, which had indeed been extravagant. Despite the fact that Ashcroft and Lyon had become practically indispensable to Clemens, Clara was finally able to persuade her father that both were cheating him. In April, Clemens angrily dismissed both of them.

Subsequently, Clemens composed a long account of what he saw as their treachery. This "Ashcroft-Lyon Manuscript" (unpublished) is an unsent "letter" to Howells, since the autobiographer was now substituting a new plan for recording his meditations — "to write letters to friends & *not send them,*" as he explained to Howells in April 1909. There are over four hundred pages of manuscript, to which are attached letters, clippings, accounts, and whatever the old man could dredge up as part of the case against the two. It is a sad document. Clemens seems to have had four reasons for writing this piece, to which he devoted many months: to display the last of his several methods of composing his autobiography, to provide his daughter Clara with a document that could be used against Ashcroft and Lyon should they bother Clara after Clemens's death, to reestablish his strained relationship with Clara, and to express his resentment and anger at Lyon's having married Ashcroft. The work engaged Clemens so fully that he wrote, ostensibly to Howells, "Howells, this great long Lyon-Ashcroft episode is just as booky as it can be; so booky that sometimes facts and realities seem . . . as if they hadn't ever happened," and he noted its resemblance to "some . . . old-time novel."[50]

But the enormous talent still flickered. In 1909, Mark Twain showed that he was still capable of turning out competent if undistinguished commercial fiction. "The International Lightning Trust" is a rather amusing satire on business practices, with greed being treated sympathetically this time. Two young men develop a scheme to offer insurance against being struck by lightning; they reap huge profits. The story got as far as a Harper editor, and there it stayed. The manuscript remained unpublished until its 1972 appearance in *Fables of Man*.

In June 1909, Mark Twain traveled with Paine to Baltimore to give what proved to be his last speech, at the graduation of one of his angelfish. It was on this trip that he first experienced angina pectoris, a symptom of the affliction that would kill him. Thereafter pain was to come again and again, often reduced by morphine shots. Elizabeth Wallace, who knew him in Bermuda, quotes a letter from him, reporting: "I was warned to stop smoking, which I did, for two or three days, but it was too lonesome, and I have resumed — in a modified way — 4 smokes a day instead of 40." But in his next letter to her he wrote, "I read, and read, and read, and smoke, and smoke, and smoke *all* the time (as formerly), and it's a contented and comfortable life." In fact, he was very much alone at the remote Stormfield, especially after the dismissal of Lyon and Ashcroft. Although Jean returned home in the spring of 1909, her presence did little to brighten her father's life. Now only Paine, living in a nearby cottage, was regularly available as company.

In the fall of 1909, Mark Twain wrote for *Harper's Bazar* an essay on "The Turning Point of My Life." It was to have been part of a series by literary figures on the topic. Mark Twain's original version began with what Paine called "one of his impossible burlesque fancies,"[51] but Paine's — and Jean Clemens's — disapproval seems to have brought on not only a revision but also an attack of angina pectoris. The abortive burlesque told of the fortunes of two apples, Tom Crab and William Greening. At first the latter seems to have all the luck, but Crab is selected by Luther Burbank and is so nurtured that he produces "a great spray of hitherto unimaginable roses." Later revised in Bermuda, with the apple adventure dropped, it was published in February 1910. In this essay he applied his deterministic philosophy to explain how he came to be a writer. The account is a not altogether accurate survey of a chain of circumstances that led to Mark Twain's career, beginning with the illness the writer suffered when he was a boy. "I can say with truth that the reason I am in the literary profession is because I had the measles when I was twelve years old." The essay is a polished, engaging piece of prose demonstrating that Mark Twain could still be a craftsman at age seventy-four.

In October 1909, Mark Twain returned once more to "dangerous" writings, and this time he produced something that would have shocked his readers far more than "Little Bessie" had it been published at the time. In August, the writer had warmed up for this work by composing under an assumed name a letter (first published in a 1973 collection) on God as the author of evil. It insisted that "if our Maker *is* all powerful for good or evil, He is not in His right mind."[52] The thirteen "Letters from the Earth," some seventeen thousand words written in October and later, begin as reports from Satan to Saint Michael and Saint Gabriel from the Earth, where Satan is suffering a temporary banishment. He is bewildered by man's strange Christianity. Soon the fiction is largely forgotten, and Mark Twain expresses his mature opinions on the folly of man's worship of God and the hypocrisy of Christianity; the ignorance of the writers of the Bible, with the story of Noah receiving extended treatment; the stupidity of the Bible's teachings; and God as the author of illness. Although the letters begin by attacking man for his crazy theology, they soon shift subtly to attacks on the "real" God, as Mark Twain had called Him in his 1906 dictations. While the work is not rounded off, the writing is exceptionally vital and brisk. Topics he had taken up elsewhere in a bitterly pessimistic, even angry, mood here are treated with good-humored detachment, perhaps because of the fictional pose.

One major source of Samuel Clemens's hostility to God is that he identified Christianity with simpleminded fundamentalism. He had become convinced that Christianity was invariably associated with hellfire and damnation. His visit to the Holy Land in 1867 had made him think that the Bible was full of errors. Later he seems to have decided that the Old Testament portrayal of God was largely accurate, and such a God he heartily despised. His anger extended even to Jesus. In "Letters from the Earth," he asserts that Jesus "devised hell and proclaimed it! Which is to say, that as the meek and gentle Savior he was a thousand billion times crueler than ever he was in the Old Testament — oh, incomparably more atrocious than ever he was at his very worst in those old days!"[53]

In his autobiography, Mark Twain devoted one dictation to an account of his conversation with Elinor Glyn, an English novelist, with whom he had talked openly about sex. In the dictation he expresses surprise at his own frankness but reluctantly categorizes himself as a servant of convention, without which mankind would be plunged into "confusion and disorder and anarchy."[54] But at the very end of his life, he cast aside his inhibitions — he was writing now, not dictating to a stenographer — and in "Letters from the Earth," hiding behind only a thin fiction, he acknowledges sexual pleasure as one of man's (and by implication his own) chief concerns. Intercourse is described as the greatest delight of heaven. Repeatedly the writer stresses the superiority of woman's sexuality: she is "competent every day, competent every night." On the other hand, man

> is competent from the age of sixteen or seventeen thenceforward for thirty-five years. After 50 his performance is of poor quality, the intervals between are wide, and its satisfactions of no great value to either party; whereas his great-grandmother is as good as new. There is nothing the matter with her plant. Her candlestick is as firm as ever, whereas his candle is increasingly softened and weakened by the weather of age, as years go by, until at last it can no longer stand, and is mournfully laid to rest in the hope of a blessed resurrection which is never to come.[55]

One can only wonder if this zesty report is not the result of Twain's liberation from the inhibitions that he had uncomfortably lived with during his years with Olivia Clemens — literary inhibitions, that is. Obviously he was in good spirits when he began these letters; only in the last of them do the jokes fade and personal grievances begin to take over. A long but self-sufficient fragment, "Letters from the Earth," was not released until 1962. (Bernard DeVoto tried to publish it in 1939 but was prevented by the objection of Mark Twain's daughter Clara.) The publication drew wide attention. A better text was published in *What Is Man? and Other Philosophical Writings* (1973).

There was still a place for pleasure of sorts in the life of Samuel Clemens. On October 6, 1909, Stormfield was the scene of the marriage of Clara, at age thirty-five, to Ossip Gabrilowitsch, the pianist she had met in Vienna. Joseph Twichell officiated, and Jean Clemens was maid of honor. Gabrilowitsch had by this time established himself; he had made his debut with the

New York Symphony Orchestra in 1900, when he played Tchaikovsky's First Piano Concerto. He was to have a notable career as an orchestra conductor. At the wedding Clemens appeared in a white suit, plus his red Oxford gown and cap. The couple intended to settle in Europe.

In November, Clemens was joined by Albert Bigelow Paine for another visit to Bermuda, but they returned home to celebrate Christmas with Jean at Stormfield. On the morning of December 24, Jean died, having drowned in the bathtub during an epileptic fit. Her father referred to her death as "this final disaster."[56] In an effort to control his reaction, he wrote a last essay. He told Paine, who published "The Death of Jean" in *Harper's Magazine* in December 1910, that it might serve as the "final chapter" of his autobiography. The essay looks back at the author's griefs, the losses of Susy, Olivia, and his friends, too. It describes the circumstances of Jean's death and his recent happy talks with her. A sentimental essay, it is a kind of farewell to life. Clemens did not attend her funeral in Elmira; he was too ill.

Early in 1910, Clemens and Howells had their last meeting together over dinner in New York. On January 5, Clemens, now in poor health, visited Bermuda once again. There he wrote one more sketch, "Advice to Paine," offering suggestions on polite deportment on one's arriving at heaven's gates or the "other place." As a last attempt at humor, it is remarkably successful. Paine published a few selections in his biography, but the whole of this amusing piece appeared only in 1995, with the added title "Etiquette for the Afterlife." It begins: "In hell it is not good form to refer, even unostentatiously, to your relatives in heaven, if persons are present who have none there." Other suggestions: "Do not try to show off. St. Peter dislikes it. The simpler you are dressed, the better it will please him. He cannot abide showy costumes. Above all things, avoid *over*-dressing. A pair of spurs & a fig-leaf is a plenty." Also, "Be careful about etiquette when invited to dinner. For evening dress, leave off your spurs."[57] With these parting instructions, the writer faced the next world, having finished with this one.

But not quite. He recorded in his notebook during the last year of his life, "Clara, when I am dead, continue to employ my lawyers (Stanchfield) at $1000 a year, & submit all business matters to them & the M. T. Co, always."[58] These instructions would be followed for a very long time; indeed, they are still in force, although in time the Mark Twain Company would evolve into the Mark Twain Foundation.

On March 25, Clemens knew from chest pains that he had little time left. He wrote to Paine from Bermuda on March 28, "I have been having a most uncomfortable time for the past four days with that breast-pain, which turns out to be an affection of the heart, just as I originally suspected."[59] The information was not new, but it was only now that Clemens, facing imminent death, recognized that the cause of his illness was smoking. He wanted to return home. He could not walk three hundred yards or "take a couple of extra smokes without paying the penalty in a severe pain in his heart." And he admitted that his belief "that a man could smoke any time or all the time without any injury to his health" had been "shattered at last by the condition in which he now found himself."[60]

Just how much Clemens associated smoking with his career as a writer is shown by a letter he had written in 1882.

> I find cigar smoking to be the best of all inspirations for the pen, and, in my particular case, no sort of detriment to the health. . . . During the family's summer vacation . . . I work five hours every day, and five days in every week, and allow no interruption under any pretext. I allow myself the fullest possible marvel of inspiration: consequently I ordinarily smoke fifteen cigars during my five hours' labours, and if my interest reaches the enthusiastic point, I smoke more. I smoke with all my might, and allow no intervals.[61]

Paine went to Bermuda to help Clemens return to New York, then to Stormfield. In Bermuda, Clemens recommended to Paine Thomas Hardy's gloomy novel *Jude the Obscure,* the last book read by the great American writer.[62] At Stormfield, on April 21, Clemens died, talking at the last of dual personality, Jekyll and Hyde. The value of his estate was just less than half a million dollars,[63] but it proved to be far more valuable in the long run. After a funeral service at the Brick Presbyterian Church in New York, with Joseph Twichell offering an emotional prayer, his body was laid in an Elmira plot, alongside Langdon, Susy, Olivia, and Jean.

"Mark Twain" proved impossible to kill, and his image and writings still live on. Since April 21, 1910, a whole library of his previously unpublished works has appeared. That omnium gatherum, his autobiography, still waits, requiring years of somebody's attention before it can be said to be published.

A household name, Mark Twain resides at the center of our concept of what the world views as American literature. Howells was discerning in comparing him to Lincoln. Even periodic controversies and disputes about Mark Twain's language and shortcomings seem unlikely to dislodge him from this commanding position. He possessed his nation's strengths and also absorbed its weaknesses. His fame and respect are likely to last as long as his country and its culture remain recognizable.

Afterword: Whys and Wherefores

The man whose highly original works are indelibly identified with the heartland of America and the vernacular became a writer of books only after pursuing several other vocations. He began writing following stints at typesetting, Mississippi River boat piloting, silver mining, and journalism. Subsequently, his career continued to be shaped to a remarkable degree by happenstance. His first successful book, *The Innocents Abroad,* was written because a subscription publisher invited him to prepare it, and it was therefore written according to the requirements of subscription books.

After *The Innocents Abroad,* Mark Twain returned to this travel formula three times, in *A Tramp Abroad* (an incoherent work, padded with appendixes — though admittedly some of them excellent), *Life on the Mississippi* (stuffed with borrowings), and *Following the Equator* (written through determination rather than inspiration). Once he had finally found a narrative manner that led to the creation of a masterpiece, he casually put his manuscript aside to write what his bourgeois family and friends wanted him to publish. Eventually he had difficulties in reconciling the persona he had created in the West, "Mark Twain," with a genteel lifestyle.

Having married an eastern lady and settled in New England, he limited his writing time to the summer, when he devoted much of his effort to composing sequels. He himself referred in 1896 to what he called "my stupid notion that I could do no work at home," a notion that dominated him "for many years," including his best ones. He told an interviewer in 1896:

The fact of it is that for many years while at home, in America, I have written little or nothing on account of social calls upon my time. There is too much social life in my city for a literary man, and so for twenty years I gave up the attempt to do anything during nine months of the twelve I am at home. It has only been during the three months that I have annually been on vacation, and have been supposed to be holiday-making that I have written anything. It has been the same during the five years that I have been away from America. I have done little or no work. I wish now that I had done differently and had persisted in writing when at home. I could easily have done it, although I thought I could not. I seemed to think then that I was never going to grow old, but I know better than that now.[1]

Although he was exaggerating in this statement of belated recognition of an ill-spent life, it is true that during long periods he let his attention be distracted, not only by social calls but both by ill-conceived literary ideas, especially his belief that he could reap rich profits as a dramatist, an idea that died hard, and by business ambitions that wasted his time and led to traumatic disappointment.

At the height of his career, he decided to give up writing to devote himself to more remunerative activities. After suffering the consequences of two bad judgments — establishing a publishing house with an incompetent businessman in charge and investing hundreds of thousands of dollars — he found that he was obliged to write potboilers and make his home in Europe for a decade. Although he should have realized that he was at his best when drawing on his own experiences, Mark Twain wrote three books that focus on the remote past: *The Prince and the Pauper,* a historical novel; *A Connecticut Yankee in King Arthur's Court,* his most ambitious novel, in which he tries to contrast the virtues of his own age with those of the days of King Arthur, about which he knew very little; and *Joan of Arc,* a fictionalized biography about a young woman whose heroism and saintliness he deeply admired, although he thought of the Deity in wholly disparaging terms. Yet he retained a fondness for his earlier creations. During his round-the-world tour, he included many pieces told either by a vernacular narrator or by the Mark Twain of old, such as Baker's blue jay yarn and the Mexican Plug story from *Roughing It.* He continued to find pleasure in the effect of reading aloud such stories as "Captain Stormfield's Visit" and the one about the Reverend Sam Jones entering heaven. (After reading "Stormfield" at a dinner party in New York in 1894, he wrote to Olivia, "It is a raging pity that that book has never been printed.")

Mark Twain remained by temperament and talent a humorist even while he judged himself more and more worthy to play the role of sage and philosopher. Still, he felt obliged to defend his earlier identity long after he had taken steps to abandon it. In 1888 he called his literary work "a worthy calling: that with all the lightness and frivolity it has one serious purpose, one aim, one specialty, and it is constant to it—the deriding of shams, the exposure of pretentious falsities, the laughing of stupid superstitions out of existence."[2]

In his later years, the greatest American humorist found that he wanted to express in his writings his increasingly pessimistic outlook, but he was deeply apprehensive that he might destroy the image of himself he had created and thereby lose his popularity. At the end of the century, finding himself in Vienna because of his daughter's desire to study with a celebrated pianist, he responded to the cultural capital's acclaim by returning effectively to the writing of imaginative literature. Toward the end of his life, he thought of himself as a philosopher—but then he almost stopped writing because he found it easier to pretend he was dictating an autobiography without order or plan.

His identification as a humorist and as an author of subscription books has misled many of those who think they know Samuel Clemens, or Mark Twain. The writer himself was largely responsible for the myths about himself. He pretended, for example, to be not much of a reader; presumably he thought that he would be more acceptable to his audience if he appeared less sophisticated than he was. It is now known that he was a very bookish man, devoted to reading.[3] His decision to appear otherwise has made him seem far more limited than he was.

Mark Twain's native and developed abilities as storyteller and humorist were shaped by his commercial bent, although his ideas about what he could publish were often limited. He expressed his view of magazine writing—and indirectly of his wife's censorship—in a letter to the publisher of the *Ladies' Home Journal,* who had requested portions of his autobiography in 1898. He explained that what he had written "would not answer for your magazine. Indeed a great deal of it is written in too independent a fashion for any magazine. One may publish a *book* and print whatever his family shall approve and allow to pass, but it is the Public that edits a Magazine, and so by the sheer necessities of the case a magazine's liberties are rather limited." It is striking to find a writer explaining to an editor the latter's responsibilities; striking, too, that Mark Twain supposed that the general rule was that a writer's *family* decided what he might be permitted to publish.

Because he began by writing long subscription books, he always measured his creativity by quantity. His work went well when he "piled up manuscript." One finds him boasting to Howells about his autobiography in June 1906: "I've dictated, (from Jan. 9) 210,000 words, & the 'fat' adds about 50,000 more. The 'fat' is old pigeon-holed things of the years gone by, which I or the editors dasn't to print." In the author's eyes, much of the value of the autobiography was enhanced by what he conceived to be its scandalous dimensions.

Perhaps quantity was emphasized so much because Mark Twain was uncertain about his ability to judge quality. His attitude toward his own artistic principles was frequently modest — and for good reason. In a letter of 1888, published in *The Art of Authorship,* edited by George Bainton (1890), he wrote, "Upon consideration, I am not sure that I have methods in composition. I do suppose I have — but they somehow refuse to take shape in my mind; their details refuse to separate and submit to classification and description; they remain a jumble."[4] Perhaps this vagueness was responsible for his willingness to permit editors and publishers to make a jumble of such works as *Life on the Mississippi, Tom Sawyer Abroad,* and *Following the Equator,* although what he originally included in *A Connecticut Yankee* demonstrates how ill-equipped he was to be a critic of his own creation. Moreover, the huge collection of unpublished, mostly unfinished works that he left at his death reinforces one's sense that in his last years he was often a fumbling artist, painfully uncertain of how to harness his genius. He attempted to write sequels or to adopt current fads, such as the detective story, and he presented repeatedly his fixed philosophical ideas or, almost obsessively, another fictional portrait of his brother Orion.

But his greatest problem as a writer may have been the trial of coping with himself. In 1906 he referred to "periodical and sudden changes of mood in me, from deep melancholy to half-insane tempests and cyclones of humor" that were "among the curiosities of my life."[5] This condition may help explain the unevenness in tone of his writings — and may be another source of the author's abiding fascination with doubles and multiple personalities, an interest that was still with him even on his deathbed.

Prodigal of his talents, Mark Twain poured himself out brilliantly at times, even in unsent letters. Many of the remarkable quantity of letters he sent have survived and are now being published. Such collections as the two-volume selection that Paine edited in 1917 and the correspondence with Howells published in 1960 suggest the brilliance of what he wrote. Some letters are as good as his best sketches. Angry, funny, more revealing than his autobiography — these tell the story of the life of Samuel Clemens and reveal his mind and heart. Candid comments in letters are marked *"private."*

One fact about Mark Twain's literary career that has been given too little attention is that he flourished during an undistinguished period in the history of American literature. Some of the other notable writers of his day, such as Emily Dickinson and Walt Whitman, were not permitted to contribute much to contemporary cultural life; another, Henry James, left America for more congenial surroundings in England. Mark Twain's years abroad were valuable to him intellectually, no doubt, but they had little effect on *how* he wrote, except for his time in Vienna. In America, his was an age when sentimental novelists were creating a new audience of middlebrows, with serious writers facing ostracism. He contributed to this milieu, but it victimized him as well.

He was very close to the accommodating William Dean Howells, who was invaluable to him as editor and literary friend, but the other editors and writers with whom Clemens associated were limiting rather than tolerant. Henry M. Alden, Thomas Bailey Aldrich, Frederick Duneka, Richard Watson Gilder, Edmund Clarence Stedman, Charles Dudley Warner, and their like were essentially minor talents; these friends and associates shaped a literary epoch that was tame, thin, and ultimately uninteresting. Hampered by doubts concerning his own stature, Mark Twain was not the man to improve the standards of his day. He thrived despite, not because of, his literary environment. He might have compensated for his milieu through reading, but while he read avidly and widely, he read chiefly for content, for ideas and information. He borrowed episodes rather than techniques, although the example of Robert Browning seems to have supplied models for the writing of the soliloquies of the czar and King Leopold.

At the end of his life, Mark Twain apparently recognized his literary milieu. Isabel Lyon recorded in 1905 that he found that

> the world is full now of young writers who admire each other just as the young writers admired each other in those early days. . . . Dr Holmes and Emerson and those fine Boston men were a generation ahead of Mr Clemens & he didn't see more of them than just to go up to Boston for their "seventy" birthdays. For himself there are only Mr Howells and Mr Aldrich, and he surprised me into recognizing the truth by telling me that he hasn't had much of a literary friendship with men, and he hasn't — Hartford is presumably between New-York & Boston, but it isn't.[6]

On the credit side of the ledger, the long life of Samuel Clemens brought him close to his country's history and its regional characters. He moved through the Border South, the Deep South, and the Frontier West; in Boston he met Emerson, Longfellow, Holmes, and Whittier, writers from an earlier age; he knew Grant and the Standard Oil vice president Henry H. Rogers; he was familiar with slavery and the political corruptions of the post–Civil War years, the "Gilded Age"; he loaned his pen to attacks on turn-of-the-century imperialism. Moreover, he encountered the world beyond, from his residences in Austria, England, France, Germany, Italy, and Switzerland and from his trip around the world. Reading his books serves as an introduction to Clemens's three-quarters of a century. At its best, this reflection was far from mere reportage, for the author mixed in an awareness of injustice and suffering, clusters of nostalgic memories, and an appealing and distinctive personality. Not always wisely, he journeyed beyond what he knew to the imagined worlds of King Arthur's court or a drop of water or the life of a microbe; to investigations of a new religion, Christian Science; and to questions regarding the authorship of Shakespeare's plays.

Mark Twain's popularity, in his time and ours, is undeniable. One reason for it is suggested by William Dean Howells in his essay "The Man of Letters as a Man of Business." Here Howells asserts, "The only thing that gives [a] writer positive value is his acceptance with the reader."[7] Mark Twain has been popular largely because in his writings he usually did not take himself too seriously—at the same time that he explored matters of permanent human concern. For example, in "The Facts Concerning the Carnival of Crime in Connecticut," he revealed what a hideous time his conscience had been giving him. In *My Mark Twain,* Howells observed of the piece, "It was, of course, funny; but under the fun it was an impassioned study of the human conscience."[8] Readers usually have a strong sense of their author in Mark Twain's work: again to quote Howells, he gives us "the companionship of a spirit that is at once delightfully open and deliciously shrewd."[9] That openness, combined with a good deal of self-mockery, appears to be permanently attractive. Despite his commercial bent, his squandering of time for writing, and his inability to judge his own work, Mark Twain produced a body of writing that is enduring. Indeed, almost every year some of his previously unpublished work appears. It is gratifying to think that more of Mark Twain's writing will continue to appear.

Abbreviations

AD	Autobiographical Dictations, Mark Twain Papers, University of California, Berkeley
Berg	Henry W. and Albert A. Berg Collection, New York Public Library, Astor, Lenox, and Tilden Foundations.
CT1	*Collected Tales, Sketches, Speeches, and Essays, 1852–1890*, ed. Louis J. Budd. New York: Library of America, 1992.
CT2	*Collected Tales, Sketches, Speeches, and Essays, 1891–1910*, ed. Louis J. Budd. New York: Library of America, 1992.
CY	*Connecticut Yankee in King Arthur's Court*, ed. Bernard L. Stein, with an introduction by Henry Nash Smith. Berkeley: University of California Press, 1979.
ET&S1	*Early Tales and Sketches*. Volume 1, 1851–1864. Ed. Edgar M. Branch and Robert H. Hirst. Berkeley: University of California Press, 1979.
ET&S2	*Early Tales and Sketches*. Volume 2, 1864–1865. Ed. Edgar M. Branch and Robert H. Hirst. Berkeley: University of California Press, 1981.
Galaxy	*Contributions to "The Galaxy," 1868–1891*, ed. Bruce R. McElderry Jr. Gainesville, Florida: Scholars' Facsimiles and Reprints, 1961.
Letters (1917)	*Mark Twain's Letters*, ed. Albert Bigelow Paine. 2 vols. New York: Harper, 1917.
Morgan Library	Pierpont Morgan Library, New York City.
Ms(s)	Manuscript(s).

MTA	*Mark Twain's Autobiography,* ed. Albert Bigelow Paine. 2 vols. New York: Harper and Brothers, 1924.
MTB	Albert Bigelow Paine, *Mark Twain, a Biography: The Personal and Literary Life of Samuel Langhorne Clemens.* 3 vols. New York: Harper, 1912.
MTCH	*Mark Twain: The Critical Heritage,* ed. Frederick Anderson and Kenneth M. Sanderson. New York: Barnes and Noble, 1971.
MTE	*Mark Twain in Eruption: Hitherto Unpublished Pages About Men and Events,* ed. Bernard DeVoto. New York: Harper, 1940.
MTL1	*Mark Twain's Letters.* Volume 1, 1853–1866. Ed. Edgar M. Branch, Michael B. Frank, and Kenneth A. Sanderson. Berkeley: University of California Press, 1988.
MTL2	*Mark Twain's Letters.* Volume 2, 1867–1868. Ed. Harriet E. Smith and Robert Bucci. Berkeley: University of California Press, 1990.
MTL3	*Mark Twain's Letters.* Volume 3, 1869. Ed. Victor Fischer and Michael B. Frank. Berkeley: University of California Press, 1992.
MTL4	*Mark Twain's Letters.* Volume 4, 1870–1871. Ed. Victor Fischer and Michael B. Frank. Berkeley: University of California Press, 1995.
MTL5	*Mark Twain's Letters.* Volume 5, 1872–1873. Ed. Lin Salamo and Harriet Elinor Smith. Berkeley: University of California Press, 1995.
MTM	Mark Twain Memorial, Hartford, Connecticut
MTP	Mark Twain Papers, University of California, Berkeley.
N&J1	*Mark Twain's Notebooks and Journals.* Volume 1 (1855–1873). Ed. Frederick Anderson, Michael B. Frank, and Kenneth M. Anderson. Berkeley: University of California Press, 1975.
N&J2	*Mark Twain's Notebooks and Journals.* Volume 2 (1877–1883). Ed. Frederick Anderson, Lin Salamo, and Bernard L. Stein. Berkeley: University of California Press, 1975.
N&J3	*Mark Twain's Notebooks and Journals.* Volume 3 (1883–1891). Ed. Robert Pack Browning, Michael B. Frank, and Lin Salamo. Berkeley: University of California Press, 1979.
OLC	Olivia Langdon Clemens
PH	Photocopy
SLC	Samuel L. Clemens

Notes

PREFACE

1 Notebook 48, transcript p. 2. Subsequent quotations of previously unpublished words are also © 1999 by Richard A. Watson and Chase Manhattan Bank as Trustees of the Mark Twain Foundation and are signaled by ** in their citations. Unless otherwise specified, Mark Twain's writings cited hereafter appear in *The Works of Mark Twain*, Stormfield Edition (1929).

CHAPTER 1: MARK TWAIN ASSEMBLED

1 "Hannibal, Missouri," published March 25, 1852; *ET&S1*, pp. 67–68. The population was closer to 1,000. Unless otherwise stated, all of the writings referred to in this chapter can be found in this collection, *ET&S2*, or in the superbly edited *MTL1* and *MTL2*. Unfortunately, two categories of Mark Twain's early writings do not appear in *ET&S*: literary criticism and social and political criticism.

2 *MTA*, 1, pp. 109–10.

3 Quoted in Wecter, *Sam Clemens of Hannibal*, pp. 104–5.

4 See Ensor, "The 'Tennessee Land.'"

5 *Hannibal, Huck, and Tom*, ed. Blair, pp. 44–45.

6 SLC to A. Arthur Reade, March 14, 1882; in Reade, *Study and Stimulants; or, The Use of Intoxicants and Narcotics in Relation to Intellectual Life*, p. 121.

7 "Samuel Langhorne Clemens," Morgan Library, MA 1405, p. 1.** I am grateful to the Pierpont Morgan Library, New York, the owner of this manuscript, for permission to quote from it. Mark Twain wrote this autobiographical sketch in January 1873 for an entry on himself in a new edition of the *Cyclopedia of American Literature*. See *MTLs*, pp. 283–87.

8 "Samuel Langhorne Clemens," Morgan Library, p. 1.**

9 *MTB*, p. 80. The biographical information here is derived from Wecter, *Sam Clemens of Hannibal*, but corrected by the chronology in *CT*.

10 SLC to A. A. Reade, as cited above. Sam obtained cigars from a shopkeeper as a reward for "fetching a bucket of water from the village pump, whether he needed water or not." *MTA*, 2, p. 101.

11 *Mark Twain Speaking*, ed. Fatout, pp. 464–65. In his autobiography he was more specific; there he reports that he was "a smoker from my ninth year — a private one during the first two years, but a public one after that — that is to say, after my father's death." *MTA*, 2, p. 100.

12 Quoted in Wecter, *Sam Clemens*, p. 258.

13 *Autobiographical Sketch* (written for Samuel Moffett), p. 3.

14 AD March 29, 1906; *MTA*, 2, p. 288.

15 Quoted in Lorch, *The Trouble Begins at Eight*, p. 8. Lorch provides a full treatment of "Mark Twain in Iowa."

16 The same letter refers to Clemens's reading of Thomas Hood. He expressed great admiration for Laurence Sterne's *Tristram Shandy* in an 1867 letter to Olivia Langdon. See *MTL2*, pp. 344–45. He expressed his affection for Curtis's book, *The Howaji in Syria*, during his *Quaker City* trip; see "Letters from Emma B. Thayer and S. L. Severance" (to Albert Bigelow Paine).

17 *MTB*, p. 1445.

18 On Clemens's reading of Dickens and Thompson, see McKeithan, "Mark Twain's Letters of Thomas Jefferson Snodgrass," and Gribben, *Mark Twain's Library*, pp. 186–92, 701–2. The writer later forgot that he had ever written the Snodgrass letters. See AD September 10, 1906; *MTE*, pp. 228–39. On the large matter of the influence of Dickens, see Gardner, "Mark Twain and Dickens," and Baetzhold, "Mark Twain and Dickens: Why the Denial?"

19 *The Adventures of Thomas Jefferson Snodgrass*, ed. Charles Honce, p. 32.

20 Ibid., pp. 37, 41, 44, 47. McKeithan provides a parallel passage from Thompson in "Mark Twain's Letters of Thomas Jefferson Snodgrass."

21 "Samuel Langhorne Clemens," Morgan Library, pp. 2–3.** See also AD March 29, 1906; *MTA*, 2, p. 289. Clemens left Cincinnati on February 16, 1857, on the *Paul Jones*, with Bixby as pilot. According to Bixby's account, Clemens asked Bixby to teach him the river even before the ship had reached New Orleans; Clemens had tried his hand on the way south. See Branch, "Bixby vs. Carroll," pp. 2, 11 n. 8, and *MTL1*, pp. 70–71.

22 Clemens's March 19, 1858, deposition concerning the collision has been published by Marleau, " 'The Crash of Timbers Continued — the Deck Swayd under Me': Samuel Langhorne Clemens, Eyewitness to the Race and Collision Between the *Pennsylvania* and the *Vicksburg*."

23 Clemens's account is in *MTLI*, pp. 81–82; see also Branch's two accounts, *Men Call Me Lucky: Mark Twain and the "Pennsylvania"* and *Mark Twain and the Starchy Boys.*

24 *Autobiographical Sketch* (written for Samuel Moffett), pp. 5–6.

25 AD September 10, 1906; *MTE*, p. 228.

26 Letter dated June 29, 1874, published in facsimile in *The Eighteenth Yearbook 1919*, p. 123. In the year before, he had written, "Part of the time reported Legislative proceedings for my paper (from Carson the capital.) Wrote a letter every Saturday to sum up results, & therefore needed a signature. In the nick of time Capt. Sellers's death came over the wires & I 'jumped' his nom de plume before the old man was cold": "Samuel Langhorne Clemens," Morgan Library, p. 8.** This part of the document was published in facsimile for the first time in the most thorough study of the complicated issue of how Clemens adopted his pen name: Kruse, "Mark Twain's *Nom de Plume:* Some Mysteries Resolved."

27 All four were located and republished by Branch in "Sam Clemens, Steersman of the *John H. Dickey*" and "A New Clemens Footprint: Soleleather Steps Forward."

28 *Autobiographical Sketch* (written for Samuel Moffett), p. 4.

29 See Miller, "Samuel Langhorne Clemens and Orion Clemens vs. Mark Twain and His Biographers." In his 1872–73 autobiographical sketch, Mark Twain wrote, "Early in 1861, my brother was appointed Secretary to the then Territory of Nevada, & I went out there with him as his private Secretary": "Samuel Langhorne Clemens," Morgan Library, p. 6.**

30 *Hannibal, Huck and Tom*, p. 34. On the writer's attitude toward the Indians, see McNutt, "Mark Twain and the American Indian"; Harris, "Mark Twain's Response to the Native American," and Hanson, "Mark Twain's Indians Reexamined."

31 "Samuel Langhorne Clemens," Morgan Library, p. 7.**

32 AD October 2, 1906; *MTE*, pp. 390–92.

33 Miller, "The Editor's Page."

34 See Miller et al., eds., *Reports of the 1863 Constitutional Convention of the Territory of Nevada.*

35 *Enterprise*, January 14, 1864; *Mark Twain of the "Enterprise,"* p. 139.

36 Regan, *Unpromising Heroes*, pp. 32–33.

37 Cox, *Mark Twain: The Fate of Humor*, p. 11.

38 Copy in Scrapbook 2, p. 43, MTP; quoted in *ET&S1*, p. 248.

39 Quoted from the *Call* of January 9, 1863, in *Clemens of the "Call,"* p. 8.

40 "Letter to *San Francisco Call*," *ET&S1*, p. 260.

41 Quoted by Paine in *Letters* (1917), I, 89.

42 Quoted in *ET&S1*, p. 267 and 269.

43 "A Couple of Sad Experiences," *CT1*, p. 392.

44 Quoted in a letter of protest by the ladies of Carson City in the *Virginia City Union*, May 25, 1864; in *MTL1*, p. 289.

45 Quoted in *MTL1*, p. 291.

46 *Autobiographical Sketch* (written for Samuel Moffett), pp. 6, 8.

47 Both are quoted in Fatout, *Mark Twain in Virginia City*, pp. 211, 212.

48 My analysis here draws on Schmidt's thoughtful dissertation, "Mark Twain's Techniques as a Humorist, 1857–72."

CHAPTER 2. JOURNALIST AND LECTURER

1 June 26, 1864, quoted in *ET&S2*, p. 9. Unless otherwise stated, writings by Mark Twain discussed in this chapter are be found in this edition.

2 Branch in *Clemens of the "Call."*

3 *Clemens of the "Call,"* p. 40; also *ET&S2*, p. 426.

4 *Clemens of the "Call,"* pp. 147–48; also *ET&S2*, pp. 435–36.

5 AD June 13, 1906; *MTE*, p. 256. The criticism of the *Call* policy appeared in the *San Francisco Dramatic Chronicle* for December 12, 1865; it may be found in *ET&S2*, p. 511.

6 AD July 7, 1908; *MTE*, p. 304.

7 Pemberton, *The Life of Bret Harte*, pp. 74–75. According to this account, Mark Twain told Harte the jumping frog story. Harte then "asked him to write it out for *The Californian*. He did so, and when published it was an emphatic success." This part of the account is obviously false.

8 Near the end of his life, June 13, 1906, Mark Twain dictated a long chapter of his autobiography devoted largely to his relationship to Bret Harte. See *MTE*, pp. 264–92.

9 "Samuel Langhorne Clemens," Morgan Library, p. 8.**

10 AD May 26, 1907; *MTE*, pp. 360–61.

11 *N&J1*, p. 70, 74–75, 80.

12 *N&J1*, p. 82.

13 See *ET&S2*, p. 145.

14 See Cyril Clemens, *Young Sam Clemens*, pp. 209–17 and Mark Twain's own "Private History of the Jumping Frog Story."

15 Clemens was paid $100 a month for his *Enterprise* chores and was paid too by the *San Francisco Dramatic Chronicle* and the *Youths' Companion* of San Francisco. Selections appear in *ET&S2*, pp. 2, 235, 242, 244–45, 298–99. See also *MTL1*, p. 321.

16 AD February 20, 1906; *MTA*, 2, 125.

17 Rogers, *Mark Twain's Burlesque Patterns*, pp. 31–34; Gribben, *Mark Twain's Library*, p. 191.

18 *Mark Twain and Hawaii*, ed. Walter Francis Frear, pp. 412, 277. Frear's edition

contains only one of the below-mentioned contributions to the *Daily Hawaiian Herald,* on pp. 460–61.

19 *Mark Twain and Hawaii,* p. 288.

20 These contributions have been made available by Barbara Schmidt on the Internet at the following URL: ⟨http://www.tarleton.edu/activities/pages/faculty-pages/schmidt/dhhindex.html⟩ (April 19, 1999).

21 *N&J1,* p. 163.

22 *MTA,* 1, pp. 242–43.

23 *Mark Twain Speaking,* p. 5. There are two good accounts of Mark Twain's lecturing: Lorch, *The Trouble Begins at Eight,* and Fatout, *Mark Twain on the Lecture Circuit.*

24 *Sketches of the Sixties,* p. 210.

25 " 'Mark Twain's' Farewell," *Alta California,* December 15, 1866.

26 *N&J1,* 253.

27 From the *Alta California* of uncertain date, reprinted in the *Yreka Weekly Union,* Yreka City, Calif., March 23, 1867; reprinted in *Mark Twain Speaks for Himself,* ed. Fatout, pp. 39–40.

28 *Mark Twain's Travels with Mr. Brown,* ed. Walker and Dane, pp. 43, 39. Hereafter references to this book are cited in the text.

29 "Female Suffrage: Views of Mark Twain," *St. Louis Missouri Democrat,* March 12, 13, and 15; "Female Suffrage," *New York Sunday Mercury,* April 7, 1867; all of these are reprinted in *CT1,* pp. 214–27.

30 Lorch, *The Trouble Begins at Eight,* pp. 52–59. He also lectured in Keokuk, Iowa, and in Quincy, Illinois.

31 Reprinted in *CT1,* pp. 235–37.

32 *Mark Twain Speaking,* ed. Fatout, pp. 65–68; *MTA,* I, 135–43.

33 The editing is fully discussed in *ET&S1,* pp. 503–46. A survey of the works in which the bachelor Mark Twain shows his interest in women and sex is provided by Budd in "Mark Twain Plays the Bachelor." Webb's relationship to Clemens is discussed by Zall in *Mark Twain Encyclopedia,* pp. 778–79.

34 *MTL2,* p. 58; Baetzhold, *Mark Twain and John Bull,* pp. 4–5; Welland, *Mark Twain in England,* pp. 15–16.

35 *MTL2,* pp. 40–44; Lorch, *The Trouble Begins at Eight,* pp. 60–67; Fatout, *Mark Twain on the Lecture Circuit,* pp. 78–82.

36 *MTL2,* pp. 46–50; *CT1,* p. 961.

CHAPTER 3. TURNING POINT

1 Statement by John J. Murphy, New York agent of the *Alta,* included in *MTL2,* pp. 23–24.

2 AD April 1904; *MTA,* 1, 243.

3 *Traveling with the Innocents Abroad,* ed. McKeithan, p. 84. Hereafter references to this book appear in the text.

4 G. R. Brown, ed., *Reminiscences of Senator William M. Stewart of Nevada,* pp. 219–20.

5 Quoted in *MTL2,* p. 194.

6 Published in the *Galaxy,* May 1868, later included in *Sketches, New and Old;* reprinted in *CT1,* pp. 257–61. The "Frozen Truth" lecture is discussed by Fatout, *Mark Twain on the Lecture Circuit,* pp. 85–86.

7 Barbara Schmidt has made much of Mark Twain's early journalism available on the Internet as follows: six *Republican* letters of 1868, forty *Alta* letters (not including letters from the *Quaker City* trip) of 1866–69, and eleven *Enterprise* letters of 1867–68. See bibliography.

8 Letter of December 4, published December 22, 1867.

9 Letter of January 20, published February 19, 1867.

10 This piece was not published, perhaps because Mark Twain heard that Johnson was dangerously ill. It appears in *MTL3,* pp. 458–66. The quotation is from pp. 464–65.

11 Letter dated February 14, published February 19, 1868.

12 Reprinted in the *Twainian,* 5 (May–June 1946), 1 and in *Life as I Find It.*

13 Reprinted in *CT1,* pp. 240–46.

14 Quoted in *MTL2,* p. 120.

15 The contract appears as appendix F in *MTL2,* pp. 421–22. Another form of the contract appears as a letter to Elisha Bliss Jr., dated January 27, 1868. Here Clemens acknowledges the stipulation that the manuscript is to be ready by "about the first of August" —*MTL2,* p. 169.

16 *MTL2,* pp. 205–10.

17 Quoted by Fatout in *Mark Twain on the Lecture Circuit,* p. 88.

18 *MTL2,* pp. 205–8, 212; Lorch, *The Trouble Begins at Eight,* pp. 77–78.

19 *Mark Twain Speaking,* p. 26.

20 Fatout quotes from the *Alta,* for April 16, 1868, in *Mark Twain on the Lecture Circuit,* p. 90.

21 *MTA,* 1, pp. 245–46.

22 McKinney Papers, Vassar College, item A-22.

23 August 17, 1868, letter from New York published in *Chicago Republican,* August 23, 1868.

24 *N&J1,* pp. 499–506. The sketch also appears in *Satires and Burlesques,* ed. Rogers, pp. 33–49, and in *CT1,* pp. 262–68.

25 *Mark Twain in Elmira,* ed. Jerome and Wisbey, provides much valuable information on the Langdons and Elmira, as does Steinbrink, *Getting to Be Mark Twain.* Olivia Langdon is the subject of a biography, Willis, *Mark and Livy,* and her

health history is explored by Skandera-Trombley, *Mark Twain in the Company of Women,* pp. 82–96.

26 Published in the *Alta,* September 6, 1868; reprinted in the *Twainian,* 7 (November–December 1948): 5–7.

27 *CT1,* p. 278.

28 I am grateful to Louis Budd, who has supplied me with a photocopy of this sketch. Steinbrink in *Getting to Be Mark Twain,* pp. 9–12, provides an extended reading of this sketch, which has not been republished.

29 Fatout, *Mark Twain on the Lecture Circuit,* pp. 103–18.

30 *Mark Twain Speaking,* pp. 27, 28.

31 Quoted in *MTL2,* pp. 286–87 n. 3.

32 Hutchinson, "Two Opinions of Twain," *San Francisco Call,* April 24, 1910; quoted in *MTL3,* p. 57 n. 6.

33 See the excellent discussion by Michelson, "The Form of *The Innocents Abroad.*" Another useful essay exploring the organization is Robinson, "Patterns of Consciousness in *The Innocents Abroad.*"

34 *St. Louis Republic,* June 1, 1902, as quoted by Budd in *Our Mark Twain,* p. 37.

35 Reprinted in Howells, *My Mark Twain,* ed. Marilyn A. Baldwin, p. 92.

36 Baetzhold, *Mark Twain and John Bull,* p. 5; Welland, *Mark Twain in England,* pp. 33–34, 36–40.

37 See *ET&S1,* p. 551.

38 The sketch first appeared in the August 1869 issue of *Packard's Monthly;* it is reprinted in *CT1,* pp. 296–99.

39 Reproduced in *MTL3,* p. 471.

40 *Buffalo Express,* September 25, 1869; text provided by Joseph McCullough and Janice McIntire-Strasburg, eds. *Mark Twain at the Buffalo "Express,"* forthcoming.

41 *Buffalo Express,* February 12, as quoted in "Ford Letters from 'Around the World' Trip," p. 2.

42 Reigstad, "Professor Ford, Editor Clemens, and Their Collaborative 'Around the World' Fiasco."

43 Lorch, *The Trouble Begins at Eight,* pp. 105–11. A version of the lecture appears in *Mark Twain Speaking,* pp. 4–15.

44 Howells, *My Mark Twain,* p. 83. See also Eble, *Old Clemens and W.D.H.*

45 So he told Annie Fields in 1876; see Howe, ed., *Memories of a Hostess,* pp. 244–45.

46 At least once, Clemens showed recognition of the effects of his smoking on others. He remembered sharing a room on shipboard with Matthew B. Cox on his 1868 trip from New York to San Francisco, with Cox "swallowing my smoke, and coughing and barking, and yet swearing that tobacco smoke never inconvenienced him." Letter dated May 1, published May 2, 1868, *Chicago Republican,* p. 2. Olivia Clemens's experience with her husband's smoking is neglected in several recent studies where it might have been explored.

47 Emerson, "Mark Twain's Quarrel with God," pp. 36–38. Susan Harris notes that Olivia's "professions of dependence on God cease to be evident fairly soon after her marriage." See Harris, *Courtship of Olivia Langdon and Mark Twain,* p. 139.

48 *Galaxy,* p. 37. All of the *Galaxy* items cited are in this volume.

49 Reprinted in *CT1,* pp. 285–90.

50 The subject is well explored in *ET&S1,* pp. 586–99.

51 *N&J1,* p. 147.

52 Brief histories of the book are in *MTL3,* pp. 313–14 n. 7, and *The Bible According to Mark Twain,* pp. 91–96. Mark Twain took up the project again in 1909.

53 See Steinbrink, *Getting to Be Mark Twain,* pp. 126–29.

54 Howells, "The Man of Letters as a Man of Business," *Scribner's,* October 1893; collected in Howells, *Literature and Life,* p. 15.

55 Howells, "Editor's Study," *Harper's,* December 1886, p. 162.

56 *MTB,* p. 452 n. 1. But in 1882, Clemens told an interviewer that he had offered the publisher a choice of titles, "and the publisher casts his experienced eye over them and guides me in the selection. That's what I did in *Roughing It,*" Budd, ed. *Interviews with Samuel Langhorne Clemens,* p. 38. See also *Roughing It* (1993), p. 863 n. 190.

57 SLC to A. Arthur Reade, March 14, 1882, published in Reade, *Study and Stimulants,* p. 122. Another account appears in chapter 1 of *Following the Equator.* Mark Twain told this story elsewhere as well.

58 So thinks Steinbrink, *Getting to Be Mark Twain,* pp. 159–60.

59 Two years later, Clemens wrote to Thomas Bailey Aldrich, "There is one discomfort which I fear a man must put up with when he publishes by subscription & that is wretched paper & vile engravings." A very full discussion of the composition and publication of the book appears in *Roughing It* (1993).

60 Emerson, "Mark Twain's Move to Hartford."

61 Howells in a March 21, 1874, letter quoted in *Mark Twain-Howells Letters,* 1, 16 n. 1. Good discussions of the Nook Farm community can be found in Andrews, *Nook Farm: Mark Twain's Hartford Circle,* and Why, *Nook Farm.* A briefer treatment is Comfort's "Nook Farm" in *The Mark Twain Encyclopedia,* pp. 544–46.

62 *Overland Monthly,* June 1872; reprinted in *MTCH,* p. 162.

63 Reprinted in Howells, *My Mark Twain,* p. 96.

64 These reviews appear in *Roughing It* (1993), pp. 885–87; other reviews are also quoted.

65 "Samuel Langhorne Clemens," Morgan Library, p. 11.**

CHAPTER 4. FUMBLING, SUCCESS, UNCERTAINTY

1 These documents are all at MTP. The contract appears in *MTL4,* p. 567.

2 Lorch, *The Trouble Begins at Eight,* pp. 98–134; Fatout, *Mark Twain on the Lecture*

Circuit, pp. 149–72. Susan Harris notes that between the years 1871 and 1874 Clemens was obliged to lecture because he needed money, especially for building his Hartford house. His English lectures, discussed below, were similarly motivated. See *Courtship of Olivia Langdon and Mark Twain,* pp. 165–67.

3 *N&J2,* p. 417. The question is quoted in Caroline Harnsberger, *Mark Twain's Views of Religion,* p. 43.

4 *CT1,* pp. 528–38.

5 Cummings, *Mark Twain and Science,* pp. 528–42.

6 *MTB,* pp. 476–77. Other interesting accounts of the genesis of the novel are to be found in *MTLs,* pp. 259–60.

7 C. D. Warner to Whitelaw Reid, April 7, 1873; in Royal Cortissoz, *Life of Whitelaw Reid,* 1, p. 273.

8 *Chicago Tribune,* February 1, 1874; quoted in Hill, *Mark Twain and Elisha Bliss,* p. 81.

9 Welland, *Mark Twain in England,* pp. 41–46.

10 See SLC's August 2, 1873, letter to Elisha Bliss (*MTLs,* 425), and DV268, notes to Samuel C. Thompson's letter, p. 2; MTP. See also *MTLs,* p. 431, n. 2. I quote the letters as they appear in *Europe and Elsewhere.*

11 *Number One* was distributed by the American News Company of New York. See *MTLs,* pp. 384–85 n. 1.

12 Stoddard, *Exits and Entrances,* pp. 62–63.

13 Quoted by Harris in *Courtship,* p. 167.

14 Lorch, *The Trouble Begins at Eight,* pp. 139–146.

15 Quoted in Budd, *Our Mark Twain,* p. 58.

16 Stoddard's reminiscences and an 1874 letter, quoted in James, "How Mark Twain Was Made," and James, "Charles Warren Stoddard." See also *MTLs,* 476–78.

17 Interview by Richard Whiteing, originally published in the *New York Herald,* May 11, 1879; reprinted in Budd, ed., *Interviews with Mark Twain,* pp. 33–34.

18 See Regan, "'English Notes': A Book Mark Twain Abandoned." Mark Twain left a bit of trivia behind in England, a slight sketch called "Magdalen Tower," which appeared in an Oxford undergraduate publication, the *Shotover,* in its October 17, 1874, issue. It describes, good-naturedly, the responses of members of Mark Twain's English audience to his deliberately ignorant reference to their tower. In the same year, he published three sketches that were to have been parts of his English book, each labeled "From the Author's Unpublished English Notes." They are "A Memorable Midnight Experience," about a visit to Westminster Abbey; "Rogers"; and "Property in Opulent London," all in *Mark Twain's Sketches. Number One.* Two years later he published, most obscurely, "Some Recollections of a Storm at Sea [Being an Extract from Chapter III, of a Book Begun Three Years Ago, But Afterwards Abandoned]." Five other pieces survive.

Two paragraphs, "An Expatriate" and "Stanley and the Queen," appear in Paine's biography, and Paine's successor as literary executor, Bernard DeVoto, published "The Albert Memorial," "Old Saint Paul's," and "The British Museum." Although all these pieces are worth reading, none is remarkable. See *MTLs*, p. 540 n. 2.

19 Ida Langdon, "My Uncle Mark Twain," in *Mark Twain in Elmira*, ed. Jerome and Wisbey, p. 53.

20 The circumstances surrounding the play are set forth in Schirer, *Mark Twain and the Theatre*, pp. 41–44; in *Mark Twain-Howells Letters*, 2, pp. 861–63, and in Jerry Thomason's extended introduction to the play, "Col. Sellers: A Drama in Five Acts," Ph.D. diss. University of Missouri, 1991. Thomason's edition of the play, published in 1995, is based on Paine 163a at the Mark Twain Papers.

21 Fishkin, *Was Huck Black?* pp. 16–27; the text of "Sociable Jimmy" is reprinted in this volume. Mark Twain's interest in recording what he calls "negro talk" is shown in his September 20, 1874, letter to Howells.

22 DV226; PH, MTP. Much of this work is reproduced by Harnsberger in her *Mark Twain: Family Man*.

23 Gribben argues that Mark Twain's reading of Thomas Bailey Aldrich's *Story of a Bad Boy* (1869) "prompted Mark Twain to value at last the wealth of literary material lying unclaimed in his recollections of prewar Hannibal." See Gribben, "'I Did Wish Tom Sawyer Was There': Boy-Book Elements in *Tom Sawyer* and *Huckleberry Finn*," p. 154.

24 AD, August 30, 1906; *MTE*, p. 197. In his September 4, 1874, letter to Dr. John Brown, written during the composition of *Tom Sawyer,* the author made a similar observation: "I must burn up the day's work, and do it all over again. It was plain that I had worked myself out, pumped myself dry." *Letters* (1917), p. 224.

25 Quoted in Brander Matthews's report on what Mark Twain told him in 1890 about the composition of *Tom Sawyer.* See "Memories of Mark Twain," in Matthews, *Tocsin of Revolt*, pp. 265–66.

26 *Tom Sawyer* (1980), pp. 8–9.

27 See AD March 8, 1906; *MTA*, 1, pp. 102, 105 (written 1897–98) II, 179.

28 Portland *Oregonian*, August 11, 1893; reprinted in Budd, ed., *Interviews with Samuel Langhorne Clemens*, p. 52. Mark Twain explains the relationship of his fiction to his own experiences in *MTA*, 1, pp. 102, 104–5 (written 1897–98); AD March 8, 1906, 2, pp. 175, 179. The autobiographical elements of *Tom Sawyer* have been examined at length. Evans's *A Tom Sawyer Companion* is described as *An Autobiographical Guided Tour with Mark Twain*. Norton's *Writing Tom Sawyer* includes two chapters on the topic.

29 San Juan, "A Source for *Tom Sawyer.*"

30 Stone, *Innocent Eye,* pp. 65–90; Gribben, "Boy-Book Elements in *Tom Sawyer.*"

31 Thomas S. Perry, in a review of *Huckleberry Finn* in the *Century Magazine*, May 18, 1885, pp. 171–72; reprinted in *MTCH*, pp. 128–30.

32 Towers, "'I Never Thought We Might Want To Come Back': Strategies of Transcendence in *Tom Sawyer*"; Fetterley, "The Sanctioned Rebel."

33 Cynthia Wolff, "*The Adventures of Tom Sawyer*: Nightmare Vision of American Boyhood." For an altogether different reading of the book, see Robinson, *In Bad Faith*, esp. pp. 20–26, 107.

34 *Mark Twain-Howells Letters*, p. 111.

35 Ibid., p. 123, n. 3.

36 Howells, *My Mark Twain*, pp. 18, 41.

37 A valuable examination of the illustrations is provided by David, *Mark Twain and His Illustrators*, vol. 1 (1869–1875), p. 220; and by David and Sapirstein, "Reading the Illustrations in *Tom Sawyer*."

38 *Athenaeum*, June 24, 1876.

39 *New York Times*, January 13, 1877; reprinted in *MTCH*, pp. 70–71.

40 The original *Atlantic* installments have been reprinted by Fred Lewis Pattee in the American Writers Series volume on Mark Twain: *Representative Selections*; the quotation is from p. 266. As noted below, Mark Twain revised his "Old Times" pieces for inclusion in *Life on the Mississippi*.

41 *MTB*, p. 1368. Paine is reporting what Clemens told him late in his life.

42 *N&J2*, pp. 449–50.

43 Quoted passages are from Pattee, ed., *Representative Selections*, pp. 295, 241, 250, 251, 266–67.

44 A useful discussion is Burde, "Mark Twain: The Writer as Pilot," but see also Branch, "Mark Twain: The Pilot and the Writer."

45 Pattee, ed., *Representative Selections*, pp. 267–68.

46 Branch, an authority on Samuel Clemens's early life, explains how much of "Old Times" is fictionalizing in his 1990 article, "'Old Times on the Mississippi.': Biography and Craftsmanship."

47 The piece has been helpfully discussed by Lee, "Fossil Feuds," pp. 5–7.

48 Review of *Sketches, New and Old* in the *Atlantic Monthly*, December 1875; reprinted in Howells, *My Mark Twain*, p. 103.

49 *Atlantic Monthly*, December 1875; reprinted in *My Mark Twain*, p. 103.

50 Reprinted in *CT1*, pp. 634–35.

51 *Mark Twain-Howells Letters*, p. 97.

52 See *The List of Members of the Monday Evening Club*. Camfield in *Sentimental Twain* carefully explores Clemens's developing philosophical sophistication and his changing attitude toward moral philosophy.

53 *Mark Twain-Howells Letters*, p. 124.

54 Twichell journal, January 24, 1876; quoted in *Mark Twain-Howells Letters*, p. 120.

A good treatment of the sketch may be found in Quirk, *Mark Twain: A Study of the Short Fiction,* pp. 65–69.

55 AD July 31, 1906; *MTE,* pp. 206–7. The Oxford Mark Twain includes a photographic facsimile of the first authorized American edition, printed at West Point in 1882. The passage quoted appears on p. iii.

56 *N&J2,* p. 303.

57 Quoted by Mark Twain in *MTE,* pp. 203–4.

58 The play was published by the Book Club of California in 1961.

59 See Duckett, *Mark Twain and Bret Harte.*

60 DV 56, Paine 197; MTP.

61 *N&J1,* p. 511. The incomplete sketch is on pp. 511–16.

62 A privately printed copy is in MTP. The manuscript is in the Humanities Research Center of the University of Texas at Austin. A full discussion is provided by McClain in "'A Murder, a Mystery, and a Marriage': Mark Twain's Hannibal in Transition." McClain reports how two men who had purchased the manuscript tried to publish the story in a limited edition but were stopped by an attorney representing the Mark Twain estate. See also Sattelmeyer's discussion in the *Mark Twain Encyclopedia,* pp. 526–27.

63 *Mark Twain-Howells Letters,* p. 186; SLC to JHT, June 27, 1877; MTP.

64 Olivia writing to her mother in 1879, quoted in Skandera-Trombley, *Mark Twain in the Company of Women,* p. 59.

65 Fulton to SLC, March 12, 1877; MTP.

66 The play was published in *Satires and Burlesques* (1967).

67 *Mark Twain-Howells Letters,* p. 207. The novel fragment was first published as a book in 1963, *Simon Wheeler, Detective;* it is included in *Satires and Burlesques* (1967).

68 *Mark Twain Speaking,* pp. 110–14.

69 A full treatment of the occasion and responses to it is H. N. Smith, "That Hideous Mistake of Poor Clemens's." Lowry, in *Littery Man,* pp. 24–37, provides a valuable study of the speech and its circumstances. In "The Mythic Struggle between East and West," Bush considers what literary scholars have made of the speech, especially those who think that Mark Twain was a significant representative of the West.

70 Howells, *My Mark Twain,* pp. 50–54.

71 AD January 11, 1906; *Mark Twain's Speeches,* ed. Albert Bigelow Paine, p. 68; AD January 23, 1906; *MTA,* II, 5; May 25, 1906; quoted in Smith, "That Hideous Mistake of Poor Clemens's," p. 175. Information about newspaper response to the speech is from Smith's notable essay.

72 Gauvreau, *My Last Million Readers,* pp. 81–82. Isabella Beecher Hooker, who came to know Clemens well during his early visits to Hartford, for instance,

called him a "parvenu" who admitted that he had no taste and so relied on what "an established house" said about an article. He was sensitive to the fact that his lack of taste was being talked about, according to Hooker's diary, pp. 193–95.

73 Transcription of notebook #42 for 1900, p. 50.**

74 AD February 9, 1906, as quoted by Skandera-Trombley, *Mark Twain in the Company of Women,* p. 9.

75 *Mark Twain Speaking,* p. 118.

CHAPTER 5. CONTRACTS, INSPIRATIONS, OBLIGATIONS

1 OLC to Mrs. Langdon, May 26, 1878; Mark Twain Memorial, Hartford.

2 SLC paid his friend's expenses. SLC to Twichell and Bissell and Co., May 23, 1878; MTP.

3 The brief "Paris Notes" appeared in *The Stolen White Elephant Etc.* (1882), and in *Letters from the Earth* (1962) Bernard DeVoto published "The French and the Comanches," wherein Mark Twain celebrates the ability of the French to execute massacres. He mentions several, including "their peerless St. Bartholomew's."

4 Interview by Richard Whiteing in the *New York World,* May 11, 1879, reprinted in Budd, ed., *Interviews with Samuel Langhorne Clemens,* p. 32.

5 *N&J2,* p. 348.

6 Presumably other portions of the voluminous remaining materials will one day be published, including a long description of the Grand Prix race. In his papers can be found chapters on European dwelling houses; the purchase of a music box; a comparison of public transportation in Europe and America; an "art-lesson 'from the nude'" in Rome; a commentary on a French book on courtship; and a discussion of German university requirements, intended to follow the account of dueling but squeezed out by the need to go on to lighten the tone of the book. Some other parts of the book, in addition to the aforementioned pieces on France, were salvaged and published elsewhere, such as "The Stolen White Elephant" and "The Invalid's Story," which first appeared in *Merry Tales* (1892). The "invalid" piece, which Mark Twain described in a January 26, 1879, letter to Twichell as "the yarn about the Limburger cheese and the box of guns," he had heard from Twichell. It is derived from a kind of frontier humor about smells that he had always liked, and was originally written for "Some Rambling Notes"; Howells recommended that it not be included in the *Tramp.*

7 *MTB,* p. 668.

8 *Athenaeum,* April 24, 1880; reprinted in *MTCH,* pp. 73–76.

9 Quoted in Tenney, *Mark Twain: A Reference Guide,* p. 9.

10 The review was reprinted in Howells's *My Mark Twain;* the passage quoted is on page 109.

11 Baggett, "Copyright," in *Mark Twain Encyclopedia,* pp. 183–84.

12 Quoted by Davis in "Mark Twain's Religious Beliefs as Indicated by Notations in His Books," p. 5.

13 Baetzhold, "Mark Twain's 'The Prince and the Pauper'"; Gribben, *Mark Twain's Library*, p. 792.

14 Taine, *The Ancient Regime*, p. 202. My discussion of Mark Twain's debt to Taine is largely based on Cummings's excellent discussion in *Mark Twain and Science*.

15 Blair, "The French Revolution and *Huckleberry Finn*."

16 *N&J2*, p. 39.

17 *MTB*, p. 598.

18 *N&J2*, p. 49.

19 Andrews reprinted it in his *Nook Farm*, pp. 243–46.

20 *MTB*, p. 696. Paine quotes a letter from SLC to his sister.

21 Goodman to SLC, October 24, 1881; MTP. The letter was written before Goodman had seen the book.

22 July 20, 1880; MTP.

23 December 22, 1880; MTP.

24 Susy Clemens, *Papa: An Intimate Biography of Mark Twain*, ed. Neider, pp. 106–7.

25 January 4, 1882; *Mark Twain to Mrs. Fairbanks*, p. 245.

26 *N&J3*, p. 287.

27 Goodman to SLC, October 24, 1881; MTP.

28 E. Purcell in the *Academy*, December 20, 1881; reprinted in *MTCH*, pp. 90–91.

29 *Atlanta Constitution*, December 25, 1881.

30 *New York Daily Tribune*, October 25, 1881, p. 6. This review was not included in Howells's *My Mark Twain*.

31 Clark, "Mark Twain at 'Nook Farm' (Hartford) and Elmira," p. 26.

32 *N&J2*, p. 491.

33 *N&J2*, p. 353; *The Prince and the Pauper* (1979), p. 12 n. 41; *Mark Twain, Businessman*, pp. 153–61.

34 Financial documents for 1881, MTP.**

35 Willis, *Mark and Livy*, p. 109. Clemens's 1880 expenses included $418 for badges made for the Saturday Morning Club (each of the nineteen engraved with a young lady's name). *N&J2*, p. 371 n.

36 See, for example, SLC to Louis Pendleton, August 4, 1888; *Letters* (1917), p. 497.

37 Twichell, "Mark Twain," p. 817.

38 Quoted in *MTB*, p. 730.

39 AD, August 30, 1906; quoted in *Mark Twain's Quarrel with Heaven*, p. 19.

40 *Report from Heaven, Mark Twain's Quarrel with Heaven*, and *The Bible According to Mark Twain*. The last of these includes valuable notes.

41 Browne in *Mark Twain's Quarrel with God*, pp. 20–27.

42 AD August 29, 1906; *MTE*, p. 246. He began writing the story after he heard

Captain Edgar Wakeman describe his dream of visiting heaven. *N&J1*, pp. 241–43. Notes on the story appear in 1878 in *N&J2*, pp. 55, 56, 66, 68, and 275.

43 Published in *Mark Twain's Quarrel with Heaven*, p. 33. Hereafter references to *The Bible According to Mark Twain* appear in the text.

44 AD August 29, 1906; *MTE*, p. 248.

45 Quirk provides a valuable reading of the story in his *Mark Twain: A Study of the Short Fiction*, pp. 116–22.

46 Quoted in Henderson, *Mark Twain*, p. 183.

47 Brooks, *The Ordeal of Mark Twain* (1920), p. 116. Brooks's chapter "The Candidate for Gentility" is still worth reading, although its argument has been attacked frequently. Susan Harris argues that Mark Twain, Olivia, and her parents had much in common, such as "assuming in the depths of their being that their race, age, culture were superior; . . . [holding] the same class values — the value of chastity, for instance, or of education, or of fiscal and moral responsibility. . . . also [holding] the same assumptions about the material bases of good living, and . . . [agreement] on the essential rightness of an ever-increasing horizon of activities, experiences, and expectations." *Courtship of Olivia Clemens and Mark Twain*, p. 10.

48 Susy Clemens, *Papa: An Intimate Biography of Mark Twain*, p. 188.

49 *Huckleberry Finn: A Facsimile of the Manuscript*, ms. p. 210.

50 *Love Letters*, p. 333.

51 *MTB*, p. 524.

52 Howe, ed., *Memoirs of a Hostess*, p. 256.

53 "In Memory of Olivia Susan Clemens," pp. 29–30, ms., MTP, as quoted by Skandera-Trombley, *Mark Twain in the Company of Women*, p. 26.

54 Howells to SLC, *Mark Twain-Howells Letters*, p. 359.

55 *Satires and Burlesques*, p. 69.

56 *MTB*, p. 729.

57 *N&J2*, p. 448.

58 *N&J2*, pp. 457, 458.

59 *N&J2*, p. 479.

60 *Life on the Mississippi*, ed. J. M. Cox, p. 290. This edition restores passages to their original position in the text. Hereafter page citations appear in the text.

61 MTP.

62 Memo dated October 29, 1882, MTP.

63 *N&J2*, p. 527.

64 Scott, "Mark Twain Revises *Old Times on the Mississippi*."

65 See David and Sapirstein, "Reading the Illustrations in *Life on the Mississippi*," pp. 25–30. Fortunately the pages that Mark Twain had stolen from the unfinished *Huck Finn* manuscript are especially well illustrated; they can appropriately

appear in the chapter when it is restored to a properly full text of *Huckleberry Finn,* as in the University of California Press edition.

66 *Letters to His Publishers,* pp. 77, 93, and 156. In the 1873 case the judge granted Mark Twain an injunction against a publisher who had pirated his work, but the writer was awarded only ten dollars in costs. The quotation is from a letter by Clemens's lawyer, Simon Sterne, to Dan Slote, dated June 27, 1879. Apparently the 1873 case was "Mark Twain's only successful use of trademark as a deterrent against literary piracy." *N&J2,* p. 271 n. 112. The idea that "Mark Twain" could be treated as a common-law trademark would, of course, have rendered the basic copyright procedures meaningless. See Feinstein, "Mark Twain's Lawsuits," pp. 33–43. According to Harnsberger, who discusses the substantial sums going to Clara Clemens in the 1960s, "A large part of the income to the Estate has come through granting permission for the use of this name [Mark Twain] in reprints, etc." *Mark Twain's Clara,* p. 185.

67 *Congregationalist* (British), quoted in Tenney, *Mark Twain: A Reference Guide,* p. 12.

68 *New Orleans Times Democrat,* May 30, 1883; reprinted in *MTCH,* pp. 109–10.

69 *Athenaeum,* June 2, 1883; reprinted in *MTCH,* p. 116.

CHAPTER 6. A NEW VOICE

1 Another passage has been identified as a possible basis for the sequel. In chapter 29 of *Tom Sawyer,* Huck tells Tom that he has a friendly, reciprocal relationship with a slave named Uncle Jake. "That's a mighty good nigger, Tom. He likes me, becuz I don't ever act as if I was above him. Some times I've set right down and eat with him." See Burde, "Slavery and the Boys."

2 See Fetterley, "Disenchantment: Tom Sawyer in *Huckleberry Finn.*"

3 D. Smith, "Huck, Jim, and American Racial Discourse."

4 The passage appears in *Adventures of Huckleberry Finn,* ed. Victor Doyno, pp. 62–65.

5 Blair and Fischer, the editors of the scholarly 1988 edition of *Huckleberry Finn,* the text cited in this chapter, write that "Clemens evidently restored the episode" to the typescript "when it was no longer needed as copy for *Life on the Mississippi*" (p. 446 of this edition, cited hereafter in the text). This supposition proved valid when the missing portion of the manuscript was recovered; the manuscript serves as copy text for the episode in the Doyno edition.

6 Quoted in *Huckleberry Finn* (1988), p. 446.

7 Some of the justifications for including the chapter include Doyno, *Writing "Huck Finn,"* p. 260; Manniere, "On Keeping the Raftsmen's Passage"; Beidler, "The Raft Episode in *Huckleberry Finn.*" In the 1988 edition, the copy text of the raftsmen passage is what appears in *Life on the Mississippi,* but a better copy text is

in the first half of the manuscript, discovered in 1990 after the California edition was published. The editors at the Mark Twain Project at the University of California, Berkeley, expect to reedit Mark Twain's masterpiece, using the recently located ms.

8 *Huckleberry Finn* (1988), pp. 723, 730.

9 Ibid., pp. 714, 717, 718, 721.

10 Budd, "The Southern Currents Under Huckleberry Finn's Raft."

11 This matter is explored by Sattelmeyer in *One Hundred Years of "Huckleberry Finn,"* ed. Sattelmeyer and Crowley, pp. 367–70. See also Hunting, "Mark Twain's Arkansaw Yahoos."

12 It is taken up in chapter 29, but this portion of the chapter was omitted from original publication of the book; it can be found in Cox's 1984 edition, p. 219.

13 *Saturday Review,* January 31, 1885; reprinted in *MTCH,* pp. 122–23.

14 *Huckleberry Finn* (1988), p. 806.

15 Pearce, "Yours truly, Huck Finn," in *One Hundred Years of "Huckleberry Finn,"* ed. Sattelmeyer and Crowley, p. 314.

16 My comments here are indebted to H. N. Smith, *Democracy and the Novel,* pp. 105–14, and Trachtenberg, "The Form of Freedom in *Adventures of Huckleberry Finn.*"

17 *MTA,* I, 131 (written around 1898).

18 Carlyle, *French Revolution,* I, 354 ("Arrears and Aristocrats"). See Blair, "The French Revolution and *Huckleberry Finn,*" and Baetzhold, *Mark Twain and John Bull,* pp. 87–90. Blair notes that Mark Twain's favorite Dickens novel, *A Tale of Two Cities,* had suggested to him how powerful the presentation of mob scenes in fiction could be.

19 *Life on the Mississippi* (1984), pp. 332–36.

20 *Adventures of Huckleberry Finn* (1988), p. 740.

21 *Adventures of Huckleberry Finn: A Facsimile,* pp. 149–50.

22 The revisions are discussed briefly by Budd in ibid. and at length by Doyno in *Writing "Huck Finn."*

23 Cited by Fischer, *"Huck Finn* Reviewed," p. 15.

24 Budd, "'A Nobler Roman Aspect' of *Adventures of Huckleberry Finn,*" in Sattelmeyer and Crowley, ed., *One Hundred Years of "Huckleberry Finn,"* pp. 27–40.

25 *MTB,* p. 772.

26 Quoted by David and Sapirstein, "Reading the Illustrations in *Huckleberry Finn,*" pp. 34–35.

27 Quoted by Briden, "Kemble's 'Specialty' and the Pictorial Countertext of *Huckleberry Finn.*" Briden provides many samples of Kemble's Negro portraiture; some look like apes. See also Kemble, "Illustrating *Huckleberry Finn.*"

28 Draft of a note from Clemens to Fred J. Hall, July 19, 1889, quoted by H. N. Smith in his introduction to *Connecticut Yankee* (1979), p. 14.

29 *Huckleberry Finn* (1988), pp. 481–83.

30 *British Quarterly Review* 81 (January-April 1885), 465–66; *Westminster Review,* n.s., 67 (April 1885), p. 596.

31 Fischer, "*Huck Finn* Reviewed"; the quotations are from pp. 8, 9, 10, and 32.

32 The letter was published in the *Boston Daily Advertiser,* April 2, 1885; quoted by Fischer in "*Huck Finn* Reviewed," pp. 25–26.

33 Susy Clemens, *Papa: An Intimate Biography of Mark Twain,* pp. 106–7, and AD February 9, 1906; *MTA,* 2, p. 88.

34 Hemingway's statement is on pp. 22–23; Ralph Ellison's in his *Going to the Territory,* p. 140; Fishkin, *Was Huck Black?* pp. 9, 139.

35 The letter was published by Edwin McDowell in the *New York Times* for March 14, 1985: "From Twain: A Letter on Debt to Blacks," pp. 1, 16. McDowell's article cites Thurgood Marshall as calling McGuinn (who was commencement speaker at the graduation of his class) "one of the greatest lawyers who ever lived." On McGuinn, see also Fishkin, *Lighting Out for the Territory,* pp. 99–107. For another instance of Clemens's help to a black man, see Riggio, "Charles Ethan Porter and Mark Twain." Howells asserted that Clemens held himself "responsible for the wrong which the white race has done the black race in slavery"—*My Mark Twain,* p. 30. A valuable commentary on the race issue in *Huckleberry Finn* is provided by Arac in *Huckleberry Finn as Idol and Target.*

36 *Mark Twain-Howells Letters,* p. 442.

37 The tale was first published in *Satires and Burlesques* (1967). For the author's use of the *Arabian Nights,* see Gribben, *Mark Twain's Library,* p. 26.

38 Howells, *My Mark Twain,* p. 22.

39 Schirer, *Mark Twain and the Theatre,* pp. 83–87.

40 Sumida has intelligently speculated about the novel in "Reevaluating Mark Twain's Novel of Hawaii."

41 The play was published in *Hannibal, Huck and Tom,* pp. 258–324; its composition and history are discussed on pp. 243–57.

42 Schirer, *Mark Twain and the Theatre,* pp. 83–87.

43 It was published in *Hannibal, Huck and Tom,* pp. 92–140, and also in *Huck Finn and Tom Sawyer Among the Indians,* pp. 33–81.

44 *What Is Man?* pp. 26–59.

45 Quoted in *MTB,* p. 412.

46 *MTA,* 2, p. 13. See also *What Is Man?* pp. 585–86.

CHAPTER 7. RETIREMENT THWARTED

1 *MTB,* p. 830.

2 Susy Clemens, *Papa: An Intimate Biography of Mark Twain,* p. 187.

3 AD November 8, 1906; *Mark Twain's Own Autobiography,* ed. Kiskis, p. 190.

4 *MTA,* 1, pp. 43–44, dated 1885. See Emerson, "Smoking and Health."

5 SLC to Orion Clemens, January 22, 1888; MTP.**

6 *N&J3,* pp. 167–69, 403–4, 461.

7 See Fatout, "Mark Twain, Litigant."

8 This "Dinner Speech" appears in *Mark Twain Speaking,* pp. 106–9.

9 The extended correspondence consists of Johnson to SLC, March 16 and 18, May 11, July 16, August 15 and 22, November 13, 1885; SLC to Johnson, March 18, July 28, September 8, 1885; typescripts, MTP. Notebook 19, typescript p. 22, MTP; quoted in *Mark Twain-Howells Letters,* p. 542 n. 1.

10 These studies either correct Mark Twain's account or provide useful analyses of it: Lorch, "Mark Twain and the 'Campaign That Failed'"; Gerber, "Mark Twain's 'Private Campaign'"; Armstrong, "John L. RoBards—A Boyhood Friend of Mark Twain"; Mattson, "Mark Twain on War and Peace." See also Quirk, "Life Imitating Art," in *Coming to Grips with "Huckleberry Finn."*

11 Quoted in *Love Letters,* p. 247.

12 Howells, *My Mark Twain,* p. 61.

13 Ibid., p. 62.

14 Gribben notes that Clemens had an earlier interest in Malory. See Gribben, "'The Master Hand of Old Malory': Mark Twain's Acquaintance with *Le Morte d'Arthur.*" As noted below, Mark Twain may have also been inspired by a story by Max Adeler, "The Fortunate Island."

15 *N&J3,* p. 78.

16 Mary Boewe, who discovered Mark Twain's use of Lecky's *Rationalism,* discusses it in her "Twain on Lecky: Some Marginalia at Quarry Farm" and "Morgan vs. Merlin: The Case for Magic and Miracle in *A Connecticut Yankee in King Arthur's Court.*"

17 *N&J3,* pp. 86, 216, 217.

18 Susy Clemens, *Papa: An Intimate Biography of Mark Twain,* pp. 191–92.

19 E. J. Park, "A Day with Mark Twain," *Chicago Tribune,* September 19, 1886, p. 12; reprinted in Budd, ed., *Interviews with Mark Twain,* p. 42.

20 Baetzhold, "The Autobiography of Sir Robert Smith of Camelot: Mark Twain's Original Plan for *A Connecticut Yankee.*"

21 See Hill, "Barnum, Bridgeport, and *The Connecticut Yankee.*"

22 See R. H. Wilson, "Malory in the *Connecticut Yankee.*"

23 *Century,* November 1889, p. 74.

24 Gribben, *Mark Twain's Library,* pp. xx; Baetzhold, *Mark Twain and John Bull,* pp. 111–113.

25 See Aspiz, "Lecky's Influence on Mark Twain," and Boewe, "Twain on Lecky" and "Morgan vs. Merlin."

26 Budd, *Mark Twain, Social Philosopher,* pp. 118–20. The text of the speech is in *Mark Twain Speaking,* pp. 257–60.

27 N&J3, p. 415.

28 Gribben, *Mark Twain's Library*, pp. 43, 400–403; Baetzhold, *Mark Twain and John Bull*; personal communication, Mary Boewe.

29 Valuable discussions of the composition of the book are H. N. Smith, introduction to *CY*, pp. 1–15; J. D. Williams, "Revision and Intention in Mark Twain's *A Connecticut Yankee*"; Baetzhold, "The Course of Composition of *A Connecticut Yankee*"; and Russell, "The Genesis, Sources, and Reputation of Mark Twain's *A Connecticut Yankee*."

30 Kruse provides important new information in "Mark Twain's *A Connecticut Yankee*: Reconsiderations and Revisions"; see p. 469.

31 The publication that Mark Twain seems to have read is *The Fortunate Island and Other Stories* (1882); the book was copyrighted in 1881, as the verso of the title page shows, by "Chas. Heber Clark." Ketterer has twice explored the relationship of the two works; see "'Professor Baffin's Adventures' by Max Adeler: The Inspiration for *A Connecticut Yankee in King Arthur's Court*?" and "'The Fortunate Island' by Max Adeler: Its Publication History and *A Connecticut Yankee*."

32 The relevant part of the interview appears on pp. 33–34 in Ketterer's "Professor Baffin's Adventures."

33 The letter appears in Kruse, "Mark Twain's *A Connecticut Yankee*," p. 72. See also the observations in *Mark Twain-Howells Letters*, p. 622 n. 1.

34 The issue is well treated by Kruse, "Mark Twain's *A Connecticut Yankee*."

35 *Century*, November 1889, p. 77. No irony, apparently, was intended.

36 Rejected preface, *CY*, p. 517.

37 Budd, *Mark Twain, Social Philosopher*, p. 141.

38 Stedman to SLC, July 7, 1889; quoted in *CY*, pp. 519–22.

39 *CY*, p. 667. Subsequent references to this edition appear in the text.

40 The speech appears in *CT1*, pp. 883–90. For commentary, see Budd, *Mark Twain: Social Philosopher*, pp. 114–15, and Carter, "Mark Twain and the American Labor Movement."

41 *CY*, pp. 517, 518.

42 See Baetzhold, *Mark Twain and John Bull*, p. 56, and Gribben, *Mark Twain's Library*, p. 174.

43 Good discussions of the illustrations are provided by David in "The Unexpurgated *A Connecticut Yankee*" and by David and Sapirstein in "Reading the Illustrations in *A Connecticut Yankee*."

44 Webster's responsibility for Clemens's financial situation has been debated. See Gold, "What Happened to Charley Webster?" and Hoffman, *Inventing Mark Twain*, pp. 286–342, 348–49, 368–69.

45 Advertising prospectus of Charles L. Webster and Company, quoted in *CY*, p. 18.

46 Quoted in *CY*, p. 25; Tenney, *Mark Twain: A Reference Guide*, pp. 17–19.

47 *Scots Observer,* January 18, 1890; reprinted in *MTCH,* p. 165. For other reviews, see *CY,* pp. 17–28; see also Baetzhold, *Mark Twain and John Bull,* pp. 162–64.

48 On the poor sales of *Connecticut Yankee* and, as a result, Mark Twain's other books in England, see Baetzhold, *Mark Twain and John Bull,* pp. 164, 354. Hall's explanation of the failure of the book to make money is set forth in an August 8, 1890, letter to Clemens: "It has been a very expensive book to make and a very expensive book to push." Quoted in *N&J3,* p. 481.

49 SLC to Rev. C. D. Crane, January 20, 1887; photocopy, MTP.

50 See Gribben, "'I Detest Novels, Poetry & Theology': Origins of a Fiction Concerning Mark Twain's Reading."

51 *MTB,* p. 1536; Waggoner, "Science in the Thought of Mark Twain"; Gribben, *Mark Twain's Library,* pp. 518, 600, 676–77.

52 The title is from Richard S. Rosenthal's 1882 textbook, *The Meisterschaft System: A Short and Practical Method of Acquiring Complete Fluency of Speech in the German Language.*

53 Only after someone improved Mark Twain's German. But he himself noted, "There is some tolerably rancid German here and there in this piece. It is attributable to the proof-reader."—*MTB,* p. 849 n.; Paine quotes from SLC's manuscript.

54 DV344; quoted in Baetzhold, *Mark Twain and John Bull,* p. 165.

55 DV313A, MTP.

56 *MTB,* p. 917.

57 Box 32, MTP.

58 Lampton, "Jesse M. Leathers" in *Mark Twain Encyclopedia;* see also Grimm, "*The American Claimant:* Reclamation of a Farce."

59 The best discussion of the novel is by Messent, afterword to *The American Claimant* (1996).

60 Tenney, *Mark Twain: A Reference Guide,* pp. 20–21.

CHAPTER 8. SEARCHING

1 AD June 4, 1906; *Autobiography,* ed. Neider, p. 327.

2 *Mark Twain's Own Autobiography,* ed. Kiskis, p. 125. See also Dolmetsch, "Berlin," in *Mark Twain Encyclopedia,* ed. LeMaster and Wilson, pp. 70–71.

3 "Mental Telepathy?" DV254, published in *Mark Twain's Quarrel with Heaven,* p. 119. This collection includes "A Singular Episode."

4 *N&J1,* pp. 506, 511.

5 SLC explains all this in a letter to Fred J. Hall; *Letters to His Publishers,* pp. 313–15.

6 *Tom Sawyer Abroad,* in *The Adventures of Tom Sawyer, Tom Sawyer Abroad, Tom Sawyer, Detective,* ed. Gerber et al., pp. 302, 255, 341, 294. The best discussion of

Tom Sawyer Abroad is by Michelson, in *Mark Twain on the Loose,* pp. 108–14. In *Tom Sawyer Abroad,* the adventures of the three balloonists show definite borrowings from Jules Verne's story; Mark Twain's three characters in fact resemble Verne's three. Both groups see a lion at an oasis and see a mirage; both stories tell of hovering over a caravan buried in the sand, and in both stories one of the travelers jumps from the balloon into a lake.

7 Unpublished portion of "My Platonic Sweetheart," p. 36a recto, Box 15, No. 3A, MTP.

8 Box 8, No. 9, MTP, published in part by Arlin Turner in "Mark Twain and the South," p. 511.

9 Susan L. Crane to her cousin Elizabeth Ford Adams, December 5, 1892, *Mark Twain Society Bulletin* 19 (July 1996), 3. At this time, Crane explains, the Clemenses were "in Florence for the winter & hope the quiet of their life may do her good, together with the opportunity to be out of doors much of the time. Her difficulty is of the heart, which necessitates a quiet life." She does not note, as she might have, that being outdoors delivered Olivia from her husband's tobacco smoke.

10 My discussion is indebted to Gillman, *Dark Twins;* see p. 54.

11 Quoted in McKeithan, *The Morgan Manuscript of Mark Twain's "Pudd'nhead Wilson,"* p. 36.

12 My discussion is indebted to Robinson, "The Sense of Disorder in *Pudd'nhead Wilson,*" in Gillman and Robinson, ed., *Mark Twain's "Pudd'nhead Wilson,"* pp. 22–45. The composition of the work and the resulting problem of interpretation are explored by Parker in *Flawed Texts and Verbal Icons,* pp. 115–45. The most recent and most fair-minded treatment is by David Smith in his afterword to *Pudd'nhead Wilson.*

13 See Gillman, *Dark Twins,* pp. 53–95.

14 See Spangler, *"Pudd'nhead Wilson:* A Parable of Property."

15 See Ross, "Mark Twain's *Pudd'nhead Wilson.*"

16 All three British reviews are reprinted in the Norton Critical Edition of *Pudd'nhead Wilson,* pp. 215–18.

17 In 1882, the author had recorded the basis of the story from his memories; see *N&J2,* pp. 453–54.

18 Hall, August 7, 1893; quoted in *Letters to His Publishers,* p. 352 n. 4. Millet, the name of the artist in "Is He Living or Is He Dead?" is derived not from the eminent nineteenth-century French painter François but from Francis Millet, an American artist who had painted the writer's portrait in 1876, according to Rasmussen, *Mark Twain A to Z,* p. 315.

19 Quoted by Charles S. Underhill Jr., "Is the Garden of Eden at Niagara Falls? Mark Twain says 'Yes,'" p. 15 (copy at MTP).

20 Ibid., pp. 14, 18–19.

21 Box 15, No. 4, PH, MTP.

22 Box 15, Nos. 4 and 13, MTP.

23 Pages 8–16. More about the complicated history of the publication appears in *The Bible According to Mark Twain*, pp. 3–7.

24 Notebook 33, typescript, pp. 47–48.** A little earlier (pp. 6–7) the author had recorded in his notebook that he had been told that 10,000 machines would be produced "with all possible dispatch. The above machines are for this country alone."**

25 Notebook 33, typescript, p. 51.**

26 The author himself tells the story in AD June 1, 1906; *MTE*, pp. 186–195. Here Mark Twain painfully describes Webster's failings as a businessman.

27 AD of sometime in 1909; *MTA*, I, 259.

28 First published in *Letters from the Earth* (1962), also found in *CT2*, pp. 193–200; the passage quoted is on p. 198.

29 *MTB*, pp. 81–83, 1262.

30 Notebook 31, typescript pp. 6, 13, MTP.

31 OLC's journal, cited in Salsbury, *Susy and Mark Twain*, p. 204.

32 *MTB*, pp. 953–57; *Letters* (1917), p. 580.

33 Notebook #26A, pp. 54–55; as quoted by Maik, *A Reexamination of Mark Twain's "Joan of Arc,"* pp. 3–4.

34 So says Albert Bigelow Paine in *Letters* (1917), p. 615.

35 Alden to SLC, quoted in *Joan of Arc*, in *Mark Twain's Works*, Stormfield Edition, p. vii.

36 *Correspondence with Henry Huddleston Rogers*, pp. 143–44 and n. 2.

37 Horn speculates about this possibility, inferring that Mark Twain was retaliating against Alden for turning down his satire of Samuel Royston — *Mark Twain and William James*, p. 74.

38 Michelet, *Jeanne D'Arc*, p. 10; Mark Twain's copy, MTP; quoted in Albert E. Stone, "Mark Twain's *Joan of Arc*," p. 6.

39 Stahl, *Mark Twain, Culture and Gender*, p. 127.

40 Mark Twain's copy, MTP; quoted in Salomon, *Twain and the Image of History*, p. 175.

41 *Joan* ms., vol. 2, pp. 341–42, 344; PH, MTP; a version is quoted in Salomon, *Twain and the Image of History*, p. 182.

42 Both quotations are from the draft of a memorial to Olivia Susan Clemens, Box 31, no. 4, pp. 30–31, 46½, MTP. The bracketed part is deleted on this unpublished manuscript.

43 All of these quotations are from Welland, *Mark Twain in England*, p. 166.

44 *Idler*, August 1896, pp. 112–14.

45 *Bookman* [London], July 1896, pp. 207–10.

46 Hutton, *Harper's Magazine*, June 1896, sup. pp. 1–2.

47 *Bookman* [New York], May 1896, pp. 207–10.

48 *Dial*, June 16, 1896, pp. 351–57.

49 *Speaker*, July 18, 1896, p. 76.

50 *Harper's Weekly*, May 30, 1896, pp. 335–36; reprinted in Howells, *My Mark Twain*, pp. 129–35.

51 Shaw, *Complete Plays*, 2, 265–318.

52 Ballorain, "Mark Twain's Capers," in *American Novelists Revisited*, ed. Fleischmann, pp. 162–64. See also Stahl, *Mark Twain, Culture and Gender*, pp. 120–50; Zwarg, "Woman as Force in Twain's *Joan of Arc*."

53 Bay, "*Tom Sawyer, Detective:* The Origins of the Plot"; La Cour, "The Scandinavian Crime-Detective Story"; introduction to *Tom Sawyer, Detective*, in *The Adventures of Tom Sawyer, Tom Sawyer Abroad, Tom Sawyer, Detective* (1980), pp. 351–52.

54 Clara Clemens, *My Father, Mark Twain*, p. 97.

CHAPTER 9. THE HOUSE BURNS DOWN

1 Quoted in Shillingsburg, *At Home Abroad*, p.22.

2 Edith Salsbury has explored this subject in *Susy and Mark Twain*, esp. pp. 339, 354, 367, 370, 381, 385–96; see also Lawton, *A Lifetime with Mark Twain*, p. 130; Neider, introduction to Susy Clemens, *Papa: An Intimate Biography of Mark Twain*, pp. 10–58; and Stoneley, *Mark Twain and the Feminine Aesthetic*, pp. 98–103.

3 Karanovich and Gribben, eds., *Overland with Mark Twain*, p. 15.

4 "Mark Twain's Plan of Settlement," *New York Times*, August 17, 1895, p. 8. The phrasing seems to have come from an "interview" publicized by Clemens's nephew, Samuel Moffett. See Budd, *Our Mark Twain*, p. 125.

5 Shillingsburg, *At Home Abroad*, pp. 91, 99, 115. Shillingsburg has provided a full account of part of the trip in "Down Under Day by Day with Mark Twain."

6 Quoted in ibid., p. 209.

7 Notebook 34 typescript, p. 24, dated November 1, 1895, MTP.**

8 The passage is quoted by Camfield in "'I Wouldn't Be as Ignorant as You for Wages,'" p. 147.

9 *Bombay Times of India*, January 23, 1896; quoted in Rodney, *Mark Twain Overseas*, p. 180.

10 *Bombay Times of India*, January 25, 1896; quoted in Salsbury, *Susy and Mark Twain*, p. 377.

11 Mutalik, *Mark Twain in India*, p. 66. An entire issue of the *Mark Twain Journal* is devoted to Ahluwalia's "Mark Twain's Lecture-Tour in India."

12 This account is indebted to Rodney, *Mark Twain Overseas*.

13 This essay first appeared in *Fables of Man* (1972); the passages quoted are on pp. 86 and 88.

14 The agreement appears in *Correspondence with Henry Huddleston Rogers*, pp. 678–81.

15 Johnson, *A Bibliography of the Works of Mark Twain*; Long, *Mark Twain Handbook*; Rodney, *Mark Twain International*. See also Budd, "Mark Twain's Books Do Furnish a Room: But a Uniform Edition Does Still Better."

16 The agreements appear in *Mark Twain's Correspondence with Rogers*, pp. 691–708. In 1967, federal funding from the Office of Education was provided for a new edition of Mark Twain's writings; under the funding arrangement Harper would not have had full control of the editions that were to be published. Harper withdrew as Mark Twain's exclusive publisher. See Gerber, "The Iowa Years of *The Works of Mark Twain:* A Reminiscence." I am grateful to John Gerber for providing me with an advance copy of his essay. The volumes included as parts of "The Works of Mark Twain" series were published for the Iowa Center for Textual Studies by the University of California Press through the publication of *Adventures of Huckleberry Finn* in 1988; thereafter the volumes have been published solely by the University of California Press.

17 Notebook 36, typescript p. 15, quoted in *Mark Twain's Correspondence with Rogers,* p. 540 n. 1.

18 Ms., *More Tramps Abroad,* p. 953; Berg.

19 See Krause, "Olivia Clemens's 'Editing' Reviewed," and Carter, "Olivia Clemens Edits *Following the Equator.*"

20 See Welland, "Mark Twain's Last Travel Book," and Madigan, "Mark Twain's Passage to India: A Genetic Study of *Following the Equator.*"

21 See Messent, "Racial and Colonial Discourse in Mark Twain's *Following the Equator.*"

22 Tenney, *Mark Twain: A Reference Guide*, pp. 25–29; *MTCH*, pp. 210–15.

23 AD February 2, 1906; *MTA*, 2, p. 34.

24 AD February 2, 1906; *MTA*, 2, p. 40.

25 Notebook 42, typescript pp. 28–34, MTP.

26 *Fables of Man,* p. 131.

27 Notebook 39, typescript p. 22; Notebook 41, typescript pp. 57–58, MTP; quoted in *Hannibal, Huck and Tom,* p. 153.

28 Notebook 45, typescript 20, MTP.

29 The quotations are from *Hannibal, Huck and Tom,* pp. 167 and 163. The best analysis of "Tom Sawyer's Conspiracy" is that of Michelson, *Mark Twain on the Loose,* pp. 114–22.

30 See Howard, "The Ending to Mark Twain's 'Villagers of 1840–3.'"

31 *Satires and Burlesques,* pp. 199, 187.

32 Dolmetsch has suggested that since this part of the story was written while Mark Twain was living in Vienna, where transvestism was not uncommon, he may have obtained the idea there. See Dolmetsch, *"Our Famous Guest,"* p. 240.

33 Paine 212, MTP.

CHAPTER 10. SECOND HARVEST

1 I have profited greatly from Dolmetsch, *"Our Famous Guest."* This important contribution to biography sheds a great deal of light on Mark Twain's experiences.

2 Notebook 40, p. 20; quoted in Dolmetsch, *"Our Famous Guest,"* p. 153. In "Diplomatic Pay and Clothes," which Mark Twain wrote in early 1899, he suggests that he would have been receptive to being appointed American ambassador to Austria; he may not have made the observation facetiously.

3 Quoted by Albert Bigelow Paine in *Mark Twain's Notebook,* pp. 353–54, from a *New York Times* article of 1930 by Gabrilowitsch, "Memoirs of Leschetizky." Clara Clemens, in *My Husband Gabrilowitsch,* published in 1938, reports that while she was coming to know her husband-to-be, he told her, "I wish you to know something about me that you may not have heard. You and I are not of the same race. I descend from the Jewish people." Or, as he expressed it in German: "Ich stamme aus juedischer Herkunft" (p. 6).

4 Clemens's admiration for the Jews was shown in his responses to a questionnaire sent him by the *American Hebrew.* He reported that he found Jews superior intellectually as well as in other ways. His reply was published for the first time in *Fables of Man,* pp. 446–48. Kahn's "Mark Twain's Philosemitism" is an extended discussion of Mark Twain's attitude toward the Jews. The fullest discussions of the context of "Concerning the Jews" are both by Dolmetsch: "Mark Twain and the Viennese Anti-Semites" and *"Our Famous Guest,"* especially pp. 160–80.

5 Dolmetsch, *"Our Famous Guest,"* pp. 124–26.

6 In his notebook Mark Twain made notes for other plays: "Make plays — with a German for Principal character (Dutchy), an Irishman, a Scotchman, A Chinaman, a Japanese, a Negro (George), Uncle John Quarles who was very like the Yankee farmer in Old Homestead"; on "the *Comedy* side of hypnotism"; "The *Footprint.*" Quoted by Schirer, *Mark Twain and the Theatre,* pp. 95–96.

7 Wagner-Martin, "What Is Man?" in *Mark Twain Encyclopedia.*

8 SLC to Carl Thalbitzer, November 26, 1902; copy belonging to Brita Thalbitzer Hartz.** I am indebted to her for permission to quote this previously unpublished letter, which was brought to my attention by Hamlin Hill. Two letters from Thalbitzer are at MTP.

9 I quote from the 1973 edition, *What Is Man? and Other Philosophical Writings.*

10 Dolmetsch, *"Our Famous Guest,"* p. 228. Dolmetsch also identifies other authors that Clemens read in Vienna.

11 Cummings, *Mark Twain and Science,* p. 210.

12 *Mark Twain's Rubaiyat,* "Introduction" by Gribben, pp. 27–28. The verses quoted are found on page 46.

13 *MTA,* I, pp. 111–12.

14 "My Platonic Sweetheart," pp. 36a verso, 37–38; Box 15, no. 3A, MTP. Mark Twain recorded in Notebook 34 in 1901 an idea for a story: "divorce of the McWilliams on account of his dream-wife and family"—quoted by Gibson in *The Mysterious Stranger Manuscripts,* p. 29. This notebook reference has been cited as evidence that Clemens was feeling estrangement from his wife (Hill, *Mark Twain: God's Fool,* pp. 36–37).

15 "My Platonic Sweetheart," ms. pp. 43–44.

16 *Mark Twain's Notebook,* p. 365.

17 *Which Was the Dream?* p. 124.

18 Ibid., p. 125 n.

19 Ibid., p. 566.

20 Quoted from Notebook 32, typescript, in *Which Was the Dream?* p. 19.

21 November 8, 1899; MTP.

22 Notebook 40, typescript p. 50; quoted in *Mysterious Stranger Manuscripts,* p. 428.

23 *Mysterious Stranger Manuscripts,* p. 216.

24 Ibid., p. 438 ff.

25 *MTA,* I, p. 117.

26 In late 1895, Mark Twain had suggested in his notebook his desire to write a book "without reservations": "It is the strangest thing that the world is not full of books that scoff at the pitiful world, and the useless universe and violent, contemptible human race — books that laugh at the whole paltry scheme and deride it. Curious, for millions of men die every year with these feelings in their hearts. Why don't *I* write such a book? Because I have a family. Was this those other people's reason?"—*Mark Twain's Notebook,* p. 256.

27 Notebook 32a, typescript p. 37, MTP; quoted in *The Mysterious Stranger Manuscripts,* p. 17.

28 Gribben, *Mark Twain's Library,* p. 282.

29 *Mark Twain's Travels with Mr. Brown,* p. 252.

30 *The Mysterious Stranger Manuscripts,* p. 35. Citations of this edition hereafter appear in the text. Dolmetsch has shown that Eseldorf is a reflection of Mark Twain's experiences with the towns of Salzburg and Kaltenleutgeben, both in Austria. See Dolmetsch, "'It was still the Middle Ages in Austria.'"

31 *Which Was the Dream?* p. 168.

32 Compare ibid., pp. 171–74 and *MTA,* II, 84–87.

33 *Which Was the Dream?* p. 169.

34 Ibid., p. 167.

35 Isabel V. Lyon's Notebook, January 4, 1907; February 2, 1906–7. MTP. Quoted by permission of the heirs of Isabel Lyon and the Mark Twain Papers, the Bancroft Library, owner of the document.

36 *Which Was the Dream?* p. 168.

37 *MTA,* 1, p. 127.

38 *MTA,* 1, p. 132.

39 Hill, *Mark Twain: God's Fool,* p. 252; Frank, "Mark Twain and Health Food."

CHAPTER 11. THE HUMORIST AS PHILOSOPHER

1 Introduction at a Lotos Club dinner, November 10, 1900; *MTB,* 1116.

2 *Academy,* September 29, 1900, p. 258; R. E. Philips, "Mark Twain: More than Humorist"; *Book Buyer,* April 1901, p. 201; reprinted in *MTCH,* p. 242.

3 Interview published in the *New York Herald,* October 16, 1900, reprinted in *Mark Twain's Weapons of Satire,* ed. Zwick, p. 5. The United States was acting as an imperialist power: Senator Albert Beveridge had declared, "The Philippines are ours forever. . . . We will not abandon our opportunity in the Orient" — quoted in *Mark Twain's Weapons of Satire,* p. xviii.

4 Clara Clemens, *My Father, Mark Twain,* p. 216.

5 *Mark Twain Speaking,* pp. 364–65.

6 *New York Herald,* December 30, 1900, sect. 1, p. 7; quoted in *Mark Twain-Howells Letters,* p. 726.

7 Hawkins, "To the Person Sitting in Darkness," *Mark Twain Encyclopedia,* ed. LeMaster and Wilson; *Mark Twain's Weapons of Satire,* pp. xxi-xxiii.

8 It appears in *Fables of Man,* pp. 403–19. The passages quoted are on pp. 405 and 407.

9 Quoted in *Mark Twain-Howells Letters,* pp. 726–27.

10 Notebook 44, typescript p. 5, MTP.

11 *N&J3,* 45. Mark Twain also wrote a very brief statement, probably in earlier 1901, entitled "History 1,000 Years from Now," in which he identifies the American acquisition of the Philippines as the first step in the process "which after many years rescued our nation from democracy" — *Fables of Man,* p. 388.

12 *Fables of Man,* p. 321. Hereafter page references appear in the text.

13 Notebook 45, typescript p. 24, MTP; quoted in *Which Was the Dream?* p. 22.

14 AD August 30, 1906; *MTE,* p. 198.

15 See Pettit, *Mark Twain and the South,* pp. 168–73, 177.

16 *NJ3,* pp. 88, 358–59. In "Mark Twain's Travels in the Racial Occult," Gillman has drawn attention to a plot summary that Mark Twain had drafted (p. 199). The ms. is in Box 37, MTP.

17 Quoted in *MTB,* p. 1147.

18 Hill, *Mark Twain: God's Fool,* p. 39.

19 Mark Twain also drafted a review of Edwin Wildman's biography of Aguinaldo, which he had used in the "Defence." In the long but incomplete review, he compared Aguinaldo to Joan of Arc. It was first published in *Mark Twain's Weapons of Satire*, ed. Zwick, pp. 88–108.

20 "A Defence of General Funston," in *Mark Twain's Weapons of Satire*, p. 129.

21 *MTB*, p. 1162.

22 *Fables of Man*, p. 138.

23 *Mark Twain's Notebook*, p. 212.

24 Notebook 45, typescript pp. 2, 12, 13, 14, 15, 19; quoted in *Hannibal, Huck and Tom*, p. 17.

25 Notebook 45, typescript pp. 2** and 14, MTP; the latter quoted in *Hannibal, Huck and Tom*, p. 18.

26 Letter dated December 10, 1902, quoted by Rafferty in "The Lyon of St. Mark," p. 45. My exploration of Lyon's role in Clemens's life is much indebted to this valuable essay.

27 *MTA*, 2, p. 115.

28 Mary Lawton, *A Lifetime with Mark Twain: The Memories of Katy Leary*, p. 346.

29 *Mark Twain Speaking*, p. 465.

30 Howells, *My Mark Twain*, p. 39.

31 February 11, 1903; MTP.

32 *Mark Twain Speaking*, p. 458.

33 *CT2*, p. 551.

34 Quoted in *Mark Twain-Howells Letters*, p. 774.

35 *MTA*, 1, pp. xv-xvi.

36 AD August 30, 1906; *MTE*, pp. 198–99. Duneka's dislike of "No. 44" because of the presence in it of Adolf, the evil priest, is recorded in Isabel Lyon's diary for July 12, 1905 (MTP).

37 The above dating of the composition is based on the studies of Tuckey (*Mark Twain and Little Satan*), Gibson (his edition of *The Mysterious Stranger Manuscripts*), and Kahn (*Mark Twain's Mysterious Stranger*). Kahn and Malcolm ("Mark Twain's Gnostic Old Age: Annihilation and Transcendence in 'No. 44, The Mysterious Stranger'") argue that "No. 44" should be considered complete and thus Mark Twain's last major work.

38 DeVoto, *Mark Twain at Work*, p. 127.

39 *The Mysterious Stranger Manuscripts*, pp. 342–43. Hereafter page references appear in the text.

40 The following publications are all less than book length: *English as She Is Taught* (1900), *Edmund Burke on Croker and Tammany* (1901), *A Double-Barrelled Detective Story* (1902), *A Dog's Tale* (1904), *Extracts from Adam's Diary* (1904), *King Leopold's Soliloquy* (1905), *Eve's Diary* (1906), *What Is Man?* (privately printed,

1906), *A Horse's Tale* (1907), *Is Shakespeare Dead?* (1909), and *Extracts from Captain Stormfield's Visit to Heaven* (1909).

41 "How Nancy Jackson Married Kate Wilson." See Bibliography.

CHAPTER 12. STILL WRITING TILL THE END

1 *CT2,* p. 645.

2 *Fables of Man,* p. 422.

3 See Hawkins, "Mark Twain's Involvement with the Congo Movement: 'A Fury of Generous Indignation.'" As Hawkins has observed in "Mark Twain's Ant-Imperialism," Clemens's increasing pessimism silenced his interest in working for political change after 1905. In *King Leopold's Ghost,* Hochschild examines what the Belgians were doing in Africa and the public response.

4 Published by Paine in *Europe and Elsewhere* (1923) and in a more reliable text in *The Bible According to Mark Twain.*

5 Elizabeth Jordan to SLC, March 22, 1905; MTP.

6 Lyon's diary for March 17, 1905.

7 *MTB,* p. 1500.

8 Published in *Fables of Man.*

9 *N&J3,* p. 56.

10 July 27, 1905; MTP.

11 Box 15, no. 5.

12 *MTB,* p. 1226.

13 Box 15, no. 6, MTP. Howard Baetzhold, editor of *The Bible According to Mark Twain,* has suggested that the passage was probably written in 1901 or 1902. Personal communication, dated November 24, 1995. I am very grateful for Prof. Baetzhold's assistance.

14 *The Bible According to Mark Twain,* p. 62. This text provides the last seven words in a note on page 339. At one time Mark Twain planned a long work, making use of "Eve's Autobiography," to write "a documentary view of the doomed civilization." Baetzhold, McCullough, and Malcolm, "Mark Twain's Eden/Flood Parable," p. 35.

15 Minnie Maddern Fiske to SLC, September 18, 1905; MTP; *MTB,* p. 1246.

16 *New York Times,* December 6, 1905, p. 1.

17 *MTA,* 1, p. 269.

18 Isabel Lyon's diary for January 14, 1906.

19 Howells, *My Mark Twain,* p. 77.

20 *MTB,* p. 1268.

21 Isabel Lyon's diary for June 3, 1906.

22 *Mark Twain's Own Autobiography,* ed. Kiskis, p. xxiv. Kiskis's introductory essay is the best treatment of the autobiography in print. In his afterword to *Chapters*

from My Autobiography, Kiskis notes that Mark Twain's selection "emphasized tales of domesticity" and presented him "as a literary man embedded in the complexities of family life" (pp. 11, 14). Kiskis also notes that in his later years, without the family audience that he formerly had, Clemens enjoyed responding to another text, as he was doing here and as he did in the autobiography, when he used his daughter Susy's biography of her father as a text to respond to. Kiskis, "Mark Twain and Collaborative Autobiography."

23 *MTA,* p. 1.

24 AD August 30, 1906; *MTE,* p. 196.

25 *MTE,* p. 199.

26 *Mark Twain-Howells Letters,* p. 781.

27 AD October 4, 1906; MTP.

28 AD May 19, 1907; MTP.

29 *The Outrageous Mark Twain,* ed. Neider, p. 47.

30 Quoted in *MTB,* p. 1268.

31 AD June 2, 1906; *MTE,* p. 195.

32 *Mark Twain Speaking,* p. 562, at June 25, 1907, luncheon in London. This is one of five speeches that Mark Twain gave during his visit in England.

33 Sidney Brooks, "Mark Twain in England," p. 1054.

34 Quoted by Kate Douglas Wiggin in *My Garden of Memory,* p. 307.

35 DV226, Collection of James S. Copley Library, La Jolla, California. Harnsberger quotes at length from this piece in her *Mark Twain: Family Man.* In preparing this work, SLC drew on another unpublished work, written about the Clemens children in the 1870s and 1880s, "A Record of Small Foolishnesses," DV401, PH, MTP.

36 See Budd, *Our Mark Twain,* pp. 206 ff.

37 Notebook 48, typescript, p. 2.**

38 Lyon's diary for August 6, 7, and 11, 1906, and February 12, 1908.

39 Quoted by Rafferty, "The Lyon of St. Mark," p. 50.

40 Quoted in *Correspondence with Henry Huddleston Rogers,* p. 664.

41 See Hill, *Mark Twain: God's Fool,* pp. 183, 192, 212, 251, 258–59; Feinstein, "Mark Twain's Lawsuits," p. 25; and Mark Twain's will, published by Isabelle Budd, "Twain's Will Be Done."

42 LeMaster and Wilson, "Estate of Samuel Langhorne Clemens," *Mark Twain Encyclopedia,* p. 256. Clara was wealthy enough to "loan" some $350,000 to her second husband, Jacques Samossoud. See Harnsberger, *Mark Twain's Clara,* pp. 183, 185.

43 Isabelle Budd, "Clara Samossoud's Will"; Isabelle Budd, letter to the author, December 14, 1994. I am grateful to Mrs. Budd for sharing information with me.

44 See *Mark Twain's Aquarium: The Samuel Clemens Angelfish Correspondence, 1905–1910,* ed. John Cooley.

45 Lyon's diary for September 15, 1907. The fullest text of "Stormfield" is in *The Bible According to Mark Twain*.

46 Skandera-Trombley, *Mark Twain in the Company of Women*, based on Jean's diary, pp. 19, 178–79.

47 Quoted in Hill, *Mark Twain: God's Fool*, p. 220.

48 Lyon's diary for July 1, 1907.

49 Quoted from the Ashcroft-Lyon manuscript in Hill, *God's Fool*, p. 219. The ms. is #34, MTP.

50 Quoted in Skandera-Trombley, "Mark Twain's Last Work of Realism: The Ashcroft-Lyon Manuscript," p. 43. The account here of Clemens's motives for writing is derived from Skandera-Trombley's valuable essay and from Hill, "Ashcroft-Lyon Manuscript," *Mark Twain Encyclopedia*, pp. 43–44.

Henry Nash Smith, who interviewed Lyon in 1958, wrote, "Since I have some official connection with the Mark Twain Estate [he was literary editor], I should like to say that in my opinion Mark Twain did Mrs. Lyon an injustice at the time she left his employ" — October 30, 1956, letter from Smith to Lyon's nephew, David L. Moore, quoted by Rafferty, "The Lyon of St. Mark," p. 54.

51 *MTB*, p. 1528.

52 *What Is Man?* (1973), p. 400.

53 Ibid, p. 443. Mark Twain's religious thinking is explored by Brodwin in "Mark Twain's Theology" and by Emerson in "Mark Twain's Quarrel with God."

54 AD January 13, 1908; *MTE*, p. 316.

55 *What Is Man? and Other Philosophical Writings*, p. 439.

56 *MTB*, p. 1548.

57 *The Bible According to Mark Twain*, pp. 208–10.

58 Notebook 49 (1910), p. 4, MTP.**

59 Quoted in Paine, *MTB*, p. 1563. Hoffman provides a good account of Mark Twain's last days in *Inventing Mark Twain*, pp. 497–99.

60 "Mark Twain Smokes," *Danbury* (Connecticut) *Evening News*, August 3, 1909, p. 6. I owe this reference to Louis Budd.

61 SLC to A. Arthur Reade, March 14, 1882, published in Reade's *Study and Stimulants*, p. 122.

62 *MTB*, p. 1567.

63 LeMaster and Williams, "Estate of Samuel Langhorne Clemens," *Mark Twain Encyclopedia*, p. 256.

AFTERWORD. WHYS AND WHEREFORES

1 *Bombay Gazette*, January 23, 1896; reprinted in *Mark Twain Speaks for Himself*, p. 155.

2 Letter to Yale University on being awarded an honorary master's degree, *Hartford Courant*, June 29, 1888.

3 See Gribben, *Mark Twain's Library.*

4 "My Methods of Writing."

5 AD February 15, 1906; *MTE,* p. 251.

6 Isabel Lyon's diary, July 4, 1905, MTP. I am grateful to Laura Skandera-Trombley for bringing this item to my attention.

7 Howells, *Literature and Life,* p. 32.

8 Howells, *My Mark Twain,* p. 120.

9 Ibid., p. 119.

Bibliography

Works cited in the list of abbreviations are not included here.

MANUSCRIPTS BY SAMUEL L. CLEMENS (MARK TWAIN)
Unless otherwise stated, manuscripts are in the Mark Twain Papers, Bancroft Library, University of California, Berkeley (MTP). Parts of the collection are cataloged under the names of literary editors Albert Bigelow Paine and Bernard DeVoto (DV).

"Adam's Diary," additions to, Box 15, no. 5.

"Adam's Diary," unpublished fragment, Box 15, no. 6.

The American Claimant, manuscript of novel and summary, Box 32.

"The American Press," Paine no. 102A.

"Ashcroft-Lyon Manuscript," Box 48.

Autobiographical dictations and other portions of autobiography.

"A Defense of Royalty and Nobility," DV313a.

"Extract from Adam's Diary," from *The Niagara Book.* Buffalo, N.Y.: Underhill and Nichols, 1893. With author's holograph corrections, PH.

Extracts from Adam's Diary. New York: Harper and Brothers, 1904. With author's holograph corrections, PH.

"A Family Sketch," DV226. Mark Twain Collection, James S. Copley Library, La Jolla, California.

"Happy Memories of the Dental Chair," DV51.

"In Memory of Olivia Susan Clemens," draft, Box 31, no. 4.

The Innocents Abroad, manuscript drafts, McKinney Papers, Vassar College.

"Is He Dead?" Paine no. 126.

Joan of Arc, holograph manuscript, PH.

"Letters from a Dog to Another Dog Explaining & Accounting for Man: Translated from the Original Doggerel," DV344.

Life on the Mississippi, holograph manuscript, Pierpont Morgan Library, New York.

"Mental Telegraphy?" DV254.

More Tramps Abroad, holograph manuscript, Berg Collection, New York Public Library.

"My Platonic Sweetheart," Box 15, no. 3a.

"The Mysterious Chamber," DV56.

Notebooks, typescripts of unpublished, MTP.

Notes on Samuel C. Thompson's 1909 letter, DV268.

"On Progress, Civilization, Monarchy, etc.," Paine no. 102b.

"Postal Service," Paine no. 73.

Pudd'nhead Wilson, manuscript notes, Box 8, no. 9.

"A Record of the Small Foolishnesses of Susie & 'Bay' Clemens (Infants)," PH., DV401.

"Samuel Langhorne Clemens," written January 1873. Morgan Library, MA 1405.

Sandwich Islands novel fragment, DV111.

Scrapbook no. 2, MTP.

"A Singular Episode," DV329. [Also known as "The Late Reverend Sam Jones's Reception into Heaven."]

A Tramp Abroad, early drafts, Box 6, nos. 46, 47, 52.

MANUSCRIPTS BY OTHERS

Duneka, Frederick A. Mark Twain. *Extracts from Adam's Diary.* New York: Harper and Brothers, 1904. With Frederick Duneka's holograph corrections, PH.

Lyon, Isabel. Daybooks, daily reminders, and journals for 1906, 1907, and 1908. Typed transcripts and photocopies, MTP.

Twichell, Joseph H. Journals. Beinecke Rare Book and Manuscript Library, Yale University.

PUBLISHED WORKS BY SAMUEL L. CLEMENS (MARK TWAIN)

Adventures of Huckleberry Finn, ed. Walter Blair and Victor Fischer. Berkeley: University of California Press, 1988.

Adventures of Huckleberry Finn: A Facsimile of the Manuscript. Introduction by Louis J. Budd. 2 vols. Detroit: Gale Research, 1983.

Adventures of Huckleberry Finn, ed. Victor Doyno. New York: Random House, 1996.

The Adventures of Thomas Jefferson Snodgrass, ed. Charles Honce. Chicago: Pascal Covici, 1928.

The Adventures of Tom Sawyer, Tom Sawyer Abroad, Tom Sawyer, Detective, ed. John C. Gerber, Paul Baender, and Terry Firkins. Berkeley: University of California Press, 1980.

The Adventures of Tom Sawyer, ed. John C. Gerber and Paul Baender. Berkeley: University of California Press, 1982.

"Ah Sin": A Dramatic Work by Mark Twain and Bret Harte, ed. Frederick Anderson. San Francisco: Book Club of California, 1961.

"Around the World," *Buffalo Express,* October 17, 30; November 13; December 11, 18, 1869; January 8, 22, 29, 1870; PH, MTP.

Autobiographical Sketch (written for Samuel Moffett). Worcester: Privately printed, 1918. Moffett used this sketch as the basis for "Mark Twain: A Biographical Sketch," which was first published in *McClure's* in October 1899. Subsequently Moffett's piece appeared in various collected editions — for example, in the "American Artists Edition," at the end of the volume entitled "In Defense of Harriet Shelley."

The Autobiography of Mark Twain, ed. Charles Neider. New York: Harper and Brothers, 1959.

The Bible According to Mark Twain: Writings on Heaven, Eden, and the Flood, ed. Howard G. Baetzhold and Joseph B. McCullough. Athens and London: University of Georgia Press, 1995.

"The Carson Fossil-Footprints," *The San Franciscan,* February 16, 1884 (copy at Bancroft Library, University of California, Berkeley); reprinted in *Resources for American Literary Study* 10 (1980): 74–78, ed. Everett Emerson.

The Celebrated Jumping Frog of Calaveras County, and Other Sketches, ed. John Paul. New York: C. H. Webb, 1867.

The Choice Humorous Works of Mark Twain. London: John Camden Hotten [1873].

The Choice Humorous Works of Mark Twain. Revised and Corrected by the Author. London: Chatto and Windus, 1874.

Clemens of the "Call": Mark Twain in San Francisco, ed. Edgar M. Branch. Berkeley: University of California Press, 1969.

Col. Sellers. A Drama in Five Acts, ed. Jerry Thomason. *Missouri Review* 18 (1995): 109–51.

"Comments on the Moro Massacre," from AD March 12 and 14, 1906, in *Mark Twain's Weapons of Satire: Anti-Imperialist Writings on the Philippine-American War,* ed. Jim Zwick, pp. 170–78. Syracuse: Syracuse University Press, 1992.

The Complete Essays of Mark Twain, ed. Charles Neider. Garden City, N.Y.: Doubleday, 1963.

"Correspondence," *Memphis Daily Appeal,* October 24, 1858; reprinted in *American Literary Realism* 15 (1982): 201–3.

[Date, 1601.] Conversation, as it Was by the Social Fireside, in the Time of the Tudors.

[n.p., n.d.]. Reprinted in *Collected Tales, Speeches, and Essays, 1852–1890*, pp. 661–66.

Eve's Diary. New York: Harper and Brothers, 1906.

"Eve's Diary." In *Their Husbands' Wives*, ed. William Dean Howells and Henry Mills Alden. New York: Harper and Brothers, 1906.

Eye Openers: Good Things, Immensely Funny Sayings and Stories That Will Bring a Smile upon the Gruffest Countenance. London: John Camden Hotten, [1871].

Following the Equator: A Journey Around the World. Hartford: American, 1897.

Gold Miners and Guttersnipes: Tales of California. Selected, with an Introduction, by Ken Chowder. San Francisco: Chronicle Books, 1991.

The Gilded Age. A Tale of To-day. Co-author: Charles Dudley Warner. Hartford: American, 1873.

"Happy Memories of the Dental Chair." In Sheldon Baumrind, "Mark Twain Visits the Dentist." *Journal of the California Dental Association* 46 (1964): 493–96, 502.

"How Nancy Jackson Married Kate Wilson." [Title supplied by Robert Sattelmeyer, who wrote a brief introductory essay.] *Missouri Review* 10 (1987): 99–112.

How to Tell a Story and Other Essays. New York: Harper and Brothers, 1897.

Huck Finn and Tom Sawyer Among the Indians and Other Unfinished Stories, ed. Dahlia Armon and Walter Blair. Berkeley: University of California Press, 1989.

The Innocents Abroad; or, The New Pilgrim's Progress. Hartford: American, 1869.

Letters (twenty-eight) in the *San Francisco Alta California*, December 14, 1866-August 18, 1869. URL for index pages: ⟨http://www.tarleton.edu/activities/pages/facultypages/schmidt/altaindex.html⟩ (April 19, 1999). Also in *Mark Twain's Travels with Mr. Brown*, ed. Franklin Walker and Ezra C. Dane. New York: Alfred Knopf, 1940. Barbara Schmidt deserves thanks for making several groups of Mark Twain's journalism readily available.

Letters from the Earth, ed. Bernard DeVoto, with a preface by Henry Nash Smith. New York: Harper and Row, 1962.

Letters (six) in the *Chicago Republican*, February 8-August 23, 1868. URL for index pages: ⟨http://www.tarleton.edu/activities/pages/facultypages/schmidt/crindex/html⟩ (April 19, 1999).

Letters (seven) in the *Daily Hawaiian Herald*, September 5-December 13, 1866. URL for index pages: ⟨http://www.tarleton.edu/activities/pages/facultypages/schmidt/dhhindex.html⟩ (April 19, 1999).

Letters (thirteen) in the *Virginia City Territorial Enterprise*, December 22, 1867-April 7, 1868. URL for index pages: ⟨http://www.tarleton.edu/activities/pages/facultypages/schmidt/teindex.html⟩ (April 19, 1999).

Life as I Find It: Essays, Sketches, Tales, and Other Material, ed. Charles Neider. Garden City, N.Y.: Hanover House, 1961.

Life on the Mississippi. Boston: Charles R. Osgood, 1883.

Life on the Mississippi, ed. James M. Cox. New York: Penguin Books, 1984.

The Literary Apprenticeship of Mark Twain, ed. Edgar M. Branch. Urbana: University of Illinois Press, 1950.

"Magdalen Tower." In *The Shotover Papers; or, Echoes from Oxford,* October 17, 1874; reprinted in the *Twainian* 2 (January 1943): 4–5.

The Mammoth Cod, and Address to the Stomach Club, ed. Gershon Legman. Milwaukee: Maledicta, 1976.

The Man That Corrupted Hadleyburg and Other Stories and Essays. New York: Harper and Brothers, 1900.

The Man That Corrupted Hadleyburg and Other Stories and Sketches. London: Chatto and Windus; Leipzig: Bernard Tauchnitz, 1900.

Mark Twain and Hawaii, ed. Walter Francis Frear. Chicago: Lakeside Press, 1947.

Mark Twain of the "Enterprise": Newspaper Articles and Other Documents, 1862–1864, ed. Henry Nash Smith and Frederick Anderson. Berkeley: University of California Press, 1957.

Mark Twain: San Francisco Correspondent, ed. Henry Nash Smith and Frederick Anderson. San Francisco: Book Club of California, 1957.

Mark Twain Speaking, ed. Paul Fatout. Iowa City: University of Iowa Press, 1976.

Mark Twain Speaks for Himself, ed. Paul Fatout. West Lafayette, Ind.: Purdue University Press, 1979.

Mark Twain's (Burlesque) Autobiography and First Romance. New York: Sheldon [1871].

Mark Twain's Fables of Man, ed. John S. Tuckey. Berkeley: University of California Press, 1972.

Mark Twain's Hannibal, Huck and Tom, ed. Walter Blair. Berkeley: University of California Press, 1969.

Mark Twain's Letters from Hawaii, ed. A. Grove Day. New York: Appleton-Century, 1966.

Mark Twain's Mysterious Stranger Manuscripts, ed. William M. Gibson. Berkeley: University of California Press, 1969.

Mark Twain's Notebook. Prepared for publication with comments by Albert Bigelow Paine. New York: Harper and Brothers, 1935.

Mark Twain's Own Autobiography: The Chapters from the "North American Review," ed. Michael J. Kiskis. Madison: University of Wisconsin Press, 1990.

Mark Twain's Quarrel with Heaven: "Captain Stormfield's Visit to Heaven" and Other Sketches, ed. Ray B. Browne. New Haven: College and University Press, 1970.

"Mark Twain's Religious Beliefs as Indicated by Notations in His Books," ed. Chester L. Davis. *Twainian* 14 (September-October 1955): 4.

Mark Twain's Rubáiyát. Introduction by Alan Gribben. Textual Note by Kevin B.

MacDonnell. Austin and Santa Barbara: Jankins Publishing and the Karpeles Manuscript Library, 1983.

Mark Twain's Satires and Burlesques, ed. Franklin R. Rogers. Berkeley: University of California Press. 1967.

Mark Twain's Sketches, New and Old. Hartford: American, 1875.

Mark Twain's Sketches. Number One. New York: American News [1874].

Mark Twain's Sketches. Selected and revised by the author. London: George Routledge and Sons, 1872.

Mark Twain's Speeches, ed. Albert Bigelow Paine. New York: Harper and Brothers, 1923.

Mark Twain's Weapons of Satire: Anti-Imperialist Writings on the Philippine-American War, ed. Jim Zwick. Syracuse: Syracuse University Press, 1992.

Mark Twain's Which Was the Dream? and Other Symbolic Writings of the Later Years, ed. John S. Tuckey. Berkeley: University of California Press, 1968.

"Memphis — The Cotton Trade — Illinois Politics — What Tennessee Thinks of Them," *Missouri Republican,* October 22, 1858; reprinted in *American Literary Realism* 15 (1982): 199–200.

More Tramps Abroad. London: Chatto and Windus, 1897.

"My Methods of Writing." Letter written in 1888 and published in George Bainton, ed., *The Art of Authorship.* New York: Appleton, 1890. Reprinted in *Life As I Find It,* ed. Charles Neider, p. 227. Garden City, N.Y.: Hanover House, 1961.

The New Pilgrim's Progress. London: Routledge, 1872.

On the Poetry of Mark Twain: With Selections from His Verse, ed. Arthur L. Scott. Urbana: University of Illinois Press, 1966.

"Our Special River Correspondence," *Missouri Democrat,* September 1, 1858; reprinted in *American Literary Realism* 15 (1982): 197–98.

The Oxford Mark Twain, ed. Shelley Fisher Fishkin. 29 vols. New York: Oxford University Press, 1996.

The Pattern for Mark Twain's "Roughing It," ed. Franklin R. Rogers. Berkeley: University of California Press, 1961.

A Pen Warmed Up in Hell: Mark Twain in Protest, ed. Frederick Anderson. New York: Harper and Row, 1972.

The Portable Mark Twain, ed. Bernard DeVoto. New York: Viking Press, 1946.

The Prince and the Pauper, ed. Victor Fischer and Lin Salamo. Berkeley: University of California Press, 1979.

Pudd'nhead Wilson and Those Extraordinary Twins, ed. Sidney E. Berger. Norton Critical Edition. New York: Norton, 1980.

Punch, Brothers, Punch! and Other Sketches. New York: Slote, Woodman, 1878.

"Reflections on Religion." In *The Outrageous Mark Twain,* ed. Charles Neider, pp. 30–51. New York: Doubleday, 1987.

Report from Paradise, ed. Dixon Wecter. New York: Harper and Brothers, 1952.

Representative Selections, ed. Fred Lewis Pattee. New York: American Book Co., 1935.

"Rev. H. W. Beecher: His Private Habits," *Buffalo Express,* September 25, 1869, p. 1. PH, MTP.

Roughing It, ed. Franklin R. Rogers and Paul Baender. Berkeley: University of California Press, 1972.

Roughing It, ed. Harriet E. Smith and Edgar M. Branch. Berkeley: University of California Press, 1993.

Screamers: A Gathering of Scraps of Humor, Delicious Bits, and Short Stories. London: John Camden Hotten, [1871].

Simon Wheeler, Detective, ed. Franklin R. Rogers. New York: New York Public Library, 1963.

Sketches of the Sixties. By Bret Harte and Mark Twain. San Francisco: J. Howell, 1926.

Slovenly Peter. Translated by Mark Twain, with a preface by Clara Clemens. New York: Harper, 1935. Mark Twain's Introduction was published by Dixon Wecter in "Mark Twain as Translator from the German," reprinted in *On Mark Twain: The Best from "American Literature,"* ed. Louis J. Budd and Edwin H. Cady, pp. 34–35. Durham, N.C.: Duke University Press, 1987.

"Soleleather Cultivates His Taste for Music," *New Orleans Crescent,* July 21, 1859; reprinted in *American Literature* 54 (1982): 498–502.

"Some Recollections of a Storm at Sea," *The Bazaar Record* (Cleveland), January 18, 1876; reprinted in the *Twainian* 8 (July-August 1949): 1–2.

The Stolen White Elephant Etc. Boston: James R. Osgood, 1882.

"Three New Letters by Samuel Clemens in the *Muscatine Journal,*" ed. Edgar M. Branch. *Mark Twain Journal* 22 (1984): 2–7.

"To the Person Sitting in Darkness," *North American Review* (February 1901): pp. 161–76; reprinted in *Collected Tales, Sketches, Speeches, and Essays, 1891–1910,* pp. 457–73.

Tom Sawyer Abroad. London: Chatto and Windus, 1894.

Traveling with the Innocents Abroad: Mark Twain's Original Reports from Europe and the Holy Land, ed. Daniel Morley McKeithan. Norman: University of Oklahoma Press, 1958.

A True Story and the Recent Carnival of Crime. Boston: James R. Osgood, 1877.

Wapping Alice. Berkeley, Calif.: Friends of the Bancroft Library, 1981.

What Is Man? and Other Philosophical Writings, ed. Paul Baender. Berkeley: University of California Press, 1973.

The Writings of Mark Twain. Definitive Edition. 37 vols. New York: Gabriel Wells, 1923–35.

The Works of Mark Twain. Stormfield Edition. 37 vols. New York: Harper, 1929. Includes *Europe and Elsewhere.*

PERSONAL LETTERS OF SAMUEL L. CLEMENS (MARK TWAIN) [IN ADDITION TO THOSE CITED ABOVE]

" 'Dear Master Wattie': The Mark Twain-David Watson Bowser Letters," ed. Pascal Covici Jr., *Southwest Review* 45 (1960): 104–21.

Letter of June 24, 1874. In *The Eighteenth Year Book 1919.* Boston: Bibliophile Society, 1919.

The Love Letters of Mark Twain, ed. Dixon Wecter. New York: Harper and Brothers, 1949.

Mark Twain, Business Man, ed. Samuel C. Webster. Boston: Little, Brown, 1946. (Mostly letters to Charles L. Webster, also to Orion Clemens, Mollie Clemens, Jane Clemens, Pamela Clemens Moffett, and Annie Moffett.)

Mark Twain-Howells Letters, ed. Henry Nash Smith and William M. Gibson. 2 vols. Cambridge: Harvard University Press, 1960.

Mark Twain to Mrs. Fairbanks, ed. Dixon Wecter. San Marino, Calif.: Huntington Library, 1949.

Mark Twain's Aquarium: The Samuel Clemens Angelfish Correspondence, 1905–1910, ed. John Cooley. Athens: University of Georgia Press, 1991.

Mark Twain's Correspondence with Henry Huddleston Rogers, ed. Lewis Leary. Berkeley: University of California Press, 1969.

Mark Twain's Letters to His Publishers, ed. Hamlin Hill. Berkeley: University of California Press, 1967. (Mostly letters to Elisha Bliss, Frank Bliss, James R. Osgood, Charles L. Webster, and Fred J. Hall.)

Mark Twain's Letters to Mary, ed. Lewis Leary. New York: Columbia University Press, 1961. (Letters to Mary Benjamin Rogers.)

SLC to A. Arthur Reade, March 14, 1882. In A. A. Reade, *Study and Stimulants; or, The Use of Intoxicants and Narcotics in Relation to Intellectual Life,* pp. 120–22. Philadelphia: Lippincott; Manchester [U.K.]: Heywood, 1883.

"Unpublished Letters to Dan Beard." *Mark Twain Quarterly* 7 (Winter-Spring 1945): 22.

SECONDARY WORKS

(Book reviews and most interviews cited in notes are not listed here.)

Adeler, Max. *The Fortunate Island and Other Stories.* Boston: Lee and Shepard, 1882.

Ahluwalia, Harsharan Singh. "Mark Twain's Lecture-Tour in India." *Mark Twain Journal* 34 (Spring 1996): 1–48.

Aldrich, Thomas Bailey. *The Story of a Bad Boy.* Boston: Fields and Osgood, 1869.

Andrews, Kenneth R. *Nook Farm: Mark Twain's Hartford Circle.* Cambridge: Harvard University Press, 1950.

Andrews, William L. "The Source of Mark Twain's 'The War Prayer'." *Mark Twain Journal* 17 (Summer 1975): 8–9.

Arac, Jonathan. *"Huckleberry Finn" as Idol and Target.* Madison: University of Wisconsin Press, 1997.

Armstrong, C. J. "John J. RoBards — A Boyhood Friend of Mark Twain." *Missouri Historical Review* 25 (1931): 293–98.

Arnold, St. George Tucker. "The Twain Bestiary: Mark Twain's Critters and the Traditions of Animal Portraiture of the Old Southwest." *Southern Folklore Quarterly* 40 (1977): 195–211.

Aspiz, Harold, "Lecky's Influence on Mark Twain." *Science and Society* 26 (1962): 15–25.

Austen, Roger. *Genteel Pagan: The Life of Charles Warren Stoddard,* ed. John W. Crowley. Amherst: University of Massachusetts Press, 1991.

Baender, Paul. "Alias Macfarlane: A Revision of Mark Twain Biography." *American Literature* 38 (1966–67): 187–97.

——. "The Date of Mark Twain's 'The Lowest Animal'." *American Literature* 36 (1964–65): 174–79.

——. "Found: Mark Twain's 'Lost Sweetheart'." *American Literature* 44 (1972–73): 414–29.

—— "The Jumping Frog as a Comedian's First Virtue." *Philological Quarterly* 60 (1963): 192–200.

Baetzhold, Howard G. "The Autobiography of Sir Robert Smith of Camelot: Mark Twain's Original Plan for *A Connecticut Yankee.*" *American Literature* 32 (1960–61): 456–61.

——. "The Course of Composition of *A Connecticut Yankee:* A Reinterpretation." *American Literature* 33 (1961): 195–214.

——. "Mark Twain and Dickens: Why the Denial?" *Dickens Studies Annual* 16 (1987): 189–219.

——. *Mark Twain and John Bull: The British Connection.* Bloomington: Indiana University Press, 1970.

——. "Mark Twain's 'The Prince and the Pauper'." *Notes and Queries,* n.s. 1 (1954): 401–3.

Baetzhold, Howard G., Joseph B. McCullough, and Donald Malcolm. "Mark Twain's Eden/Flood Parable: 'The Autobiography of Eve'." *American Literary Realism* 24 (Fall 1991): 23–38.

Baggett, J. Mark. "Copyright." In *The Mark Twain Encyclopedia,* ed. J. R. LeMaster and James D. Wilson, pp. 183–84. New York: Garland, 1993.

Ballorain, Rolande. "Mark Twain's Capers: A Chameleon in King Carnival's Court." In *American Novelists Revisited: Essays in Feminist Criticism,* ed. Fritz Fleischmann, pp. 143–70. Boston: G. K. Hall, 1982.

Bassett, John E. *"A Heart of Ideality in My Realism" and Other Essays on Howells and Twain.* West Cornwall, Conn.: Locust Hill Press, 1991.

Bay, J. Christian. *"Tom Sawyer, Detective:* The Origin of the Plot." In *Essays Offered to Herbert Putnam by His Colleagues and Friends,* ed. William W. Bishop and Andrew Keough, pp. 80–88. New Haven: Yale University Press, 1929.

Beidler, Peter G. "The Raft Episode in *Huckleberry Finn." Modern Fiction Studies* 14 (1968): 11–20.

Beidler, Philip D. "Realistic Style and the Problem of Context in *The Innocents Abroad* and *Roughing It." American Literature* 52 (1980–81): 33–49.

Benson, Ivan. *Mark Twain's Western Years.* Stanford: Stanford University Press, 1938.

Blair, Walter. "The French Revolution and *Huckleberry Finn." Modern Philology* 55 (1957): 21–35.

———. *Mark Twain and Huck Finn.* Berkeley: University of California Press, 1960.

———. "Mark Twain's Other Masterpiece: 'Jim Baker's Blue Jay Yarn.'" *Studies in American Humor* 1 (1975): 132–47.

———. "On the Structure of *Tom Sawyer." Modern Philology* 37 (1939): 75–88.

———. "When Was *Huckleberry Finn* Written?" *American Literature* 30 (1958–59): 1–24.

Blair, Walter, and Hamlin Hill. *America's Humor: From Poor Richard to Doonesbury.* New York: Oxford University Press, 1978.

Boewe, Mary. "Twain on Lecky: Some Marginalia at Quarry Farm." *Mark Twain Society Bulletin* 8 (1985): 1–6.

———. "Morgan vs. Merlin: The Case for Magic and Miracle in *A Connecticut Yankee in King Arthur's Court." Quarry Farm Papers* 4 (1994): 29–39.

Brack, O. M., Jr. "Mark Twain in Knee Pants: The Expurgation of *Tom Sawyer Abroad." Proof* 2 (1972): 141–51.

Branch, Edgar M. "'The Babes in the Woods': Artemus Ward's 'Double Health' to Mark Twain." *PMLA* 93 (1978): 955–72.

———. "Bixby vs. Carroll: New Light on Sam Clemens's Early River Career." *Mark Twain Journal* 30 (Fall 1992): 2–22.

———. *The Literary Apprenticeship of Mark Twain.* Urbana: University of Illinois Press, 1950.

———. *Mark Twain and the Starchy Boys.* Elmira, N.Y.: Quarry Farm Papers, 1992.

———. "Mark Twain: The Pilot and the Writer." *Mark Twain Journal* 23 (Fall 1985): 28–43.

———. *Men Call Me Lucky: Mark Twain and the "Pennsylvania."* Miami, Ohio: Friends of the Library Society, 1985.

———. "'My Voice is Still for Setchell': A Background Study of 'Jim Smiley and His Jumping Frog.'" *PMLA* 82 (1967): 591–601.

———. "A New Clemens Footprint: Soleleather Steps Forward." *American Literature* 54 (1982): 497–510.

———. "'Old Times on the Mississippi': Biography and Craftsmanship." *Nineteenth-Century Literature* 45 (1990): 73–87.

———. "Sam Clemens, Steersman on the *John H. Dickey*." *American Literary Realism* 15 (1982): 195–208.

Branch, Edgar M., and Robert H. Hirst. *The Grangerford-Shepherdson Feud by Mark Twain*. Berkeley: Friends of the Bancroft Library, 1985.

Briden, Earl F. "Kemble's 'Speciality' and the Pictorial Countertext of *Huckleberry Finn*." *Mark Twain Journal* 26, no. 2 (1988): 2–14.

Bridgman, Richard. *Traveling in Mark Twain*. Berkeley: University of California Press, 1987.

Brodwin, Stanley. "Mark Twain's Theology: The Gods of a Brevet Presbyterian." in *The Cambridge Companion to Mark Twain,* ed. Forrest G. Robinson, pp. 220–48. New York: Cambridge University Press, 1995.

———. "The Useful and Useless River: *Life on the Mississippi* Revisited." *Studies in American Humor* 2 (1976): 196–209.

Brooks, Sidney. "Mark Twain in England." *Harper's Weekly* 51 (July 20, 1907): 1053–54.

Brooks, Van Wyck. *The Ordeal of Mark Twain*. New York: E. P. Dutton, 1920. Rev. ed., 1933.

Brown, George Rothwell, ed. *Reminiscences of Senator William M. Stewart of Nevada*. New York: Neal, 1908.

Browne, Ray B. "Mark Twain and Captain Wakeman." *American Literature* 33 (1961–62): 320–29.

Buckle, Thomas Henry. *History of Civilization in England*. 2 vols. New York: Appleton, 1866.

Budd, Isabelle. "Twain's Will Be Done." *Mark Twain Journal* 22 (1984): 34–39.

———. "Clara Samossoud's Will." *Mark Twain Journal* 25 (1988): 17–29.

Budd, Louis J., ed. *Interviews with Samuel L. Clemens, 1874–1910*. Arlington, Tex.: American Literary Realism, 1977.

———. "Mark Twain Plays the Bachelor." *Western Humanities Review* 11 (1957): 157–67.

———. *Mark Twain: The Ecstasy of Humor.* Elmira, N.Y.: Quarry Farm Papers, no. 6, 1995.

———. "Mark Twain's Books Do Furnish a Room: But a Uniform Edition Does Still Better." *Nineteenth-Century Prose* 25, no. 2 (Fall 1998): 91–101.

———. *Mark Twain: Social Philosopher.* Bloomington: Indiana University Press, 1962.

———. *Our Mark Twain: The Making of His Public Personality.* Philadelphia: University of Pennsylvania Press, 1983.

———. "A Recovered Mark Twain Speech: New Laws and Old Yarns." *Essays in Arts and Sciences* 23 (October 1994): 59–66.

———. "The Southern Currents Under Huckleberry Finn's Raft." *Mississippi Valley Historical Review* 46 (1959): 222–37.

Budd, Louis J., and Edwin H. Cady. *On Mark Twain: The Best from "American Literature."* Durham, N.C.: Duke University Press, 1987.

Burde, Edgar. "Mark Twain: The Writer as Pilot." *PMLA* 93 (1978): 878–92.

———. "Slavery and the Boys: *Tom Sawyer* and the Germ of *Huck Finn*." *American Literary Realism* 24 (1991): 86–90.

Bush, Harold K. "The Mythic Struggle Between East and West: Mark Twain's Speech at Whittier's Birthday Celebration and W. D. Howells' *A Chance Acquaintance*." *American Literary Realism* 27, no. 2 (Winter 1995): 53–73.

Camfield, Gregg. "'I Wouldn't Be as Ignorant as You for Wages': Huck Finn Talks Back to His Conscience." *Studies in American Fiction* 20 (1992): 169–75.

———. *Sentimental Twain: Samuel Clemens in the Maze of Moral Philosophy.* Philadelphia: University of Pennsylvania Press, 1994.

Cardwell, Guy A. *Twins of Genius.* East Lansing: Michigan State College Press, 1953.

———. *The Man Who Was Mark Twain: Images and Ideologies.* New Haven: Yale University Press, 1991.

Carlyle, Thomas. *The French Revolution: A History.* 2 vols. New York: Harper and Brothers, n.d.

Carter, Everett. "The Meaning of *A Connecticut Yankee*." *American Literature* 50 (1978–79): 418–40.

Carter, Paul J. "Mark Twain and the American Labor Movement." *New England Quarterly* 30 (1957): 382–88.

———. "Olivia Clemens Edits *Following the Equator*." *American Literature* 30 (1958–59): 194–209.

Clark, Charles H. "Mark Twain at 'Nook Farm' (Hartford) and Elmira." *Critic* 6 (January 17, 1885): 25–26.

Clark, Charles Heber. *See* Adeler, Max [pen name].

Clemens, Clara. *My Father Mark Twain.* New York: Harper and Brothers, 1931.

———. *My Husband Gabrilowitsch.* New York: Harper, 1938.

Clemens, Cyril. *Young Sam Clemens.* Portland, Me.: Leon Tebbets, 1942.

Clemens, Susy. *Papa: An Intimate Biography of Mark Twain.* Ed. Charles Neider. Garden City, N.Y.: Doubleday, 1985.

Comfort, Mary S. "Nook Farm." In *The Mark Twain Encyclopedia,* ed. J. R. LeMaster and James D. Wilson, pp. 544–46. New York: Garland, 1993.

Cooley, John. "Mark Twain's Transvestite Tragedies." *Over here: reviews in american studies* 15 (1995): 34–48.

Cortissoz, Royal. *The Life of Whitelaw Reid.* 2 vols. London: Thornton Butterworth, 1921.

Covici, Pascal, Jr. *Mark Twain's Humor: The Image of a World.* Dallas: Southern Methodist University Press, 1962.

Cox, James M. "The Muse of Mark Twain." *Massachusetts Review* 5 (1963): 127–41.

———. *Mark Twain: The Fate of Humor.* Princeton: Princeton University Press, 1966.

Crews, Frederick C. *The Critics Bear It Away: American Fiction and the Academy.* New York: Random House, 1992.

Cummings, Sherwood. "*What Is Man?* The Scientific Sources." In *Essays in Determinism in American Literature,* ed. Sydney J. Krause, pp. 108–16. Kent, Ohio: Kent State University Press, 1964.

———. *Mark Twain and Science: Adventures of a Mind.* Baton Rouge: Louisiana State University Press, 1988.

———. "Mark Twain's Social Darwinism." *Huntington Library Quarterly* 20 (1957): 163–75.

David, Beverly R. "Mark Twain and the Legends for *Huckleberry Finn.*" *American Literary Realism* 15 (1982): 155–65.

———. "Tragedy and Travesty: Edward Whymper's *Scrambles Amongst the Alps* and Mark Twain's *A Tramp Abroad.*" *Mark Twain Journal* 27, no. 1 (1989): 2–8.

———. *Mark Twain and His Illustrators.* Volume 1 (1869–1875). Troy, N.Y.: Whitston, 1986.

———. "The Pictorial *Huck Finn:* Mark Twain and His Illustrator, E. W. Kemble." *American Quarterly* 26 (1974): 331–51.

———. "The Unexpurgated *A Connecticut Yankee:* Mark Twain and His Illustrator, Daniel Carter Beard." *Prospects* 1 (1975): 98–117.

David, Beverly R., and Ray Sapirstein. "Reading the Illustrations in *A Connecticut Yankee.*" In Mark Twain, *A Connecticut Yankee in King Arthur's Court.* New York: Oxford University Press, 1996.

———. "Reading the Illustrations in *Huckleberry Finn.*" In Mark Twain, *Adventures of Huckleberry Finn.* New York: Oxford University Press, 1996.

———. "Reading the Illustrations in *Life on the Mississippi.*" In Mark Twain, *Life on the Mississippi.* New York: Oxford University Press, 1996.

———. "Reading the Illustrations in *Tom Sawyer.*" In Mark Twain, *The Adventures of Tom Sawyer.* New York: Oxford University Press, 1996.

Davis, Chester L. "Mark Twain's Religious Beliefs as Indicated by Notations in His Books." *Twainian* 14 (September-October 1955): 1–4.

Delaney, Paul. " 'You Can't Go Back to the Raft A'gin, Huck Honey!': Mark

Twain's Western Sequel to *Huckleberry Finn*." *Western American Literature* 11 (1976): 215–29.

———. "The Dissolving Self: The Narrators of Mark Twain's *Mysterious Stranger* Fragments." *Journal of Narrative Techniques* 7 (1976): 51–65.

DeVoto, Bernard. *Mark Twain at Work*. Cambridge: Harvard University Press, 1942.

———. *Mark Twain's America*. Boston: Little, Brown, 1932.

Dickinson, Leon T. "Mark Twain's Revisions in Writing *The Innocents Abroad*." *American Literature* 19 (1947–48): 139–57.

———. "Mark the Twain: The Double Vision of Samuel Clemens." *Revue des Langues Vivantes,* special U.S. Bicentennial Issue, 1976, pp. 81–91.

———. Review of Dewey Ganzel, *Mark Twain Abroad. Modern Philology* 68 (1970): 117–19.

———. "The Sources of *The Prince and the Pauper*." *Modern Language Notes* 64 (1949): 103–6.

Dolmetsch, Carl. "Berlin." In *The Mark Twain Encyclopedia,* ed. J. R. LeMaster and James D. Wilson, p. 72. New York: Garland, 1993.

———. "'It was still the Middle Ages in Austria . . . ' ." In *Images of Central Europe in Travelogues and Fiction by North American Writers,* ed. Waldemar Zacharasiewicz, pp. 94–103. Tübingen: Staffenburg Verlag, 1995.

———. "Mark Twain and the Viennese Anti-Semites: New Light on 'Concerning the Jews.'" *Mark Twain Journal* 23 (Fall 1985): 10–17.

———. *"Our Famous Guest": Mark Twain in Vienna*. Athens: University of Georgia Press, 1992.

Doyno, Victor A. *Writing "Huck Finn": Mark Twain's Creative Process*. Philadelphia: University of Pennsylvania Press, 1991.

Duckett, Margaret. *Mark Twain and Bret Harte*. Norman: University of Oklahoma Press, 1964.

Duncan, Jeffrey L. "The Empirical and Ideal in Mark Twain." *PMLA* 95 (1980): 201–12.

Eble, Kenneth E. *Old Clemens and W. D. H.: The Story of a Remarkable Friendship*. Baton Rouge: Louisiana State University Press, 1985.

Ellison, Ralph. *Going to the Territory*. New York: Random House, 1986.

Eliot, T. S. Introduction to *The Adventures of Huckleberry Finn*. London: Cressett Press, 1950.

Emerson, Everett. *The Authentic Mark Twain: A Literary Biography of Samuel L. Clemens*. Philadelphia: University of Pennsylvania Press, 1984.

———. "*A Connecticut Yankee in King Arthur's Court:* Meaning and Significance Revisited." *Over here: reviews in american studies* 15, nos. 1–2 (1995): 11–19.

———. "Mark Twain and Humiliation." *Mark Twain Journal* 29 (1991): 2–7.

———. "Mark Twain's Move to Hartford." *Mark Twain Journal* 23 (Spring 1985): 18–20.

———. "Mark Twain's Quarrel with God." In *Order in Variety: Essays in Honor of Donald E. Stanford,* ed. R. W. Crump, pp. 32–58. Newark: University of Delaware Press, 1991.

———. "A Send-Off for Joe Goodman: Mark Twain's 'The Carson Fossil Footprints.'" *Resources for American Literary Study* 10 (1980): 71–78.

———. "Smoking and Health: The Case of Samuel L. Clemens." *New England Quarterly* 70 (1997): 548–66.

———. "The Strange Disappearance of Mark Twain." *Studies in American Fiction* 13 (1985): 143–55.

Ensor, Alison. "The 'Tennessee Land' of *The Gilded Age:* Fiction and Reality." *Tennessee Studies in English* 15 (1970): 15–23.

Evans, John D. *A Tom Sawyer Companion: An Autobiographical Guided Tour with Mark Twain.* Latham, Md.: University Press of America, 1993.

Fatout, Paul. "Mark Twain's *Nom de Plume.*" *American Literature* 34 (1962–63): 1–7.

———. *Mark Twain on the Lecture Circuit.* Bloomington: Indiana University Press, 1960.

———. "Mark Twain, Litigant." *American Literature* 31 (1959–60): 30–45.

———. *Mark Twain in Virginia City.* Bloomington: Indiana University Press, 1964.

Feinstein, Herbert. "Mark Twain's Lawsuits." Ph.D. diss., University of California, Berkeley, 1962.

Ferguson, DeLancey. *Mark Twain: Man and Legend.* Indianapolis: Bobbs-Merrill, 1943.

———. "Mark Twain's Comstock Duel: The Birth of a Legend." *American Literature* 14 (1942–43): 66–70.

———. "Huck Finn Aborning." *Colophon* 3 (1938): 171–80.

Fetterley, Judith. "The Sanctioned Rebel." *Studies in the Novel* 3 (1971): 293–304.

———. "Disenchantment: Tom Sawyer in *Huckleberry Finn.*" *PMLA* 87 (1972): 69–74.

Fischer, Victor. "*Huck Finn* Reviewed: The Reception of *Huckleberry Finn* in the United States, 1885–1897." *American Literary Realism* 16 (1983): 1–57.

Fishkin, Shelley Fisher. *Lighting Out for the Territory: Reflections on Mark Twain and American Culture.* New York: Oxford University Press, 1997.

———. *Was Huck Black? Mark Twain and African-American Voices.* New York: Oxford University Press, 1993.

Florence, Don. *Persona and Humor in Mark Twain's Early Writings.* Columbia: University of Missouri Press, 1995.

Foner, Philip S. *Mark Twain: Social Critic.* New York: International, 1958.

"Ford Letters from 'Around the World.'" *Mark Twain Society Bulletin* 17, no. 1 (January 1994): 3–6.

Frank, Michael. "Mark Twain and Health Food." *Bancroftiana: Newsletter of the Friends of the Bancroft Library* (Fall 1997): 11.

Frederick, John T. *The Darkened Sky: Nineteenth-Century Novelists and Religion.* Notre Dame, Ind.: University of Notre Dame Press, 1969.

French, Bryant Morey. *Mark Twain and the Gilded Age.* Dallas: Southern Methodist University Press, 1965.

Gale, Robert L. *Plots and Characters in the Works of Mark Twain.* 2 vols. Hamden, Conn.: Archon Books, 1973.

Ganzel, Dewey. *Mark Twain Abroad: The Cruise of the "Quaker City."* Chicago: University of Chicago Press, 1968.

Gardner, Joseph H. "Mark Twain and Dickens." *PMLA* 84 (1969): 90–101.

Gauvreau, Emile. *My Last Million Readers.* New York: Dutton, 1941.

Gerber, John. "The Relationship Between Point of View and Style in the Works of Mark Twain." In *Style in Prose Fiction,* English Institute Essays, 1958, pp. 142–71. New York: Columbia University Press, 1959.

——. "Mark Twain's 'Private Campaign.'" *Civil War History* 1 (1955): 37–60.

——. "The Iowa Years of *The Works of Mark Twain:* A Reminiscence." *Studies in American Humor,* n.s. 3, no. 4 (1997): 68–87.

Giddings, Robert, ed. *Mark Twain: A Sumptuous Variety.* London: Vision Press, 1985.

Gillman, Susan. *Dark Twins: Imposture and Identity in Mark Twain's America.* Chicago: University of Chicago Press, 1989.

——. "Mark Twain's Travels in the Racial Occult: *Following the Equator* and the Dream Tales." In *The Cambridge Companion to Mark Twain,* ed. Forrest G. Robinson, pp. 193–219. New York: Cambridge University Press, 1995.

Gillman, Susan, and Forrest G. Robinson, eds. *Mark Twain's "Pudd'nhead Wilson": Race, Conflict, and Culture.* Durham, N.C.: Duke University Press, 1990.

Gold, Charles H. "What Happened to Charley Webster?" *Mark Twain Journal* 32 (Fall 1994): 11–22.

Goldman, Robert. "Mark Twain as Playwright." In *Mark Twain: A Sumptuous Variety,* ed. Robert Giddings, pp. 108–31. London: Vision Press, 1985.

Grant, Douglas. *Mark Twain.* New York: Grove Press, 1962.

Gribben, Alan. "'I Detest Novels, Poetry & Theology': Origins of a Fiction Concerning Mark Twain's Reading." *Tennessee Studies in Literature* 22 (1977): 154–61.

——. "'I Did Wish Tom Sawyer Was There': Boy Book Elements in *Tom Sawyer* and *Huckleberry Finn.*" In *One Hundred Years of Huckleberry Finn: The Boy, His Book, and American Culture,* ed. Robert Sattelmeyer and J. Donald Crowley, pp. 149–70. Columbia: University of Missouri Press, 1985.

———. " 'It Is Unsatisfactory to Read to One's Self': Mark Twain's Informal Reading." *Quarterly Journal of Speech* 62 (1976): 49–56.

———. *Mark Twain's Library: A Reconstruction.* 2 vols. Boston: G. K. Hall, 1980.

———. " 'The Master Hand of Old Malory': Mark Twain's Acquaintance with *Le Morte d'Arthur.*" *English Language Notes* 16 (1978): 32–40.

———. " 'A Splendor of Stars & Suns': Mark Twain as a Reader of Browning's Poems." *Browning Institute Studies* 6 (1978): 87–103.

Grimm, Clyde L. "*The American Claimant:* Reclamation of a Farce." *American Quarterly* 19 (1967): 86–103.

Hall, Fred J. "Fred J. Hall Tells the Story of His Connection with Charles L. Webster and Co." *Twainian* 6 (November-December 1947): 1–3.

Hanson, Elizabeth. "Mark Twain's Indians Reexamined." *Mark Twain Journal* 20 (Summer 1981): 11–12.

Harnsberger, Caroline Thomas. *Mark Twain: Family Man.* New York: Citadel, 1960.

———. *Mark Twain's Clara; or, What Became of the Clemens Family.* Evanston, Ill.: Ward Schori, 1982.

———. *Mark Twain's Views of Religion.* Evanston, Ill.: Schori Press, 1961.

Harper, J. Henry. *The House of Harper.* New York: Harper, 1912.

Harris, Helen L. "Mark Twain's Response to the Native American." *American Literature* 46 (1974–75): 495–505.

Harris, Susan K. *The Courtship of Olivia Langdon and Mark Twain.* New York: Cambridge University Press, 1996.

Hawkins, Hunt. "Mark Twain's Involvement with the Congo Movement: 'A Fury of Generous Indignation.'" *New England Quarterly* 51 (1978): 147–75.

———. "Mark Twain's Anti-Imperialism." *American Literary Realism* 25 (1993): 31–45.

———. "To the Person Sitting in Darkness." In *The Mark Twain Encyclopedia,* ed. J. R. LeMaster and James D. Wilson, pp. 738–39. New York: Garland, 1993.

Hemingway, Ernest. *The Green Hills of Africa.* New York: Scribner, 1935.

Henderson, Archibald. *Mark Twain.* New York: Stokes, 1912.

Hill, Hamlin. "Ashcroft-Lyon Manuscript." In *The Mark Twain Encyclopedia,* ed. J. R. LeMaster and James D. Wilson, pp. 43–44. New York: Garland, 1993.

———. "Mark Twain's Book Sales, 1869–1879." *Bulletin of the New York Public Library* 65 (1961): 371–89.

———. "Mark Twain: Audience and Artistry." *American Quarterly* 15 (1963): 25–40.

———. *Mark Twain and Elisha Bliss.* Columbia: University of Missouri Press, 1964.

———. *Mark Twain: God's Fool.* New York: Harper and Row, 1973.

———. "Barnum, Bridgeport, and *The Connecticut Yankee.*" *American Quarterly* 16 (1964): 615–16.

———. "The Composition and Structure of *Tom Sawyer*." *American Literature* 32 (1961–62): 379–92.

———, and Frederick Anderson. "How Samuel Clemens Became Mark Twain's Publisher: A Study of the James R. Osgood Contracts." *Proof* 2 (1972): 117–43.

Hirst, Robert. "The Making of *The Innocents Abroad*: 1867–1872." Ph.D. diss., University of California, Berkeley, 1975.

Hochschild, Adam. *King Leopold's Ghost: A Story of Greed, Terror, and Heroism in Colonial Africa*. Boston: Houghton Mifflin, 1998.

Hoffman, Andrew. *Inventing Mark Twain: The Lives of Samuel Langhorne Clemens*. New York: Morrow, 1997.

Hooker, Isabella Beecher. Diary MS. in the Connecticut Historical Society; typed copy at MTP.

Horn, Jason Gary. *Mark Twain and William James: Crafting a Free Self*. Columbia: University of Missouri Press, 1996.

Howard, Sam. "The Ending to Mark Twain's 'Villagers of 1840–3.'" *American Literary Realism* 17 (1990): 87–90.

Howe, M. A. DeWolfe, ed. *Memoirs of a Hostess: A Chronicle of Eminent Friendships Drawn Chiefly from the Diaries of Mrs. James T. Fields*. Boston: Atlantic Monthly Press, 1922.

Howells, William Dean. *My Mark Twain: Reminiscences and Criticism*, ed. Marilyn Austin Baldwin. Baton Rouge: Louisiana State University Press, 1967.

———. *Literature and Life*. New York: Harper and Brothers, 1902.

———. "Editor's Study." *Harper's Magazine* (December 1886): 162.

Hunting, Robert. "Mark Twain's Arkansaw Yahoos." *Modern Language Notes* 73 (1958): 264–67.

James, George Wharton. "Charles Warren Stoddard." *National Review* (August 1911): 659–72.

———. "How Mark Twain Was Made." *National Review* (February 1911): 1–13.

Jerome, Robert D., and Herbert A. Wisbey Jr., eds. *Mark Twain in Elmira*. Elmira, N.Y.: Mark Twain Society, 1977.

Johnson, Merle. *A Bibliography of the Works of Mark Twain*. New York: Harper and Brothers, 1935.

Jones, Alexander E. "Mark Twain and Sexuality." *PMLA* 71 (1956): 595–616.

———. "Mark Twain and the Determinism of *What Is Man?*" *American Literature* 29 (1957–58): 1–17.

Jones, Daryl E. "The Hornet Disaster: Mark Twain's Adaptation in 'The Great Dark.'" *American Literary Realism* 9 (1976): 243–47.

Kahn, Sholom J. *Mark Twain's Mysterious Stranger*. Columbia: University of Missouri Press, 1979.

———. "Mark Twain's Philosemitism: 'Concerning the Jews.'" *Mark Twain Journal* 23 (Fall 1985): 18–25.

Kaplan, Fred. Afterword to Mark Twain, *Following the Equator and Anti-imperialist Essays*. New York: Oxford University Press, 1996.

Kaplan, Justin. *Mr. Clemens and Mark Twain*. New York: Simon and Schuster, 1966.

Karanovich, Nick, and Alan Gribben, eds. *Overland with Mark Twain: James B. Pond's Photographs and Journal of the North American Lecture Tour of 1895*. Elmira, N.Y.: Center for Mark Twain Studies at Quarry Farm, 1992.

Keller, Helen. *The Story of My Life*. 1902. Garden City, N.Y.: Doubleday, 1954.

Kemble, E. W. "Illustrating *Huckleberry Finn*." *Colophon* 1 (1930): 44–45.

Ketterer, David. "'The Fortunate Island' by Max Adeler: Its Publication History and *A Connecticut Yankee*." *Mark Twain Journal* 29 (1991): 28–32.

——. "'Professor Baffin's Adventures' by Max Adeler: The Inspiration for *A Connecticut Yankee in King Arthur's Court*?" *Mark Twain Journal* 24 (1986): 24–34.

Kiskis, Michael. Afterword to Mark Twain, *Chapters from My Autobiography*. New York: Oxford University Press, 1996.

——. "Mark Twain and Collaborative Autobiography." *Studies in the Literary Imagination* 29 (1966): 27–40.

Klett, Ada M. "Meisterschaft; or, The True State of Mark Twain's German." *German-American Review* 7 (December 1940): 10–11.

Krause, Sydney J. "The Art and Satire of Twain's 'Jumping Frog' Story." *American Quarterly* 16 (1964): 363–76.

——. "Cooper's Literary Offenses: Mark Twain in Wonderland." *New England Quarterly* 38 (1965): 291–311.

——. *Mark Twain as Critic*. Baltimore: Johns Hopkins University Press, 1967.

—— "Olivia Clemens's 'Editing' Reviewed." *American Literature* 39 (1967–68): 325–35.

Kruse, Horst H. "Literary Old Offenders: Mark Twain, John Quill, Max Adeler, and Their Plagiarism Duel." *Mark Twain Journal* 29 (1991): 10–27.

——. *Mark Twain and "Life on the Mississippi."* Amherst: University of Massachusetts Press, 1981.

——. "Mark Twain's *A Connecticut Yankee*: Reconsiderations and Revisions." *American Literature* 62 (1990): 464–83.

——. "Mark Twain's *Nom de Plume*: Some Mysteries Resolved." *Mark Twain Journal* 30 (1992): 1–32.

LaCour, Tage. "The Scandinavian Crime-Detective Story." *American Book Collector* 9 (May 1959): 22–23.

Lampton, Lucius M. "Jesse M. Leathers." In *The Mark Twain Encyclopedia*, ed. J. R. LeMaster and James D. Wilson, pp. 448–50. New York: Garland, 1993.

Lawton, Mary. *A Lifetime with Mark Twain: The Memories of Katy Leary*. New York: Harcourt, Brace, 1925.

Lee, Judith Yaross. "Fossil Feuds: Popular Science and the Rhetoric of Vernacular Humor." *Essays in Arts and Sciences* 23 (October 1994): 1–19.

Leisy, Ernest. "Mark Twain's Part in *The Gilded Age.*" *American Literature* 8 (1936–37): 445–47.

LeMaster, J. R., and James D. Wilson, eds. *The Mark Twain Encyclopedia.* New York: Garland, 1993.

———. "Estate of Samuel L. Clemens (1910–1964)." In *The Mark Twain Encyclopedia,* eds. J. R. LeMaster and James D. Wilson, pp. 256–57. New York: Garland, 1993.

Lindberg, Gary. *The Confidence Man in American Literature.* New York: Oxford University Press, 1982.

The List of Members of the Monday Evening Club Together with the Records of Papers Read at Their Meetings, 1869–1954. Hartford: privately printed, 1954.

Long, E. Hudson. *Mark Twain Handbook.* New York: Hendricks House, 1957.

Lorch, Fred W. "Mark Twain in Iowa." *Iowa Journal of History and Politics* 27 (1929): 408–58.

———. "Mark Twain and the 'Campaign that Failed.'" *American Literature* 12 (1940–41): 454–70.

———. "Mark Twain's Philadelphia Letters in *The Muscatine Journal.*" *American Literature* 17 (1945–46): 348–52.

———. *The Trouble Begins at Eight: Mark Twain's Lecture Tours.* Ames: Iowa State University Press, 1968.

Lowry, Richard S. *"Littery Man": Mark Twain and Modern Authorship.* New York: Oxford University Press, 1986.

Lynn, Kenneth. *William Dean Howells: An American Life.* New York: Harcourt Brace Jovanovich, 1971.

———. *Mark Twain and Southwestern Humor.* Boston: Little, Brown, 1959.

Madigan, Francis J. "Mark Twain's Passage to India: A Genetic Study of *Following the Equator.*" Ph.D. diss., New York University, 1964.

Maik, Thomas A. *A Reexamination of Mark Twain's "Joan of Arc."* Lewiston, N.Y.: Edwin Mellen, 1992.

Malcolm, Donald. "Mark Twain's Gnostic Old Age: Annihilation and Transcendence in 'No. 44, The Mysterious Stranger.'" *American Literary Realism* 28, no. 2 (1996): 41–58.

Manierre, William R. "On Keeping the Raftsman's Passage in *Huckleberry Finn.*" *English Language Notes* 6 (1968): 118–22.

Marleau, Michael H. "'The Crash of Timbers Continued—the Deck Swayd under Me': Samuel L. Clemens, Eyewitness to the Race and Collision between the *Pennsylvania* and the *Vicksburg.*" *Mark Twain Journal* 28 (Spring 1990): 1–36.

Matthews, Brander. *The Tocsin of Revolt and Other Essays.* New York: Scribner, 1922.

Mattson, J. Stanley. "Mark Twain on War and Peace: The Missouri Rebel and 'The Campaign That Failed.'" *American Quarterly* 20 (1968): 783–94.

May, John R. "The Gospel According to Philip Traum: Structural Unity in 'The Mysterious Stranger.'" *Studies in Short Fiction* 8 (1971): 411–22.

McClain, Laurence. "'A Murder, a Mystery, and a Marriage': Mark Twain's Hannibal in Transition." *Library Chronicle of the University of Texas at Austin* n.s. 37 (1986): 52–75.

McCullough, Joseph, and Janice McIntire-Strasburg, eds. *Mark Twain at the Buffalo "Express": Sketches and Articles by America's Favorite Humorist and Social Critic.* DeKalb: Northern Illinois University Press, 1999.

McDowell, Edwin. "From Twain: A Letter on Debt to Blacks." *New York Times* (14 March 1985): 1, 16.

McKeithan, Daniel. *Court Trials in Mark Twain and Other Essays.* The Hague: Martinus Nijhoff, 1958.

———. "Mark Twain's Letters of Thomas Jefferson Snodgrass." *Philological Quarterly* 32 (October 1953): 353–65. Reprinted in *Court Trials,* cited above.

———. *The Morgan Manuscript of Mark Twain's "Pudd'nhead Wilson."* Uppsala: American Institute, Uppsala University, 1961.

McNamara, Eugene. "Huck Lights Out for the Territory: Mark Twain's Unpublished Sequel." *University of Windsor Review* 2 (1966): 68–74.

McNutt, James C. "Mark Twain and the American Indian: Earthly Realism and Heavenly Idealism." *American Indian Quarterly* 4 (1978): 223–42.

Messent, Peter. Afterword to Mark Twain, *The American Claimant.* New York: Oxford University Press, 1996.

———. "Colonial and Racial Discourse in Mark Twain's *Following the Equator.*" *Essays in Arts and Sciences* 22 (1993): 67–83.

Michelson, Bruce. "The Form of *The Innocents Abroad.*" In *The Best of Mark Twain,* ed. Louis J. Budd and Edwin H. Cady, pp. 171–84. Durham, N.C.: Duke University Press, 1987.

———. *Mark Twain on the Loose.* Amherst: University of Massachusetts Press, 1995.

Miller, William C. "Samuel L. Clemens and Orion Clemens vs. Mark Twain and His Biographers (1861–1862)." *Mark Twain Journal* 16 (1973): 1–9.

———. "The Editor's Page." *Nevada Historical Society Quarterly* 5 (January-March 1962), inside back cover.

Miller, William, et al., eds. *Reports of the 1863 Constitutional Convention of the Territory of Nevada.* Carson City: State of Nevada, 1972.

Mobley, Lawrence E. "Mark Twain and the *Golden Era.*" *Publication of the Bibliographical Society of America* 58 (1964): 8–23.

Mutalik, Keshav. *Mark Twain in India.* Bombay: Noble Publishing, 1978.

Norton, Charles A. *Writing Tom Sawyer: The Adventures of a Classic.* Jefferson, N.C.: McFarland, 1983.

Parker, Hershel. *Flawed Texts and Verbal Icons: Literary Authority in American Fiction*. Evanston, Ill.: Northwestern University Press, 1984.

Parsons, Coleman O. "Down the Mighty River with Mark Twain." *Mississippi Quarterly* 22 (1968–69): 1–18.

———. "The Devil and Samuel Clemens." *Virginia Quarterly Review* 23 (1947): 582–606.

Pearce, Roy Harvey. "Yours Truly, Huck Finn." In *One Hundred Years of Huckleberry Finn: The Boy, His Book, and American Culture*, ed. Robert Sattelmeyer and J. Donald Crowley, pp. 313–24. Columbia: University of Missouri Press, 1985.

Pemberton, E. Edgar. *The Life of Bret Harte*. New York: Dodd, Mead, 1903.

Pettit, Arthur G. *Mark Twain and the South*. Lexington: University Press of Kentucky, 1974.

Phelps, Elizabeth Stuart. *The Gates Ajar*. Boston: Fields, Osgood, 1869.

Poirier, Richard. *A World Elsewhere: The Place of Style in American Literature*. New York: Oxford University Press, 1966.

Quirk, Tom. *Coming to Grips with "Huckleberry Finn": Essays on a Book, a Boy, and a Man*. Columbia: University of Missouri Press, 1993.

———. *Mark Twain: A Study of the Short Fiction*. New York: Twayne Publishers, 1997.

Rafferty, Jennifer L. " 'The Lyon of St. Mark': A Reconsideration of Isabel Lyon's Relationship to Mark Twain." *Mark Twain Journal* 34, no. 2 (Fall 1996): 43–55.

Rasmussen, R. Kent. *Mark Twain A to Z: The Essential Reference to His Life and Writings*. New York: Facts on File, 1995.

Rees, Robert A. "*Captain Stormfield's Visit to Heaven* and *The Gates Ajar*." *English Language Notes* 7 (1970): 197–202.

Rees, Robert A., and Richard Dilworth Rust. "Mark Twain's 'The Turning Point of My Life.'" *American Literature* 40 (1968–69): 524–35.

Regan, Robert. "The Reprobate Elect in *The Innocents Abroad*." *American Literature* 54 (1982–83): 240–57.

———. " 'English Notes': A Book Mark Twain Abandoned." *Studies in American Humor* 2 (1976): 157–70.

———. *Unpromising Heroes: Mark Twain and His Characters*. Berkeley: University of California Press, 1966.

Reigstad, Tom. "Professor Ford, Editor Clemens, and Their Collaborative 'Around the World' Fiasco." *Mark Twain Society Bulletin* 16 (July 1993): 1, 3–5.

Requa, Kenneth A. "Counterfeit Currency and Character in Mark Twain's 'Which Was It?' " *Mark Twain Journal* 17 (Winter 1974–75): 1–6.

Richmond, Marion A. "The Lost Source of Freud's 'Comment on Anti-Semitism': Mark Twain." *Journal of the American Psychoanalytic Association* 28 (1980): 563–74.

Rideing, William H. *Many Celebrities and a Few Others*. Garden City, N.Y.: Doubleday, Page, 1912.

Riggio, Thomas P. "Charles Ethan Porter and Mark Twain." In *Charles Ethan Porter,* pp. 76–87. Marlborough, Conn.: Connecticut Gallery, 1987.

Robinson, Forrest G. *In Bad Faith: The Dynamics of Deception in Mark Twain's America*. Cambridge: Harvard University Press, 1986.

———. "Patterns of Consciousness in *The Innocents Abroad*." *American Literature* 58 (March 1986): 46–63.

———. "The Sense of Disorder in *Pudd'nhead Wilson*." In *Mark Twain's "Pudd'nhead Wilson": Race, Conflict, and Culture,* pp. 22–45. Durham, N.C.: Duke University Press, 1989.

Rodney, Robert M., ed. and comp. *Mark Twain International: A Bibliography and Interpretation of His Worldwide Popularity*. Westport, Conn.: Greenwood Press, 1982.

———. *Mark Twain Overseas: A Biographical Account of His Voyages, Travels, and Reception in Foreign Lands, 1866–1910*. Washington, D.C.: Three Continents Press, 1993.

Rogers, Franklin R. *Mark Twain's Burlesque Patterns*. Dallas: Southern Methodist University Press, 1960.

Ross, Michael L. "Mark Twain's *Pudd'nhead Wilson:* Dawson's Landing and the Ladder of Nobility." *Novel* 6 (1973): 244–56.

Russell, James. "The Genesis, Sources, and Reputation of Mark Twain's *A Connecticut Yankee in King Arthur's Court*." Ph.D. diss., University of Chicago, 1966.

Salls, Helen H. "Joan of Arc in English and American Literature." *South Atlantic Quarterly* 35 (1936): 167–84.

Salomon, Roger B. *Twain and the Image of History*. New Haven: Yale University Press, 1961.

Salsbury, Edith Colgate. *Susy and Mark Twain*. New York: Harper and Row, 1965.

San Juan, Pastora. "A Source for *Tom Sawyer*." *American Literature* 38 (1966–67): 101–2.

Sattelmeyer, Robert. "A Murder, a Mystery, and a Marriage." In *The Mark Twain Encyclopedia,* ed. J. R. Lemaster and James D. Wilson, pp. 526–27. New York: Garland, 1993.

Sattelmeyer, Robert, and J. Donald Crowley, eds. *One Hundred Years of Huckleberry Finn: The Boy, His Book, and American Culture*. Columbia: University of Missouri Press, 1985.

Scharnhorst, Gary, ed. *Critical Essays on "The Adventures of Tom Sawyer."* New York: G. K. Hall, 1993.

Schirer, Thomas. *Mark Twain and the Theatre*. Nuremberg, Germany: Hans Carl, 1984.

Schmidt, Paul. "Mark Twain's Techniques as a Humorist, 1857–1872." Ph.D. diss., University of Minnesota, 1951.

Schonemann, Friedrich. "Mark Twain and Adolph Wilbrandt." *Modern Language Notes* 34 (1919): 372–75.

Scott, Arthur L. *"The Innocents Adrift,* Edited by Mark Twain's Official Biographer." *PMLA* 78 (1963): 320–37.

——. "Mark Twain Revises *Old Times on the Mississippi." Journal of English and German Philology* 54 (1955): 634–38.

Sewell, David R. *Mark Twain's Languages: Discourse, Dialogue, and Linguistic Variety.* Berkeley: University of California Press, 1987.

Shaw, George Bernard. *Saint Joan.* In his *Complete Plays with Prefaces,* volume 2. New York: Dodd, Mead, 1962.

Shillingsburg, Miriam Jones. *At Home Abroad: Mark Twain in Australia.* Jackson: University Press of Mississippi, 1988.

——. "Down Under Day by Day with Mark Twain." *Mark Twain Journal* 33 (Fall 1995): 1–41.

Skandera-Trombley, Laura. *Mark Twain in the Company of Women.* Philadelphia: University of Pennsylvania Press, 1994.

——. "Mark Twain's Last Work of Realism: The Ashcroft-Lyon Manuscript." *Essays in Arts and Sciences* 23 (October 1994): 39–48.

——. " 'Why Can't a Woman Act More Like a Man?' Mark Twain's Masculine Women and Feminine Men." *Over here; reviews in american studies* 15 (1995): 49–57.

Smith, David L. Afterword to Mark Twain, *The Tragedy of Pudd'nhead Wilson and the Comedy of Those Extraordinary Twins.* New York: Oxford University Press, 1996.

——. "Huck, Jim, and American Racial Discourse." *Mark Twain Journal* 22 (Fall 1984): 4–12.

Smith, Henry Nash, ed. *Adventures of Huckleberry Finn.* Boston: Houghton Mifflin, 1958.

——. *Democracy and the Novel: Popular Resistance to Classic American Writers.* New York: Oxford University Press, 1978.

——. "Mark Twain as Interpreter of the West: The Structure of *Roughing It."* In *The Frontier in Perspective,* ed. W. D. Wyman and C. B. Kroeber. Madison: University of Wisconsin Press, 1957.

——. *Mark Twain: The Development of a Writer.* Cambridge: Harvard University Press, 1962.

——. *Mark Twain's Fable of Progress: "A Connecticut Yankee in King Arthur's Court."* New Brunswick, N.J.: Rutgers University Press, 1964.

——. "Mark Twain's Images of Hannibal: From St. Petersburg to Eseldorf." *Texas Studies in English* 37 (1958): 3–23.

———. "That Hideous Mistake of Poor Clemens's." *Harvard Library Bulletin* 9 (1955): 145–80.

Smythe, Carlyle. "The Real Mark Twain." *Pall Mall Magazine* 16 (September 1898): 29–36.

Spangler, G. W. "*Pudd'nhead Wilson:* A Parable of Property." *American Literature* 42 (1970–71): 28–37.

Spengemann, William C. *Mark Twain and the Backwoods Angel: The Matter of Innocence in the Works of Samuel L. Clemens.* Kent, Ohio: Kent State University Press, 1966.

Stahl, J. D. *Mark Twain, Culture, and Gender: Envisioning America Through Europe.* Athens: University of Georgia Press, 1994.

Steinbrink, Jeffrey. *Getting to Be Mark Twain.* Berkeley: University of California Press, 1991.

Stoddard, Charles Warren. "Mark Twain." *San Francisco Chronicle,* July 28, 1878.

———. *Exits and Entrances: A Book of Essays and Sketches.* Boston: Lothrop, 1903.

Stone, Albert E. *The Innocent Eye: Childhood in Mark Twain's Imagination.* New Haven: Yale University Press, 1961.

———. "Mark Twain's *Joan of Arc:* The Child as Goddess." *American Literature* 31 (1959–60): 1–20.

———. "The Twichell Papers and Mark Twain's *A Tramp Abroad.*" *Yale University Library Gazette* 29 (1955): 151–64.

Stoneley, Peter. *Mark Twain and the Feminine Aesthetic.* Cambridge: Cambridge University Press, 1992.

Sumida, Stephen H. "Reevaluating Mark Twain's Novel of Hawaii." *American Literature* 61 (December 1989): 586–609.

Taine, Hippolyte Adolphe. *The Ancient Regime.* Trans. John Durand. New York: Henry Holt, 1876.

Tenney, Thomas A. *Mark Twain: A Reference Guide.* Boston: G. K. Hall, 1977.

Thayer, Emma B., and S. L. Severance. "Letters from Emma B. Thayer and S. L. Severance." *Twainian* 16 (March-April 1967): 2–3.

Towers, Tom T. "I Never Thought We Might Want to Come Back: Strategies of Transcendence in *Tom Sawyer.*" *Modern Fiction Studies* 21 (1975–76): 509–20.

———. "'Hateful Reality': The Failure of the Territory in *Roughing It.*" *Western American Literature* 9 (1974): 3–15.

———. "*The Prince and the Pauper:* Mark Twain's Once and Future King." *Studies in American Fiction* 6 (1978): 194–202.

Trachtenberg, Alan. "The Form of Freedom in *Adventures of Huckleberry Finn.*" *Southern Review* 6 (1970): 954–71.

Tuckey, John S. "Mark Twain's Later Dialogue: The 'Me' and the Machine." *American Literature* 41 (1969–70): 532–42.

———. *Mark Twain and Little Satan: The Writing of "The Mysterious Stranger."* West Lafayette, Ind.: Purdue University Studies, 1963.

———, ed. *"The Mysterious Stranger" and the Critics.* Belmont, Calif.: Wadsworth, 1968.

Turner, Arlin. "Mark Twain and the South: An Affair of Love and Anger." *Southern Review* 4 (1968): 493–519.

———. *George W. Cable: A Biography.* Durham, N.C.: Duke University Press, 1956.

Twichell, Joseph. "Mark Twain." *Harper's New Monthly Magazine* 92 (1896): 817–27.

Underhill, Charles S. "Is the Garden of Eden at Niagara Falls? Mark Twain Says 'Yes.'" *Gleaner* [Buffalo, N.Y.] 1 (March 1928): 14–19.

Waggoner, Hyatt H. "Science in the Thought of Mark Twain." *American Literature* 8 (1938): 357–70.

Wagner-Martin, Linda. "What Is Man?" In *The Mark Twain Encyclopedia,* ed. J. R. LeMaster and James D. Wilson, pp. 783–85. New York: Garland, 1993.

Wallace, Elizabeth. *Mark Twain and the Happy Island.* Chicago: McClurg, 1913.

Weber, Carl J. *The Rise and Fall of James Ripley Osgood: A Biography.* Waterville, Me.: Colby College Press, 1959.

Wecter, Dixon. *Sam Clemens of Hannibal.* Boston: Houghton Mifflin, 1952.

Welland, Dennis. *Mark Twain in England.* Atlantic Highlands, N.J.: Humanities Press, 1978.

———. "Mark Twain's Last Travel Book." *Bulletin of the New York Public Library* 69 (1965): 31–48.

Why, Joseph S. *Nook Farm.* Hartford: Stowe-Day Foundation, 1975.

Wiggin, Kate Douglas. *My Garden of Memory: An Autobiography.* Boston: Houghton Mifflin, 1926.

Wiggins, Robert A. *Mark Twain: Jackleg Novelist.* Seattle: University of Washington Press, 1964.

———. "The Original of Mark Twain's 'Those Extraordinary Twins.'" *American Literature* 23 (1951–52): 355–57.

Williams, James D. "Revision and Intention in Mark Twain's *A Connecticut Yankee.*" *American Literature* 36 (1964–65): 288–97.

Willis, Resa. *Mark and Livy: The Love Story of Mark Twain and the Woman Who Almost Tamed Him.* New York: Atheneum, 1992.

Wilson, James D. *A Reader's Guide to the Short Stories of Mark Twain.* Boston: G. K. Hall, 1987.

———. "The Use of History in Mark Twain's *A Connecticut Yankee.*" *PMLA* 80 (1965): 102–10.

Wilson, Robert H. "Malory in *The Connecticut Yankee.*" *Texas Studies in English* 27 (1948): 185–206.

Wolff, Cynthia Griffin. "*The Adventures of Tom Sawyer:* Nightmare Vision of American Boyhood." *Massachusetts Review* 21 (1980): 637–52.

Wonham, Henry B. *Mark Twain and the Art of the Tall Tale.* New York: Oxford University Press, 1993.

Wood, John. *The Art of Autochrome: The Birth of Color Photography.* Iowa City: University of Iowa Press, 1993.

Yates, Norris. *William T. Porter and the "Spirit of the Times": A Study of the Big Bear School of Humor.* Baton Rouge: Louisiana State University Press, 1957.

Zacharias, Greg W. "Henry Rogers, Public Relations, and the Recovery of Mark Twain's 'Character.' " *Mark Twain Journal* 31 (1993): 2–17.

Zall, P. M. "Charles Henry Webb (1834–1905)." In *The Mark Twain Encyclopedia,* ed. J. R. LeMaster and James D. Wilson, pp. 778–79. New York: Garland, 1993.

Zladic, Thomas D. "Mark Twain's View of the Universe." *Papers on Language and Literature* 27 (1991): 338–55.

Zwarg, Christina. "Woman as Force in Twain's *Joan of Arc:* The Unwordable Fascination." *Criticism* 27 (Winter 1985): 57–72.

Index

Twain, Mark (*cont.*)

"From the 'London Times' of 1904,"
243; "Frozen Truth, The," 50; "Genuine Mexican Plug, The," 219;
"George Washington's Negro Body-Servant," 63; "German Chicago,
The," 188, 201; *Gilded Age, The*, *82–85*, 89, 90, 95, 100, 104, 159, 214;
"Golden Arm, The," 206; "Goldsmith's Friend Abroad Again," 67;
"Great Dark, The," 245, 254; *Hannibal, Huck, and Tom*, 231; "Happy
Memories of the Dental Chair," 161;
Hawaiian novel, 160; "Hellfire
Hotchkiss," 231, 232, 284; "History
of Lynching," 260; "Horse's Tale, A,"
284, 292; "House Beautiful, The,"
134; "How Nancy Jackson Married
Kate Wilson," 275, 284; "How to
Cure a Cold," 20; "How to Tell a
Story," 205; *How to Tell a Story and
Other Essays*, 233; "Huck Finn and
Tom Sawyer Among the Indians,"
161–162; "Huck Finn in Africa," 190;
Huckleberry Finn, Adventures of, 4, 7,
10, 30, 89–90, 93, 98, 127, 103, 112,
117, 119, 128, 129, 130, 134, 136,
140–159, 160, 161, 163, 167, 171, 172,
176, 188, 191, 192, 210, 213, 214,
215, 216, 217, 221, 230, 231, 260,
275, 288, 289; "Final Huck Finn
book," 265; "Huckleberry Finn
Abroad," 190; "Huckleberry Finn
and Tom Sawyer Abroad," 190;
"Imitating the Equator," 224;
"Important Correspondence," 30;
"In Defense of Harriet Shelley," 203,
204; "In Memoriam Olivia Susan
Clemens," 230; "In My Bitterness,"
230; "Indiantown," 251, 262, 270,

271; *Innocents Abroad, The*, 10, 36, 46,
52, 53, 54, 57, 58, *59–63*, 65, 68, 70,
71, 74, 76, 78, 81, 82, 85, 90, 90, 112,
114, 130, 139, 188, 207, 259, 271,
300; "Innocents Adrift, The," 188;
Innocents At Home, The, 78; "International Lightning Trust, The," 295;
"Introductory," 67; "Is He Dead?"
238; "Is He Living or Is He Dead?"
202, 238; *Is Shakespeare Dead?* 247,
287, 294; "Italian with Grammar,"
269, 271; "Italian Without a Master,"
269; "Jim Baker's Blue Jay Yarn," 226;
"Jim Smiley and His Jumping Frog,"
32–34, 38, 72, 141; "Jim Wolf and
the Cats," 253; "Jim Wolf and the
Tom-Cats," 42, 45, 90; *Joan of Arc*,
208–214, 215, 218, 226, 254, 259, 301;
"Jumping Frog, The," 219; "King of
France," 146, 149, 153, 154, 231; *King
Leopold's Soliloquy*, 277–278; "Landscape Gardening," 68; "Late Reverend Sam Jones's Reception in
Heaven, The," 188–189, 301; "Latest
Innocent Abroad, The," 224; *Latest
Innocent Abroad, The*, 71; "Legend of
the Capitoline Venus," 64; "Legend
of the Spectacular Ruin," 116; "Letters from a Dog to Another Dog,"
182; "Letters from the Earth," 182,
187, 296, 297; "Letters to Satan," 230,
248; "Lick House Ball, The," 20; *Life
on the Mississippi*, 10, 12, 112, *132–139*,
141, 144, 147, 148, 149, 152, 153,
174, 188, 190, 224, 278, 300, 303;
"Literary Nightmare, A," 101; "Little
Bessie," 293, 296; "Little Note to
M. Paul Bourget," 207; "Loves of
Alonzo Fitz Clarence and Rosannah
Ethelton, The," 105; "Luck," 183,

189; "Lucretia Smith's Soldier," 28–29; "Macfarlane," 200; "Majestic Literary Fossil, A," 181; "Major General Wood, M.D.," 270; "Mamie Grant, the Child Missionary," 54–55; "Man That Corrupted Hadleyburg, The," 4, 241, 246, 254, 255, 269; *Man That Corrupted Hadleyburg and Other Stories and Sketches, The,* 247; "Man with the Negro Blood, The," 263; "Man's Place in the Animal World," 222, 223; "Marienbad — A Health Factory," 187; *Mark Twain in Eruption,* 287; "'Mark Twain' in the Metropolis," 24, 33; *Mark Twain's (Burlesque) Autobiography and First Romance,* 72; *Mark Twain's Autobiography,* 253, 287; *Mark Twain's Sketches,* 69, 72; *Mark Twain's Sketches, New and Old,* 28, 64, 68, 69, 92, *98–100; Mark Twain's Sketches, Number One,* 86; *Mark Twain's Speeches,* 287; *Mark Twain's Travels with Mr. Brown,* 40, 44, 113; *Mark Twain's Weapons of Satire,* 270, 288; "Mark Twain Tobacco," 292; "Mark Twain Whiskey," 292; "Medieval Romance, A," 284; "Meisterschaft," 181, 189; "Memorable Assassination, The," 235; "Mental Telegraphy," 131, 183, 201; "Mental Telegraphy Again," 206; *Merry Tales,* 189; "Missionary in World Politics, The," 253; "Moral Impossibilty of Doughnuts, The," 57; "Moral Sense, The," 239; *More Tramps Abroad,* 132, 224, 226; "Mrs. Eddy in Error," 267; "Mrs. McWilliams and the Lightning," 189; "Murder, a Mystery, and a Marriage, A," 104, 190; "My Boyhood Dreams,"

252; "My Debut as a Literary Person," 36, 38, 245; "My First Lie and How I Got Out of It," 252; "My First Literary Venture," 67, 68; "My Late Senatorial Secretaryship," 50; "My Lost Sweetheart," 243; "My Platonic Sweetheart," 243, 273; "Mysterious Bridegroom, The," 104; "Mysterious Chamber, The," 104, 110; *Mysterious Stranger, The,* 242, 272; *Mysterious Stranger Manuscripts, The,* 105; "Mystery, A," 57; "New Huck Finn," 230; "New Infallibility, The," 267; "Newhouse's Jew Story," 225; *New York Sunday Mercury,* contributions to, 19, 42, 45; *New York Weekly Review,* contributions to, 35, 41; "No. 44, The Mysterious Stranger," 244, *272–274,* 281, 293; "Noah's Ark" book, 70; "Old Comrades," 259, 271; "Old Times on the Mississippi," 44, *96–98,* 110, 132, 133, 134, 138, 211; "Omar's Old Age," 240–241; "£1,000,000 Bank-Note, The," 200; *£1,000,000 Bank Note and Other New Stories, The,* 5, 159, 166, 170, 200; "1002nd Arabian Night," 159, 216, 232, 284; "On Foreign Critics," 173; *On the Poetry of Mark Twain,* 241; "Only Reliable Account of the Celebrated Jumping Frog of Calaveras County, The," 32; "Open Letter to Commodore Vanderbilt," 68; "Original Novelette," 28; "Orion's Autobiography," 105, 110; "Our Fellow Savages of the Sandwich Islands," 65; *Outrageous Mark Twain, The,* 288; "Papers of the Adam Family," 70; "People and Things," 64; "Permanent Sources of Corruption in Our Government," 135; "Personal

Twain, Mark (*cont.*)

Habits of the Siamese Twins," 63; *Personal Recollections of Joan of Arc. See Joan of Arc;* "Petition to the Queen of England, A," 181, 201; "Picturesque Incidents in History and Tradition," 166; "Plain Language from Truthful James," 103; "Playing Bear — Herrings — Jim Wolf and the Cats," 253; "Playing Courier," 187, 189, 201; "Postal Service," 188; *Prince and the Pauper, The,* 102, *118–125,* 130, 131, 132, 148, 153, 158, 161, 174, 208, 212, 259, 275, 284, 301; "Private Habits of Horace Greeley," 56; "Private History of a Campaign That Failed, The," 13, *167–168,* 169, 189, 211; "Private History of the Jumping Frog Story, The," 205; "Professor's Yarn, The," 135; "Propositions for a Postal Check," 253; *Pudd'nhead Wilson,* 2, 159, 193, *194–200,* 208, 214, 216, 219, 284; "Pudd'nhead Wilson's New Calendar," 187, 198, 225; "Punch, Brothers, Punch," 101; *Punch, Brothers, Punch,* 131; "Raft Passage," 144; "Reflections on Religion," 289; "Refuge of the Derelicts," 279; "Reminiscences of Some Uncommon Characters I Have Chanced to Meet," 81; "Rev. Henry Ward Beecher, His Private Habits," 64; "Rich Decision, A," 19; "Riley — Newspaper Correspondent," 79; "Rise and Progress of Lynching," 260; "River Intelligence," 11, 12; *Roughing It,* 12, 13, 14, 23, 24, 25, 30, 35, 40, 64, 66, *71–77,* 78, 79, 80, 85, 91, 104, 112, 115, 118, 124, 139, 211, 301; "Roughing It on the Silver Frontier," 87; "Salutation," 63; "Salutation Speech from the Nineteenth Century to the Twentieth, A," 256; *Satires and Burlesques,* 232; "Schoolhouse Hill," 247; *Screamers,* 69; "Scriptural Panoramist, The," 99, 100; "Secret History of Eddypus, The," 258, 271, 274, 281; "Selfishness," 239; "Sentimental Law Student, Ye," 21; *Simon Wheeler, Detective,* 144, 214; "Singular Episode, A," 188; *1601. See [Date 1601];* Sketches, *New and Old,* 95, 98, 99; "Slovenly Peter," 188; "Sociable Jimmy," 89; "Sold to Satan," 271; "Soleleather Cultivates His Taste for Music," 12; "Some Learned Fables, for Good Old Boys and Girls," 69, 99; "Some Rambling Notes of an Idle Excursion," 105–107, 110; "Stirring Times in Austria," 235; "Stolen White Elephant, The," 131, 214; *Stolen White Elephant, Etc., The,* 131; "Story of the Bad Little Boy, The," 28; "Story of the Good Little Boy, The," 28; *Struwwelpeter, Der,* 188; "Stupendous Procession, The," 257; *Surviving Innocent Abroad, The,* 71; "Switzerland, the Cradle of Liberty," 187; "Tale of the Lost Land, The," 170; "Taming the Bicycle," 161; "Thanksgiving Sentiment, A," 278; "$30,000 Bequest, The," 269; "Those Blasted Children," 19; "Those Extraordinary Twins," 193, 199, 199, 279; "Three Thousand Years Among the Microbes," 280–281; "To My Missionary Critics," 258; "To the Person Sitting in Darkness," 257; *Tom Sawyer* (play), 160–161; *Tom Sawyer Abroad,* 190, *191–193,*